I used to think the countryside was nice and quiet, but boy, was I wrong. The sparrows go "CHIRP" in the morning. Next, the crows go "CAW." Of course, the chickens go "CLUCK CLUCK." In the marsh, the frogs go "CROAK" and "BARRRUMP." That last one is a bullfrog. And, how could we forget the dogs that go "WOOF"? And "MEEEOWROO"? That's a cat in heat. And then there are the little brats...er, the children. For the grand finale, the weaving looms go "KACHUNK KACHUNK KACHUNK." But the loudest thing of all is our parrot..."SQUAWK!!"

—Akira Toriyama, 1982

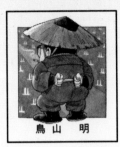

鳥山 明

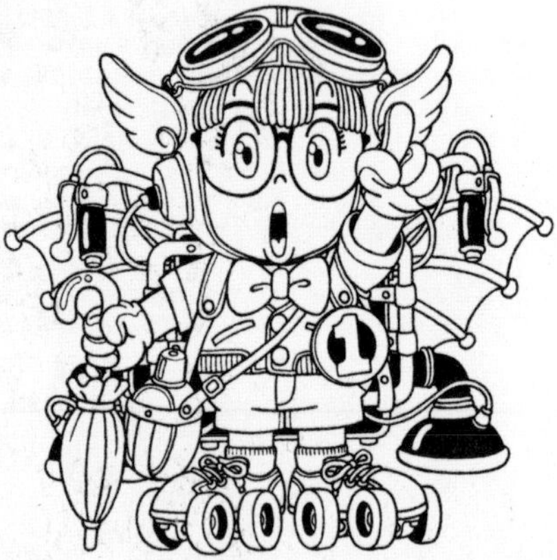

Akira Toriyama's first weekly series, **Dr. Slump**, has entertained generations of readers in Japan since it was introduced in Shueisha's **Weekly Shonen Jump** magazine in 1980. A few years later, he created his wildly popular **Dragon Ball** series, which brought him international success. Toriyama is also known for his character designs for video games, including **Dragon Warrior**, **Chrono Trigger** and **Tobal No. 1**. He lives with his family in Japan.

6/13
8°°

DR. SLUMP VOL. 8
The SHONEN JUMP Manga Edition

STORY AND ART BY
AKIRA TORIYAMA

English Adaptation & Translation/Alexander O. Smith
Touch-up Art & Lettering/Walden Wong
Cover & Interior Design/Hidemi Sahara
Editor/Yuki Takagaki

Managing Editor/Elizabeth Kawasaki
Director of Production/Noboru Watanabe
Vice President of Publishing/Alvin Lu
Vice President & Editor in Chief/Yumi Hoashi
Sr. Director of Acquisitions/Rika Inouye
Vice President of Sales & Marketing/Liza Coppola
Publisher/Hyoe Narita

Printed in the U.S.A.

Published by VIZ Media, LLC
P.O. Box 77010
San Francisco, CA 94107

SHONEN JUMP Manga Edition
10 9 8 7 6 5 4 3 2 1
First printing, July 2006

www.viz.com

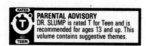

PARENTAL ADVISORY
DR. SLUMP is rated T for Teen and is
recommended for ages 13 and up. This
volume contains suggestive themes.

THE WORLD'S
MOST POPULAR MANGA

SHONEN JUMP
www.shonenjump.com

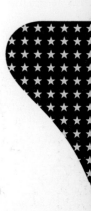

SHONEN JUMP MANGA

Dr. SLUMP™

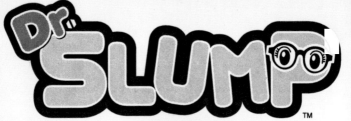

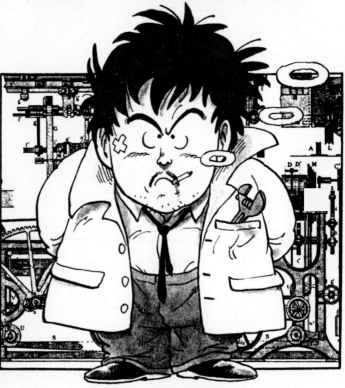

Story & Art by

Akira Toriyama

DR. SLUMP

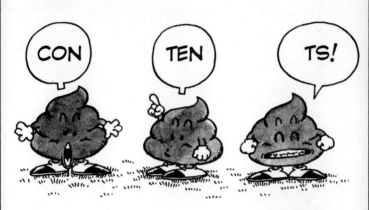

CON TEN TS!

Vol. 8

The Ho-yo-yo Gang: Part 1

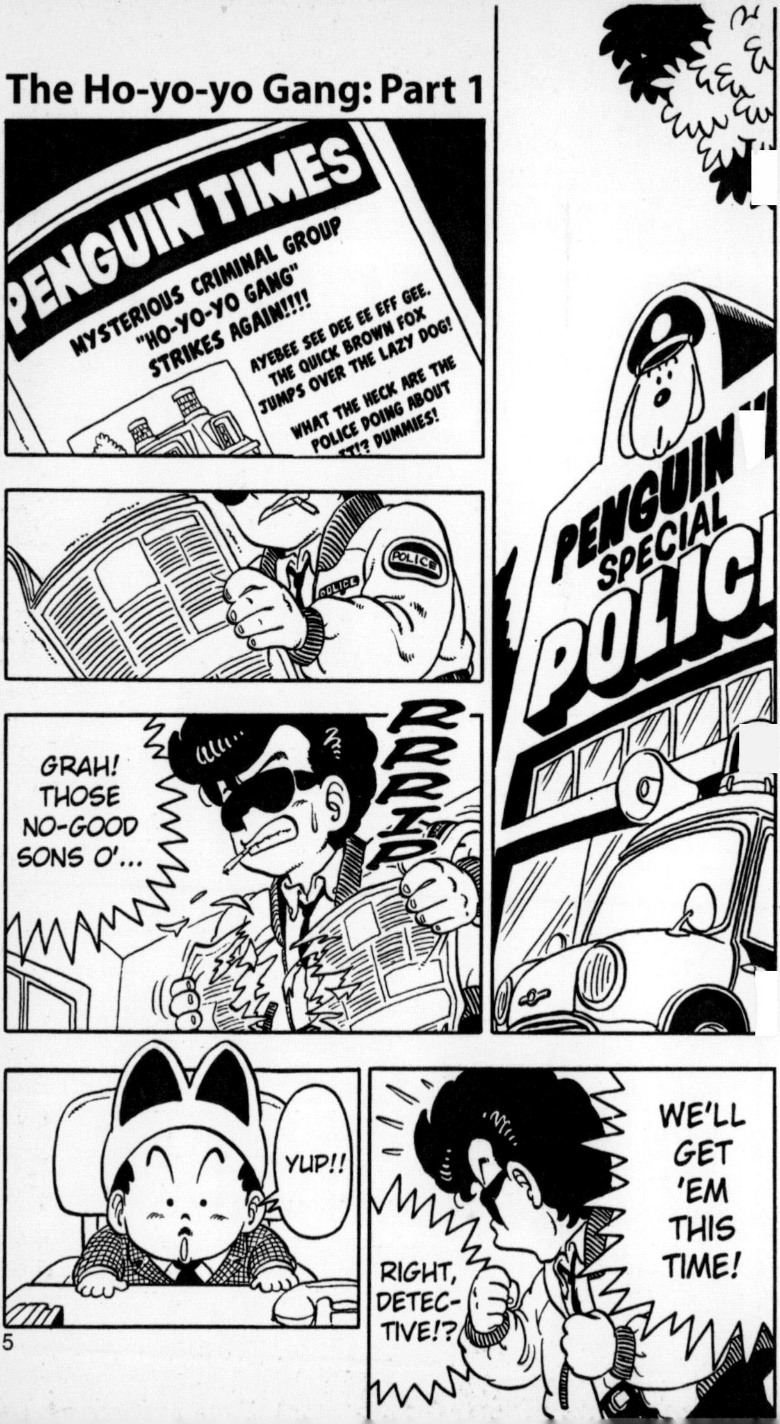
PENGUIN
SPECIAL
POLIC
PENGUIN TIMES
MYSTERIOUS CRIMINAL GROUP "HO-YO-YO GANG" STRIKES AGAIN!!!!
AYEBEE SEE DEE EE EFF GEE. THE QUICK BROWN FOX JUMPS OVER THE LAZY DOG!
WHAT THE HECK ARE THE POLICE DOING ABOUT
DUMMIES!
POLICE
GRAH! THOSE NO-GOOD SONS O'...
RRRIP
WE'LL GET 'EM THIS TIME!
RIGHT, DETECTIVE!?
YUP!!

The Ho-yo-yo Gang
Part 1

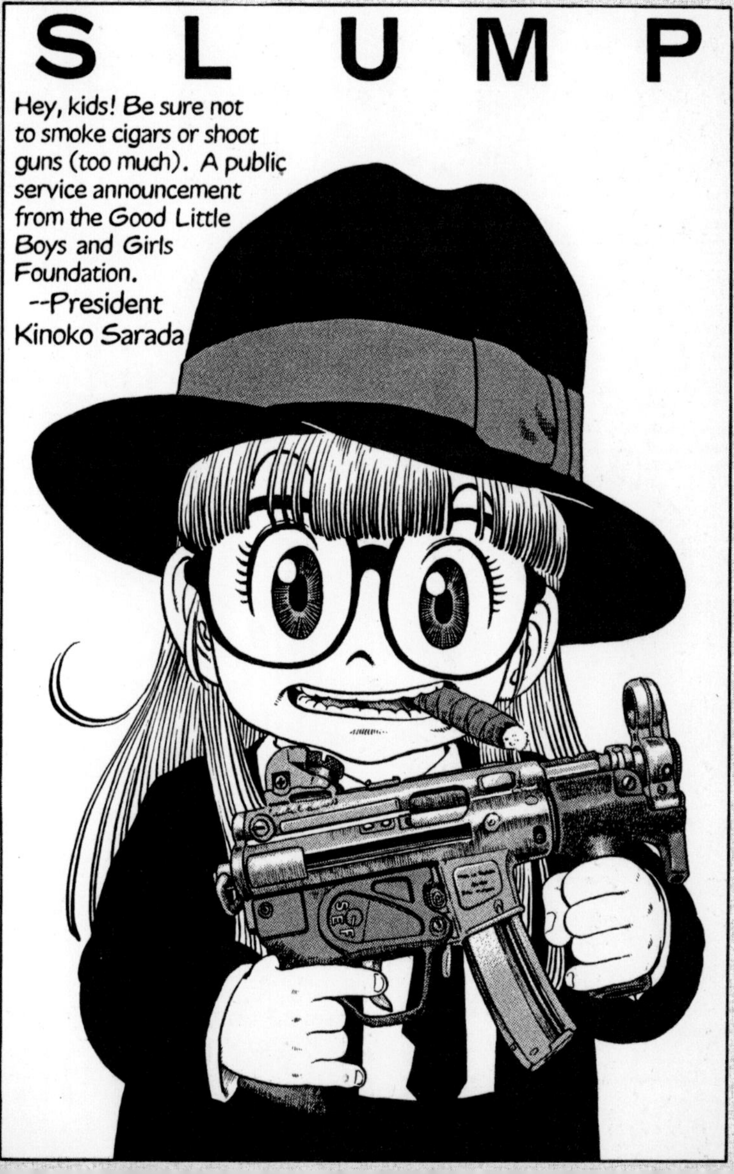
S L U M P
Hey, kids! Be sure not to smoke cigars or shoot guns (too much). A public service announcement from the Good Little Boys and Girls Foundation.
--President Kinoko Sarada

READ THIS WAY

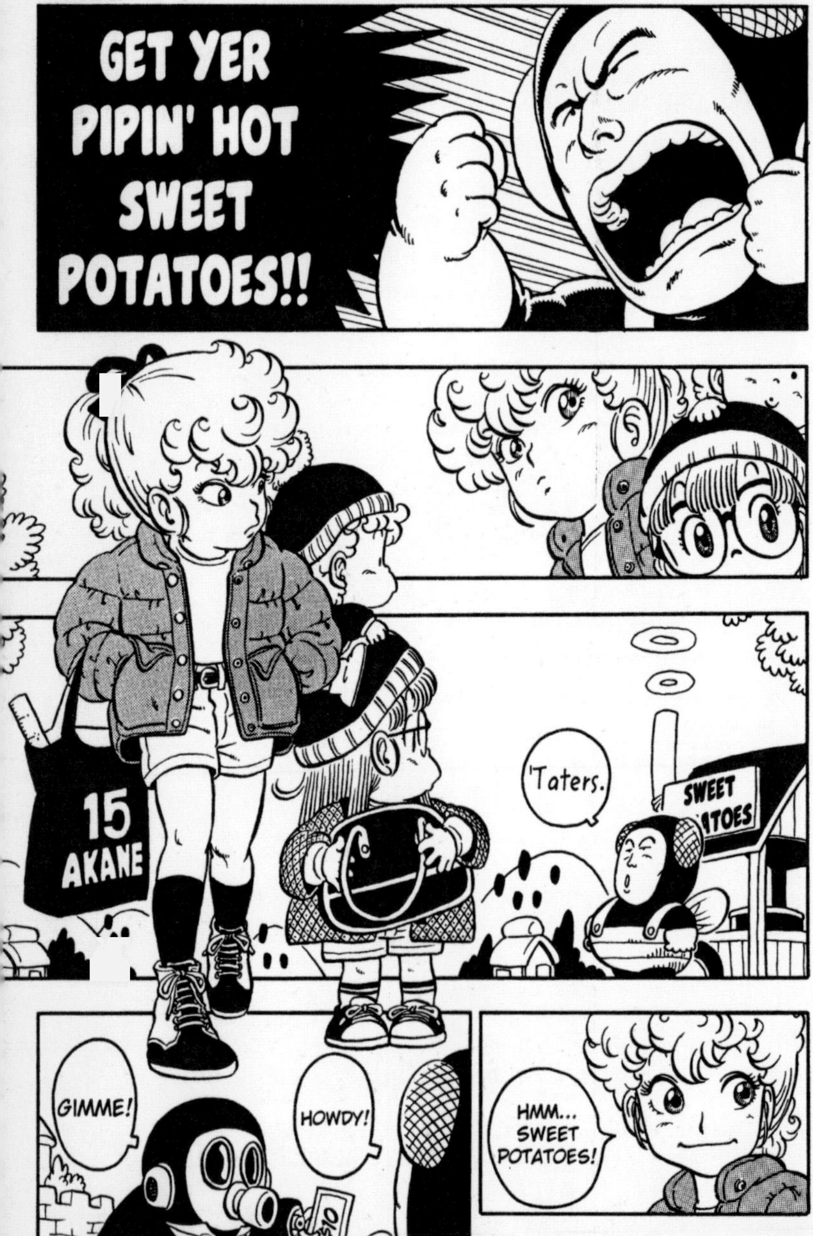
GET YER PIPIN' HOT SWEET POTATOES!!
'Taters.
15
AKANE
HMM... SWEET POTATOES!
HOWDY!
GIMME!

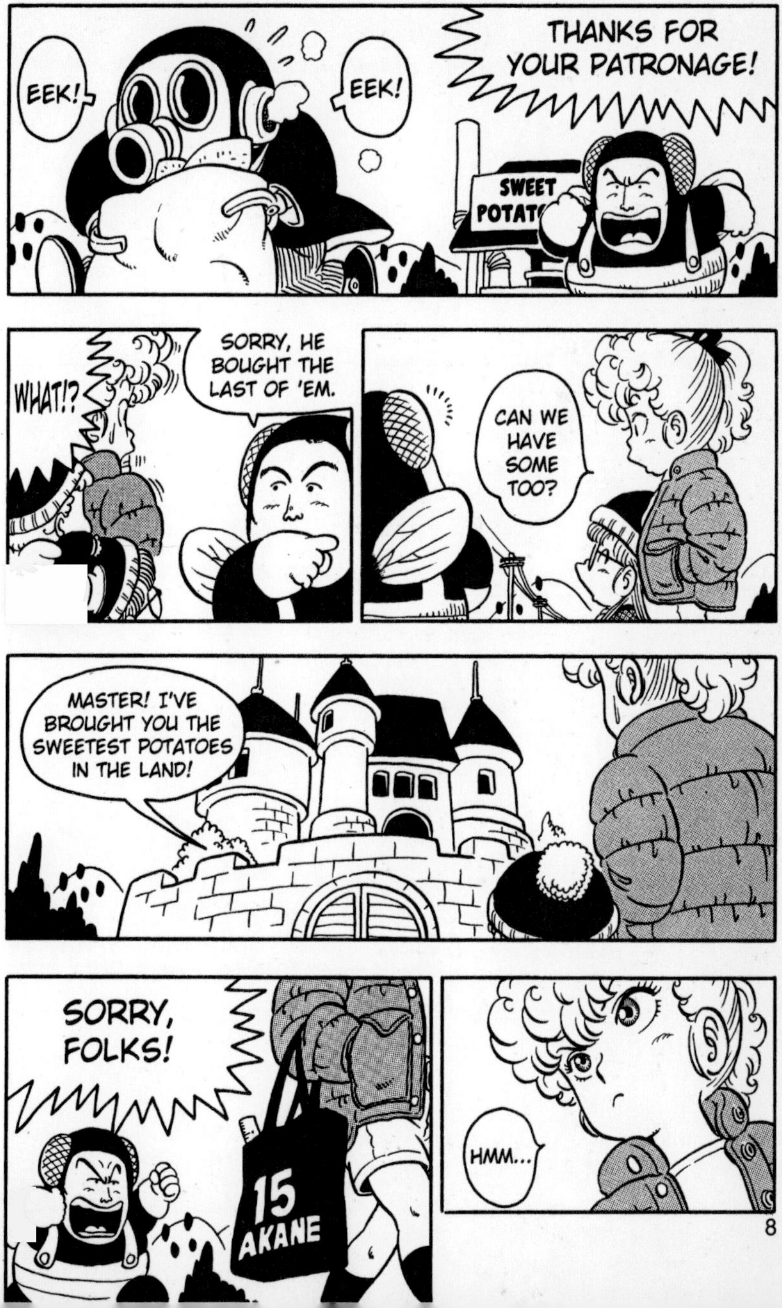
THANKS FOR YOUR PATRONAGE!
SWEET
EEK!
EEK!
CAN WE HAVE SOME TOO?
SORRY, HE BOUGHT THE LAST OF 'EM.
WHAT!?
MASTER! I'VE BROUGHT YOU THE SWEETEST POTATOES IN THE LAND!
HMM...
SORRY, FOLKS!
15
AKANE

READ THIS WAY

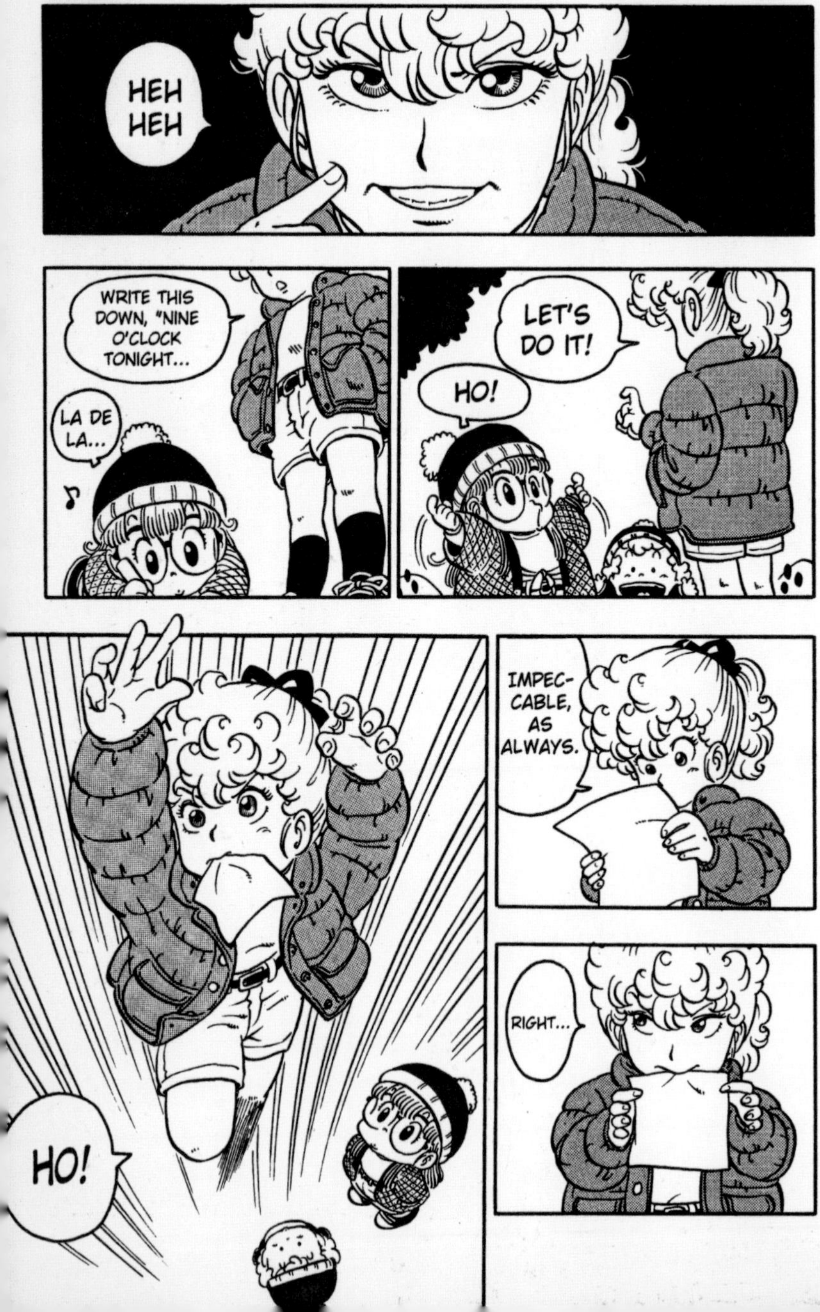
HEH HEH
LET'S DO IT!
HO!
WRITE THIS DOWN, "NINE O'CLOCK TONIGHT...
LA DE LA...
IMPEC-CABLE, AS ALWAYS.
RIGHT...
HO!

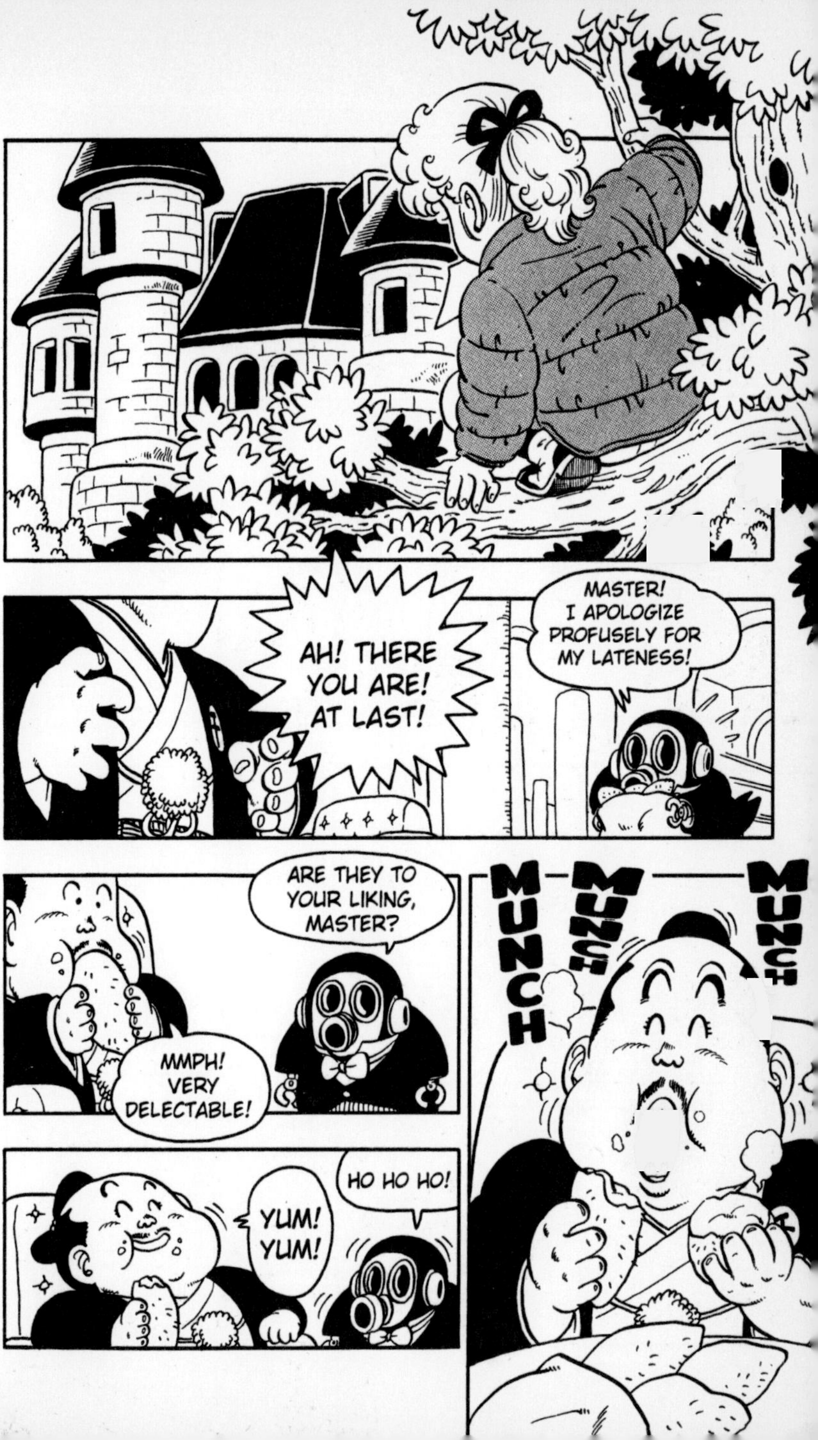
MASTER! I APOLOGIZE PROFUSELY FOR MY LATENESS!
AH! THERE YOU ARE! AT LAST!
MUNCH
MUNCH
MUNCH
ARE THEY TO YOUR LIKING, MASTER?
MMPH! VERY DELECTABLE!
HO HO HO!
YUM! YUM!

READ THIS WAY

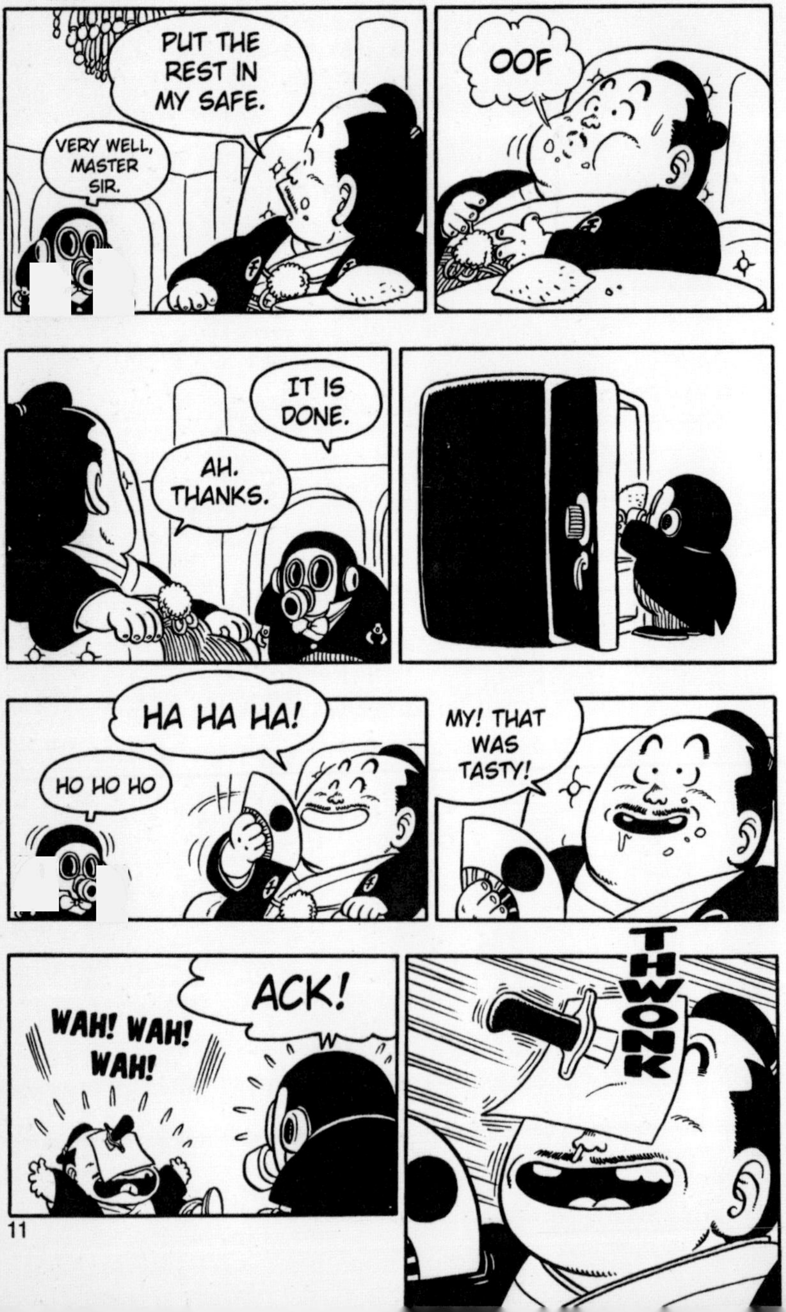
OOF
PUT THE REST IN MY SAFE.
VERY WELL, MASTER SIR.
IT IS DONE.
AH. THANKS.
MY! THAT WAS TASTY!
HA HA HA!
HO HO HO
THWONK
ACK!
WAH! WAH! WAH!

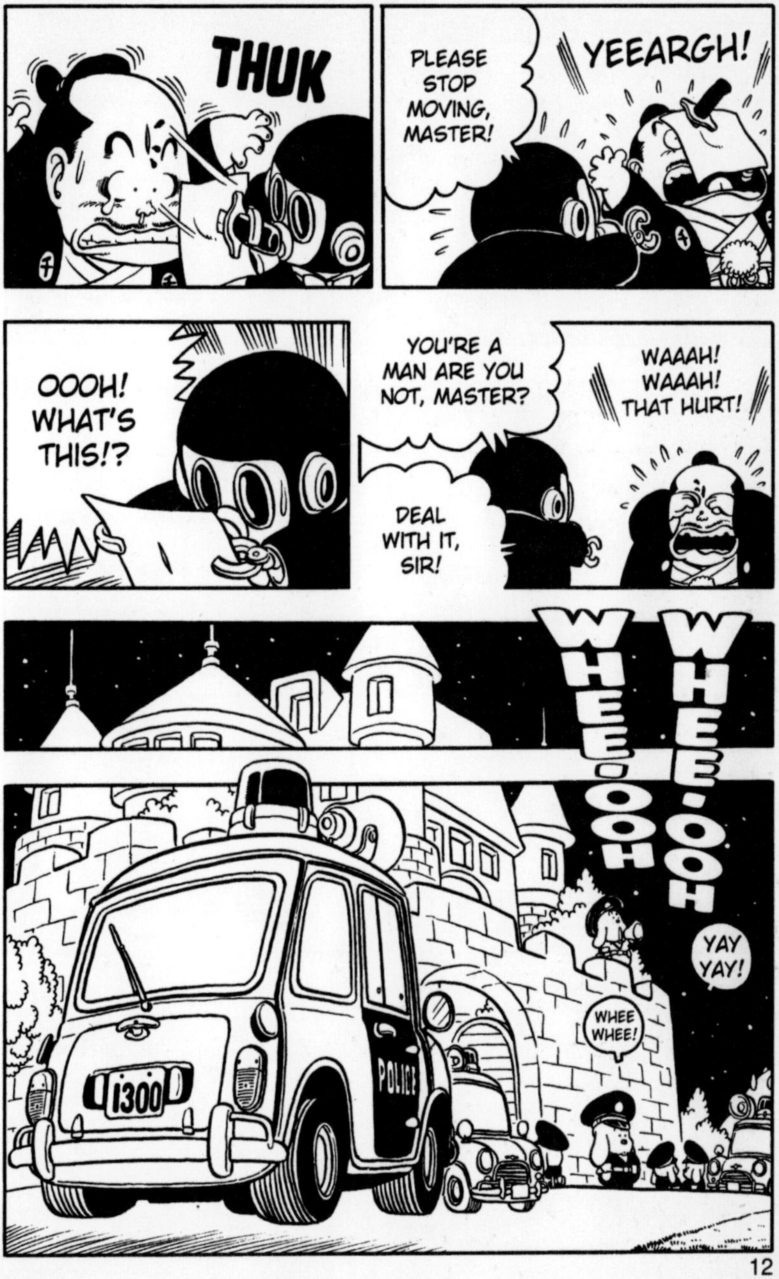
YEEARGH!
PLEASE STOP MOVING, MASTER!
THUK
WAAAH! WAAAH! THAT HURT!
YOU'RE A MAN ARE YOU NOT, MASTER?
DEAL WITH IT, SIR!
OOOH! WHAT'S THIS!?
WHEE-OOH
WHEE-OOH
YAY YAY!
WHEE WHEE!
POLICE
1300

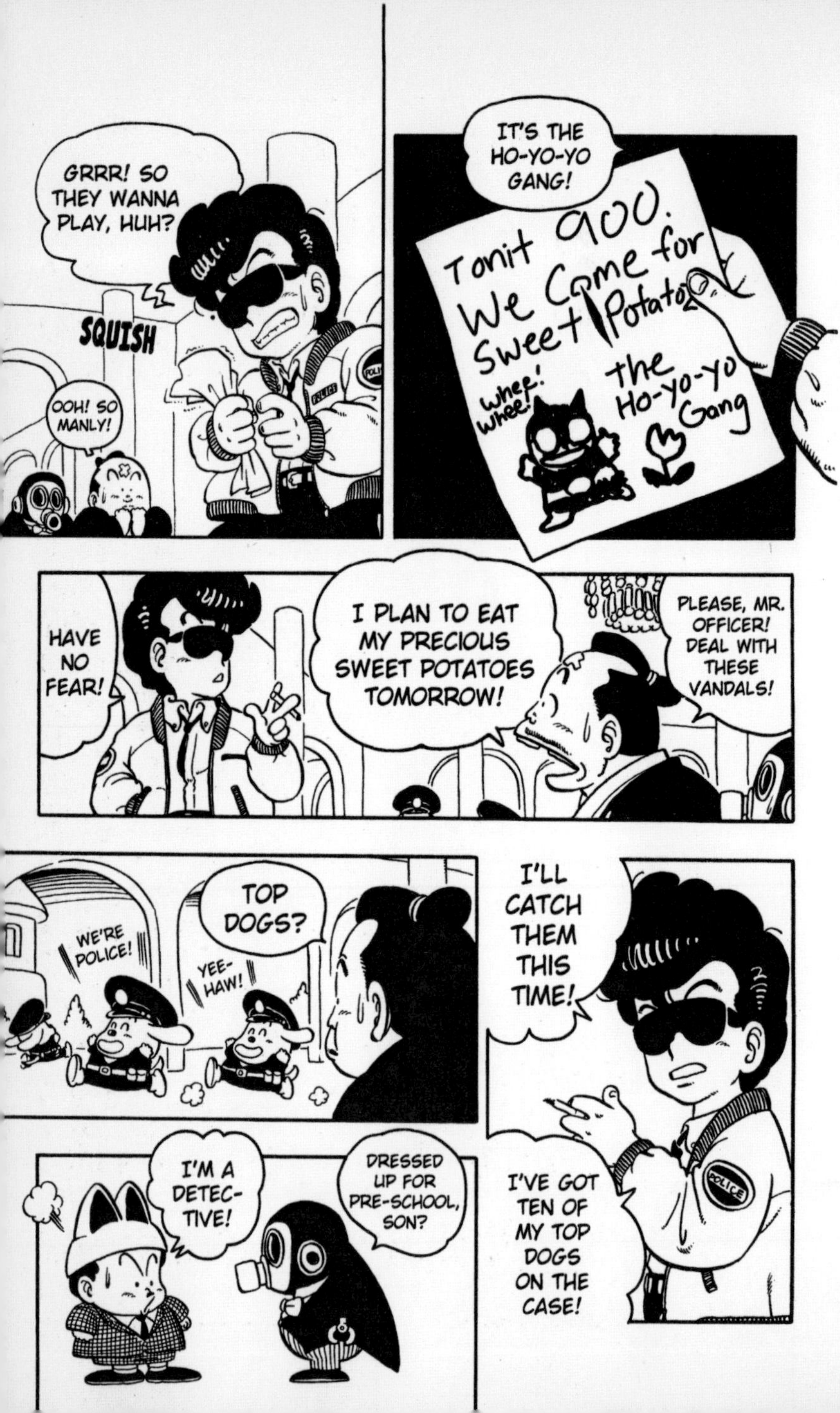
IT'S THE HO-YO-YO GANG!
Tonit 900. We Come for Sweet Potato
whee! whee!
the Ho-yo-yo Gang
GRRR! SO THEY WANNA PLAY, HUH?
SQUISH
OOH! SO MANLY!
PLEASE, MR. OFFICER! DEAL WITH THESE VANDALS!
I PLAN TO EAT MY PRECIOUS SWEET POTATOES TOMORROW!
HAVE NO FEAR!
I'LL CATCH THEM THIS TIME!
I'VE GOT TEN OF MY TOP DOGS ON THE CASE!
TOP DOGS?
YEE-HAW!
WE'RE POLICE!
DRESSED UP FOR PRE-SCHOOL, SON?
I'M A DETEC-TIVE!

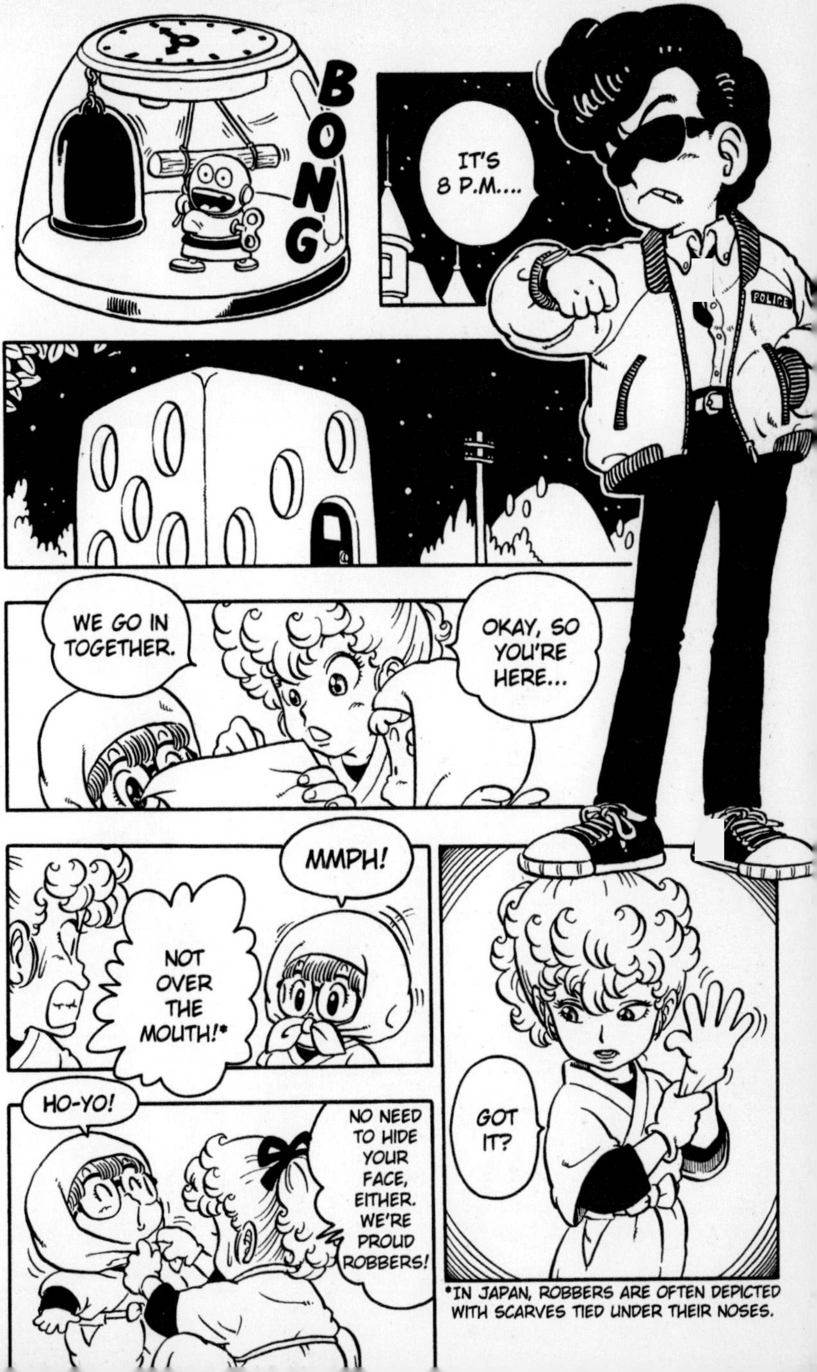
IT'S 8 P.M....
BONG
OKAY, SO YOU'RE HERE...
WE GO IN TOGETHER.
GOT IT?
MMPH!
NOT OVER THE MOUTH!*
NO NEED TO HIDE YOUR FACE, EITHER. WE'RE PROUD ROBBERS!
HO-YO!

*IN JAPAN, ROBBERS ARE OFTEN DEPICTED WITH SCARVES TIED UNDER THEIR NOSES.

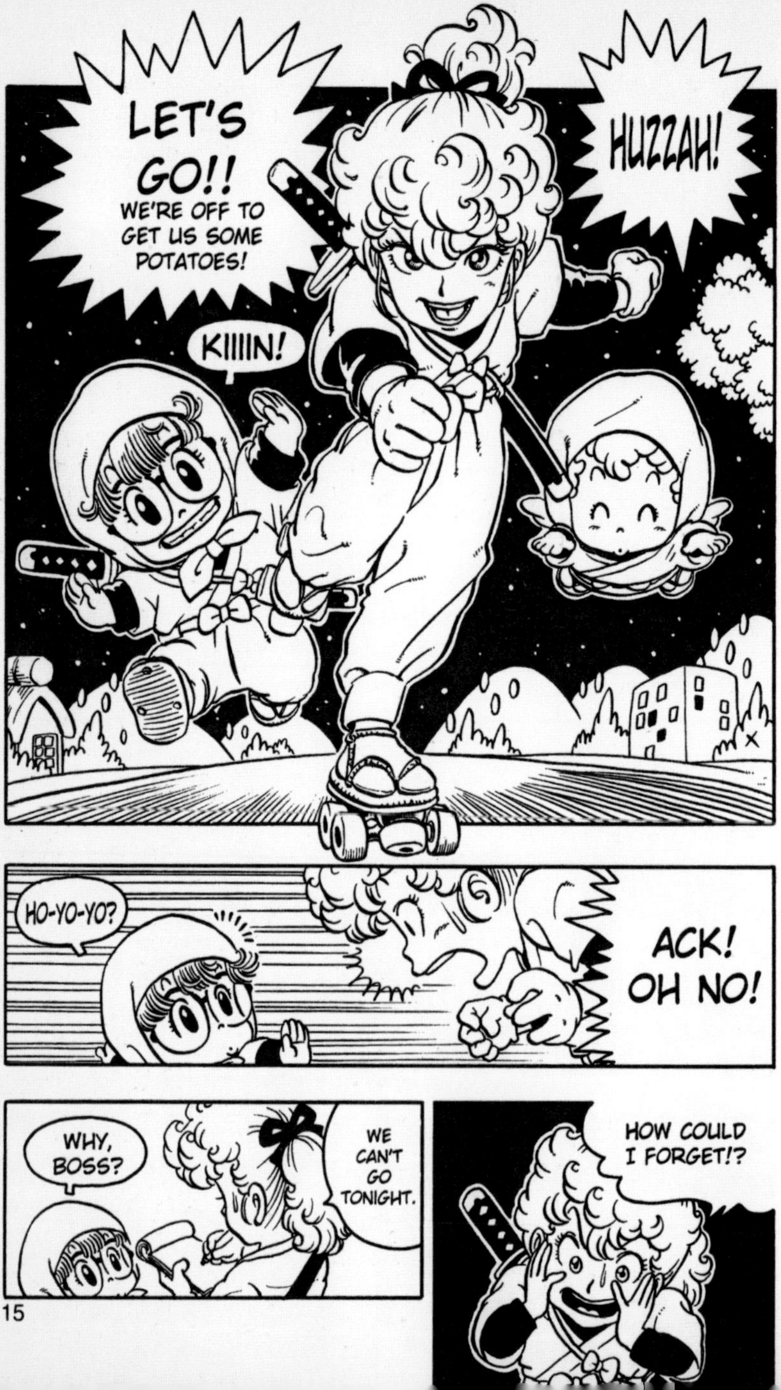
HUZZAH!
LET'S GO!! WE'RE OFF TO GET US SOME POTATOES!
KIIIIN!
ACK! OH NO!
HO-YO-YO?
HOW COULD I FORGET!?
WE CAN'T GO TONIGHT.
WHY, BOSS?

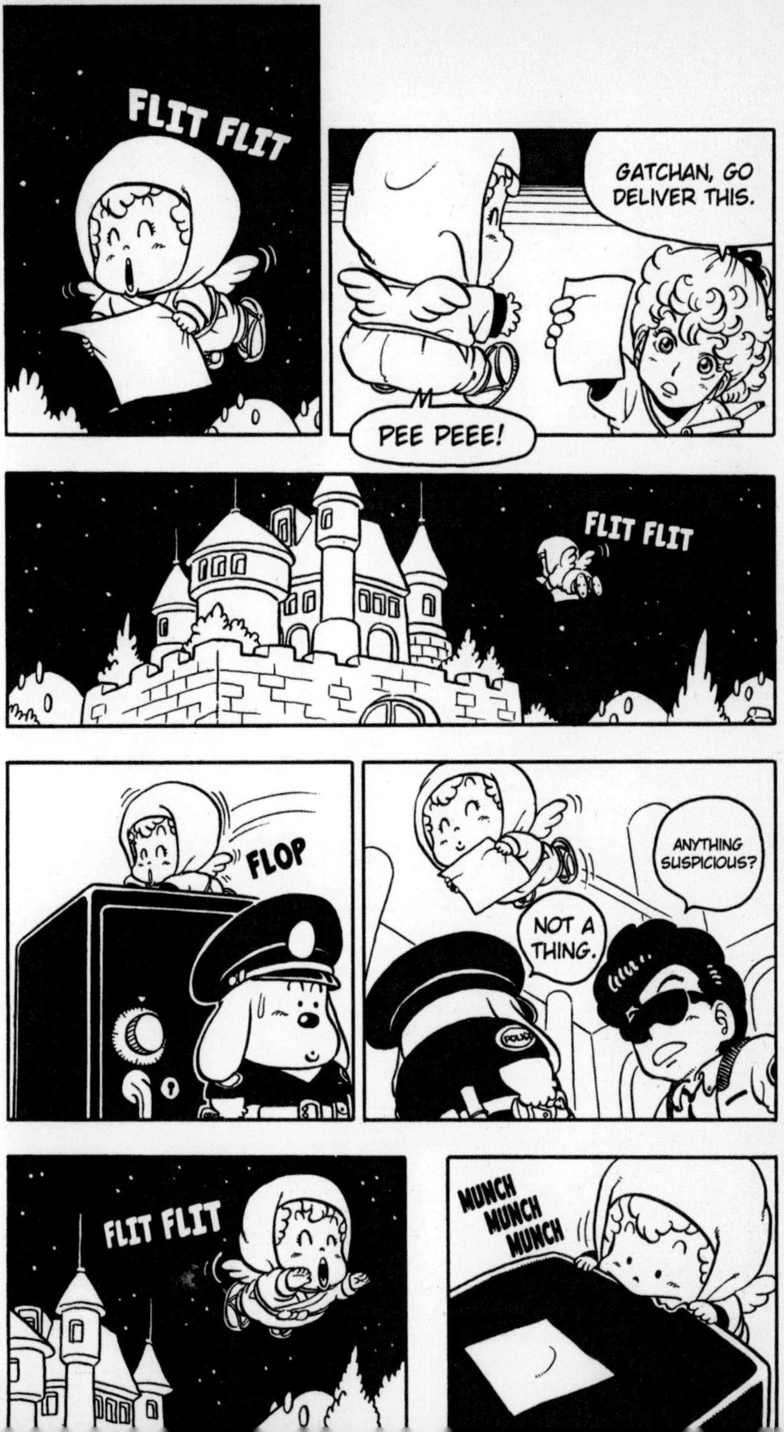
GATCHAN, GO DELIVER THIS.
PEE PEEE!
FLIT FLIT
FLIT FLIT
ANYTHING SUSPICIOUS?
NOT A THING.
FLOP
MUNCH MUNCH MUNCH
FLIT FLIT

READ THIS WAY

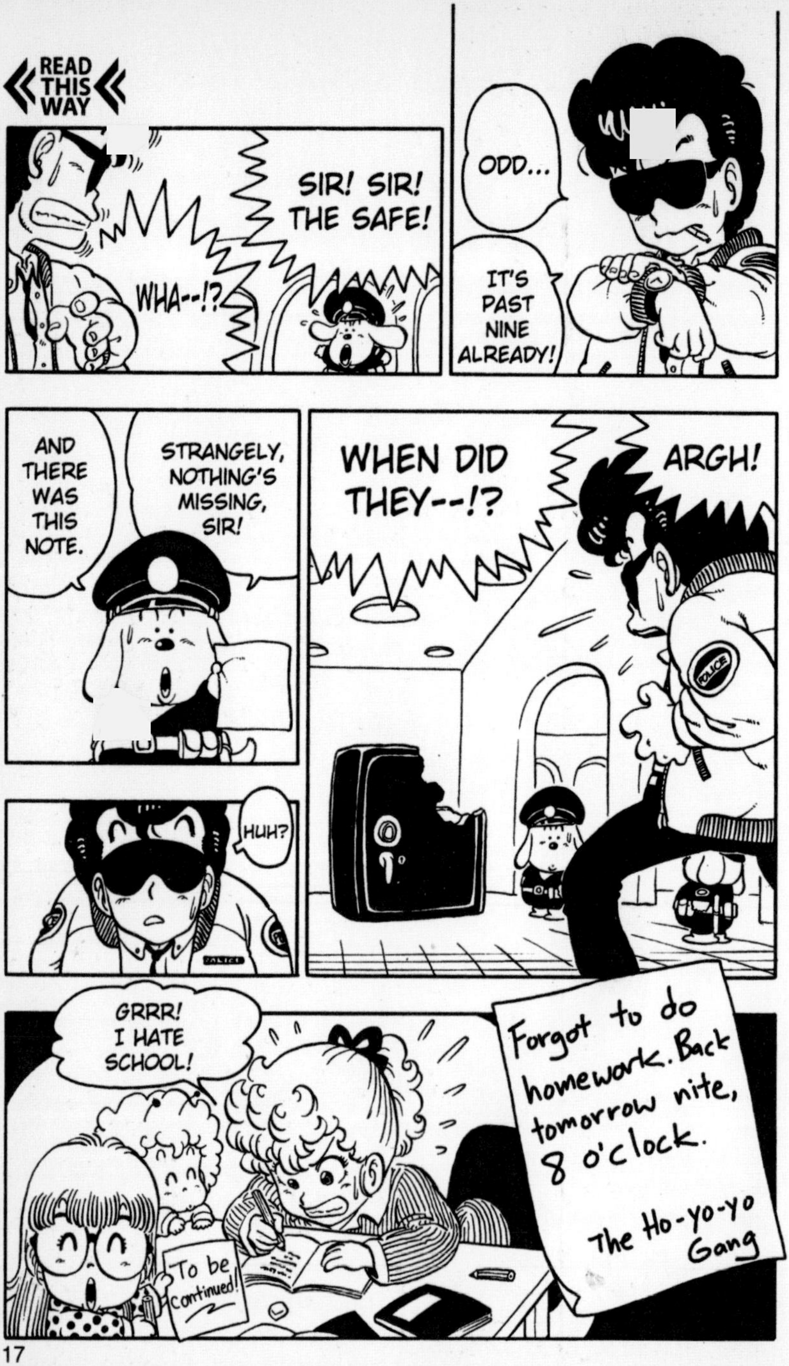

ODD...
IT'S PAST NINE ALREADY!
SIR! SIR! THE SAFE!
WHA--!?
ARGH!
WHEN DID THEY--!?
STRANGELY, NOTHING'S MISSING, SIR!
AND THERE WAS THIS NOTE.
HUH?
Forgot to do homework. Back tomorrow nite, 8 o'clock.
The Ho-yo-yo Gang
GRRR! I HATE SCHOOL!
To be continued!

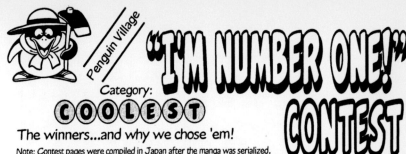

Penguin Village

"I'M NUMBER ONE!" CONTEST

Category: **COOLEST**

The winners...and why we chose 'em!

Note: Contest pages were compiled in Japan after the manga was serialized. As a result, some characters and events have yet to appear in the English edition.

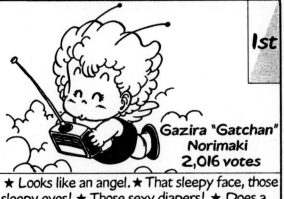

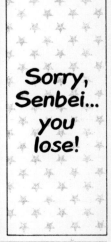

Sorry, Senbei... you lose!

1st

Gazira "Gatchan" Norimaki
2,016 votes

★ Looks like an angel. ★ That sleepy face, those sleepy eyes! ★ Those sexy diapers! ★ Does a great praying mantis impersonation. ★ Had a full head of hair from birth. ★ Drinks nectar from flowers through a straw.

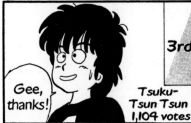

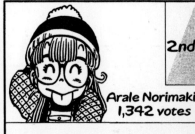

2nd

Arale Norimaki
1,342 votes

★ Wicked powerful, and "KIIIIN" is cool, too! ★ Her spunk makes me feel sluggish and boring. ★ She keeps getting shorter! ★ Alluring breasts. ★ Dumb as a doornail. ★ Ooh, her n'cha-cha dance!

3rd

Gee, thanks!

Tsuku-Tsun Tsun
1,104 votes

★ Has eyes like a hawk. ★ Women like strong men, and Tsuku-Tsun knows kung-fu! Hi-yah! ★ That froofy hair, those wavy pants, those manly eyebrows...he's so cool! ★ When women touch him, he turns goofy!

The Ho-yo-yo Gang
Part 2

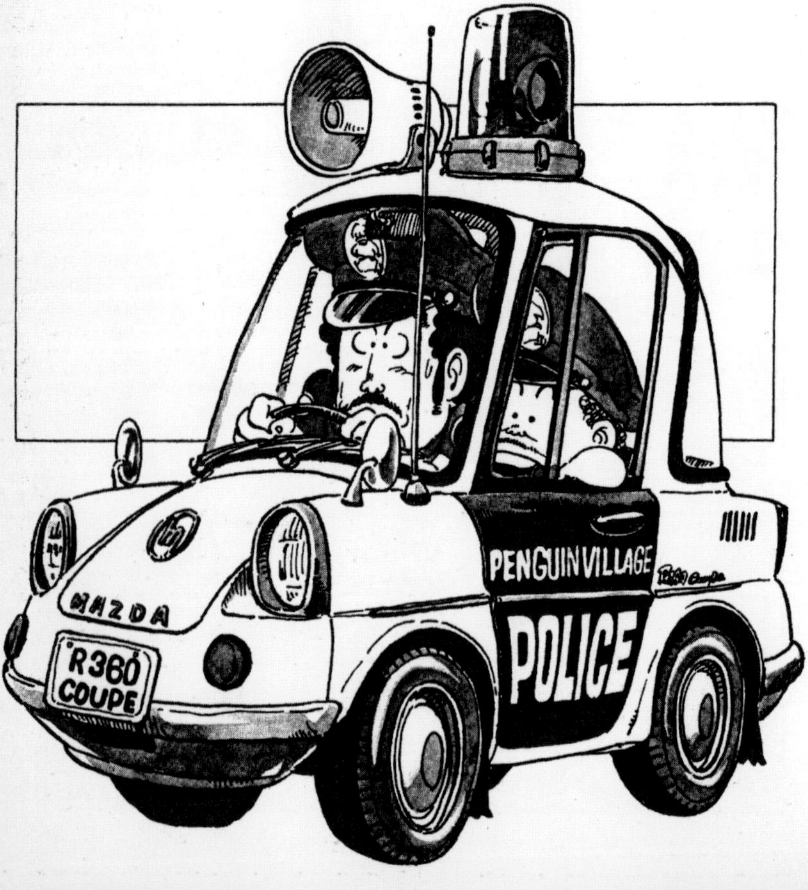
PENGUIN VILLAGE
POLICE
MAZDA
R360
COUPE

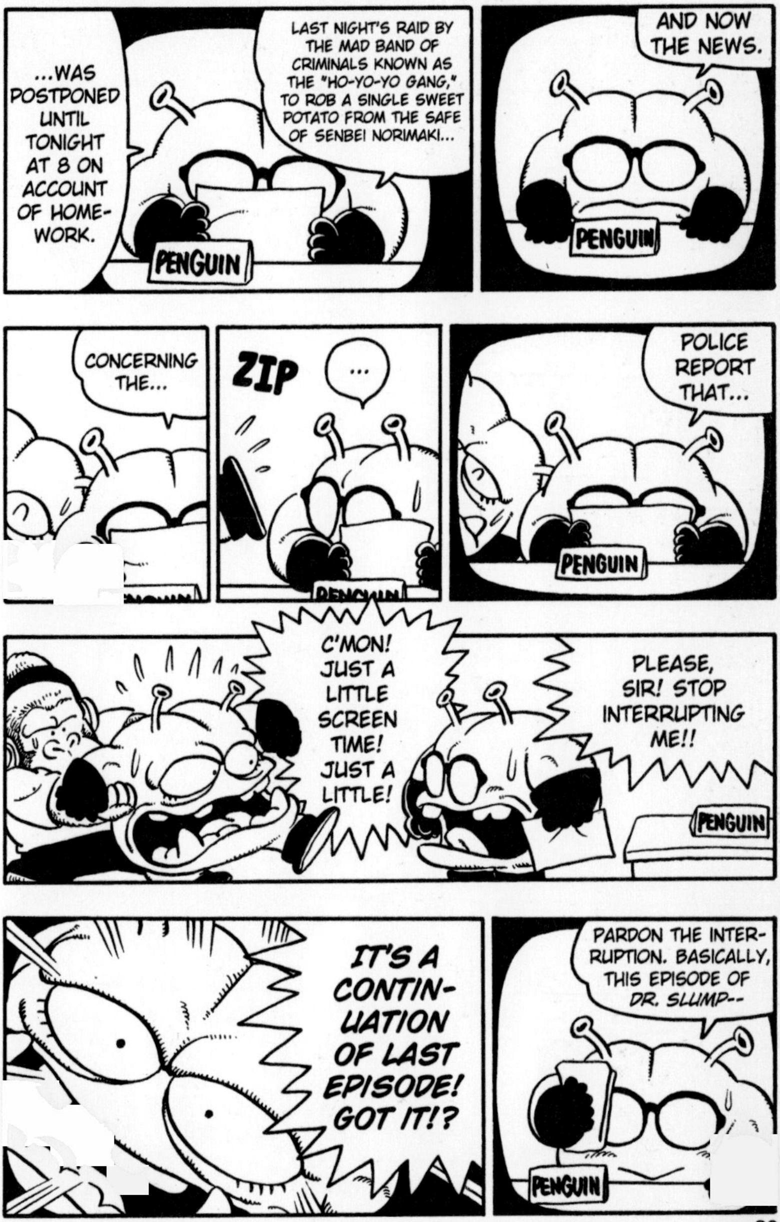
AND NOW THE NEWS.
PENGUIN
LAST NIGHT'S RAID BY THE MAD BAND OF CRIMINALS KNOWN AS THE "HO-YO-YO GANG," TO ROB A SINGLE SWEET POTATO FROM THE SAFE OF SENBEI NORIMAKI...
...WAS POSTPONED UNTIL TONIGHT AT 8 ON ACCOUNT OF HOME-WORK.
PENGUIN
POLICE REPORT THAT...
PENGUIN
...
ZIP
CONCERNING THE...
PLEASE, SIR! STOP INTERRUPTING ME!!
PENGUIN
C'MON! JUST A LITTLE SCREEN TIME! JUST A LITTLE!
PARDON THE INTER-RUPTION. BASICALLY, THIS EPISODE OF DR. SLUMP--
PENGUIN
IT'S A CONTIN-UATION OF LAST EPISODE! GOT IT!?

READ THIS WAY

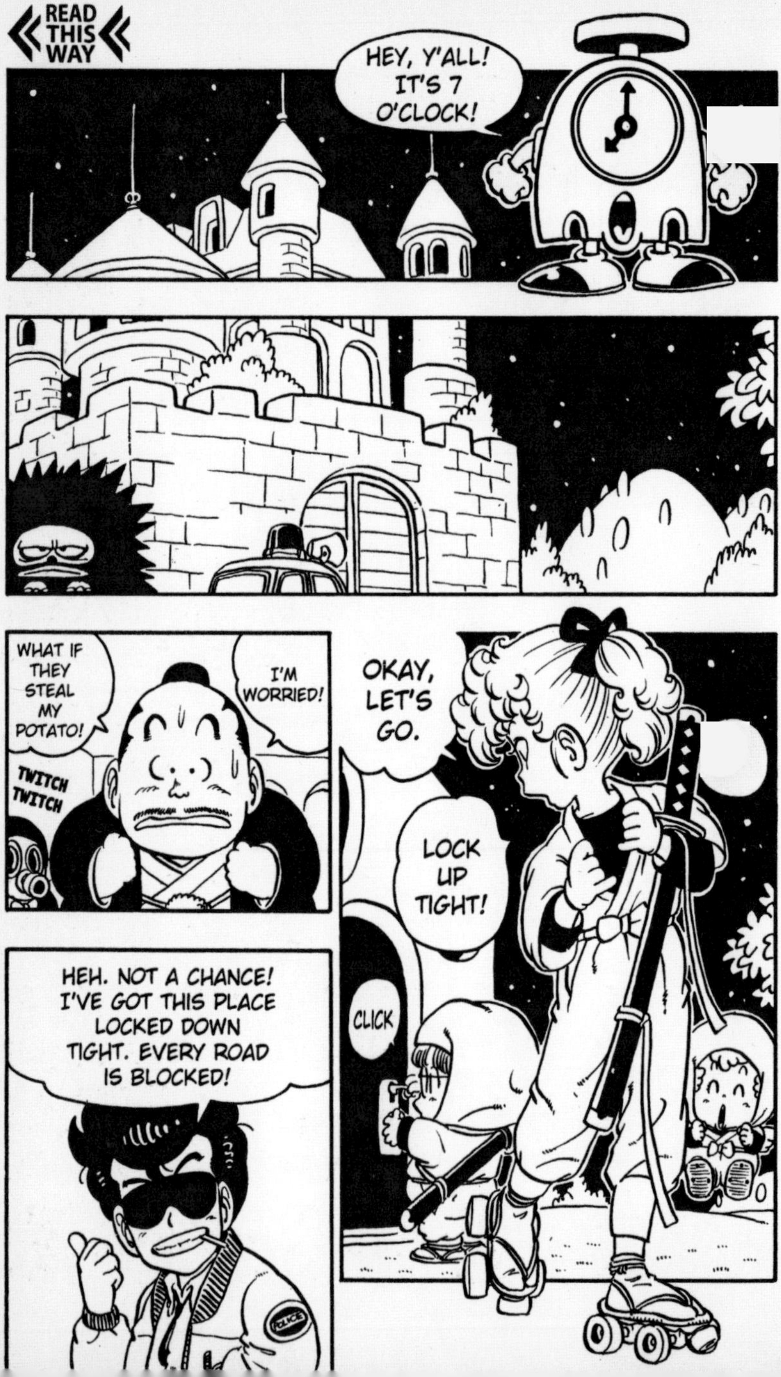
HEY, Y'ALL! IT'S 7 O'CLOCK!
OKAY, LET'S GO.
LOCK UP TIGHT!
CLICK
I'M WORRIED!
WHAT IF THEY STEAL MY POTATO!
TWITCH TWITCH
HEH. NOT A CHANCE! I'VE GOT THIS PLACE LOCKED DOWN TIGHT. EVERY ROAD IS BLOCKED!

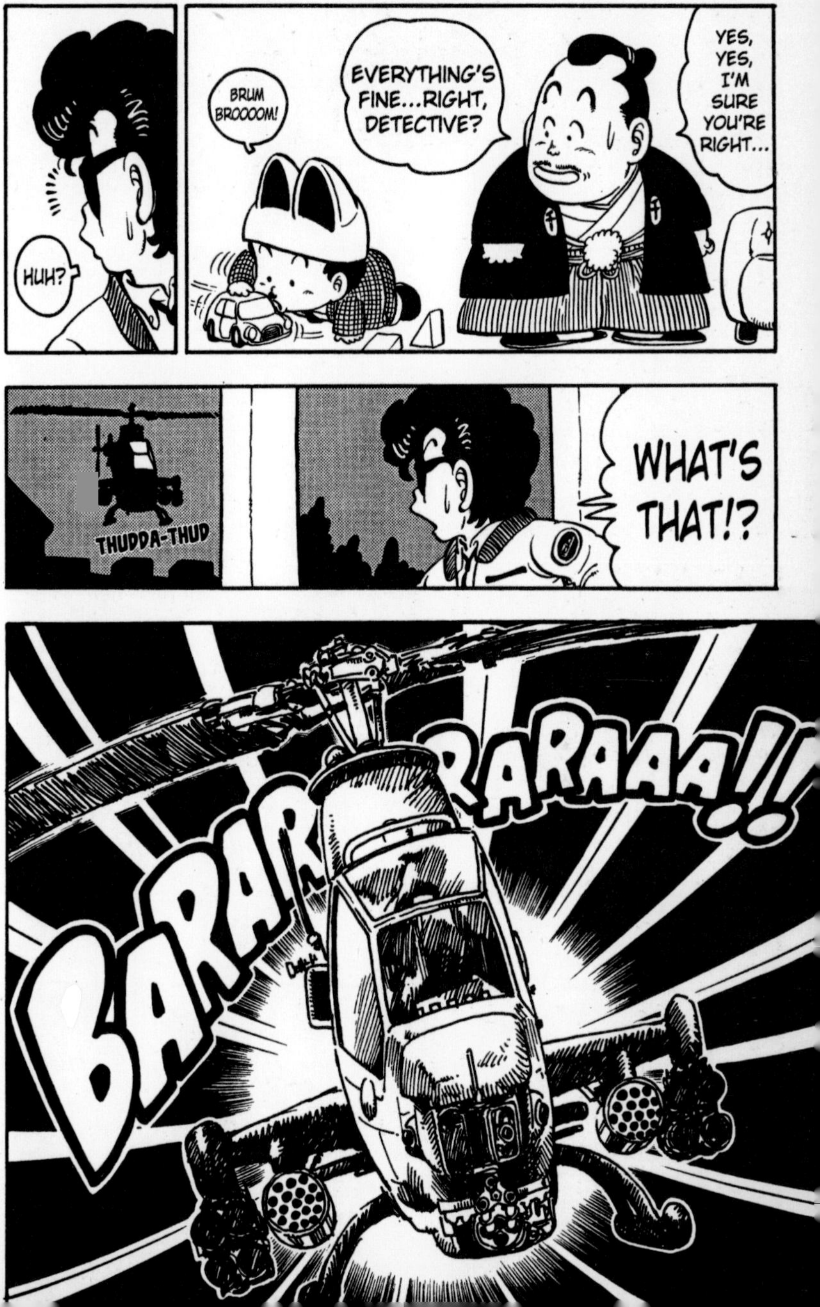
YES, YES, I'M SURE YOU'RE RIGHT...
EVERYTHING'S FINE...RIGHT, DETECTIVE?
BRUM BROOOOM!
HUH?
WHAT'S THAT!?
THUDDA-THUD
BARARRARAAA!!

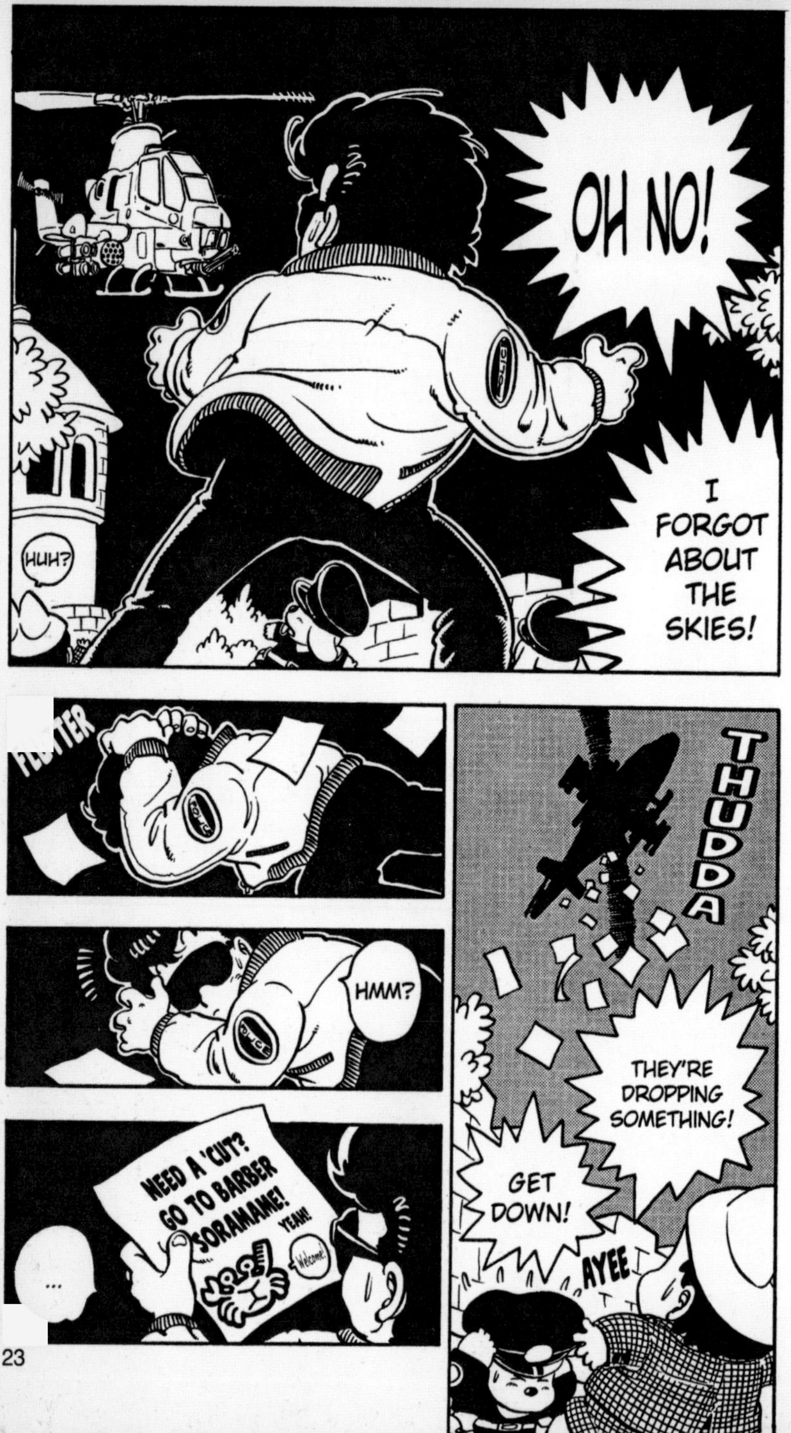

OH NO!
I FORGOT ABOUT THE SKIES!
HUH?
THUDDA
THEY'RE DROPPING SOMETHING!
GET DOWN!
AYEE
FLUTTER
HMM?
NEED A 'CUT? GO TO BARBER SORAMAME!
YEAH!
Welcome!
...

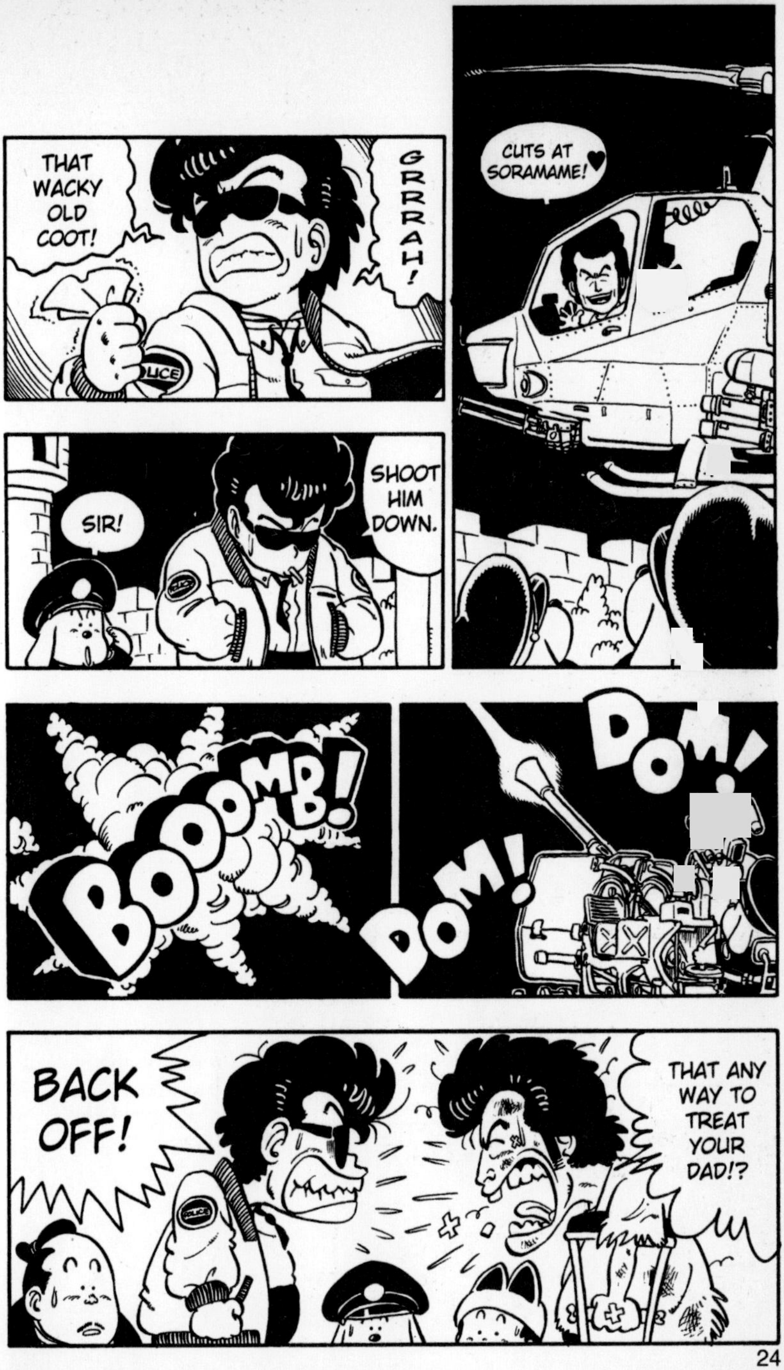
CUTS AT SORAMAME! ♥
GRRRAH!
THAT WACKY OLD COOT!
SHOOT HIM DOWN.
SIR!
DOM!
DOM!
BOOOMB!
THAT ANY WAY TO TREAT YOUR DAD!?
BACK OFF!

READ THIS WAY

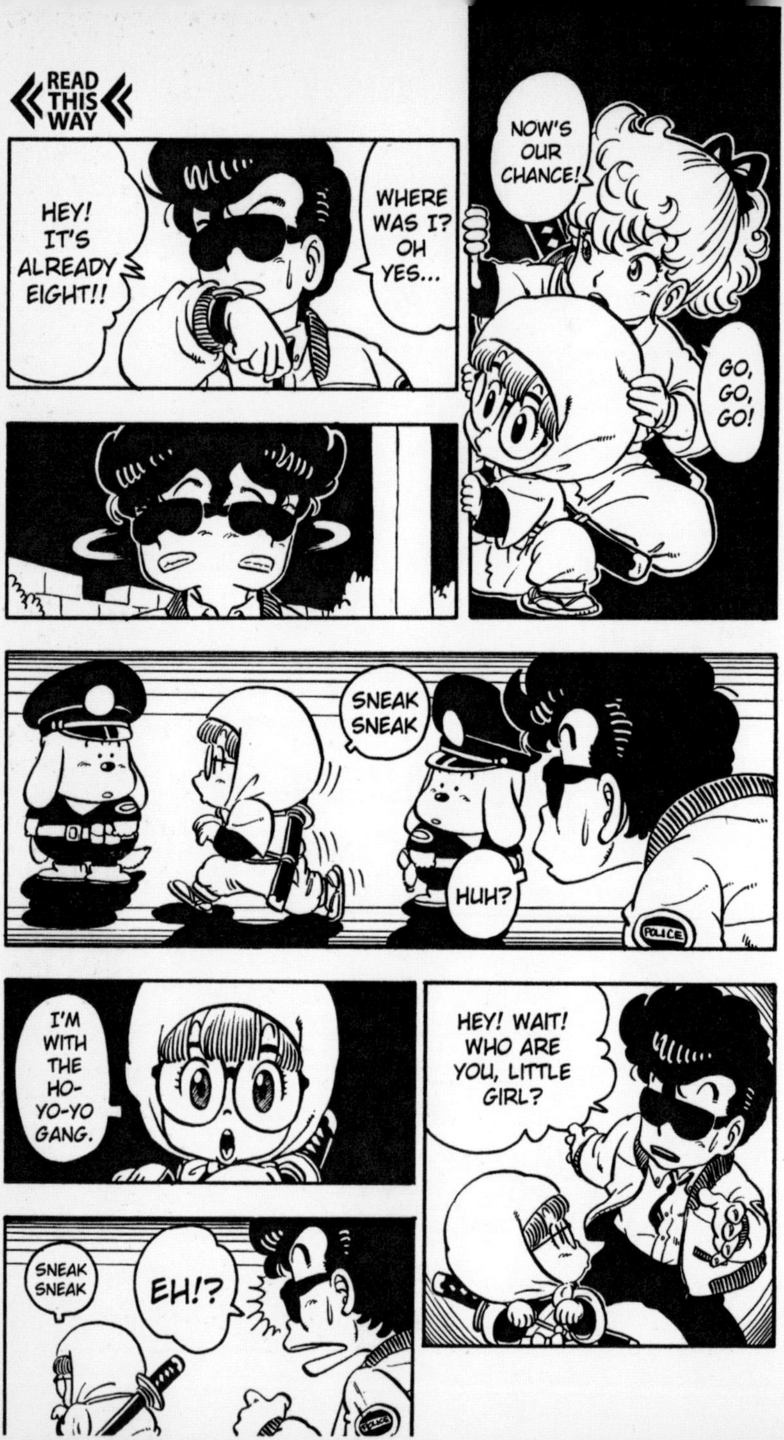
NOW'S OUR CHANCE!
GO, GO, GO!
WHERE WAS I? OH YES...
HEY! IT'S ALREADY EIGHT!!
SNEAK SNEAK
HUH?
POLICE
HEY! WAIT! WHO ARE YOU, LITTLE GIRL?
I'M WITH THE HO-YO-YO GANG.
EH!?
SNEAK SNEAK

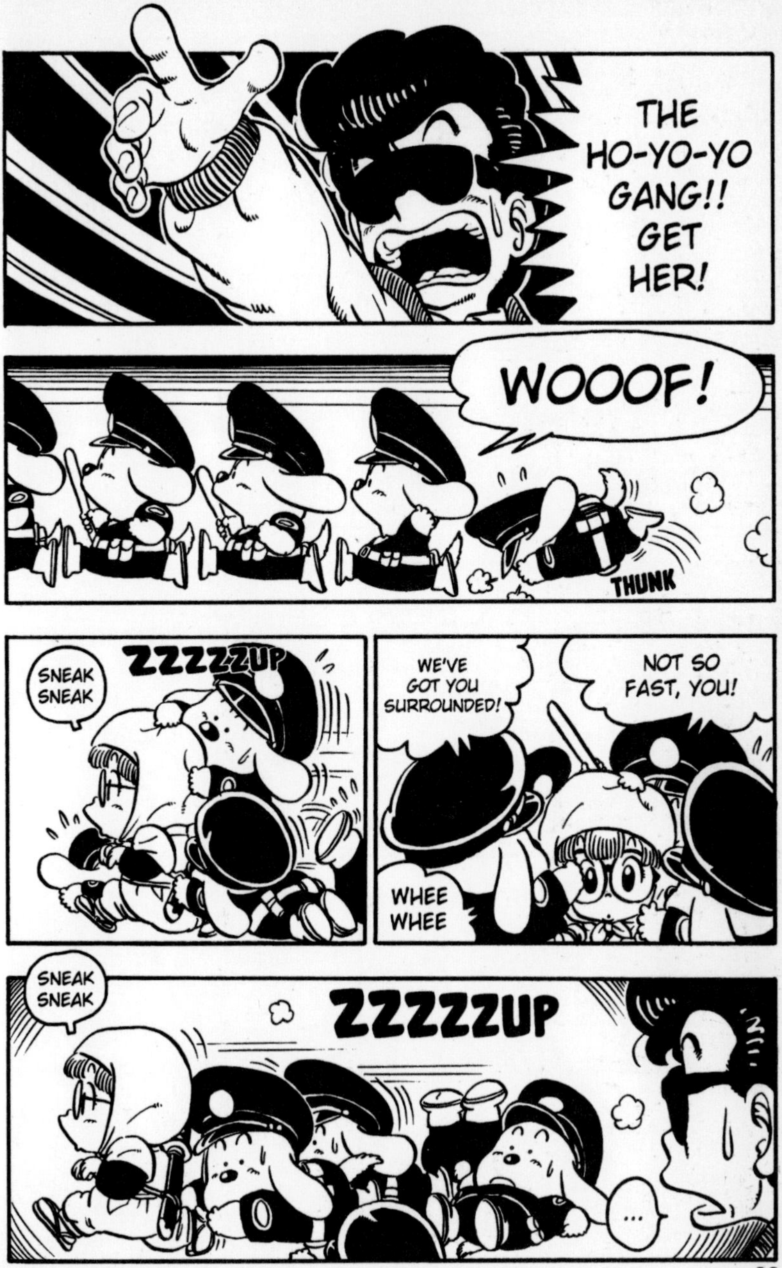
THE HO-YO-YO GANG!! GET HER!
WOOOF!
THUNK
NOT SO FAST, YOU!
WE'VE GOT YOU SURROUNDED!
WHEE WHEE
ZZZZZUP
SNEAK SNEAK
ZZZZZUP
SNEAK SNEAK
...

READ THIS WAY

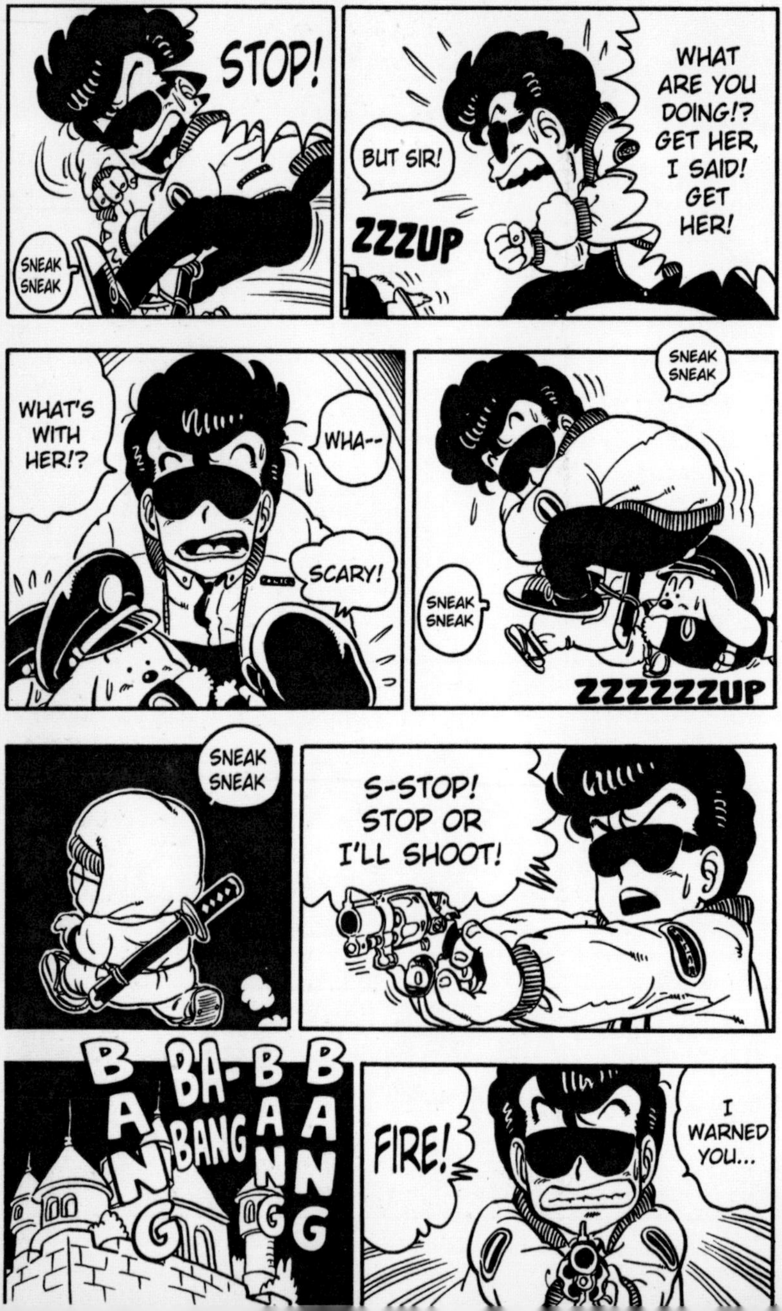

WHAT ARE YOU DOING!? GET HER, I SAID! GET HER!
BUT SIR!
ZZZUP
STOP!
SNEAK SNEAK
SNEAK SNEAK
SNEAK SNEAK
ZZZZZZUP
WHA--
SCARY!
WHAT'S WITH HER!?
S-STOP! STOP OR I'LL SHOOT!
SNEAK SNEAK
I WARNED YOU...
FIRE!
BANG
BA-BANG
BANG
BANG

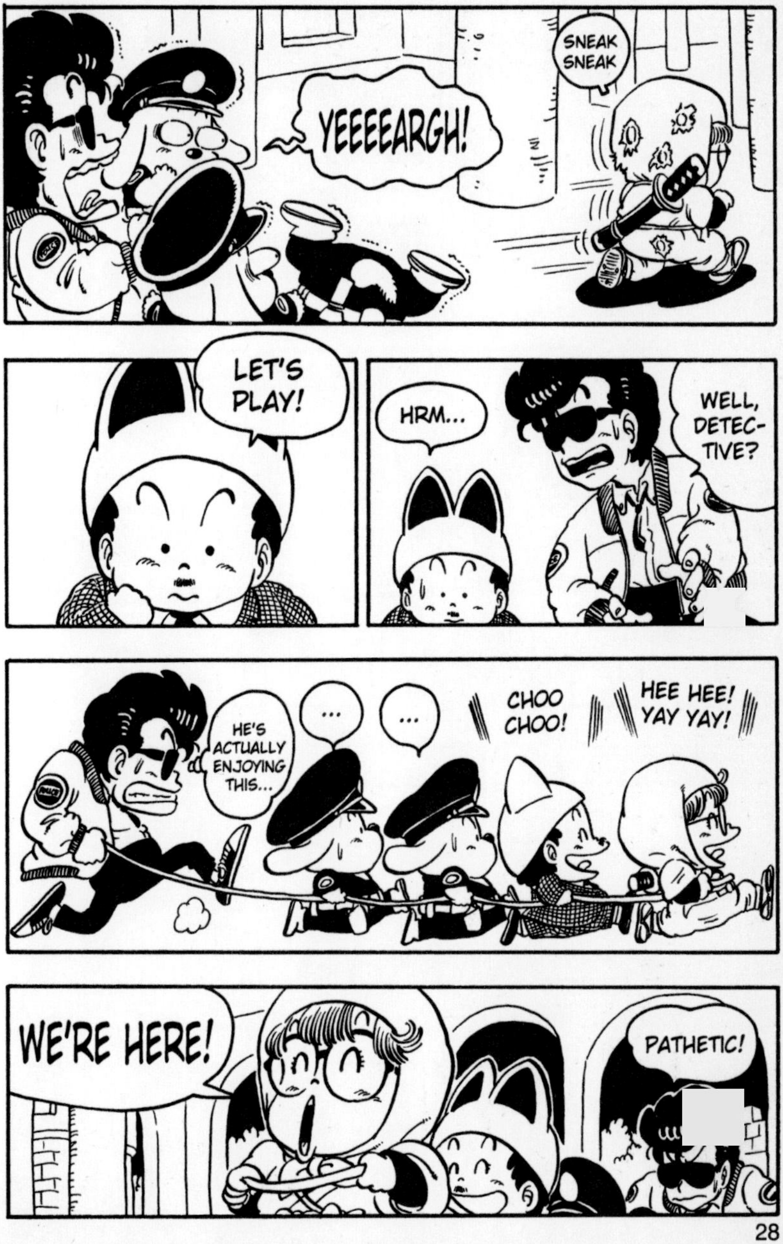
SNEAK SNEAK
YEEEEARGH!
WELL, DETECTIVE?
HRM...
LET'S PLAY!
HEE HEE! YAY YAY!
CHOO CHOO!
...
...
HE'S ACTUALLY ENJOYING THIS...
PATHETIC!
WE'RE HERE!

READ THIS WAY

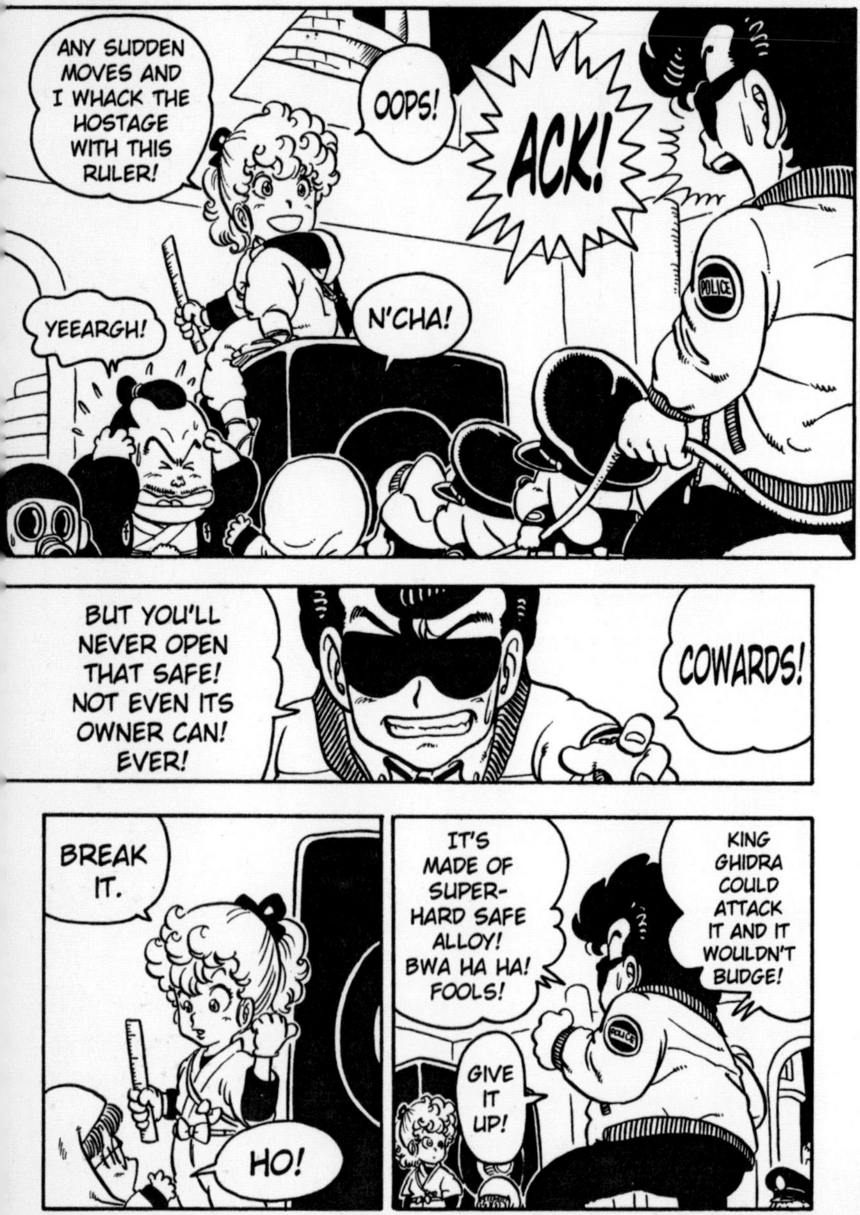
ACK!
OOPS!
ANY SUDDEN MOVES AND I WHACK THE HOSTAGE WITH THIS RULER!
N'CHA!
YEEARGH!
COWARDS!
BUT YOU'LL NEVER OPEN THAT SAFE! NOT EVEN ITS OWNER CAN! EVER!
KING GHIDRA COULD ATTACK IT AND IT WOULDN'T BUDGE!
IT'S MADE OF SUPER-HARD SAFE ALLOY! BWA HA HA! FOOLS!
GIVE IT UP!
POLICE
BREAK IT.
HO!

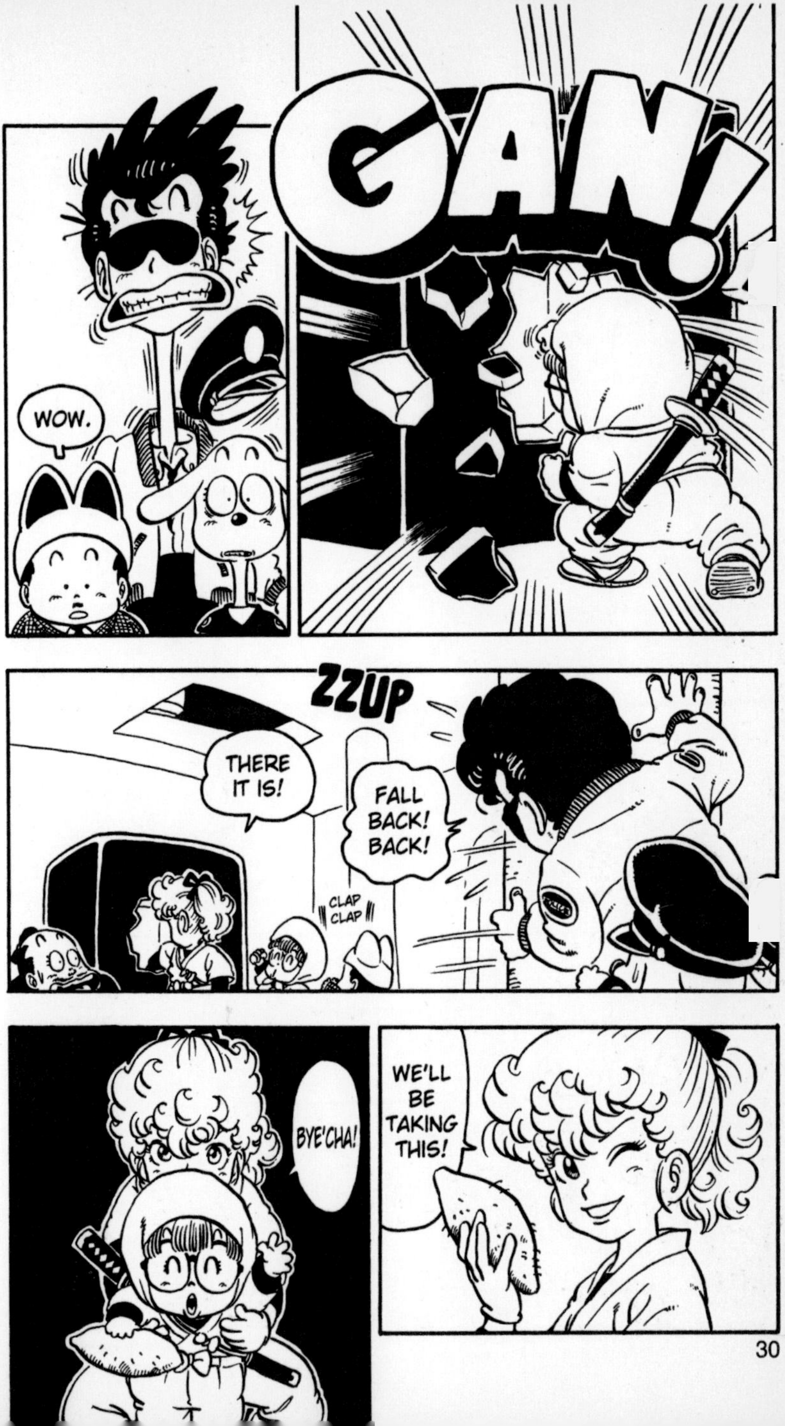
GAN!
WOW.
ZZUP
FALL BACK! BACK!
THERE IT IS!
CLAP CLAP
WE'LL BE TAKING THIS!
BYE'CHA!

READ THIS WAY

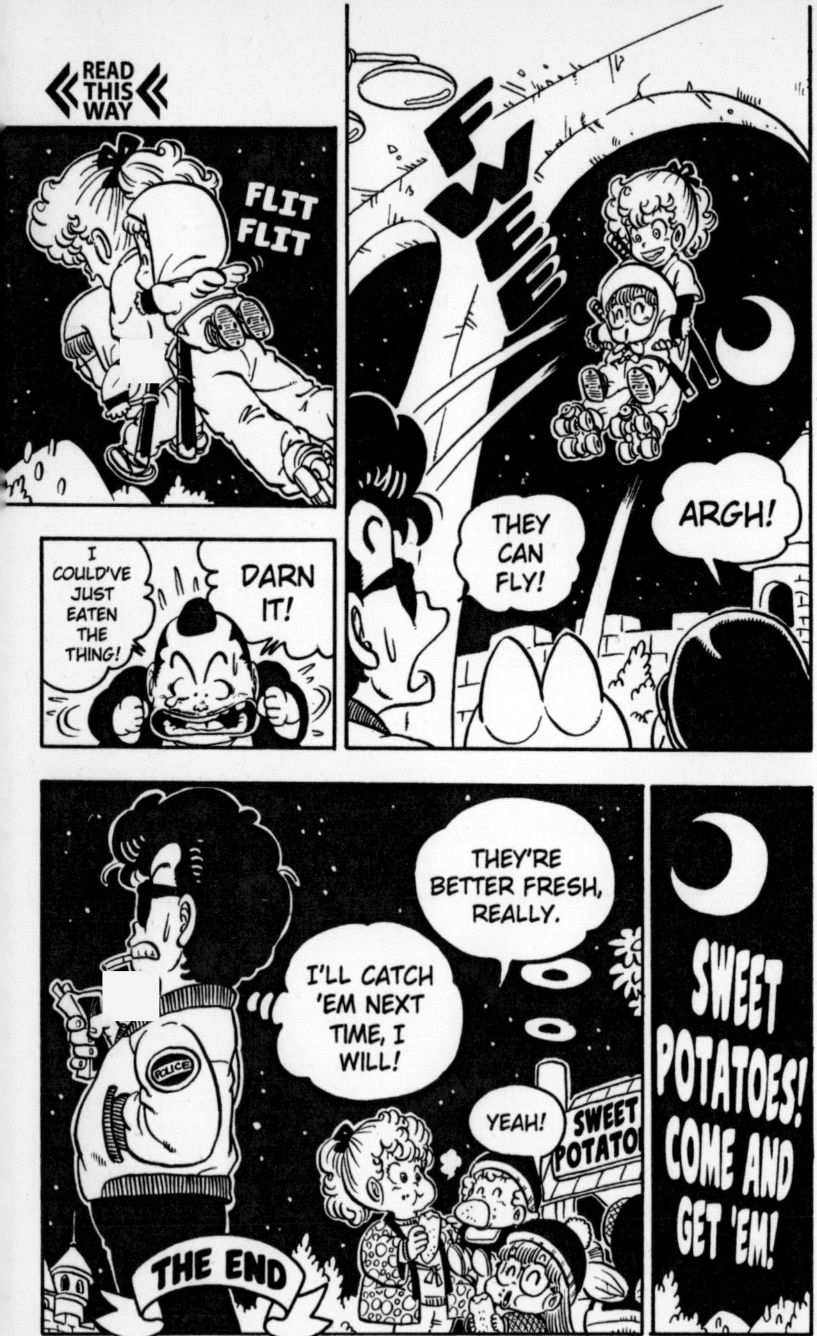

FWEEE
ARGH!
THEY CAN FLY!
FLIT FLIT
DARN IT!
I COULD'VE JUST EATEN THE THING!
SWEET POTATOES! COME AND GET 'EM!
THEY'RE BETTER FRESH, REALLY.
YEAH!
SWEET POTATO
I'LL CATCH 'EM NEXT TIME, I WILL!
POLICE
THE END

Penguin Village "I'M NUMBER ONE!" CONTEST Category: Coolest

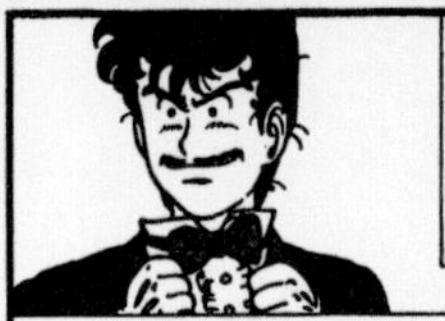

4th

Senbei Norimaki
980 votes

★ Cute pudgy belly! ★ His big ol' face! ★ That serious face that he wears for 3 minutes tops! ★ He looks just like my husband. ★ Pity vote

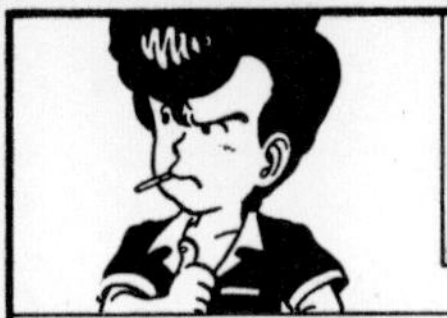

5th

Taro Soramame
692 votes

★ Cuts an imposing figure on his scooter. ★ Those beady little eyes behind his sunglasses. ★ The only real man in Penguin Village.

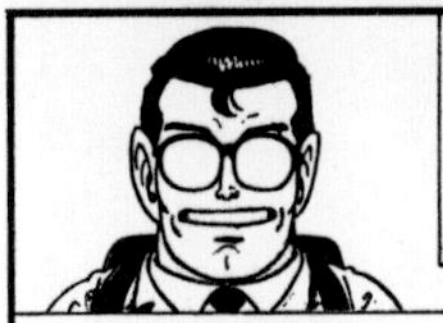

6th

Suppaman
514 votes

★ He's so cute when he picks his nose! ★ His pucker after eating pickled plums ★ His giant face ★ Such a cute necktie!

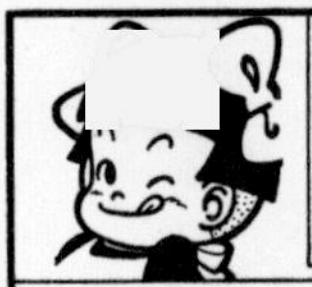

7th

Kinoko Sarada
422 votes

★ Can't get enough of her sarcasm. ★ Her buzz cut is a fashion statement. ★ That cute ribbon she wears

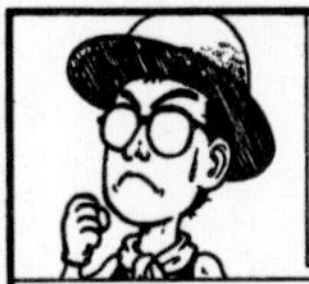

8th

Akira Toriyama
414 votes

★ We're never sure what he really looks like. ★ I just wanted a present. ★ Just kidding!

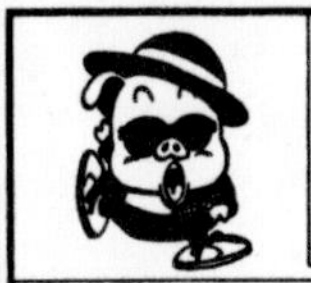

9th

Oinkety Oink
362 votes

★ C'mon, a pig wearing sunglasses? That's cool! ★ His knack for showing up in the most unlikely places!

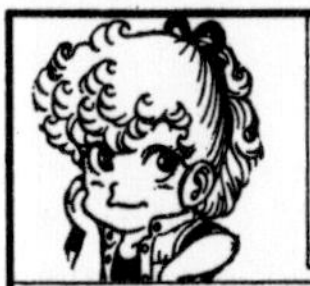

10th

Akane Kimidori
226 votes

★ Clothes and smarts. I want to make her mine! ★ A real go-getter ★ I love her. No, really. I love her.

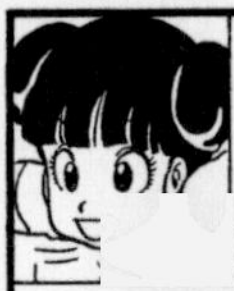

11th

Tsuru-Rin Tsun
200 votes

★ Those big eyes and that cute Chinese-style dress ★ I want to make her my bride! Hi-yah!

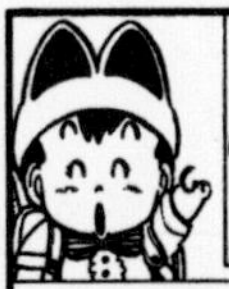

12th

Peasuke Soramame
128 votes

★ So cute when he's scared! ★ I call my boyfriend "Peasuke." ♡

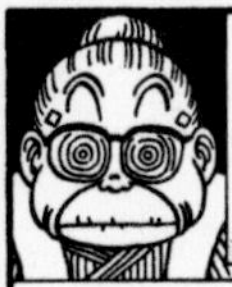

13th

Old Woman Spring
122 votes

★ Those cute whirly glasses! ★ I like how her face wrinkles! ★ That singing voice!

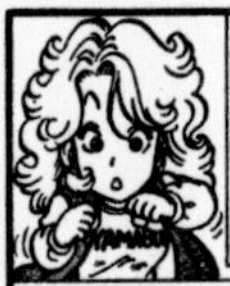

14th

Midori Norimaki (née Yamabuki)
110 votes

★ That knock-out bod ★ I can't believe she married that idiot!

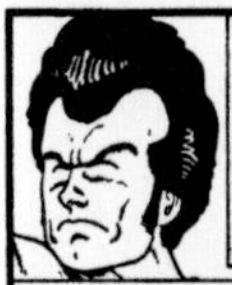

15th

Kurikinton Soramame
102 votes

★ His realistic face is so fine. ★ Who couldn't love such a dour man? ★ He can't be Peasuke's father.

Leave It to Akiko

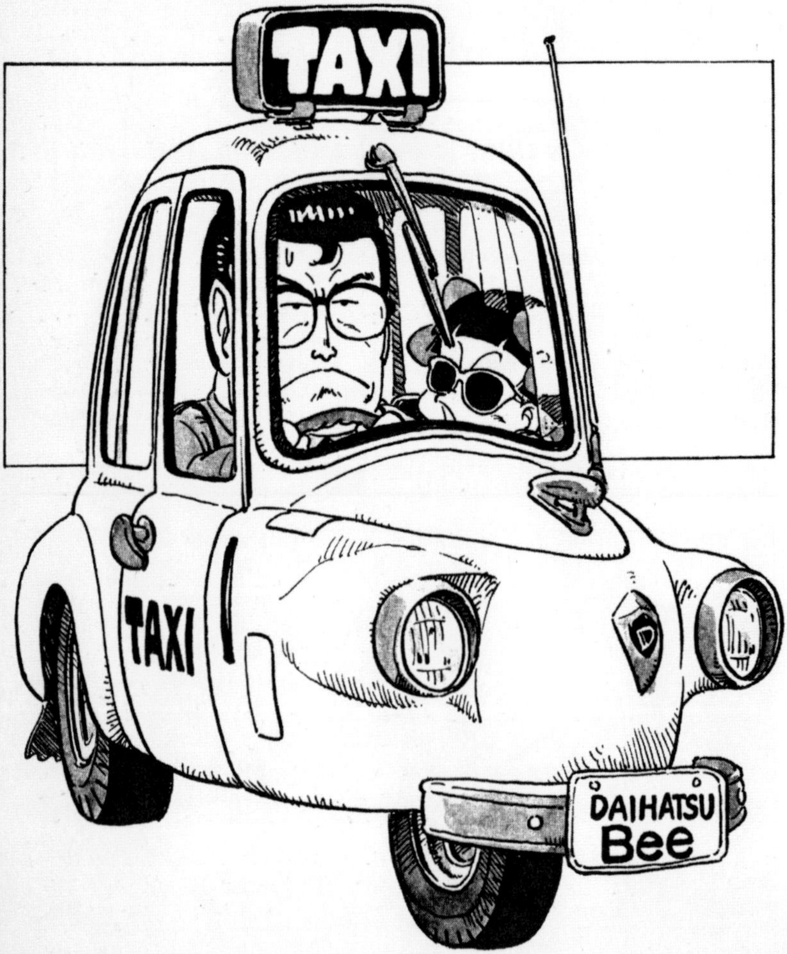
TAXI
TAXI
DAIHATSU
Bee

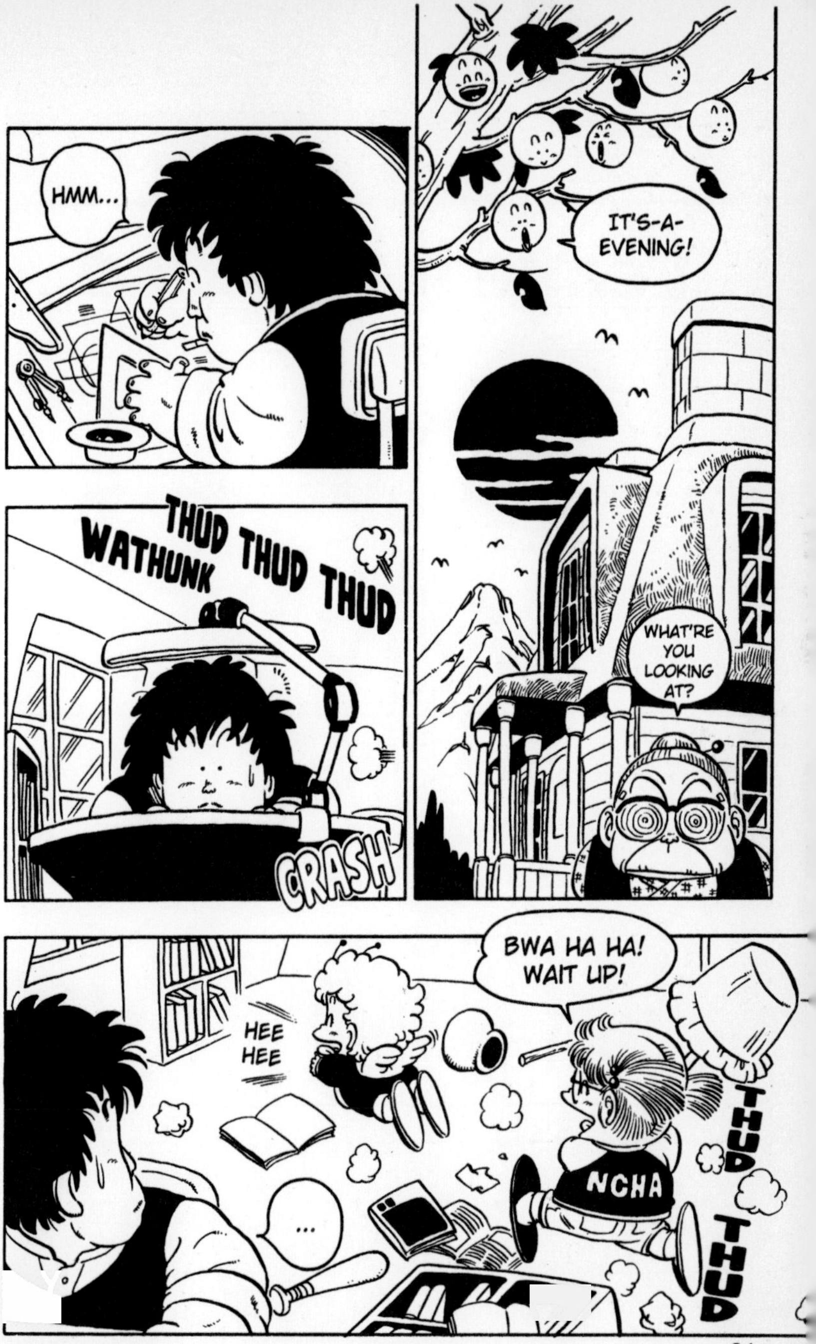
IT'S-A-EVENING!
WHAT'RE YOU LOOKING AT?
HMM...
THUD THUD THUD
WATHUNK
CRASH
BWA HA HA! WAIT UP!
THUD THUD
NCHA
HEE HEE
...

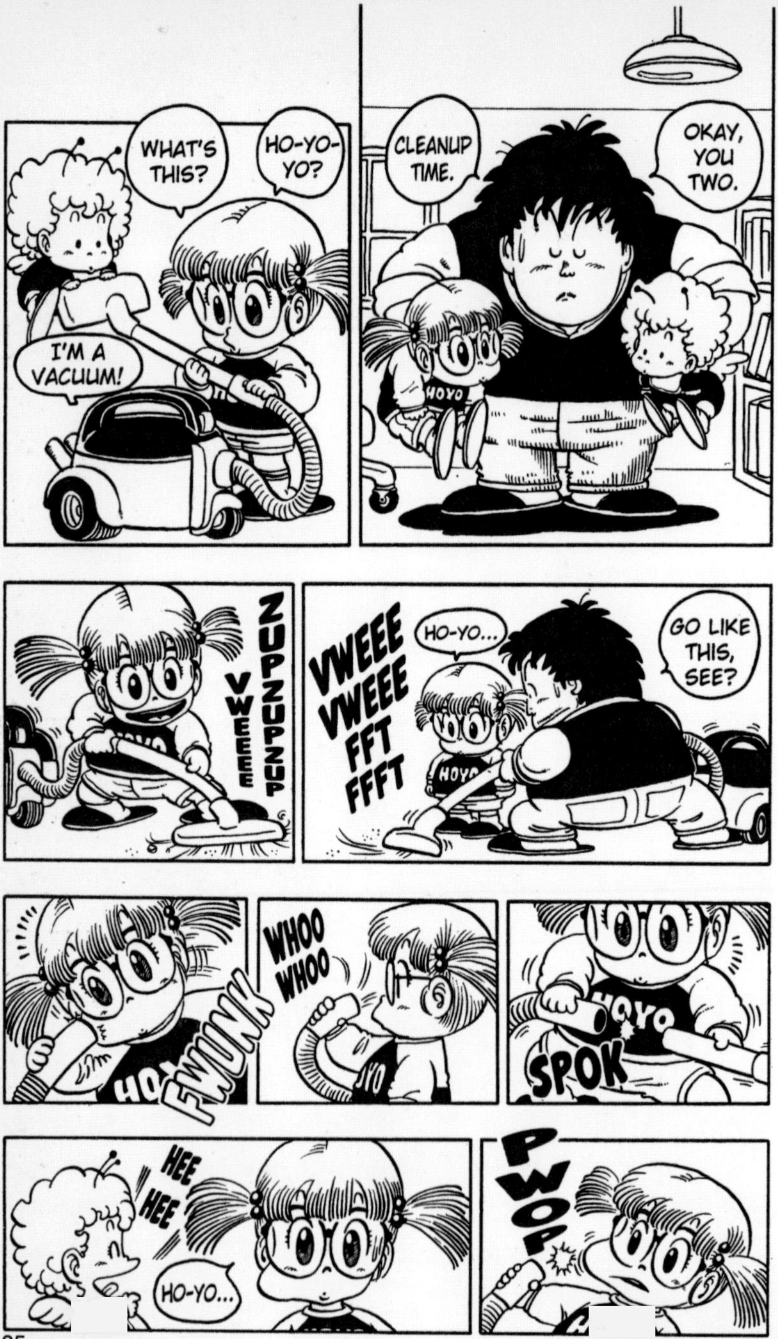
OKAY, YOU TWO.
CLEANUP TIME.
HO-YO-YO?
WHAT'S THIS?
I'M A VACUUM!
GO LIKE THIS, SEE?
HO-YO...
VWEEE VWEEE FFT FFFT
ZUPZUPZUP
VWEEEE
SPOK
WHOO WHOO
FWUNK
PWOP
HEE HEE
HO-YO...

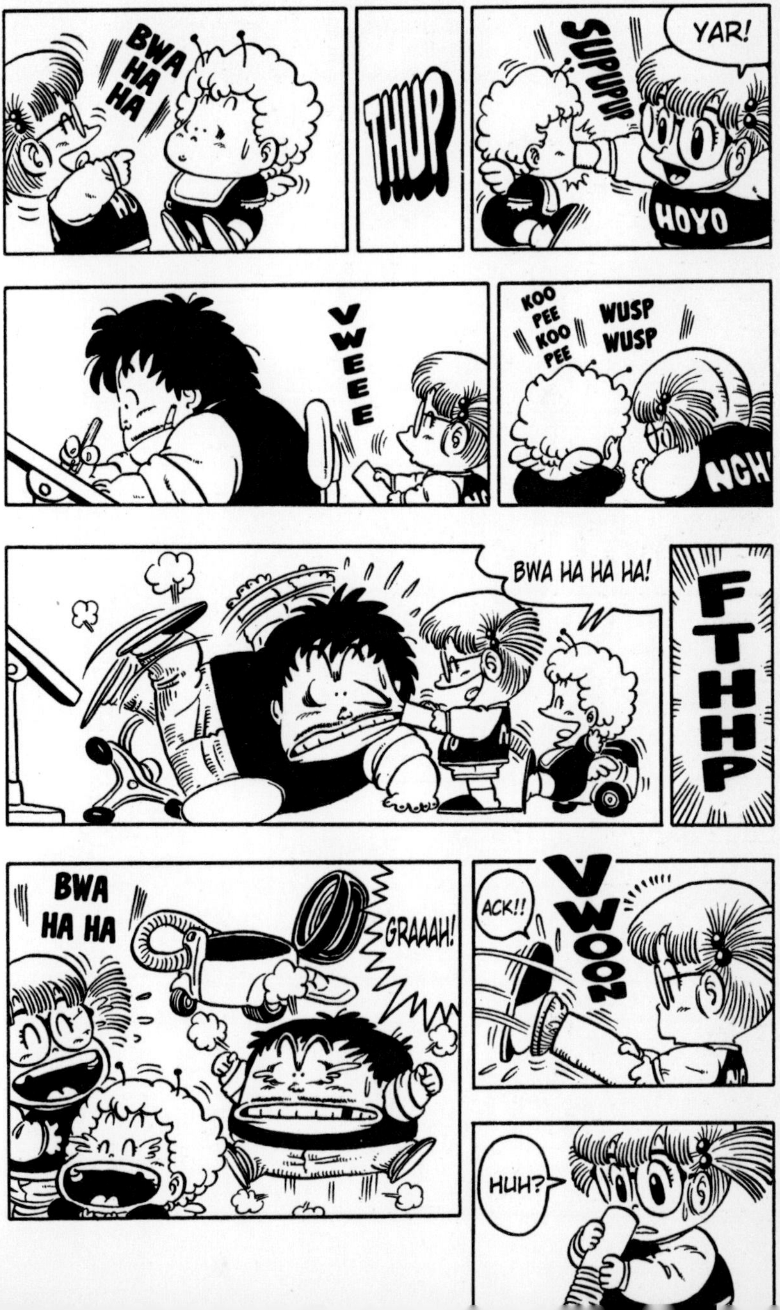
YAR!
SUPUPUP
HOYO
THUP
BWA HA HA
WUSP WUSP
KOO PEE KOO PEE
NCH
VWEEE
FTHHP
BWA HA HA HA!
VWOON
ACK!!
HUH?
GRAAAH!
BWA HA HA

READ THIS WAY

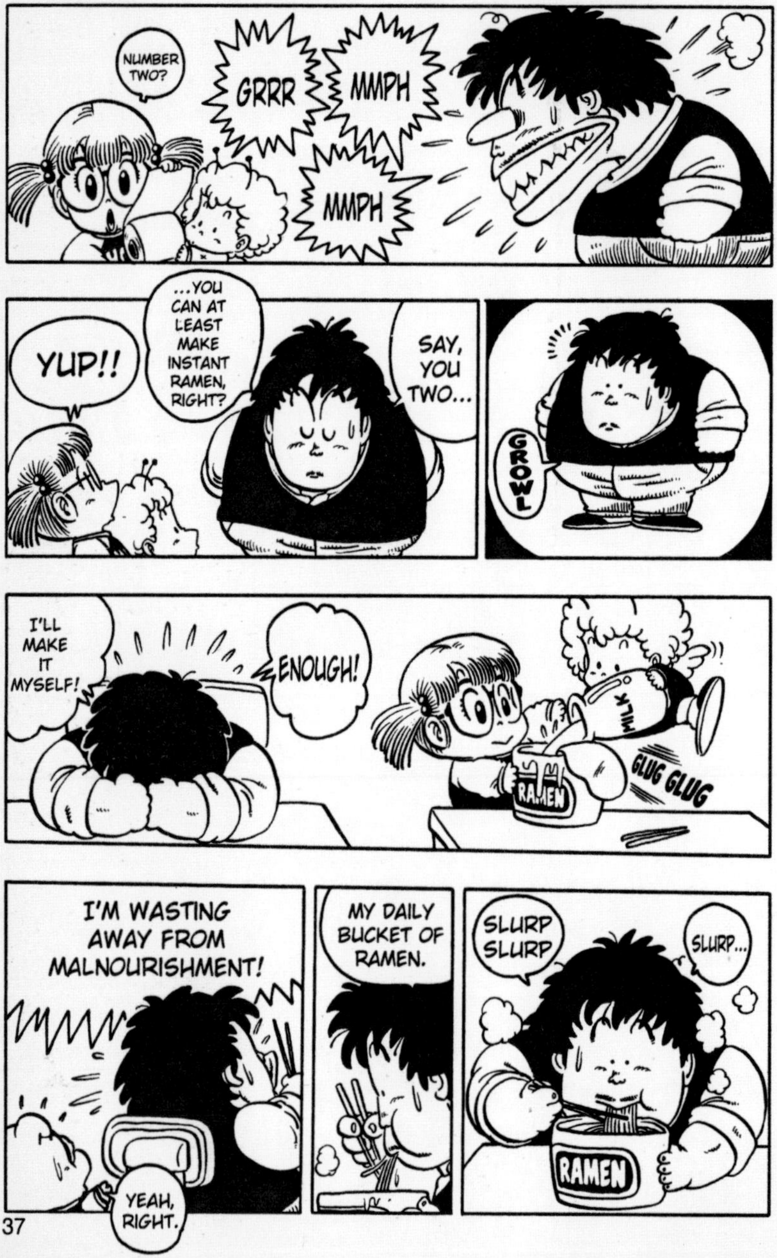
MMPH
GRRR
MMPH
NUMBER TWO?
GROWL
SAY, YOU TWO...
...YOU CAN AT LEAST MAKE INSTANT RAMEN, RIGHT?
YUP!!
MILK
GLUG GLUG
RAMEN
ENOUGH!
I'LL MAKE IT MYSELF!
SLURP...
SLURP SLURP
RAMEN
MY DAILY BUCKET OF RAMEN.
I'M WASTING AWAY FROM MALNOURISHMENT!
YEAH, RIGHT.

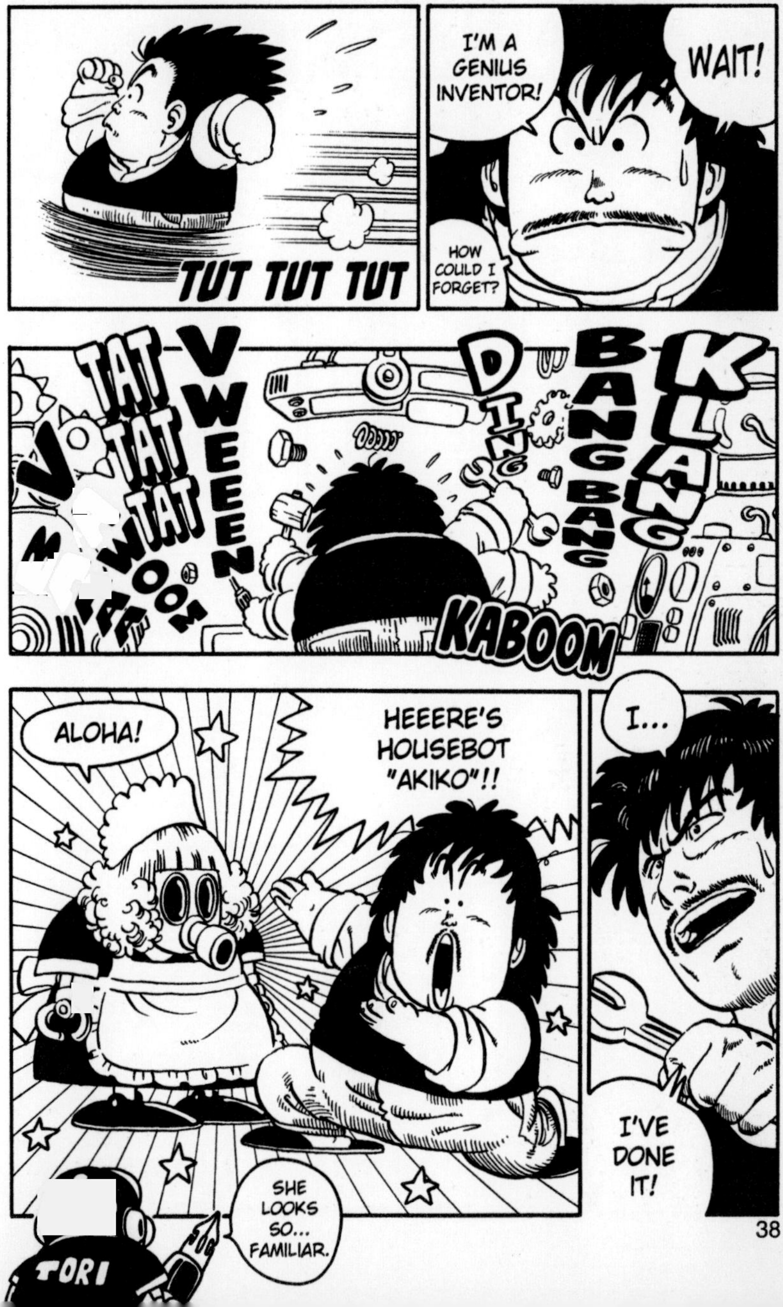
WAIT!
I'M A GENIUS INVENTOR!
HOW COULD I FORGET?
TUT TUT TUT
KLANG
BANGBANG
DING
KABOOM
VWEEEEN
TAT TAT TAT
I...
I'VE DONE IT!
HEEERE'S HOUSEBOT "AKIKO"!!
ALOHA!
SHE LOOKS SO... FAMILIAR.
TORI

READ THIS WAY

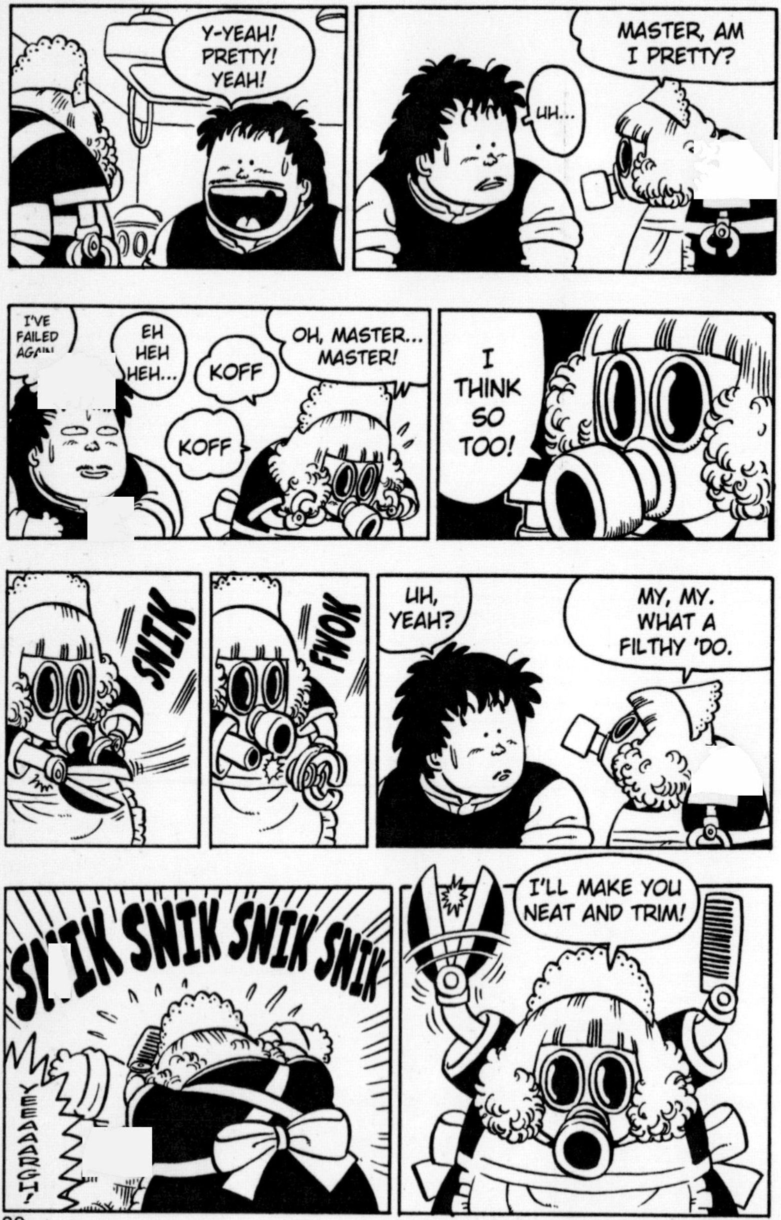
MASTER, AM I PRETTY?
UH...
Y-YEAH! PRETTY! YEAH!
I THINK SO TOO!
OH, MASTER... MASTER!
KOFF
EH HEH HEH...
I'VE FAILED
KOFF
MY, MY. WHAT A FILTHY 'DO.
UH, YEAH?
FWOK
SNIK
I'LL MAKE YOU NEAT AND TRIM!
SNIK SNIK SNIK
YEEAAARGH!

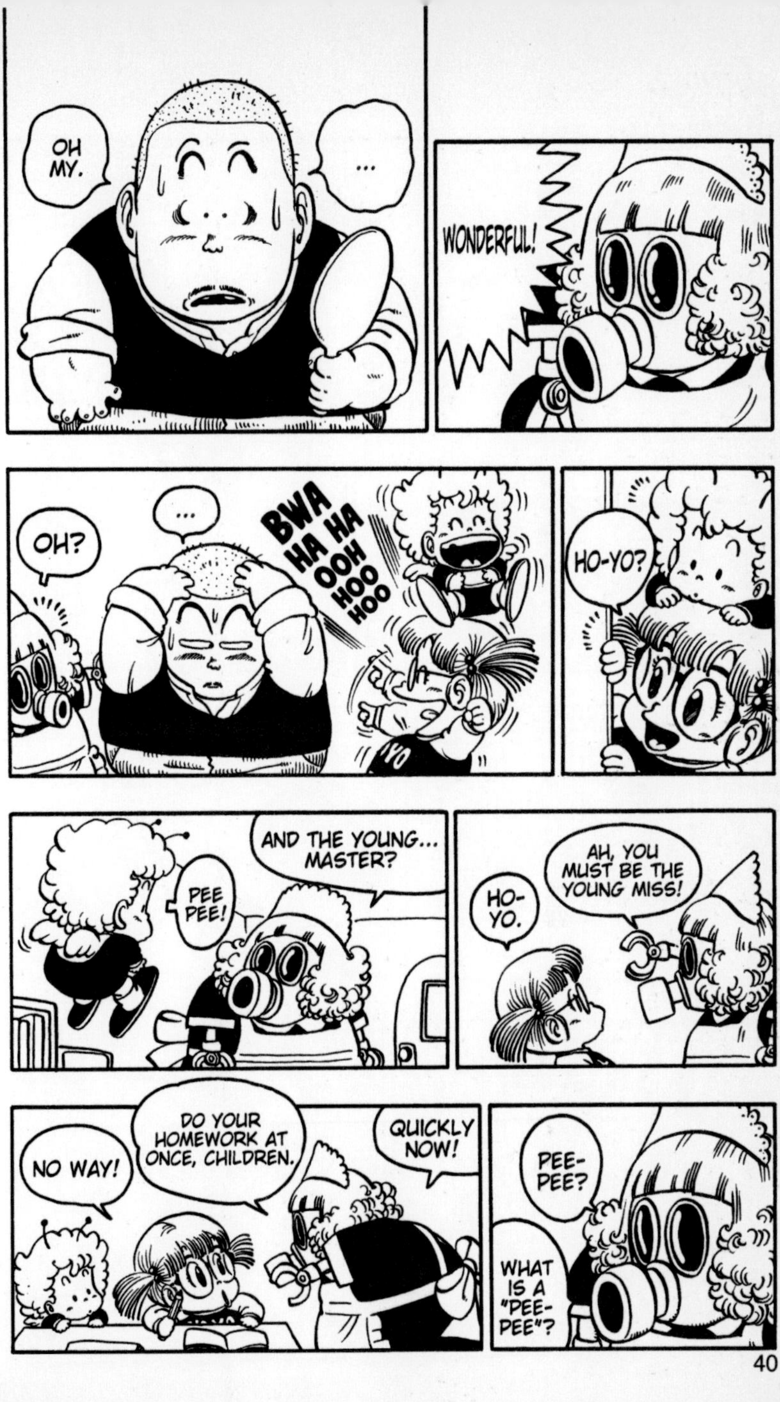
WONDERFUL!
...
OH MY.
HO-YO?
BWA HA HA OOH HOO HOO
...
OH?
AH, YOU MUST BE THE YOUNG MISS!
HO-YO.
AND THE YOUNG... MASTER?
PEE PEE!
PEE-PEE?
WHAT IS A "PEE-PEE"?
QUICKLY NOW!
DO YOUR HOMEWORK AT ONCE, CHILDREN.
NO WAY!

READ THIS WAY

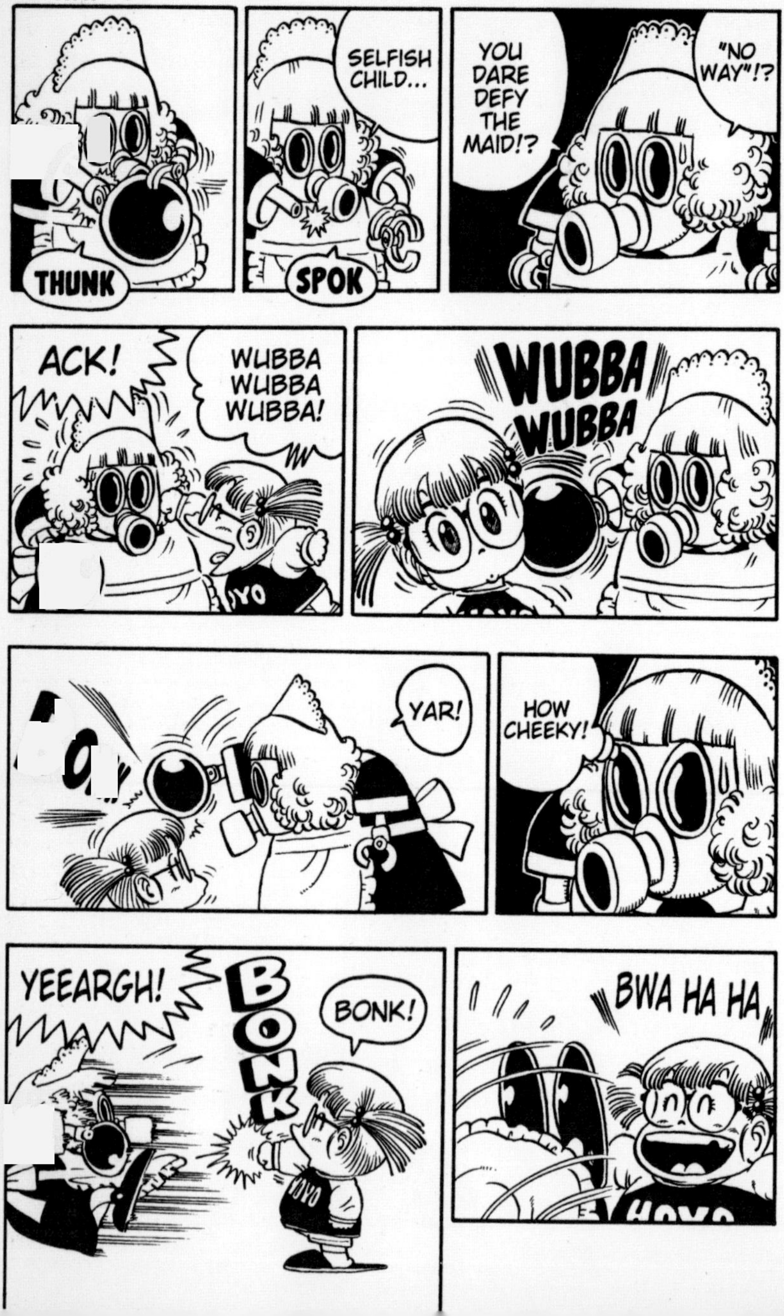
"NO WAY"!?
YOU DARE DEFY THE MAID!?
SELFISH CHILD...
SPOK
THUNK
WUBBA WUBBA
WUBBA WUBBA WUBBA!
ACK!
HOW CHEEKY!
YAR!
BWA HA HA
BONK!
BONK
YEEARGH!

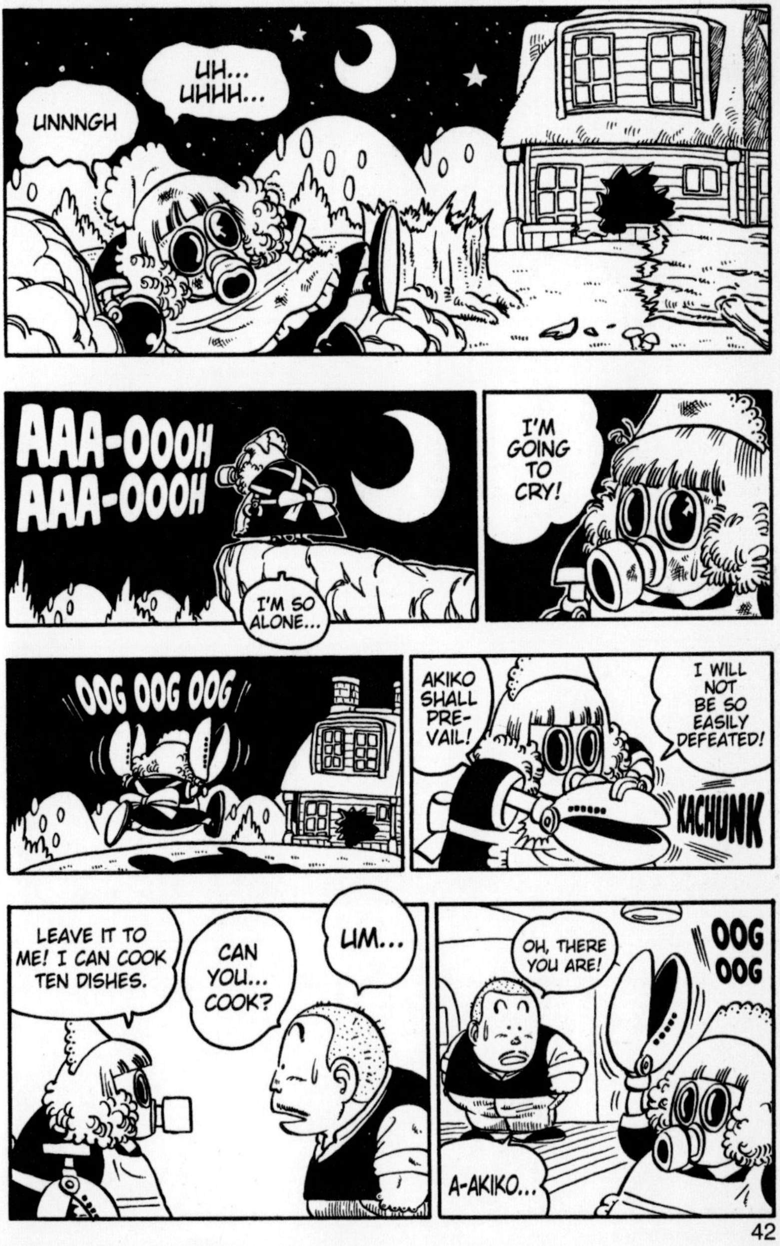
UH... UHHH...
UNNNGH
I'M GOING TO CRY!
AAA-OOOH AAA-OOOH
I'M SO ALONE...
I WILL NOT BE SO EASILY DEFEATED!
AKIKO SHALL PRE-VAIL!
KACHUNK
OOG OOG OOG
OOG OOG
OH, THERE YOU ARE!
A-AKIKO...
UM...
CAN YOU... COOK?
LEAVE IT TO ME! I CAN COOK TEN DISHES.

READ THIS WAY

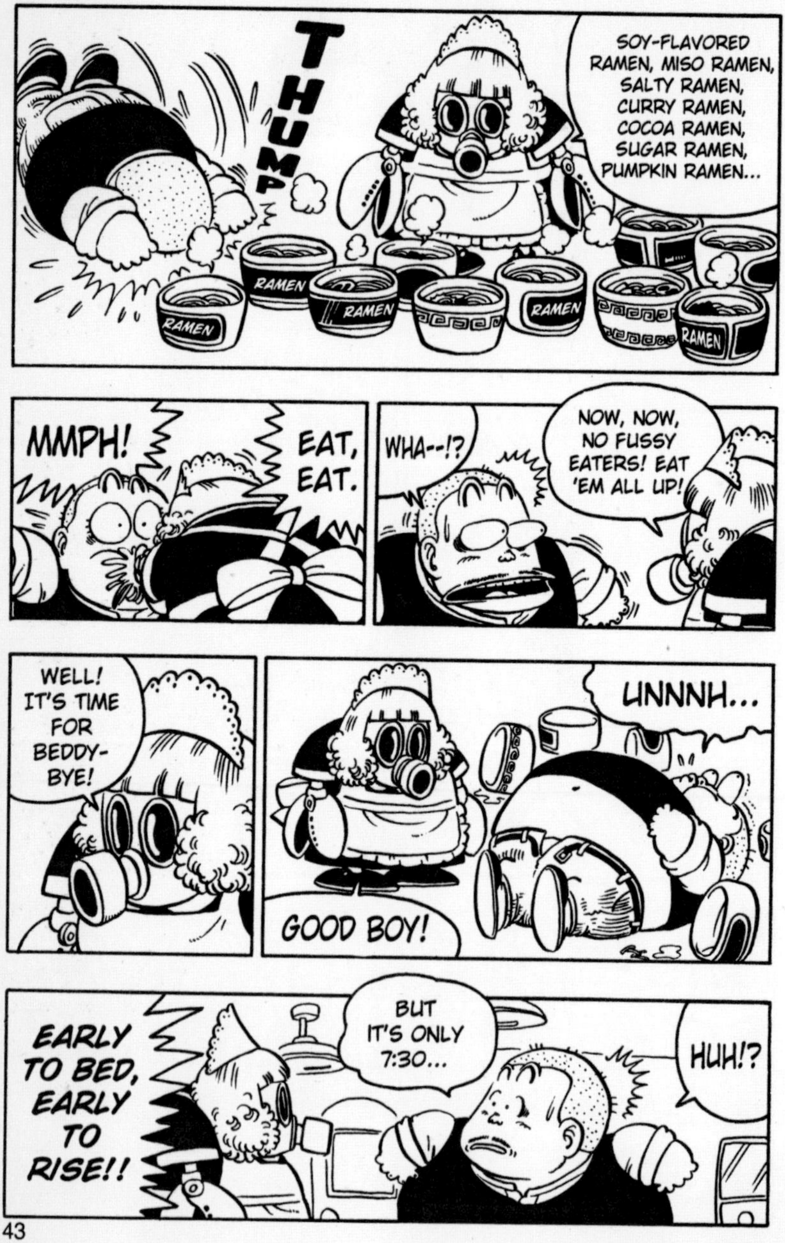
SOY-FLAVORED RAMEN, MISO RAMEN, SALTY RAMEN, CURRY RAMEN, COCOA RAMEN, SUGAR RAMEN, PUMPKIN RAMEN...
THUMP
RAMEN
NOW, NOW, NO FUSSY EATERS! EAT 'EM ALL UP!
WHA--!?
EAT, EAT.
MMPH!
UNNNH...
GOOD BOY!
WELL! IT'S TIME FOR BEDDY-BYE!
HUH!?
BUT IT'S ONLY 7:30...
EARLY TO BED, EARLY TO RISE!!

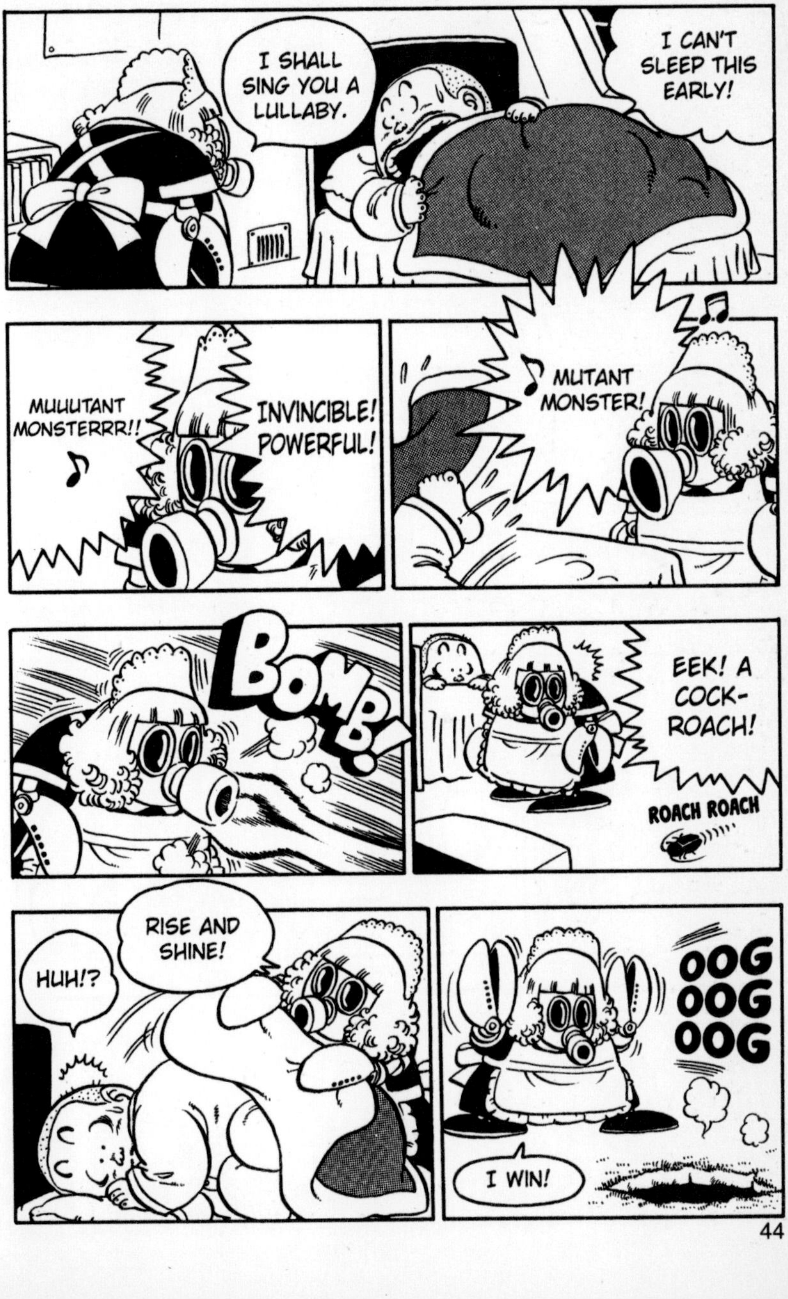
I CAN'T SLEEP THIS EARLY!
I SHALL SING YOU A LULLABY.
MUTANT MONSTER!
INVINCIBLE! POWERFUL!
MUUUTANT MONSTERRR!!
EEK! A COCK-ROACH!
ROACH ROACH
BOMB!
OOG OOG OOG
I WIN!
RISE AND SHINE!
HUH!?

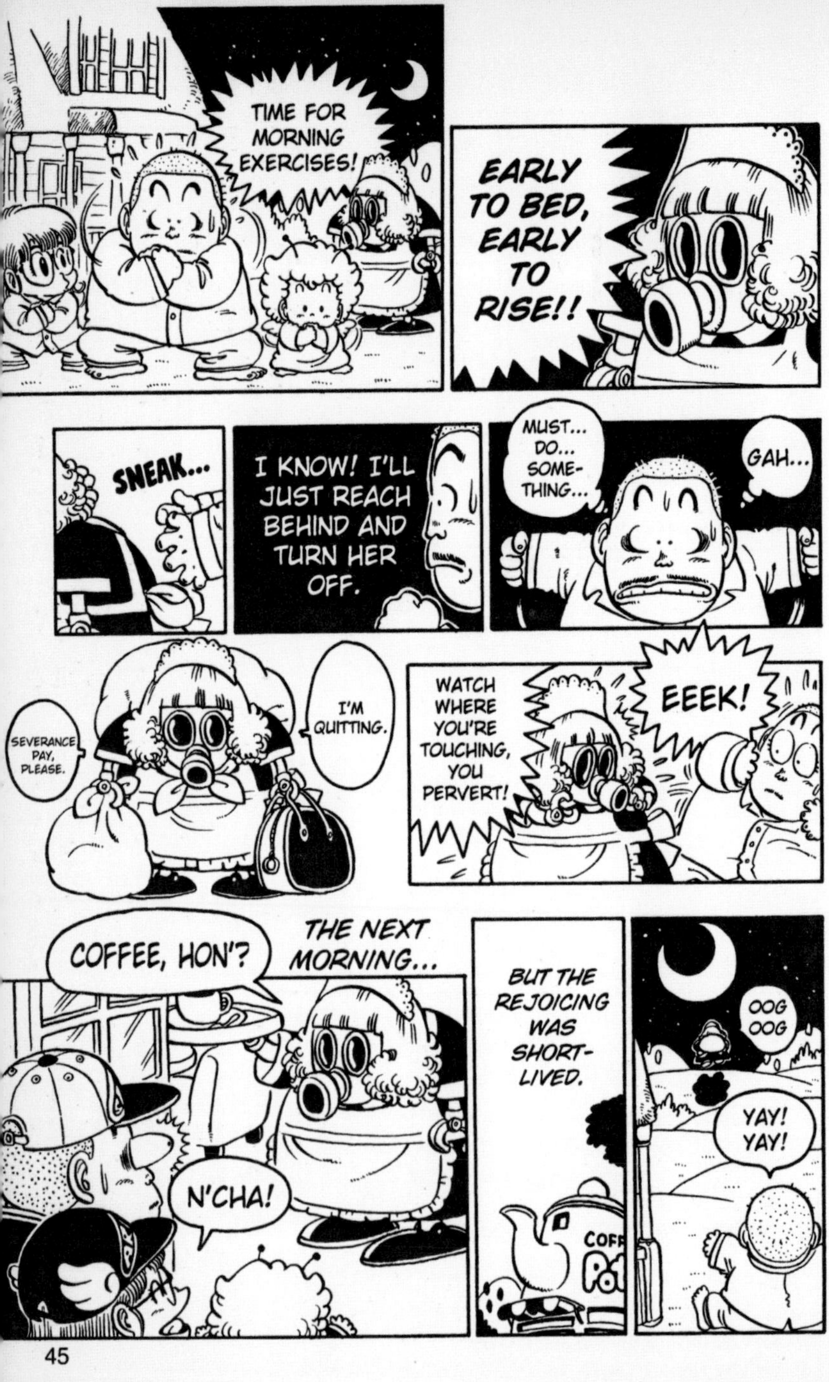
EARLY TO BED, EARLY TO RISE!!
TIME FOR MORNING EXERCISES!
GAH...
MUST... DO... SOME-THING...
I KNOW! I'LL JUST REACH BEHIND AND TURN HER OFF.
SNEAK...
EEEK!
WATCH WHERE YOU'RE TOUCHING, YOU PERVERT!
I'M QUITTING.
SEVERANCE PAY, PLEASE.
OOG OOG
YAY! YAY!
BUT THE REJOICING WAS SHORT-LIVED.
THE NEXT MORNING...
COFFEE, HON'?
N'CHA!

Penguin Village "I'M NUMBER ONE!" CONTEST Category: Coolest

20th	19th	18th	17th	16th
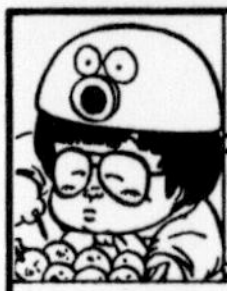	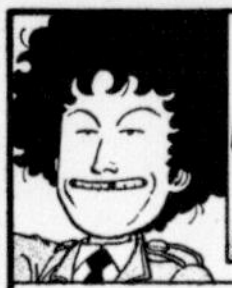	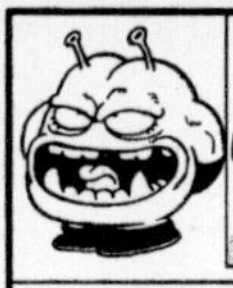	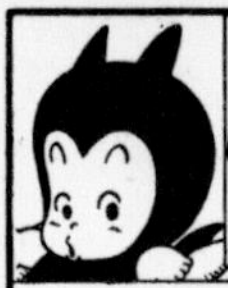	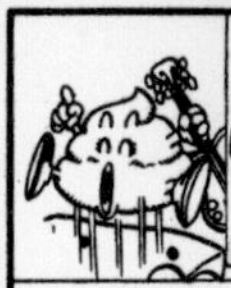
Octopus-Ball Makusa 56 votes ★His octopus hat ★His cheerful, runny-nosed grin	**Dr. Mashirito 58 votes** ★Those thin eyebrows, those diminutive eyes!	**King Nikochan 70 votes** ★I can't help but think he's playing dumb so he'll get to stay in Penguin Village.	**Chivil 76 votes** ★I like that he asks so politely for people to drop dead. ★His cute stubbornness ★His cute wee-wee	**Poop 100 votes** ★I like that he has arms and legs. ★I want a poop worthy of poking, too!

29th (tie)	29th (tie)	27th (tie)	27th (tie)	25th (tie)	25th (tie)	24th	23rd	21st (tie)	21st (tie)
Parzan 30 votes ★His hunky bod	**Ultra-man 30 votes** ★His way of eating rice-balls	**Betty from the neigh-boring town 36 votes** ★Her blushing cheeks!	**Rock-coach 36 votes** ★I want a model kit!	**Lady Trampire 38 votes** ★What lovely fangs!	**The Vacuum Car Driver 38 votes** ★He looks so serious when he drives.	**Kintaman (Koita Ojo) 40 votes** ★I like a superhero who accom-plishes nothing.	**Lazy Gramps 50 votes** ★Just looking at him makes me lazy.	**Whale Mountain 52 votes** ★He's so cute when he cries.	**Mr. Daigoro Kuri-gashira 52 votes** ★Oh, to be on the receiving end of his head-butt of love!

Here are some other responses that, though few, were nonetheless dumb. Check through volumes 1-8 and try to find them yourself!

- Vol. 1: The clerk at the women's clothing store.
- Vol. 2, page 40: Arale wipes this kid's face.
- Vol. 7, page 120: the Water Pistol
- Ultraman in festival wear
- The entire Penguin Village police force
- The bald kid in Arale's class
- The ant
- The sweating sun
- The cicada on the palm tree
- The rocket-pig

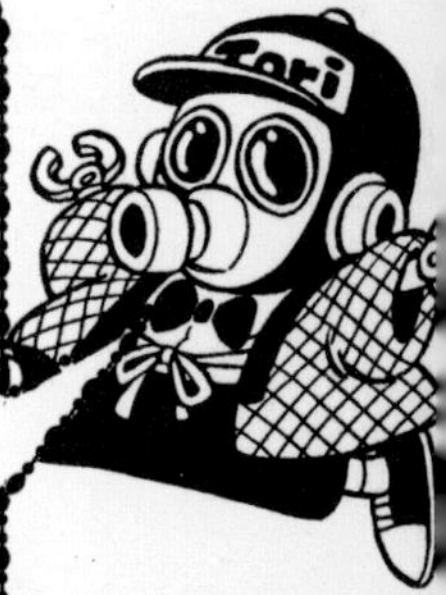
Tori

Penguin Grand Prix: Part 1

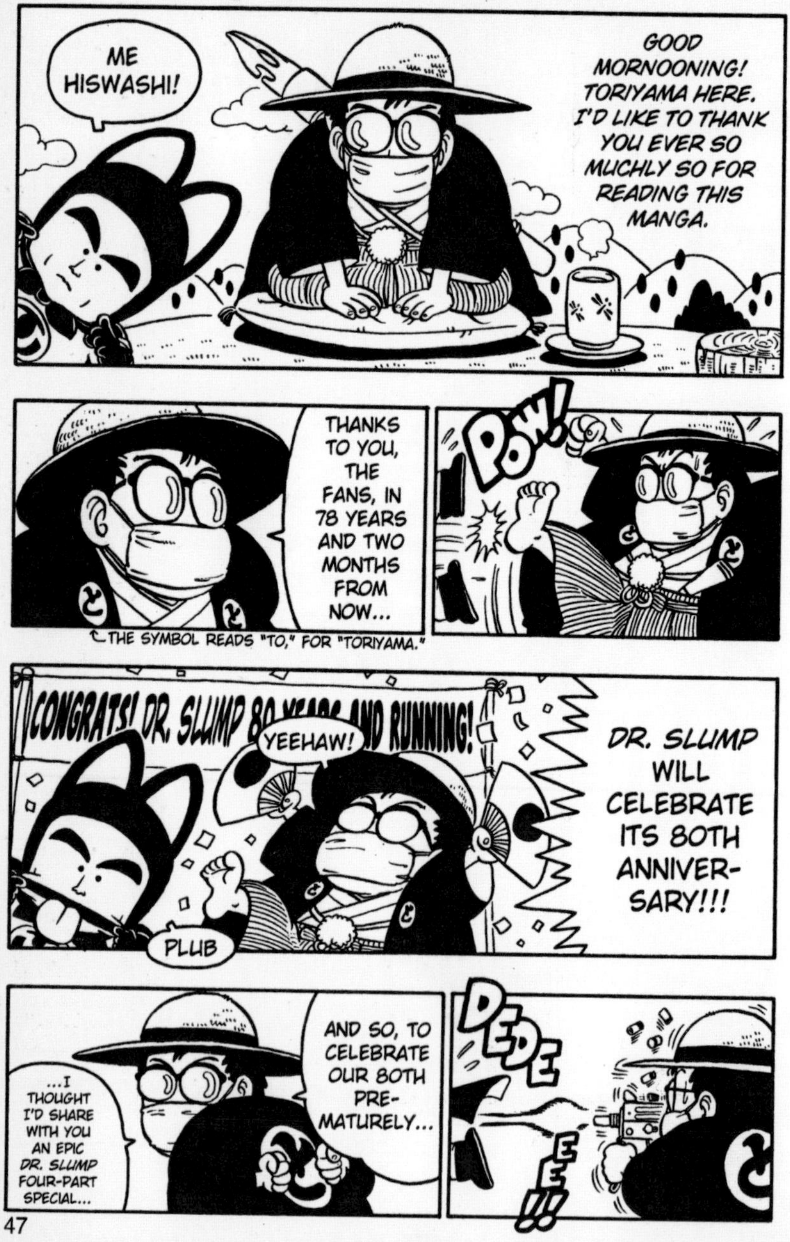
GOOD MORNOONING! TORIYAMA HERE. I'D LIKE TO THANK YOU EVER SO MUCHLY SO FOR READING THIS MANGA.
ME HISWASHI!
POW!
THANKS TO YOU, THE FANS, IN 78 YEARS AND TWO MONTHS FROM NOW...
THE SYMBOL READS "TO," FOR "TORIYAMA."
DR. SLUMP WILL CELEBRATE ITS 80TH ANNIVER-SARY!!!
CONGRATS! DR. SLUMP 80 ... ND RUNNING!
YEEHAW!
PLUB
DEDE
EE!!
AND SO, TO CELEBRATE OUR 80TH PRE-MATURELY...
...I THOUGHT I'D SHARE WITH YOU AN EPIC DR. SLUMP FOUR-PART SPECIAL...

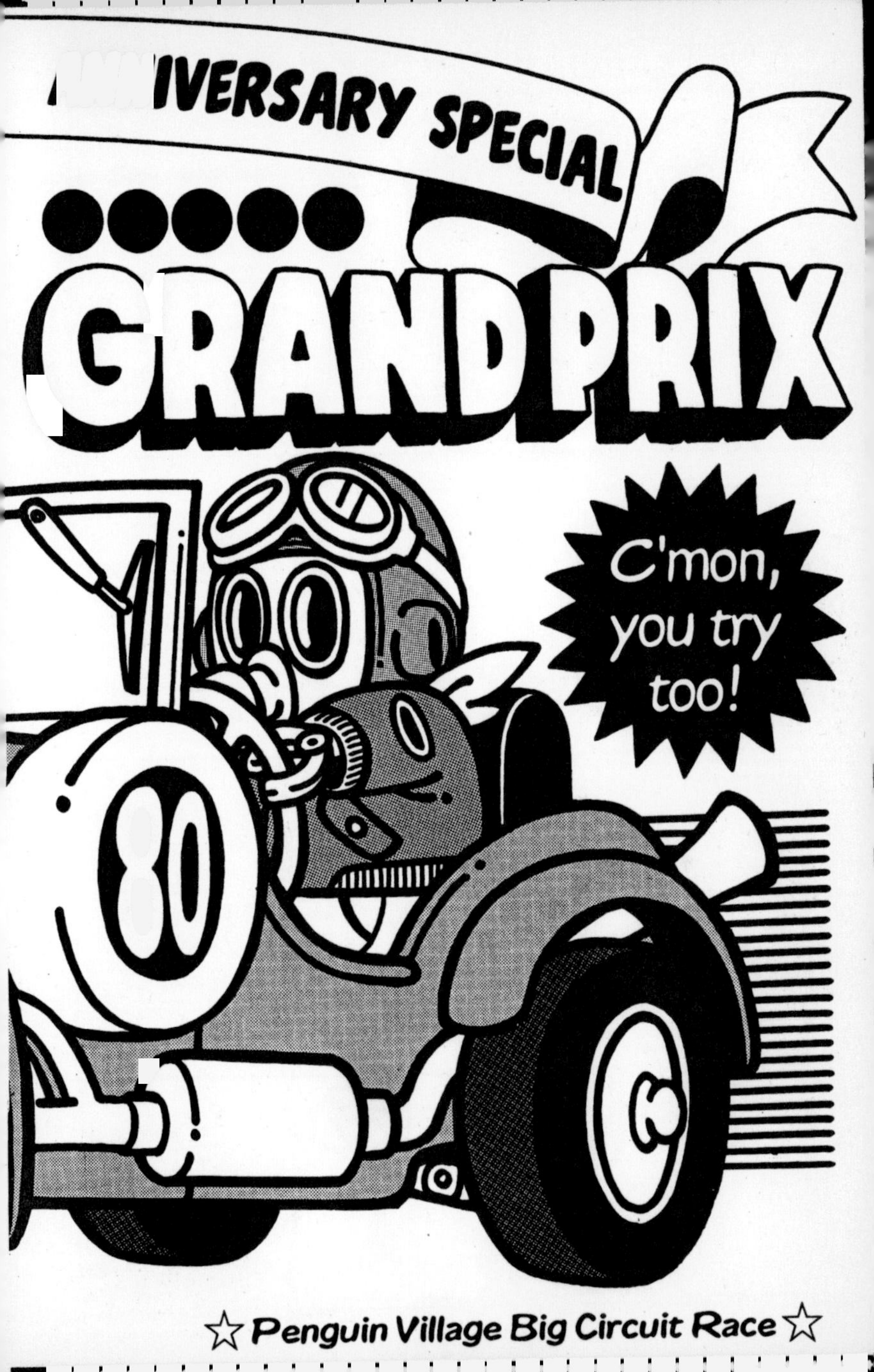
IVERSARY SPECIAL
●●●●● GRAND PRIX
C'mon, you try too!
80
☆ Penguin Village Big Circuit Race ☆

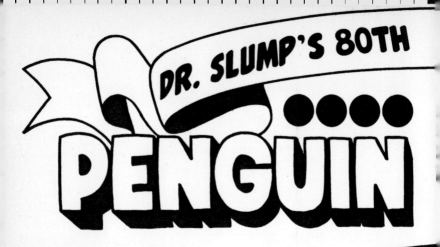

DR. SLUMP'S 80TH

●●●●● PENGUIN

‹WINNER'S PURSE› **Part 1**

$25.0000

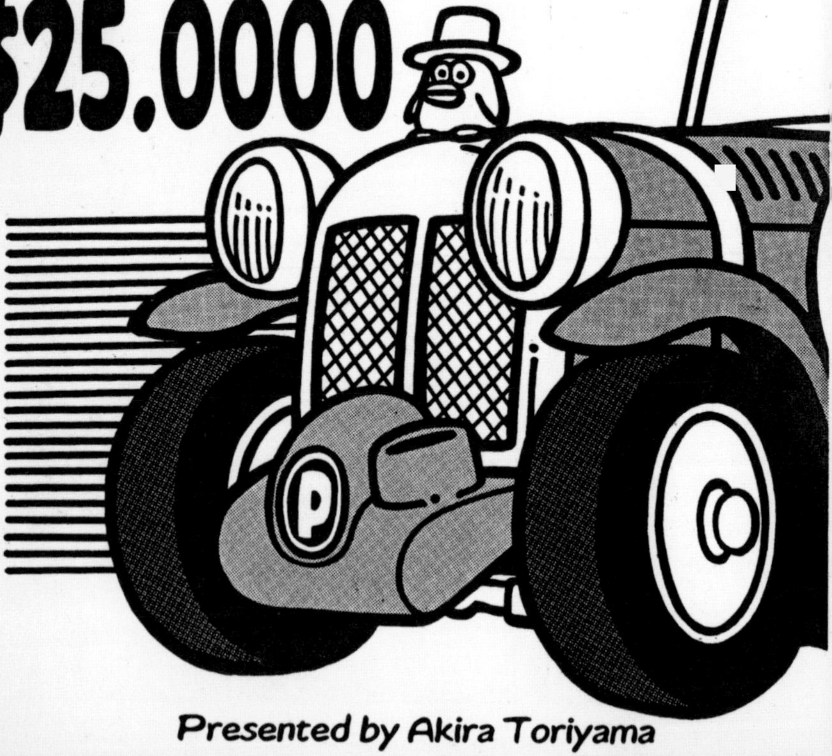

Presented by Akira Toriyama

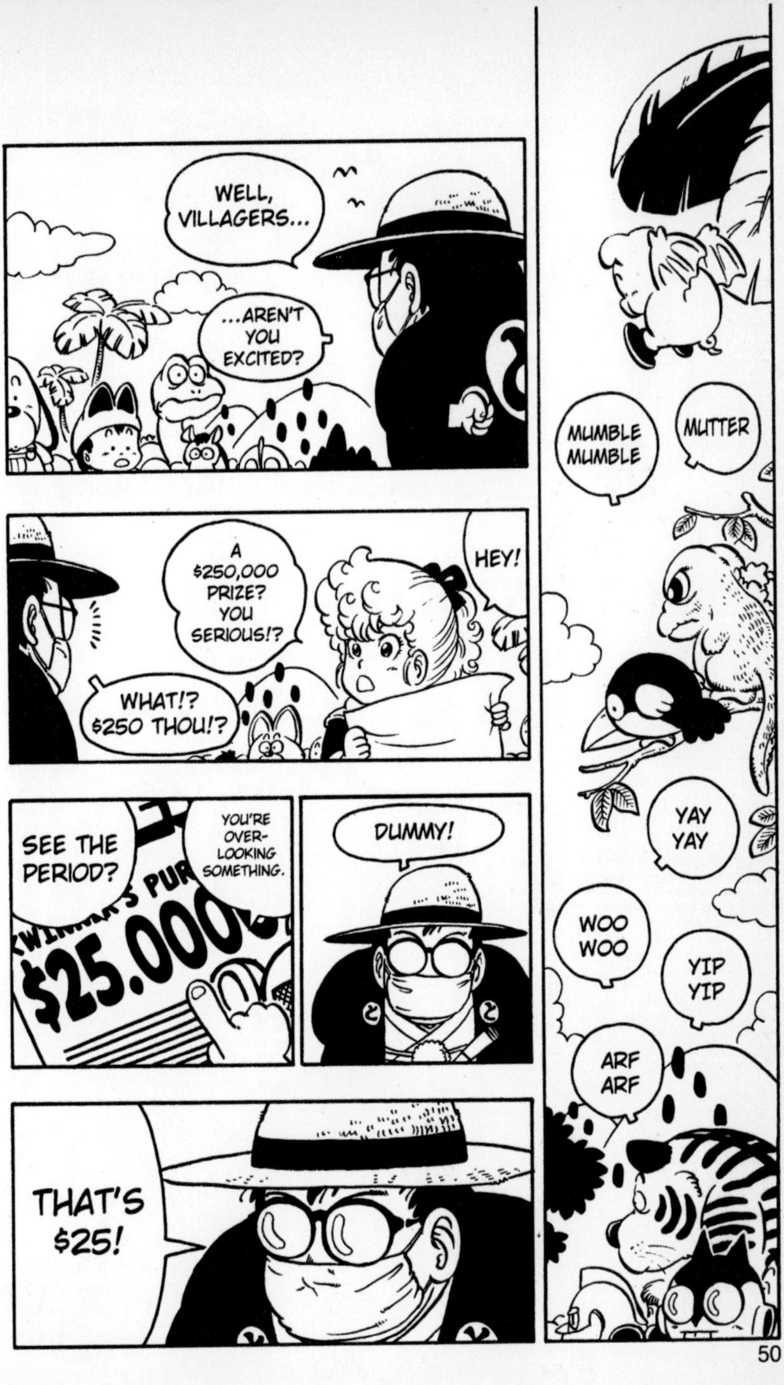
MUTTER
MUMBLE MUMBLE
YAY YAY
WOO WOO
YIP YIP
ARF ARF
WELL, VILLAGERS...
...AREN'T YOU EXCITED?
HEY!
A $250,000 PRIZE? YOU SERIOUS!?
WHAT!? $250 THOU!?
DUMMY!
YOU'RE OVER-LOOKING SOMETHING.
SEE THE PERIOD?
$25.000
THAT'S $25!

READ THIS WAY

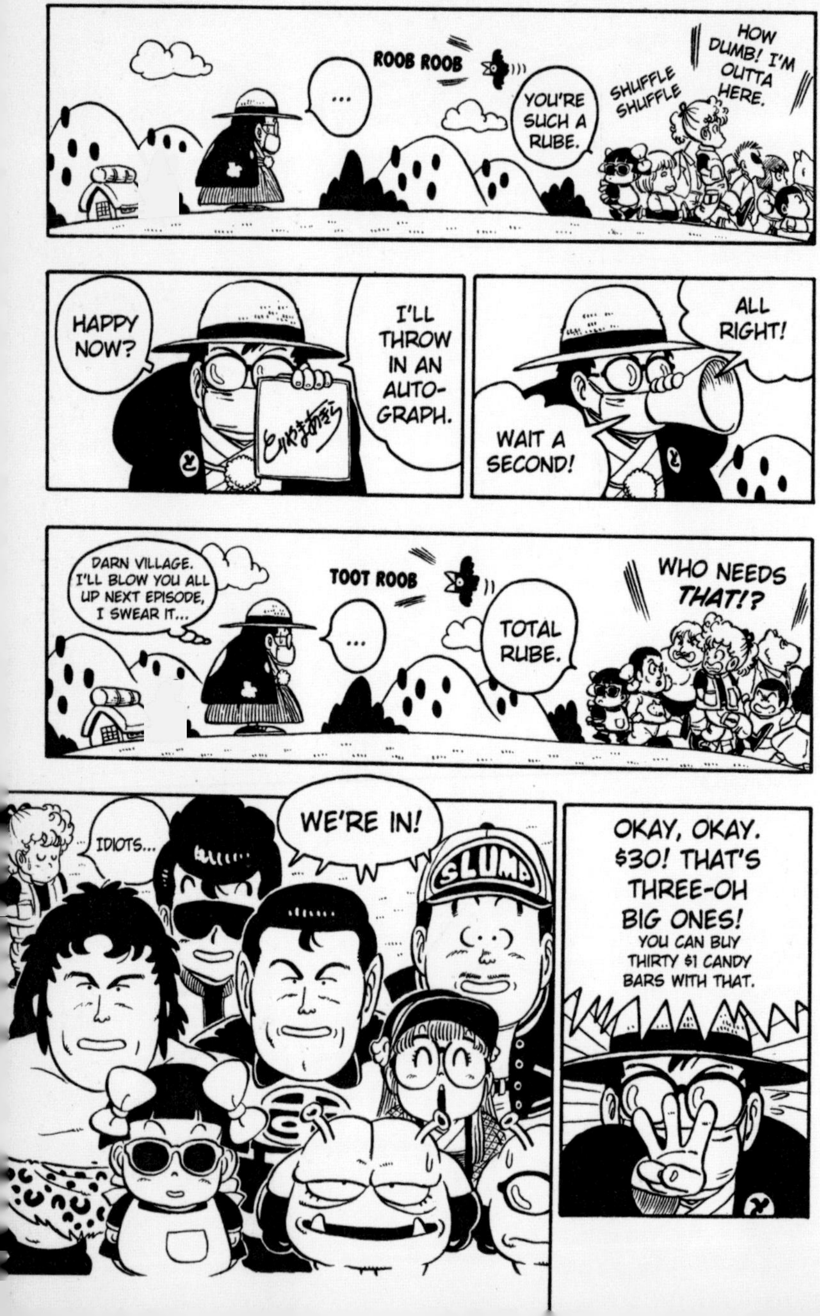
HOW DUMB! I'M OUTTA HERE.
SHUFFLE SHUFFLE
YOU'RE SUCH A RUBE.
ROOB ROOB
...
ALL RIGHT!
WAIT A SECOND!
I'LL THROW IN AN AUTO-GRAPH.
HAPPY NOW?
WHO NEEDS THAT!?
TOTAL RUBE.
TOOT ROOB
...
DARN VILLAGE. I'LL BLOW YOU ALL UP NEXT EPISODE, I SWEAR IT...
OKAY, OKAY. $30! THAT'S THREE-OH BIG ONES! YOU CAN BUY THIRTY $1 CANDY BARS WITH THAT.
WE'RE IN!
...IDIOTS...
SLUMP

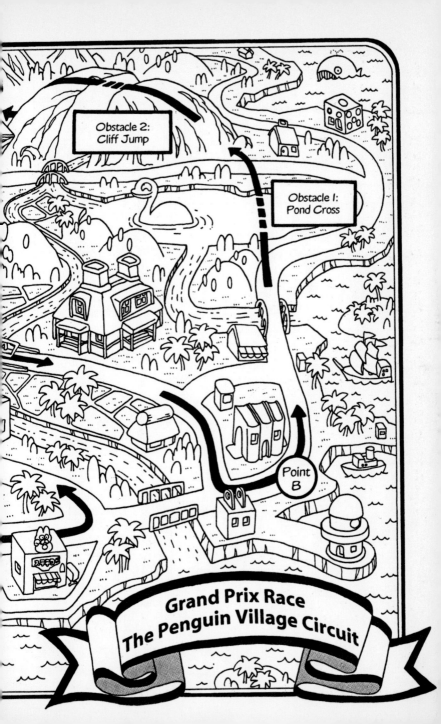

Obstacle 2:
Cliff Jump

Obstacle 1:
Pond Cross

Point
B

**Grand Prix Race
The Penguin Village Circuit**

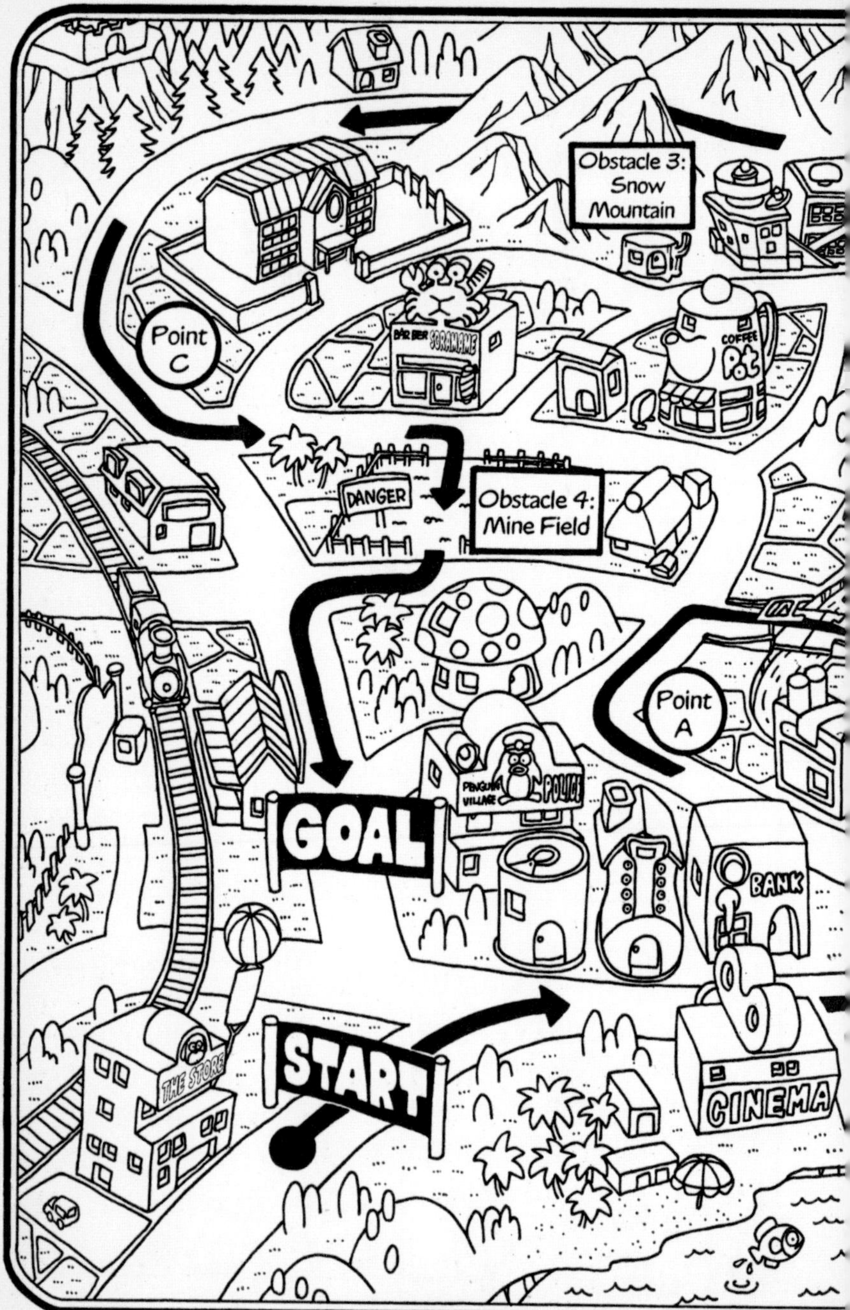
Obstacle 3: Snow Mountain
Point C
BARBER SORAMAME
COFFEE Pot
DANGER
Obstacle 4: Mine Field
Point A
PENGUIN VILLAGE POLICE
GOAL
BANK
START
THE STORE
CINEMA

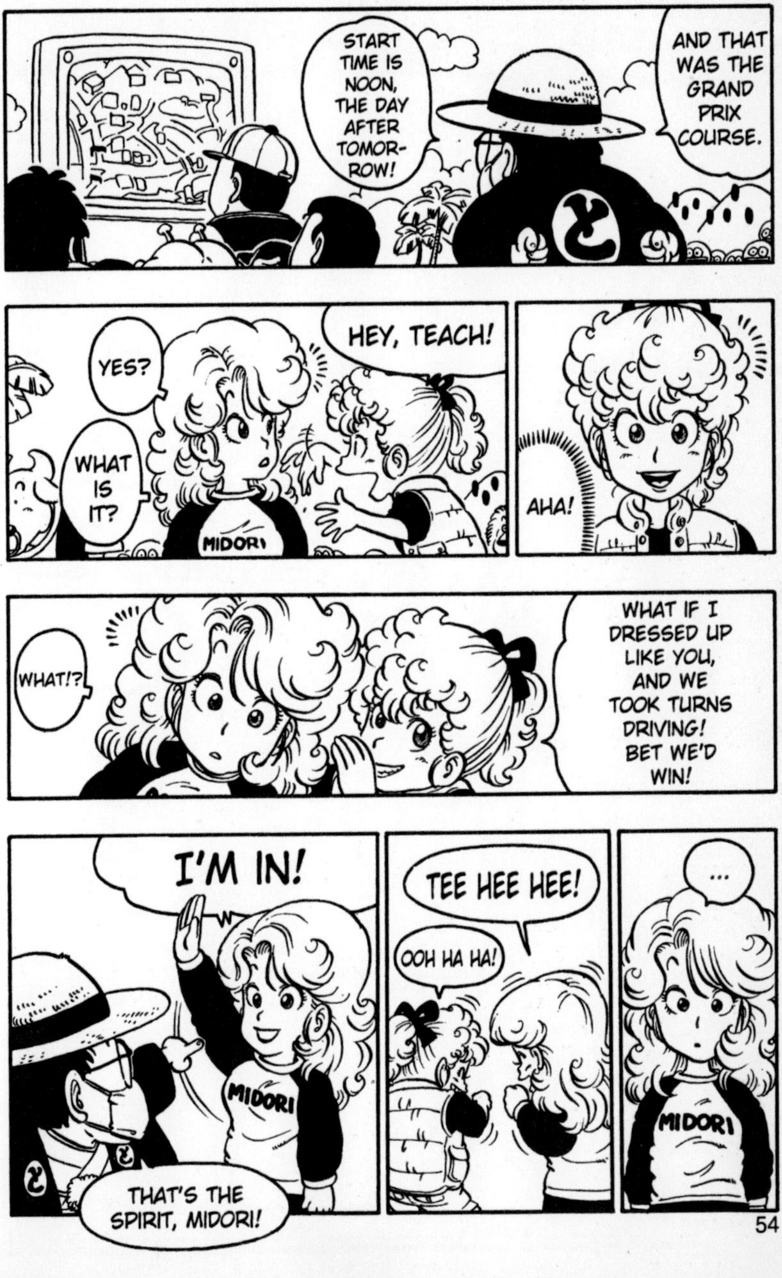
AND THAT WAS THE GRAND PRIX COURSE.
START TIME IS NOON, THE DAY AFTER TOMORROW!
AHA!
HEY, TEACH!
YES?
WHAT IS IT?
WHAT IF I DRESSED UP LIKE YOU, AND WE TOOK TURNS DRIVING! BET WE'D WIN!
WHAT!?
...
TEE HEE HEE!
OOH HA HA!
I'M IN!
THAT'S THE SPIRIT, MIDORI!

READ THIS WAY

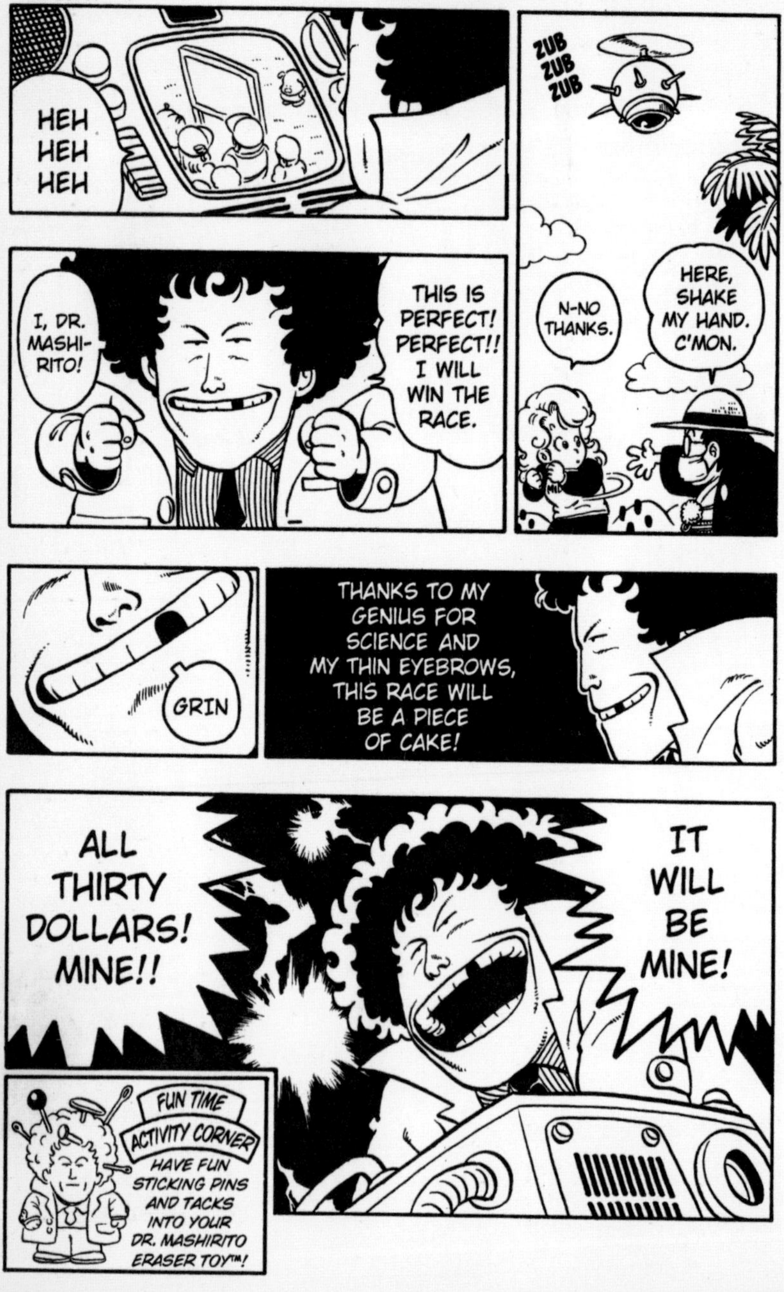

ZUB ZUB ZUB
HERE, SHAKE MY HAND. C'MON.
N-NO THANKS.
HEH HEH HEH
THIS IS PERFECT! PERFECT!! I WILL WIN THE RACE.
I, DR. MASHIRITO!
THANKS TO MY GENIUS FOR SCIENCE AND MY THIN EYEBROWS, THIS RACE WILL BE A PIECE OF CAKE!
GRIN
IT WILL BE MINE!
ALL THIRTY DOLLARS! MINE!!
FUN TIME
ACTIVITY CORNER
HAVE FUN STICKING PINS AND TACKS INTO YOUR DR. MASHIRITO ERASER TOY™!

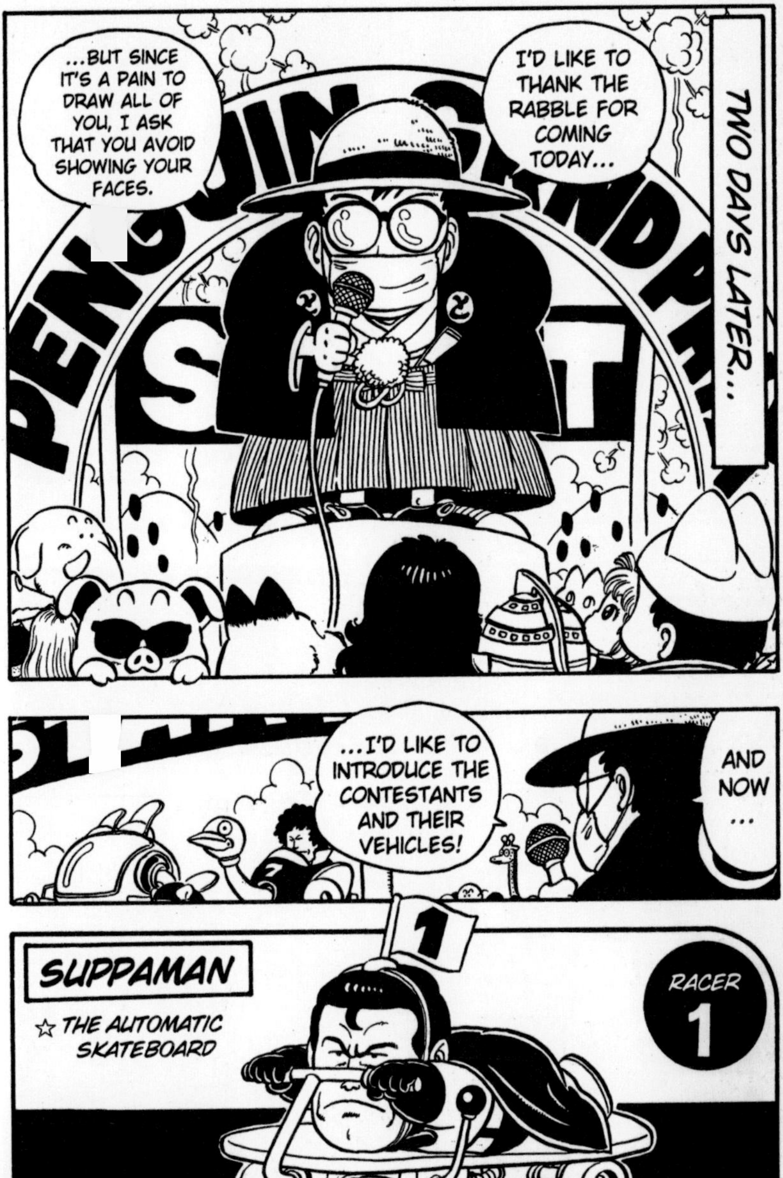
TWO DAYS LATER...
I'D LIKE TO THANK THE RABBLE FOR COMING TODAY...
...BUT SINCE IT'S A PAIN TO DRAW ALL OF YOU, I ASK THAT YOU AVOID SHOWING YOUR FACES.
AND NOW...
...I'D LIKE TO INTRODUCE THE CONTESTANTS AND THEIR VEHICLES!
1
RACER 1
SUPPAMAN
☆ THE AUTOMATIC SKATEBOARD

READ THIS WAY

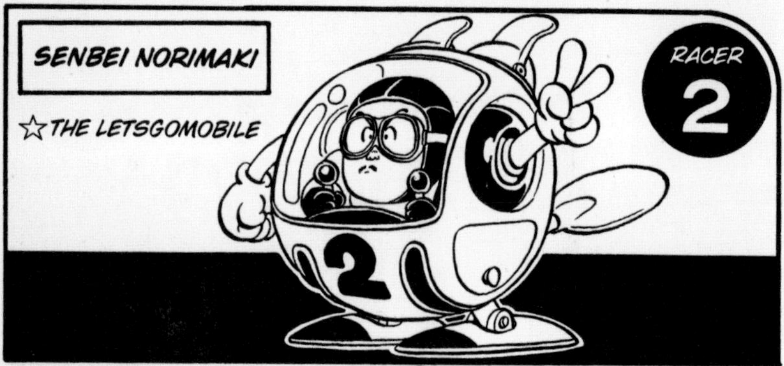
SENBEI NORIMAKI
☆THE LETSGOMOBILE
RACER
2

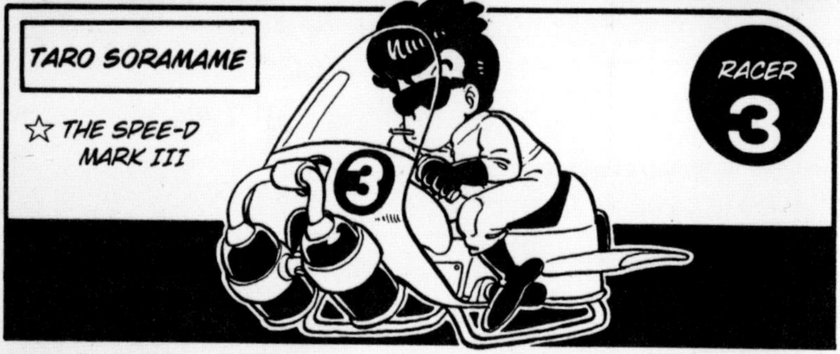
TARO SORAMAME
☆ THE SPEE-D MARK III
RACER
3

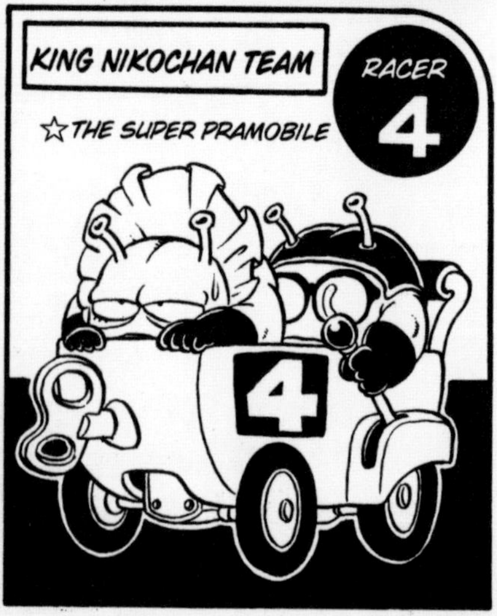
KING NIKOCHAN TEAM
☆THE SUPER PRAMOBILE
RACER
4

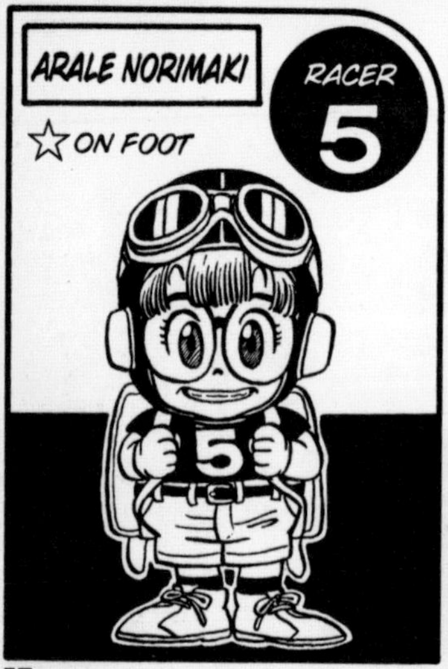
ARALE NORIMAKI
☆ON FOOT
RACER
5

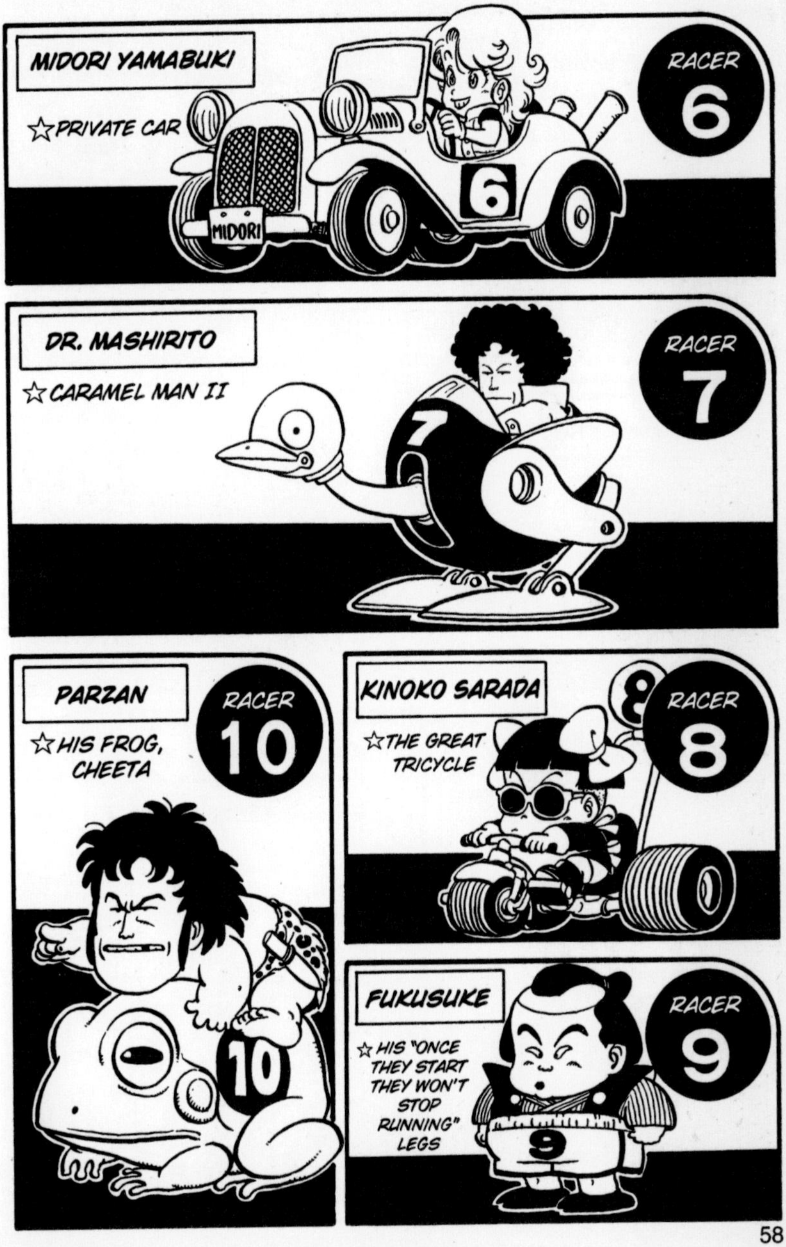
MIDORI YAMABUKI
☆PRIVATE CAR
RACER 6
MIDORI
DR. MASHIRITO
☆CARAMEL MAN II
RACER 7
KINOKO SARADA
☆THE GREAT TRICYCLE
RACER 8
FUKUSUKE
☆HIS "ONCE THEY START THEY WON'T STOP RUNNING" LEGS
RACER 9
PARZAN
☆HIS FROG, CHEETA
RACER 10

READ THIS WAY

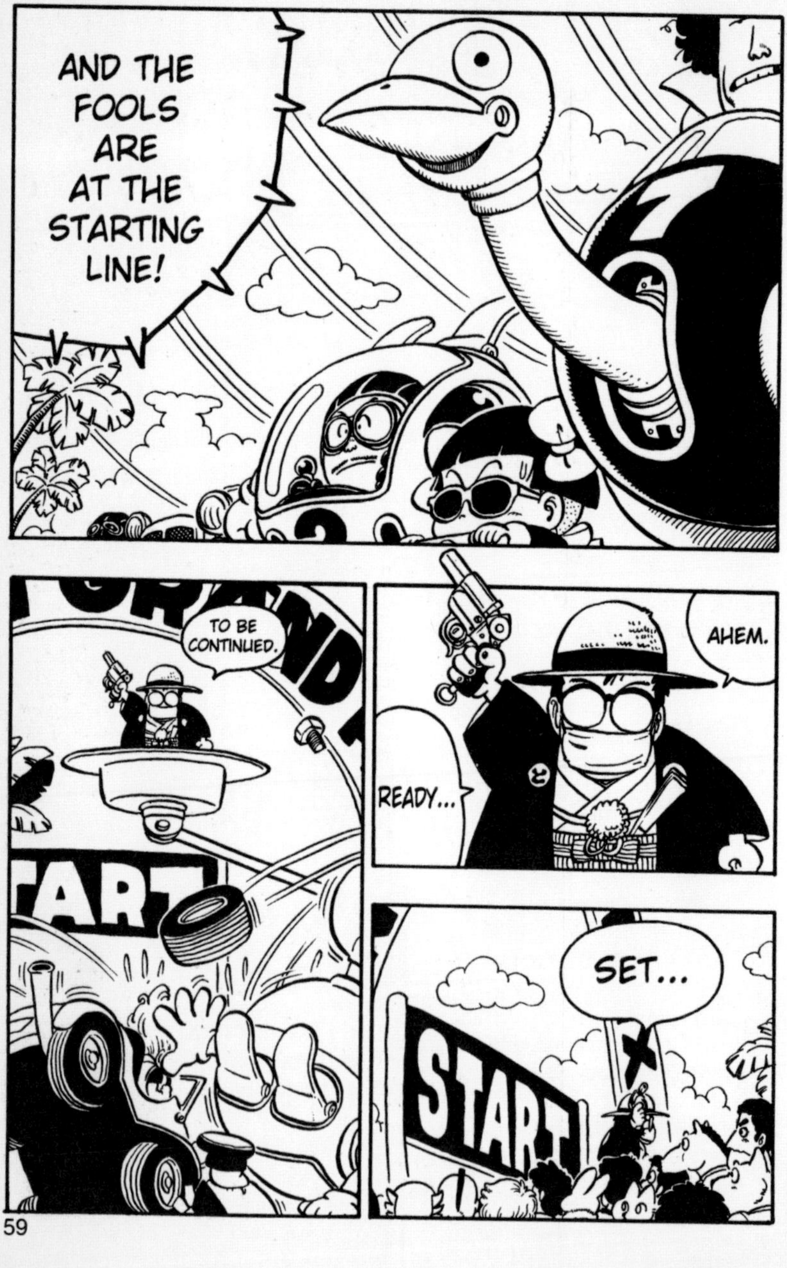
AND THE FOOLS ARE AT THE STARTING LINE!
AHEM.
READY...
SET...
START
TO BE CONTINUED.
START

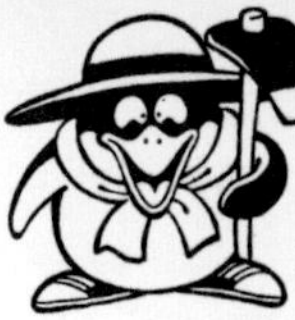

Penguin Village

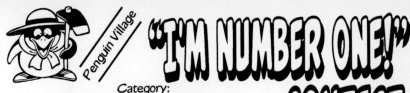

"I'M NUMBER ONE!" CONTEST

Category:

MY GENIUS FRIGHTENS ME!

Useful inventions? Not here, buddy!!

1st

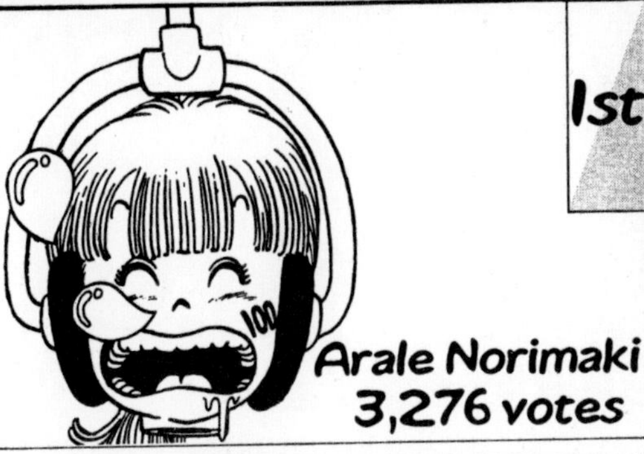

Arale Norimaki
3,276 votes

★ Hard to believe that Arale was Senbei's invention!
★ She's strong, she's good, and she's frisky!
★ She could speak at birth.
★ She's so well made, everyone thinks she's real.
★ Senbei's only *really* useful invention!

2nd

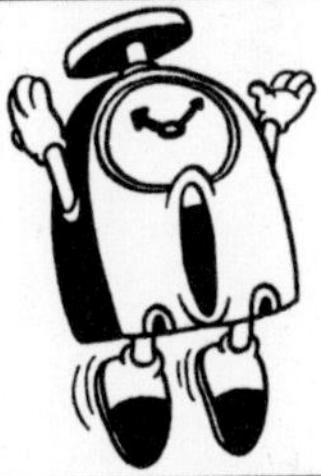

Mr. Time
1,764 votes

★ I like that he sleeps too.
★ If you really made him, you'd get the Nobel Prize.
★ I'd go back in time and show *Dr. Slump* to everyone!
★ A very imaginative invention
★ I'd visit the future and see what kind of wife I had.

3rd

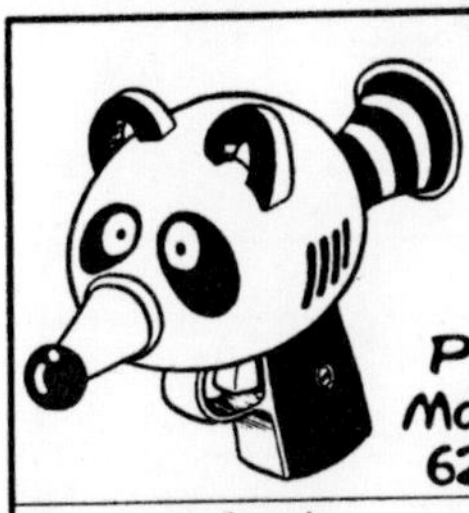

Ponpoko Morph Gun
624 votes

★ Cute face!
★ I'd use it to turn everything in the world into paper, then light a fire and create the sun.
★ I'd make myself beautiful!
★ Making cheap things into expensive things seems really useful.
★ I don't remember the other inventions.

Penguin Grand Prix: Part 2

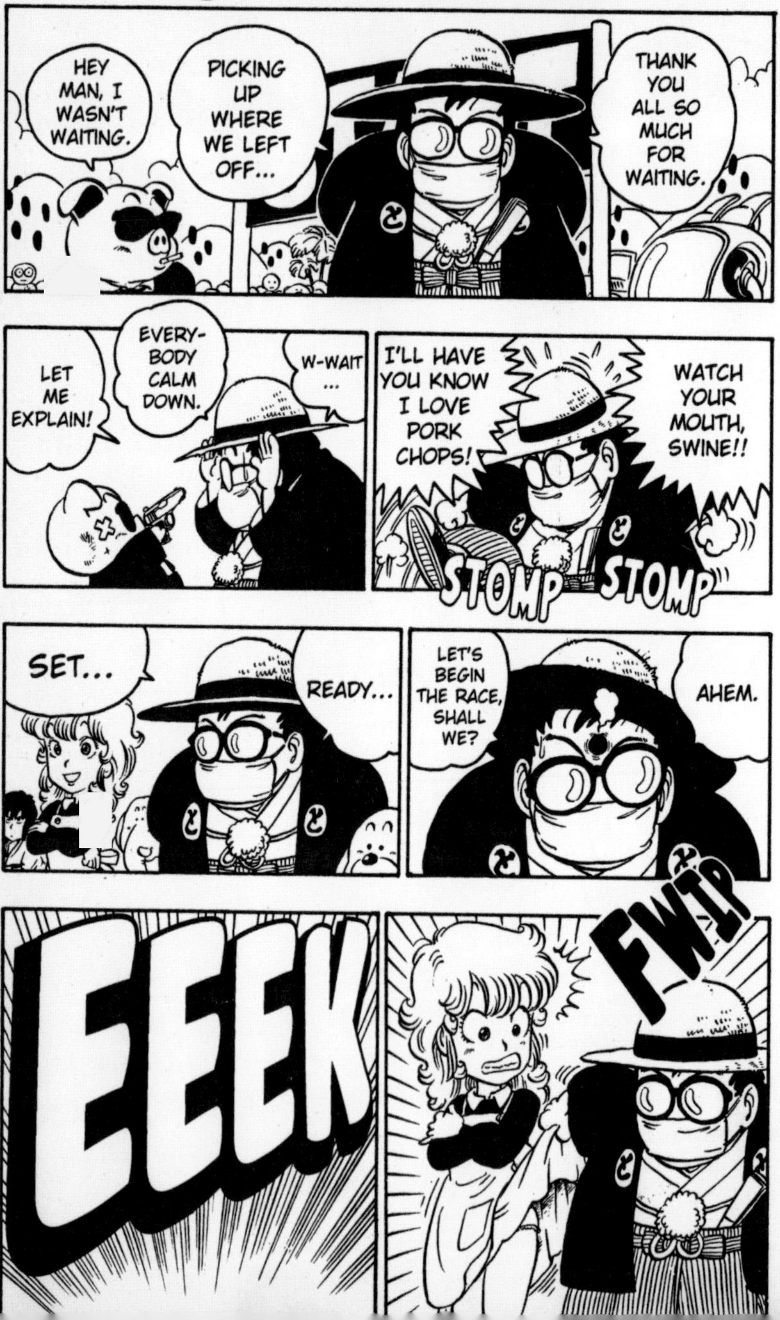

THANK YOU ALL SO MUCH FOR WAITING.
PICKING UP WHERE WE LEFT OFF...
HEY MAN, I WASN'T WAITING.
WATCH YOUR MOUTH, SWINE!!
I'LL HAVE YOU KNOW I LOVE PORK CHOPS!
STOMP STOMP
W-WAIT ...
EVERY-BODY CALM DOWN.
LET ME EXPLAIN!
AHEM.
LET'S BEGIN THE RACE, SHALL WE?
READY...
SET...
FWIP
EEEK

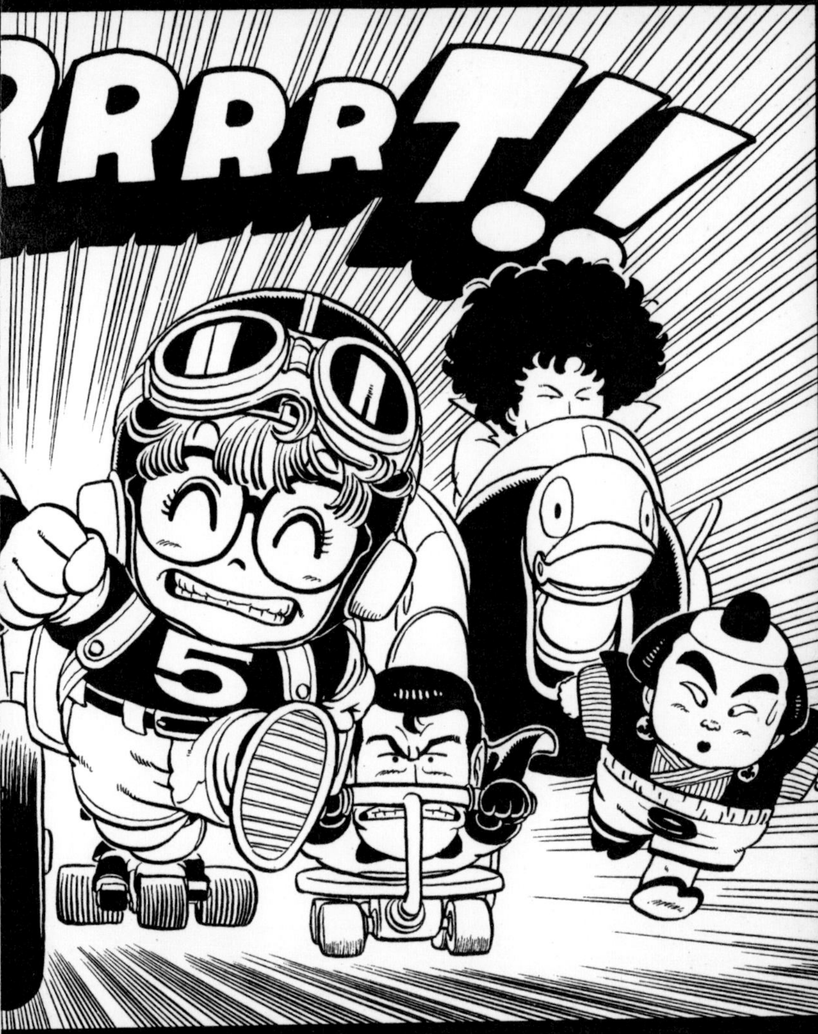
RRRRT!!

PENGUIN GRAND PRIX

Part 2

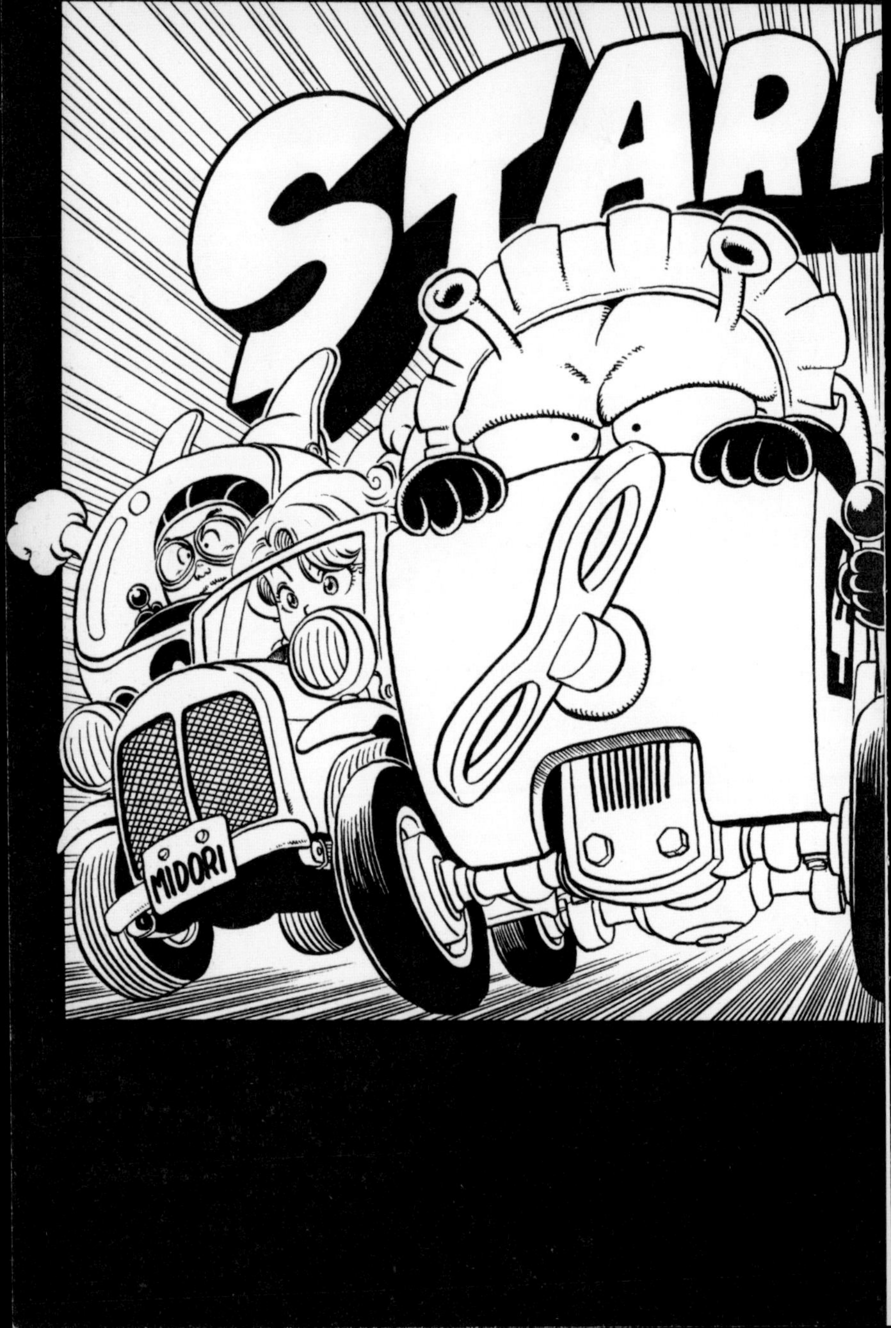
STAR
MIDORI

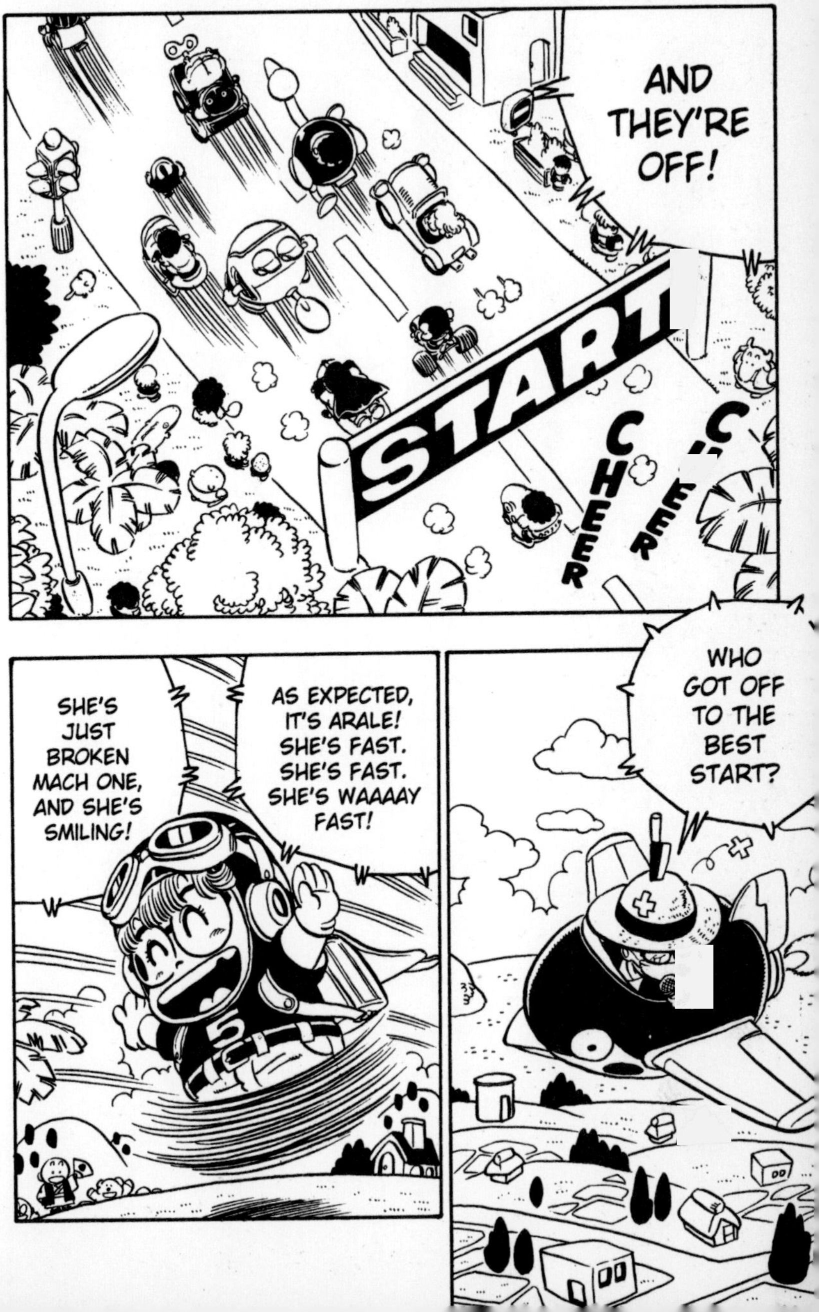
AND THEY'RE OFF!
START
CHEER
CHEER
WHO GOT OFF TO THE BEST START?
AS EXPECTED, IT'S ARALE! SHE'S FAST. SHE'S FAST. SHE'S WAAAAY FAST!
SHE'S JUST BROKEN MACH ONE, AND SHE'S SMILING!

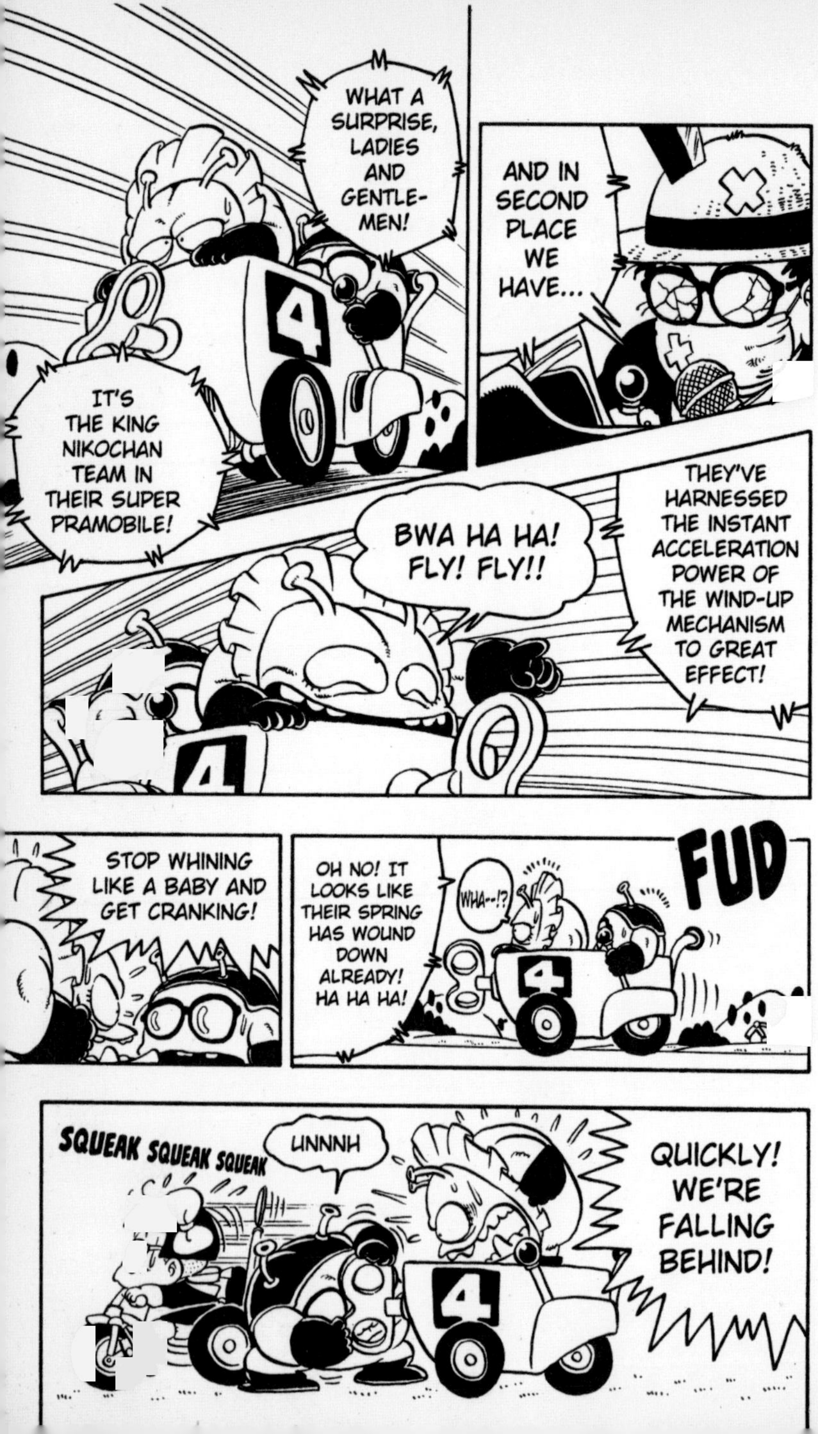
AND IN SECOND PLACE WE HAVE...
WHAT A SURPRISE, LADIES AND GENTLE-MEN!
IT'S THE KING NIKOCHAN TEAM IN THEIR SUPER PRAMOBILE!
THEY'VE HARNESSED THE INSTANT ACCELERATION POWER OF THE WIND-UP MECHANISM TO GREAT EFFECT!
BWA HA HA! FLY! FLY!!
FUD
OH NO! IT LOOKS LIKE THEIR SPRING HAS WOUND DOWN ALREADY! HA HA HA!
WHA--!?
STOP WHINING LIKE A BABY AND GET CRANKING!
QUICKLY! WE'RE FALLING BEHIND!
UNNNH
SQUEAK SQUEAK SQUEAK

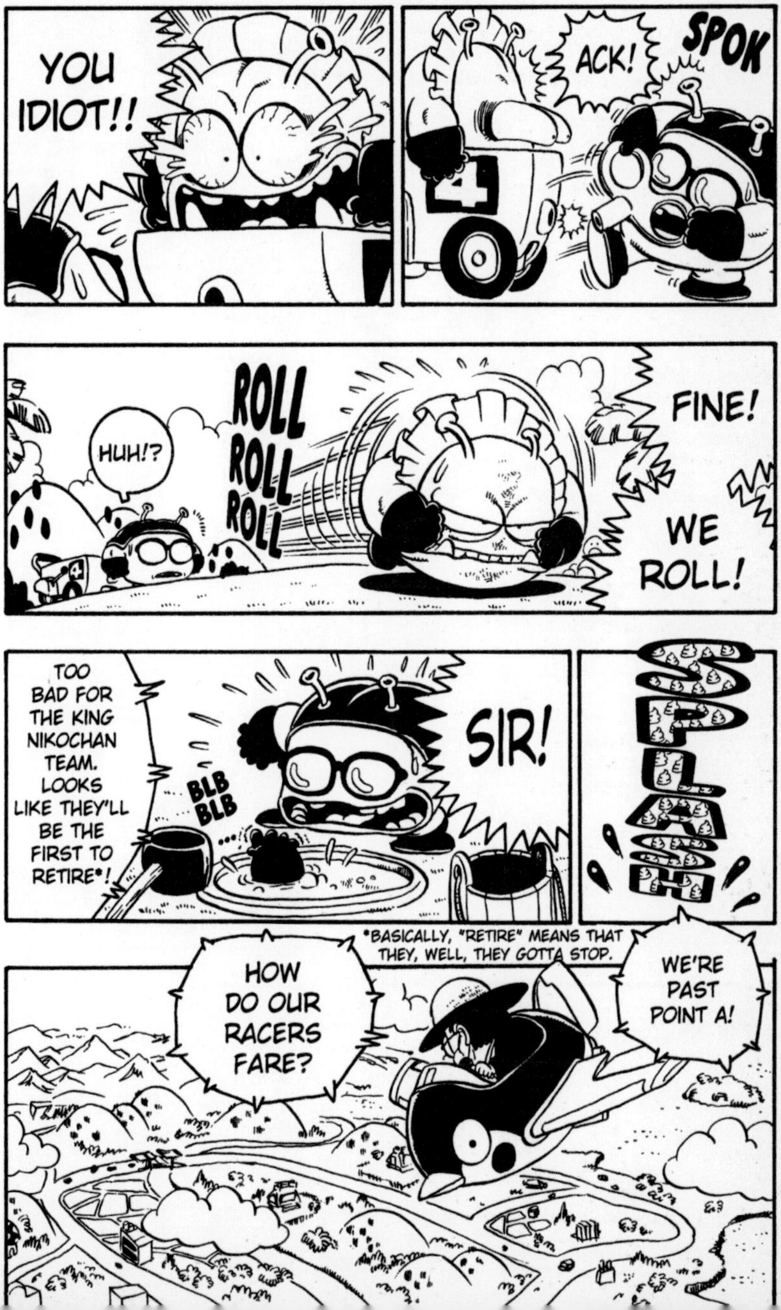

SPOK
ACK!
YOU IDIOT!!
FINE! WE ROLL!
ROLL ROLL ROLL
HUH!?
SPLASH
SIR!
BLB BLB
TOO BAD FOR THE KING NIKOCHAN TEAM. LOOKS LIKE THEY'LL BE THE FIRST TO RETIRE*!
*BASICALLY, "RETIRE" MEANS THAT THEY, WELL, THEY GOTTA STOP.
WE'RE PAST POINT A!
HOW DO OUR RACERS FARE?

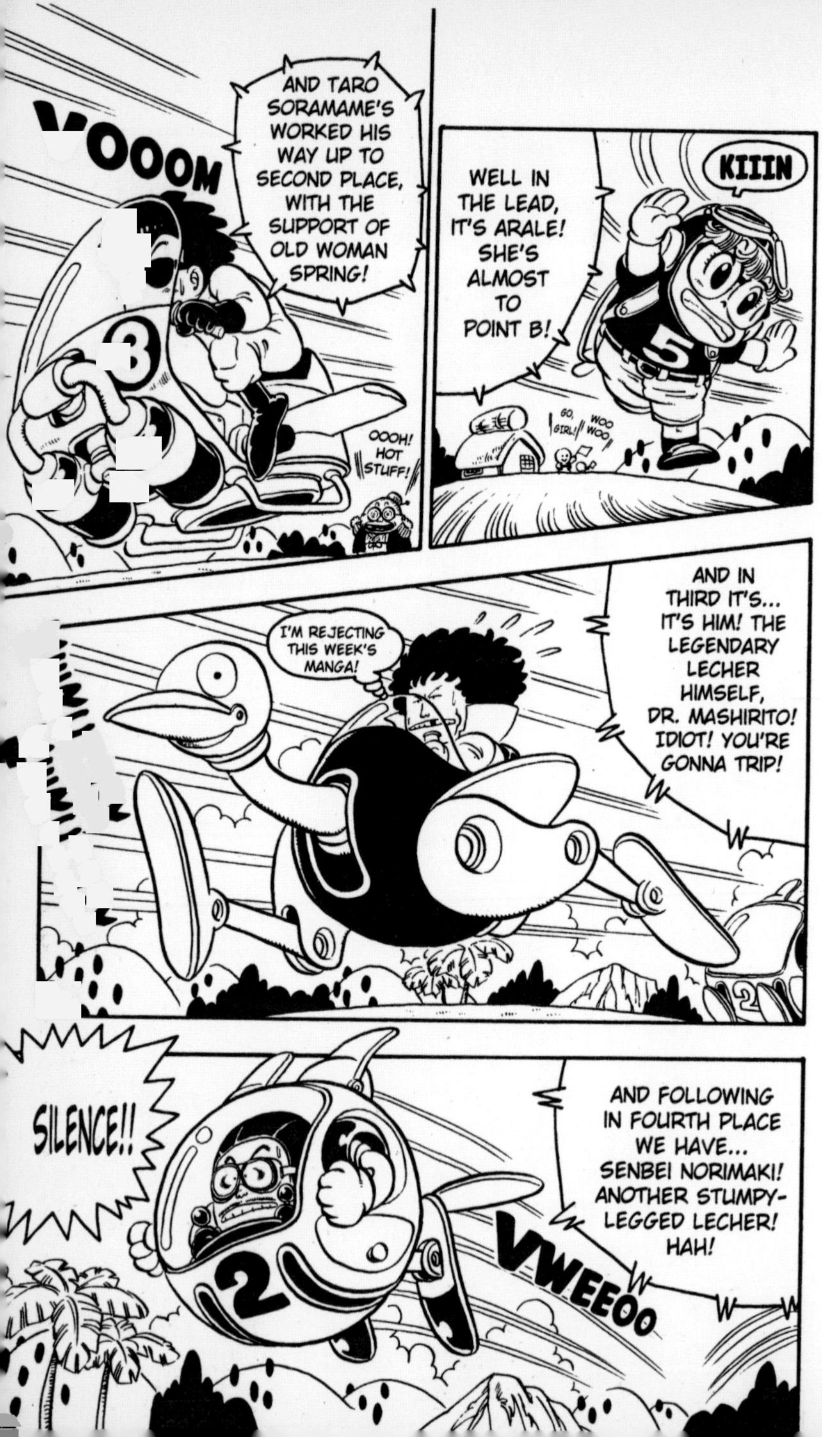
KIIIN
WELL IN THE LEAD, IT'S ARALE! SHE'S ALMOST TO POINT B!
GO, GIRL!
WOO WOO
AND TARO SORAMAME'S WORKED HIS WAY UP TO SECOND PLACE, WITH THE SUPPORT OF OLD WOMAN SPRING!
VOOOM
OOOH! HOT STUFF!
AND IN THIRD IT'S... IT'S HIM! THE LEGENDARY LECHER HIMSELF, DR. MASHIRITO! IDIOT! YOU'RE GONNA TRIP!
I'M REJECTING THIS WEEK'S MANGA!
AND FOLLOWING IN FOURTH PLACE WE HAVE... SENBEI NORIMAKI! ANOTHER STUMPY-LEGGED LECHER! HAH!
VWEEOO
SILENCE!!

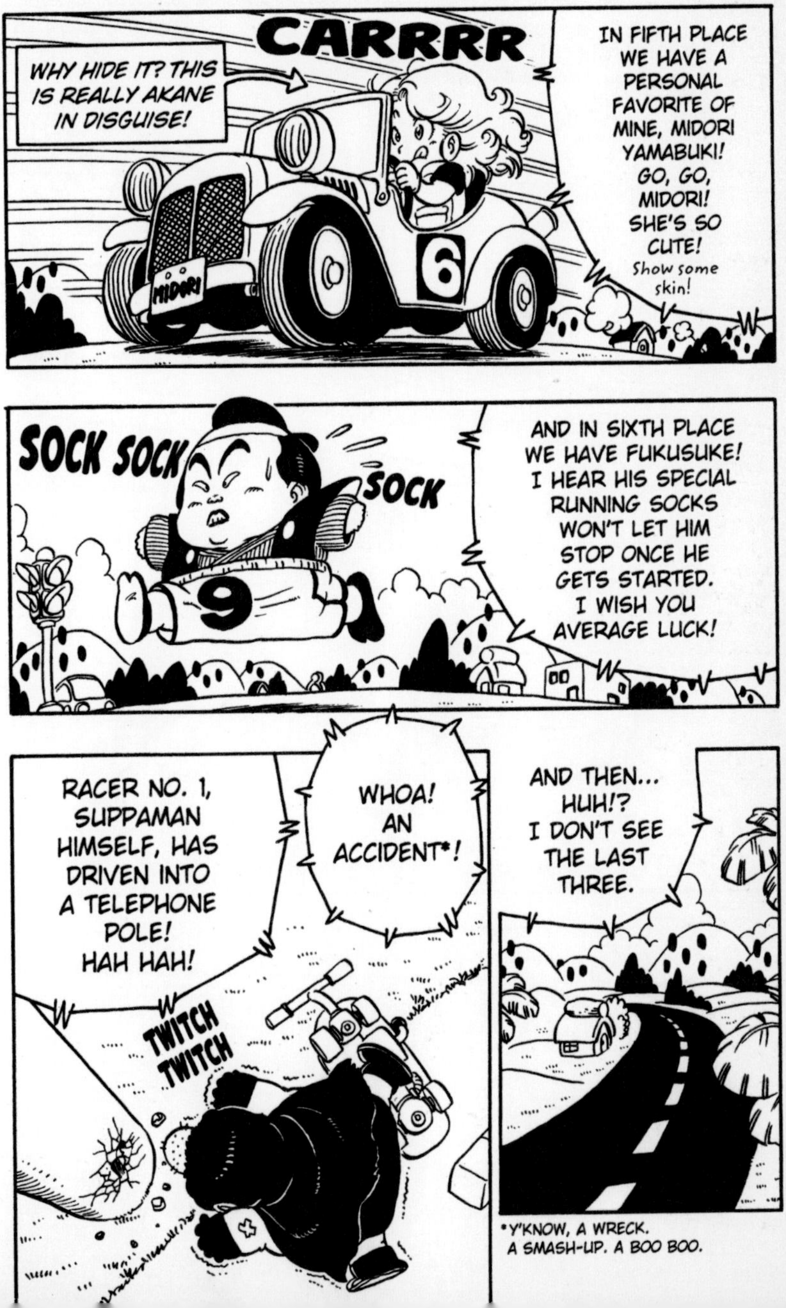
IN FIFTH PLACE WE HAVE A PERSONAL FAVORITE OF MINE, MIDORI YAMABUKI! GO, GO, MIDORI! SHE'S SO CUTE! Show some skin!
CARRRR
WHY HIDE IT? THIS IS REALLY AKANE IN DISGUISE!
MIDORI
6
AND IN SIXTH PLACE WE HAVE FUKUSUKE! I HEAR HIS SPECIAL RUNNING SOCKS WON'T LET HIM STOP ONCE HE GETS STARTED. I WISH YOU AVERAGE LUCK!
SOCK
SOCK SOCK
9
AND THEN... HUH!? I DON'T SEE THE LAST THREE.
WHOA! AN ACCIDENT*!
RACER NO. 1, SUPPAMAN HIMSELF, HAS DRIVEN INTO A TELEPHONE POLE! HAH HAH!
TWITCH TWITCH

*Y'KNOW, A WRECK. A SMASH-UP. A BOO BOO.

READ THIS WAY

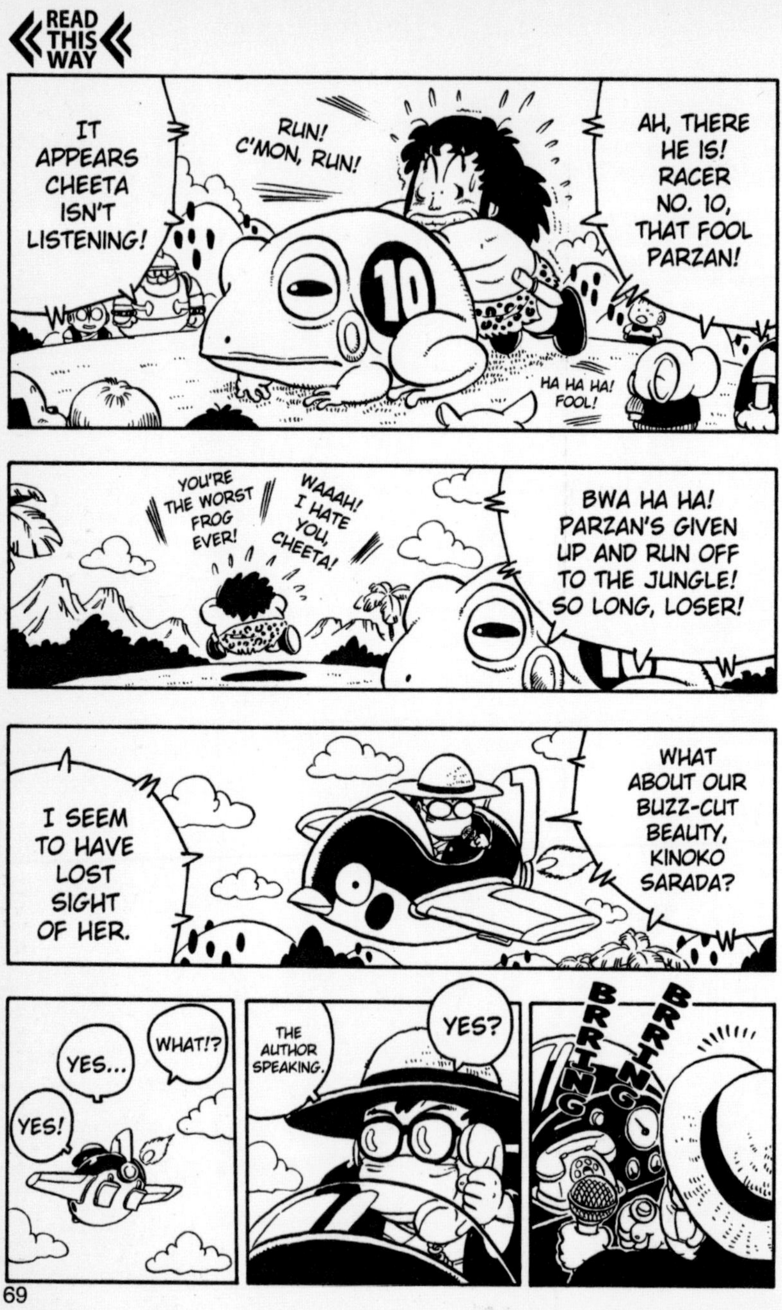
AH, THERE HE IS! RACER NO. 10, THAT FOOL PARZAN!
RUN! C'MON, RUN!
IT APPEARS CHEETA ISN'T LISTENING!
10
HA HA HA! FOOL!
BWA HA HA! PARZAN'S GIVEN UP AND RUN OFF TO THE JUNGLE! SO LONG, LOSER!
WAAAH! I HATE YOU, CHEETA!
YOU'RE THE WORST FROG EVER!
WHAT ABOUT OUR BUZZ-CUT BEAUTY, KINOKO SARADA?
I SEEM TO HAVE LOST SIGHT OF HER.
BRRING
BRRING
YES?
THE AUTHOR SPEAKING.
WHAT!?
YES...
YES!

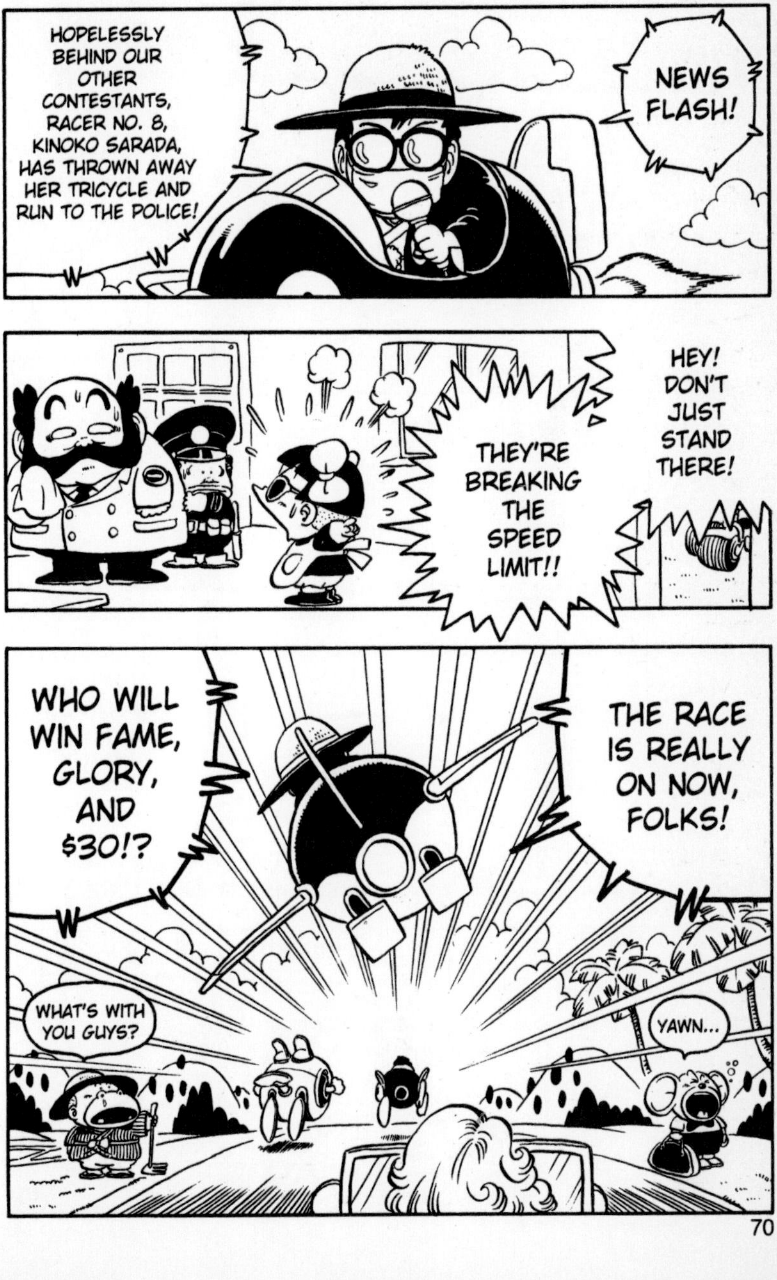
NEWS FLASH!
HOPELESSLY BEHIND OUR OTHER CONTESTANTS, RACER NO. 8, KINOKO SARADA, HAS THROWN AWAY HER TRICYCLE AND RUN TO THE POLICE!
HEY! DON'T JUST STAND THERE!
THEY'RE BREAKING THE SPEED LIMIT!!
THE RACE IS REALLY ON NOW, FOLKS!
WHO WILL WIN FAME, GLORY, AND $30!?
YAWN...
WHAT'S WITH YOU GUYS?

READ THIS WAY

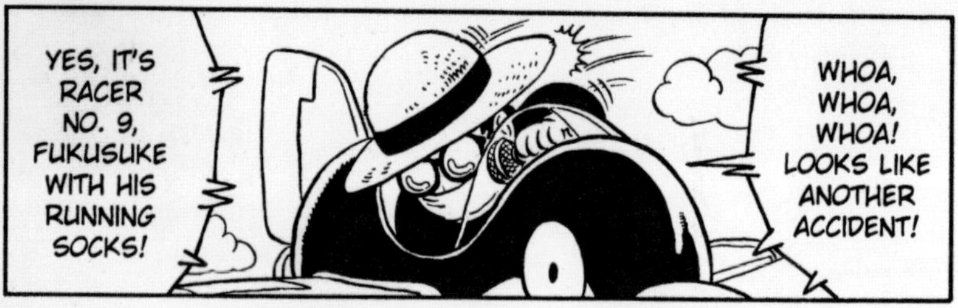
WHOA, WHOA, WHOA! LOOKS LIKE ANOTHER ACCIDENT!
YES, IT'S RACER NO. 9, FUKUSUKE WITH HIS RUNNING SOCKS!

THE SYMBOL ON HIS BACK READS "FU," FOR "FUKUSAKE."

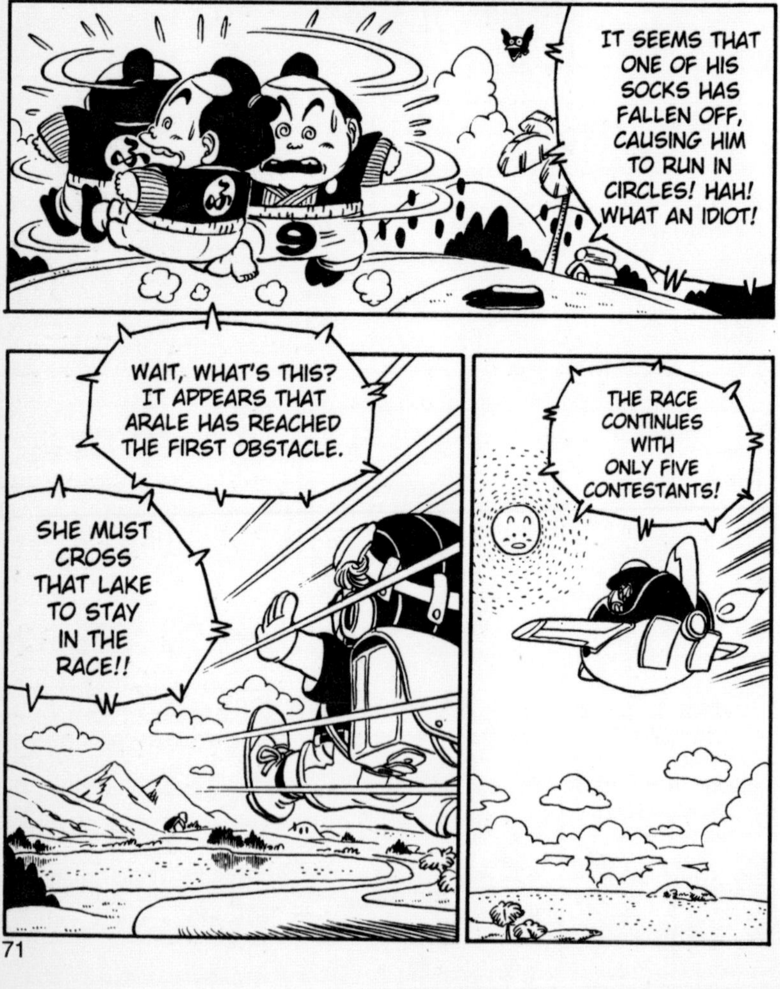
IT SEEMS THAT ONE OF HIS SOCKS HAS FALLEN OFF, CAUSING HIM TO RUN IN CIRCLES! HAH! WHAT AN IDIOT!
9
THE RACE CONTINUES WITH ONLY FIVE CONTESTANTS!
WAIT, WHAT'S THIS? IT APPEARS THAT ARALE HAS REACHED THE FIRST OBSTACLE.
SHE MUST CROSS THAT LAKE TO STAY IN THE RACE!!

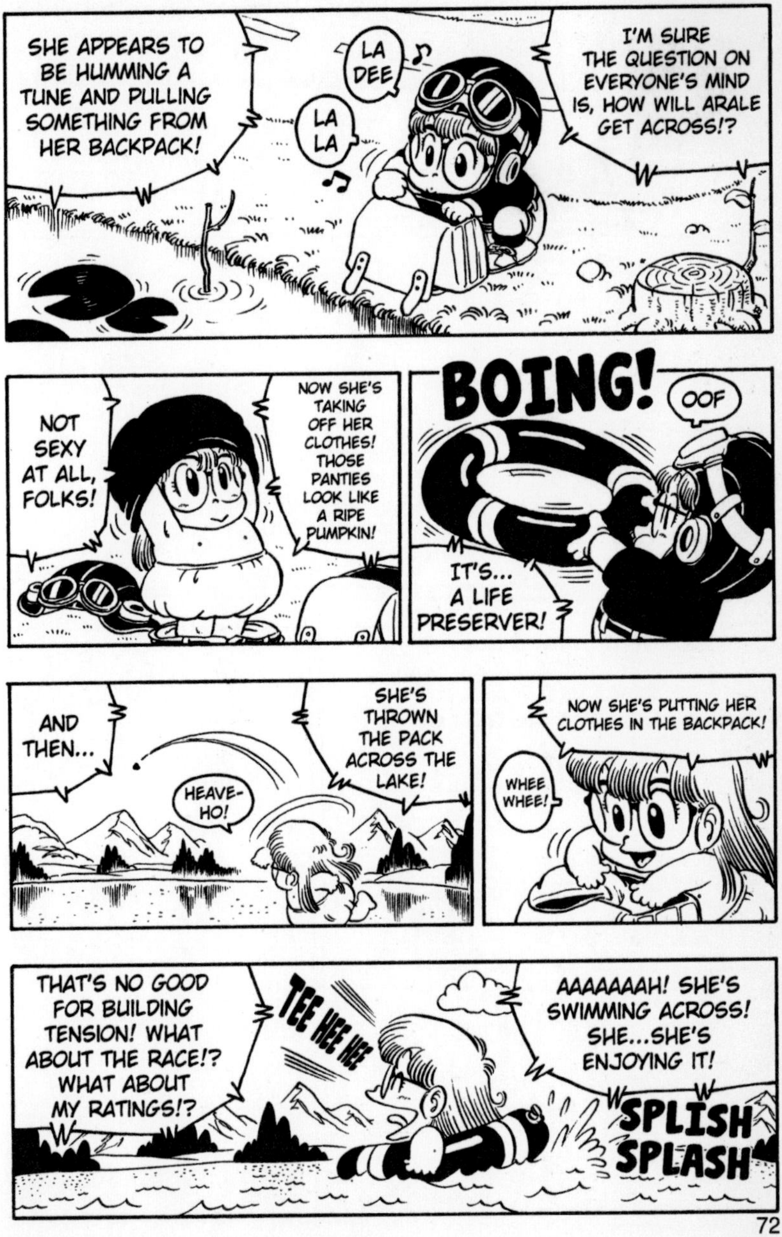
I'M SURE THE QUESTION ON EVERYONE'S MIND IS, HOW WILL ARALE GET ACROSS!?
LA DEE
LA LA
SHE APPEARS TO BE HUMMING A TUNE AND PULLING SOMETHING FROM HER BACKPACK!
BOING!
OOF
IT'S... A LIFE PRESERVER!
NOW SHE'S TAKING OFF HER CLOTHES! THOSE PANTIES LOOK LIKE A RIPE PUMPKIN!
NOT SEXY AT ALL, FOLKS!
NOW SHE'S PUTTING HER CLOTHES IN THE BACKPACK!
WHEE WHEE!
SHE'S THROWN THE PACK ACROSS THE LAKE!
HEAVE-HO!
AND THEN...
AAAAAAAH! SHE'S SWIMMING ACROSS! SHE...SHE'S ENJOYING IT!
SPLISH SPLASH
TEE HEE HEE
THAT'S NO GOOD FOR BUILDING TENSION! WHAT ABOUT THE RACE!? WHAT ABOUT MY RATINGS!?

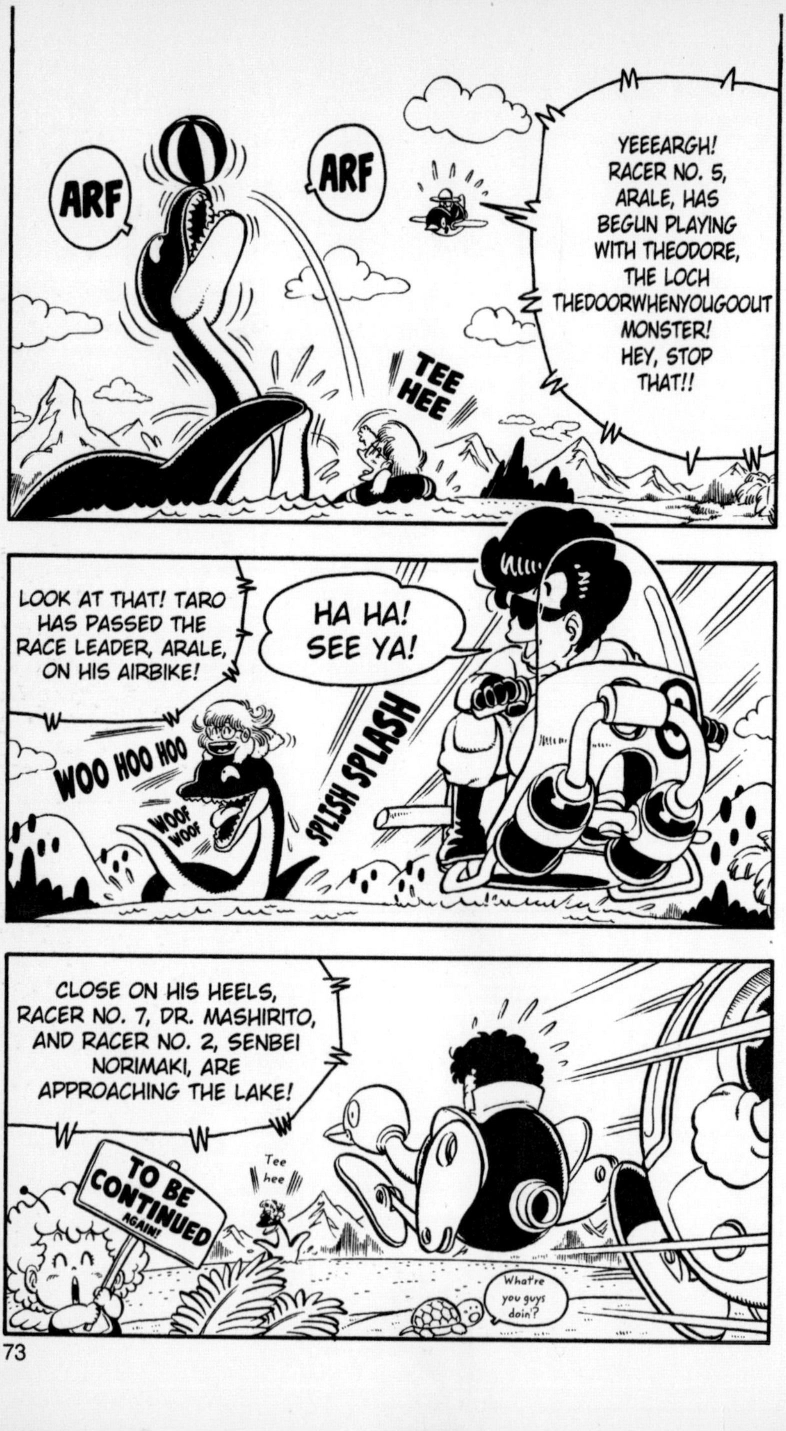
YEEEARGH! RACER NO. 5, ARALE, HAS BEGUN PLAYING WITH THEODORE, THE LOCH THEDOORWHENYOUGOOUT MONSTER! HEY, STOP THAT!!
ARF
ARF
TEE HEE
HA HA! SEE YA!
LOOK AT THAT! TARO HAS PASSED THE RACE LEADER, ARALE, ON HIS AIRBIKE!
SPLISH SPLASH
WOO HOO HOO
WOOF WOOF
CLOSE ON HIS HEELS, RACER NO. 7, DR. MASHIRITO, AND RACER NO. 2, SENBEI NORIMAKI, ARE APPROACHING THE LAKE!
Tee hee
What're you guys doin'?
TO BE CONTINUED AGAIN!

Penguin Village **"I'M NUMBER ONE!" CONTEST** Category: My Genius Frightens Me!

4th

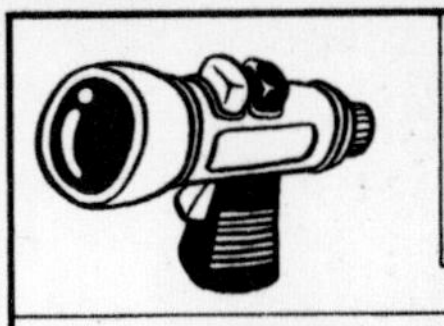

Big-Small Ray Gun
616 votes

★I'd shrink people I don't like and step on 'em!
★I want to eat a piece of chocolate as big as the moon!
★I like that it's modeled after a hair dryer. How cheap.

5th

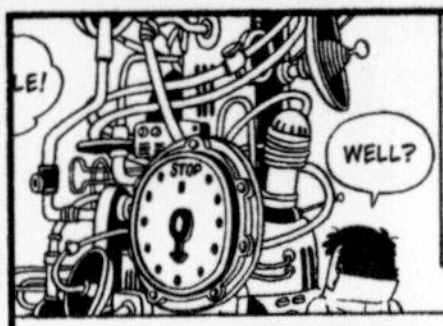
WELL?
STOP

Time Stopper
606 votes

★I like that it can only be used once.
★Wait a second, who's writing the manga now!? Yikes!

6th

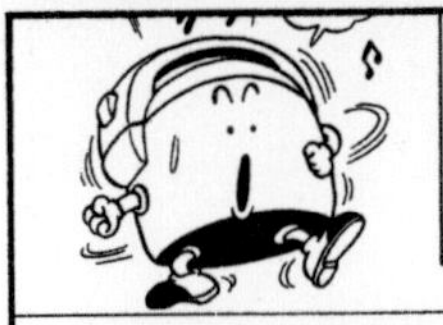

Reality Machine
560 votes

★I want to put a picture of my favorite comedian in it!
★Ooh! You could make your own dreamboat--in the buff!
★Great dance!

7th

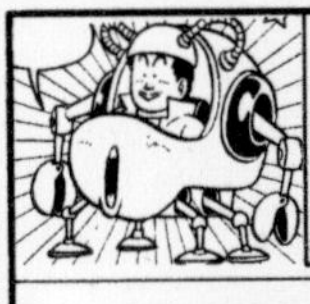

Mr. Handy
234 votes

★Kudos for fattening the already-fat Senbei even more!
★I don't care how fat I get. I want to be lazy in Mr. Handy!

8th

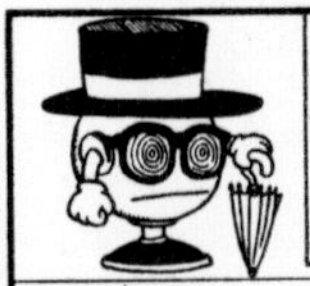

Fairy Tale Machine
214 votes

★I wish I could use this to go into a *Shonen Jump* manga!
★Imagine if you wandered into an English textbook by mistake. Yeeeargh!

9th

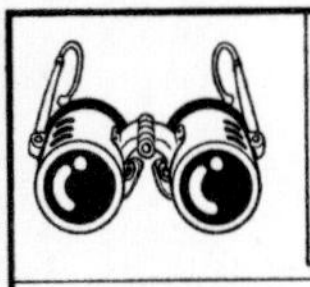

See-thru Glasses
212 votes

★Mankind's ultimate dream
★Makes me want to go to teen idol concerts.
★Tee hee hee!

10th

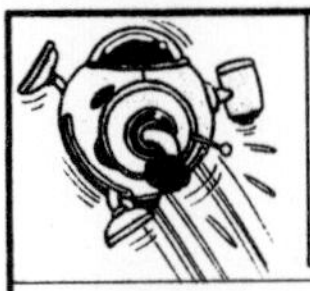

Super-Mecha "Ping-pong"
170 votes

★It's amphibious! And it can even fly through space!
★Great for going on dates.

11th

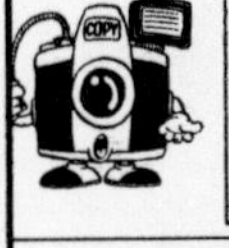
COPY

Mr. Copy
154 votes

★I would make a copy of myself to take my exams.
★Good for making someone to play games with. I'd always win!

12th

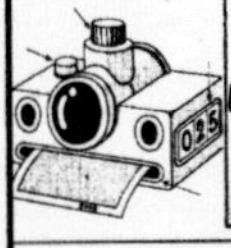

Future Camera
152 votes

★I'd take pics of my friends to depress them!
★I don't want to see my own photo.

13th

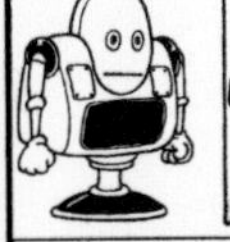

Robot Hair-dresser "Barberman"
130 votes

★I like the bold "self-destruct on first sign of danger" programming.
★Barbers are good at cutting hair and talking. This robot isn't.

14th

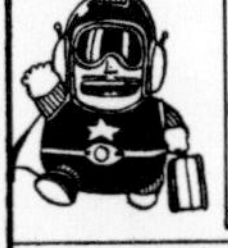

Super Senbei robot
124 votes

★So much like Senbei, even Arale can't tell them apart!

15th

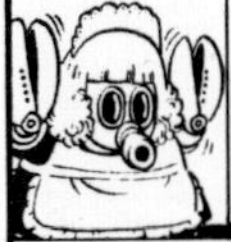

Housebot Akiko
104 votes

★Ugly, but strong!
★Cool and calculating.

Penguin Grand Prix
Part 3

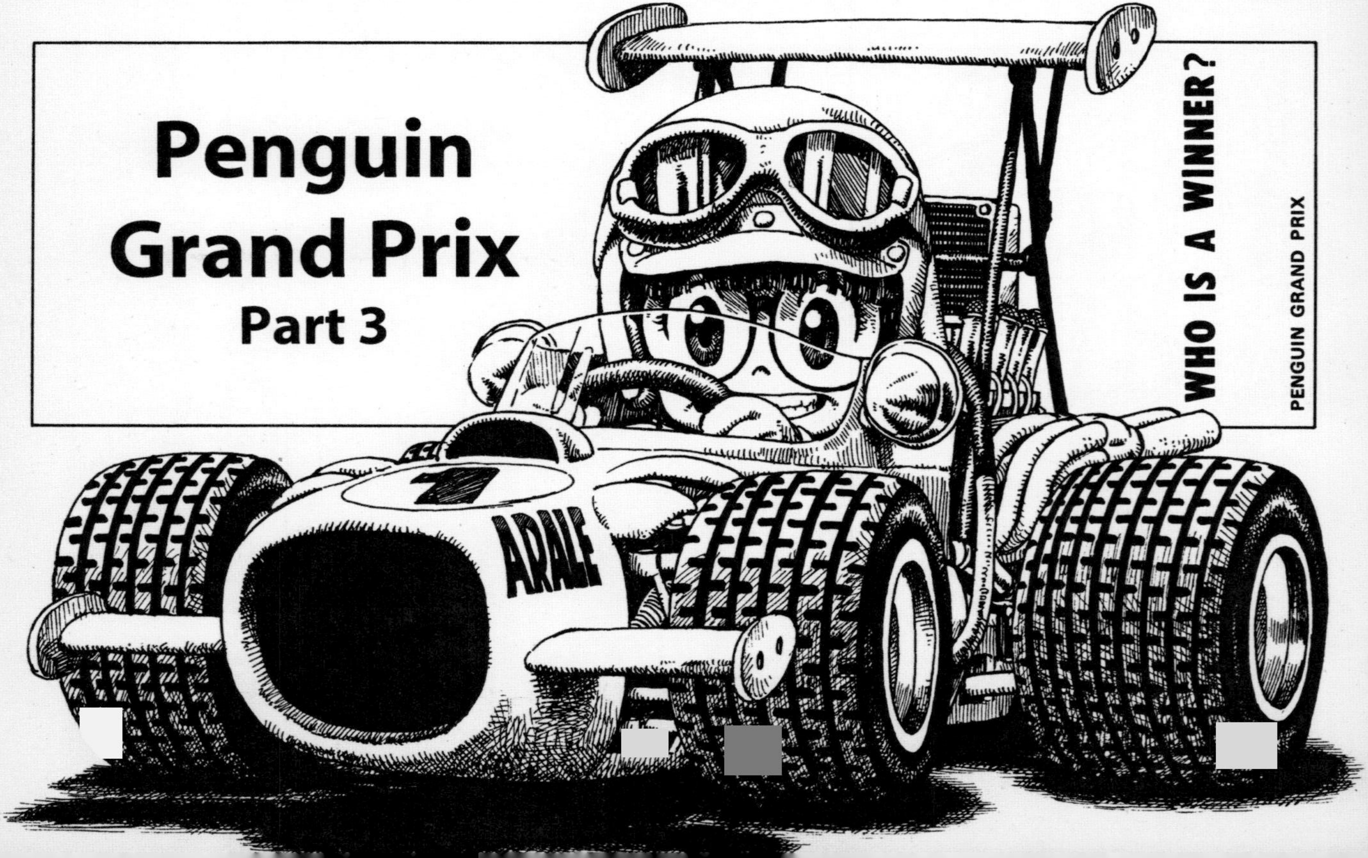
ARALE
1

WHO IS A WINNER?

PENGUIN GRAND PRIX

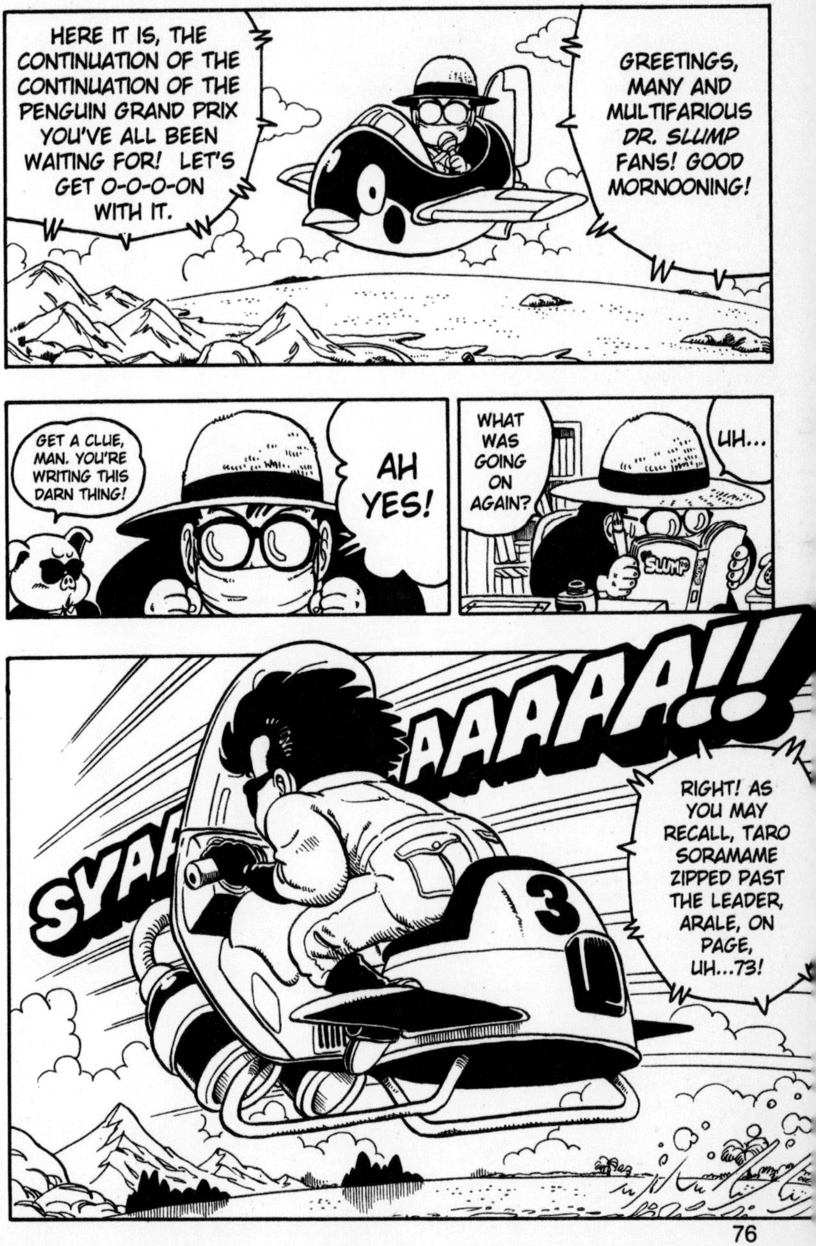
GREETINGS, MANY AND MULTIFARIOUS *DR. SLUMP* FANS! GOOD MORNOONING!
HERE IT IS, THE CONTINUATION OF THE CONTINUATION OF THE PENGUIN GRAND PRIX YOU'VE ALL BEEN WAITING FOR! LET'S GET O-O-O-ON WITH IT.
UH...
WHAT WAS GOING ON AGAIN?
SLUMP
GET A CLUE, MAN. YOU'RE WRITING THIS DARN THING!
AH YES!
SYA
AAAAAA!!
RIGHT! AS YOU MAY RECALL, TARO SORAMAME ZIPPED PAST THE LEADER, ARALE, ON PAGE, UH...73!
3

READ THIS WAY

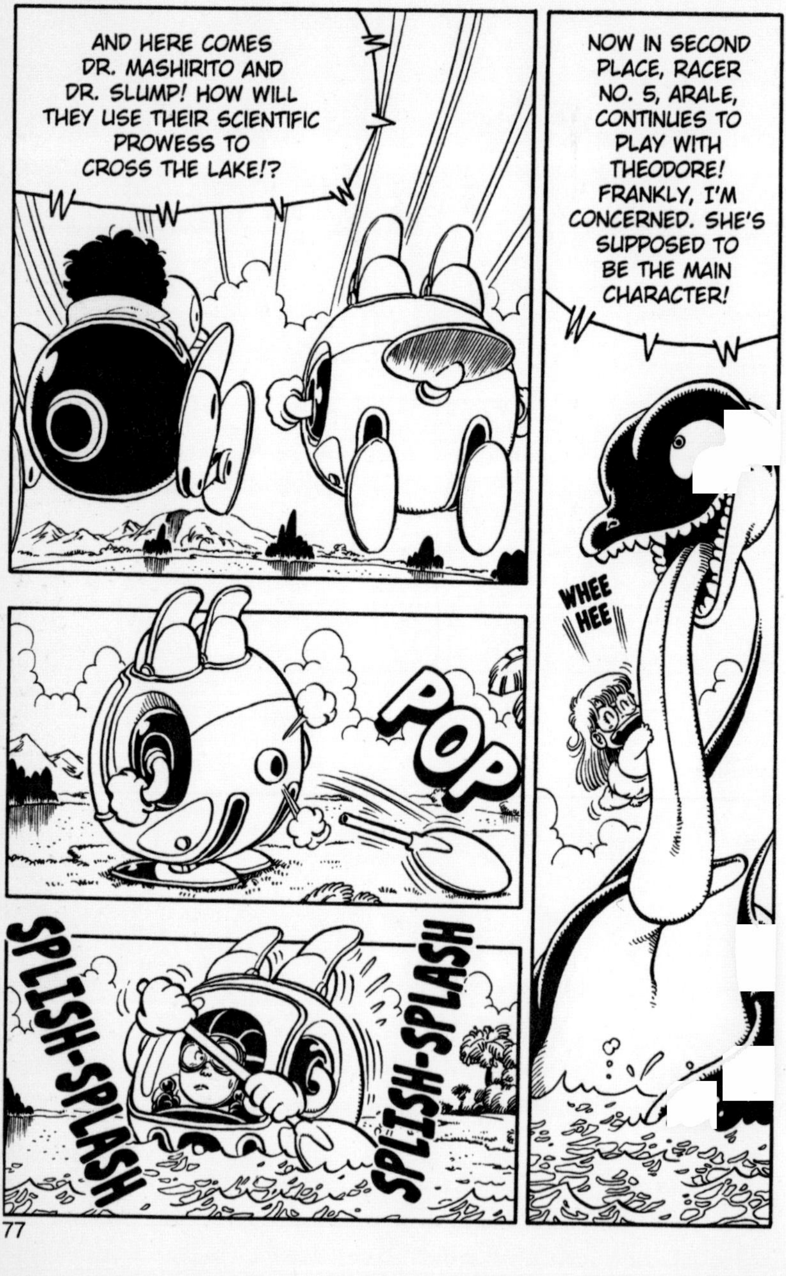
NOW IN SECOND PLACE, RACER NO. 5, ARALE, CONTINUES TO PLAY WITH THEODORE! FRANKLY, I'M CONCERNED. SHE'S SUPPOSED TO BE THE MAIN CHARACTER!
WHEE HEE
AND HERE COMES DR. MASHIRITO AND DR. SLUMP! HOW WILL THEY USE THEIR SCIENTIFIC PROWESS TO CROSS THE LAKE!?
POP
SPLISH-SPLASH
SPLISH-SPLASH

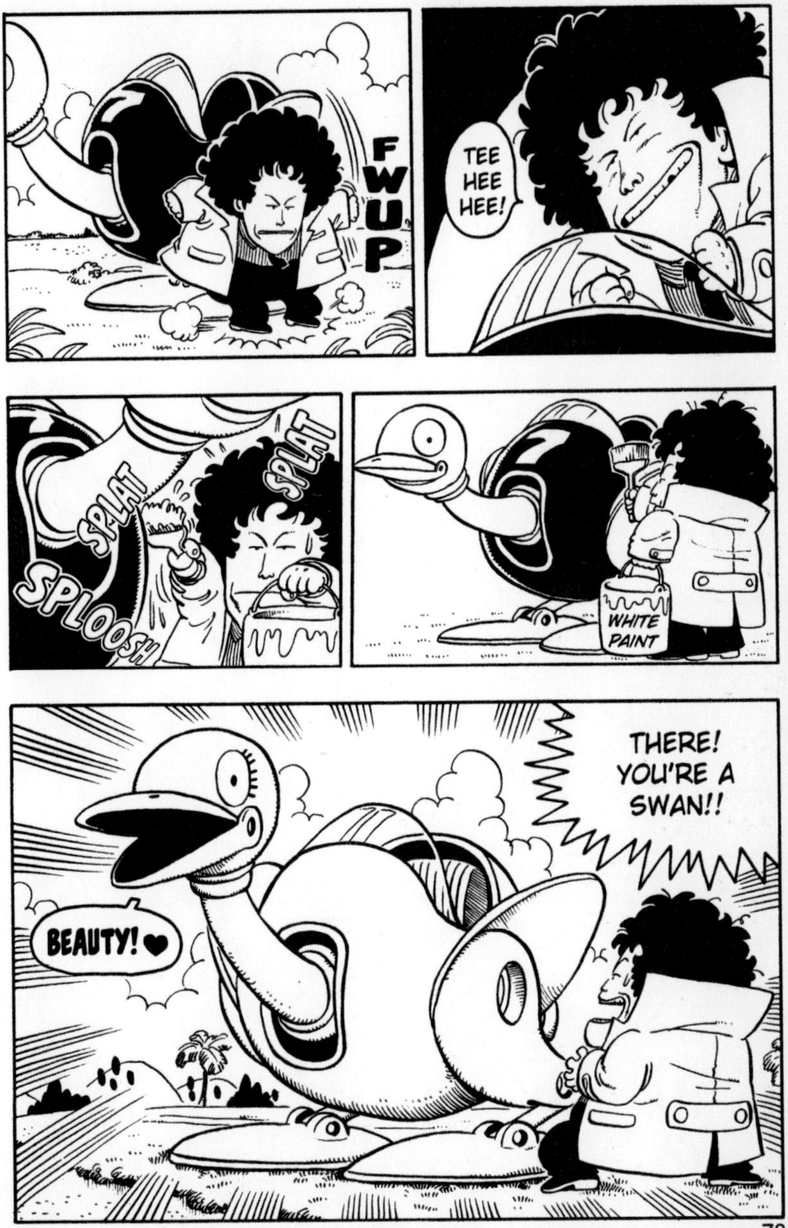
TEE HEE HEE!
FWUP
WHITE PAINT
SPLAT
SPLAT
SPLOOSH
THERE! YOU'RE A SWAN!!
BEAUTY! ♥

READ THIS WAY

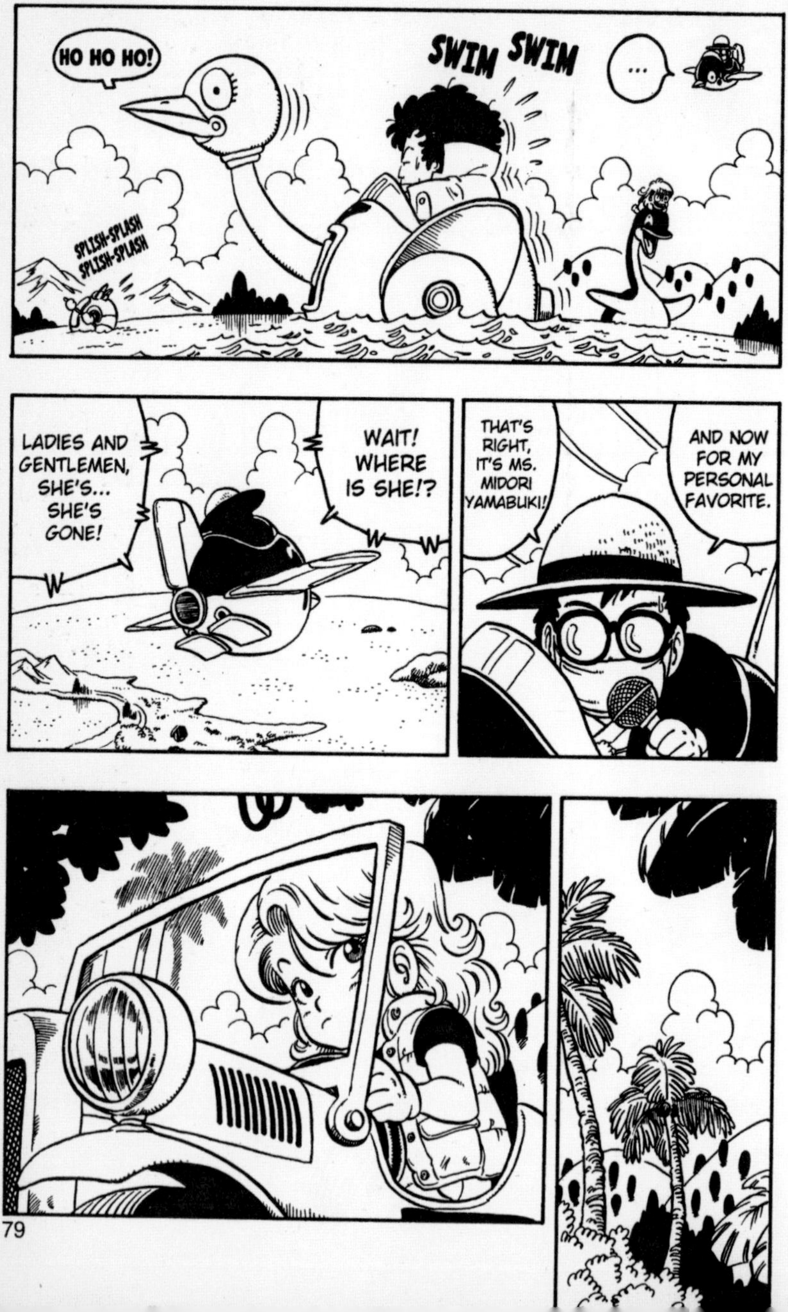
...
SWIM SWIM
HO HO HO!
SPLISH-SPLASH SPLISH-SPLASH
AND NOW FOR MY PERSONAL FAVORITE.
THAT'S RIGHT, IT'S MS. MIDORI YAMABUKI!
WAIT! WHERE IS SHE!?
LADIES AND GENTLEMEN, SHE'S... SHE'S GONE!

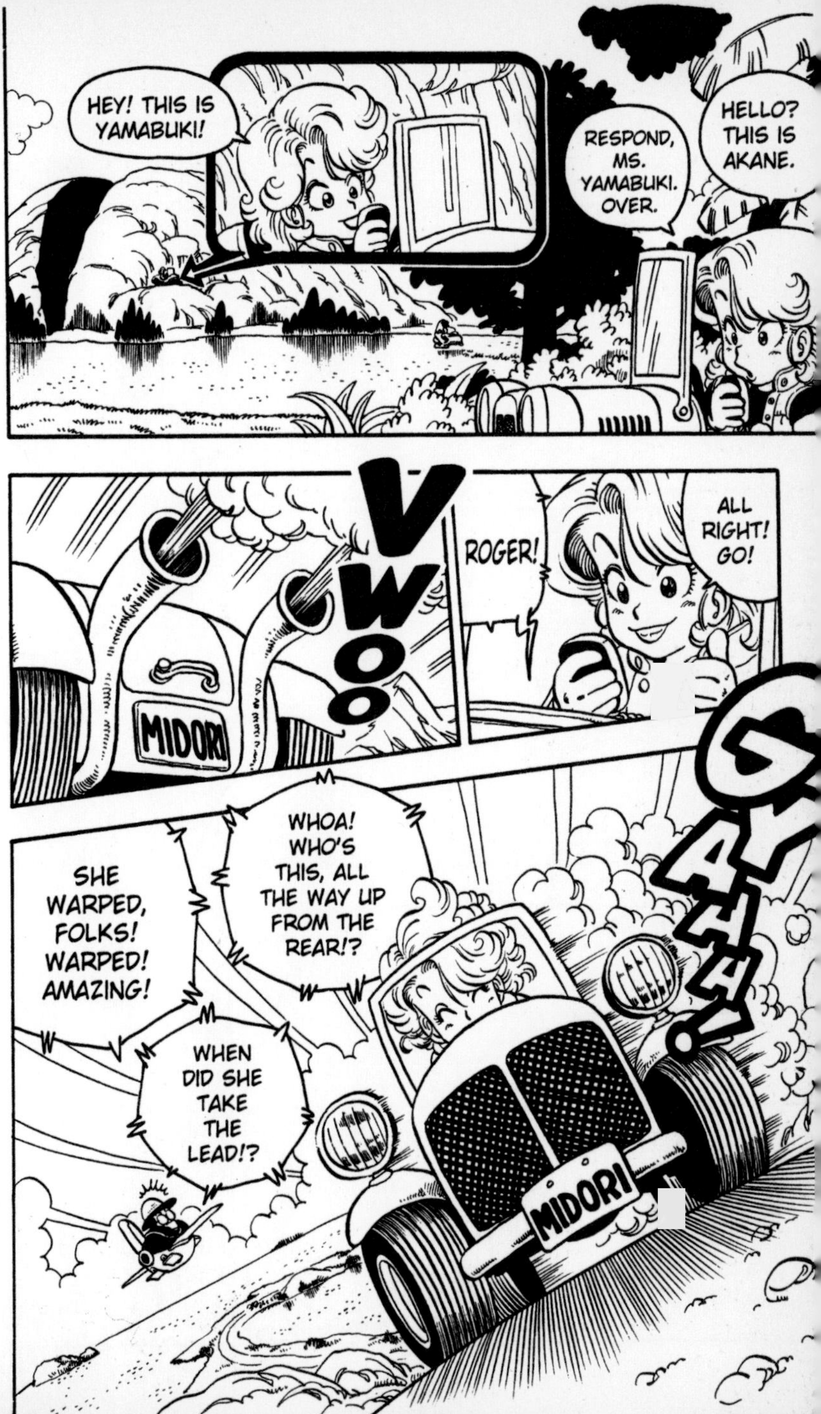
HELLO? THIS IS AKANE.
RESPOND, MS. YAMABUKI. OVER.
HEY! THIS IS YAMABUKI!
ALL RIGHT! GO!
ROGER!
VWOO
GYAAAA!
WHOA! WHO'S THIS, ALL THE WAY UP FROM THE REAR!?
SHE WARPED, FOLKS! WARPED! AMAZING!
WHEN DID SHE TAKE THE LEAD!?
MIDORI

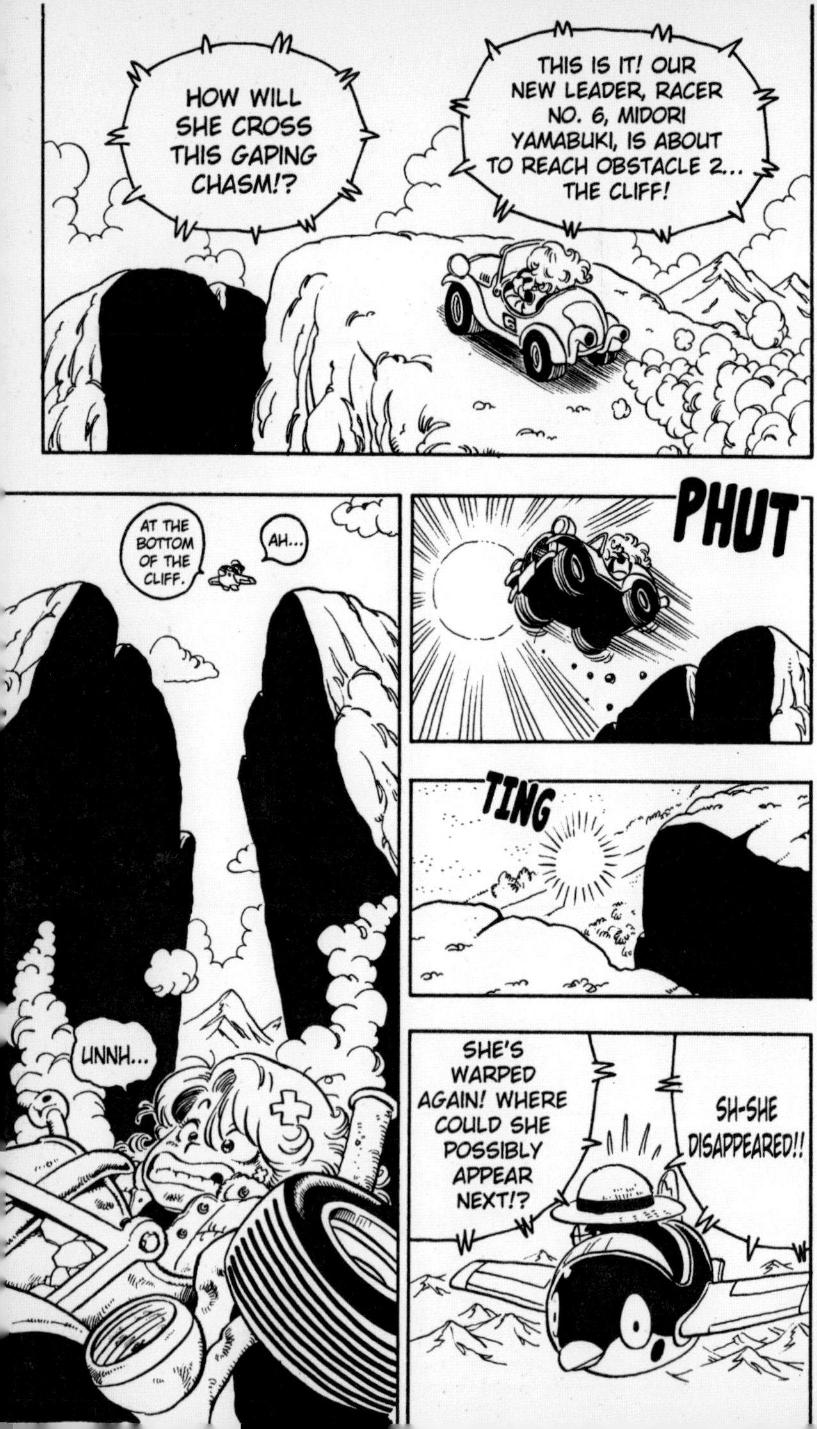
THIS IS IT! OUR NEW LEADER, RACER NO. 6, MIDORI YAMABUKI, IS ABOUT TO REACH OBSTACLE 2... THE CLIFF!
HOW WILL SHE CROSS THIS GAPING CHASM!?
PHUT
TING
SH-SHE DISAPPEARED!!
SHE'S WARPED AGAIN! WHERE COULD SHE POSSIBLY APPEAR NEXT!?
AH...
AT THE BOTTOM OF THE CLIFF.
UNNH...

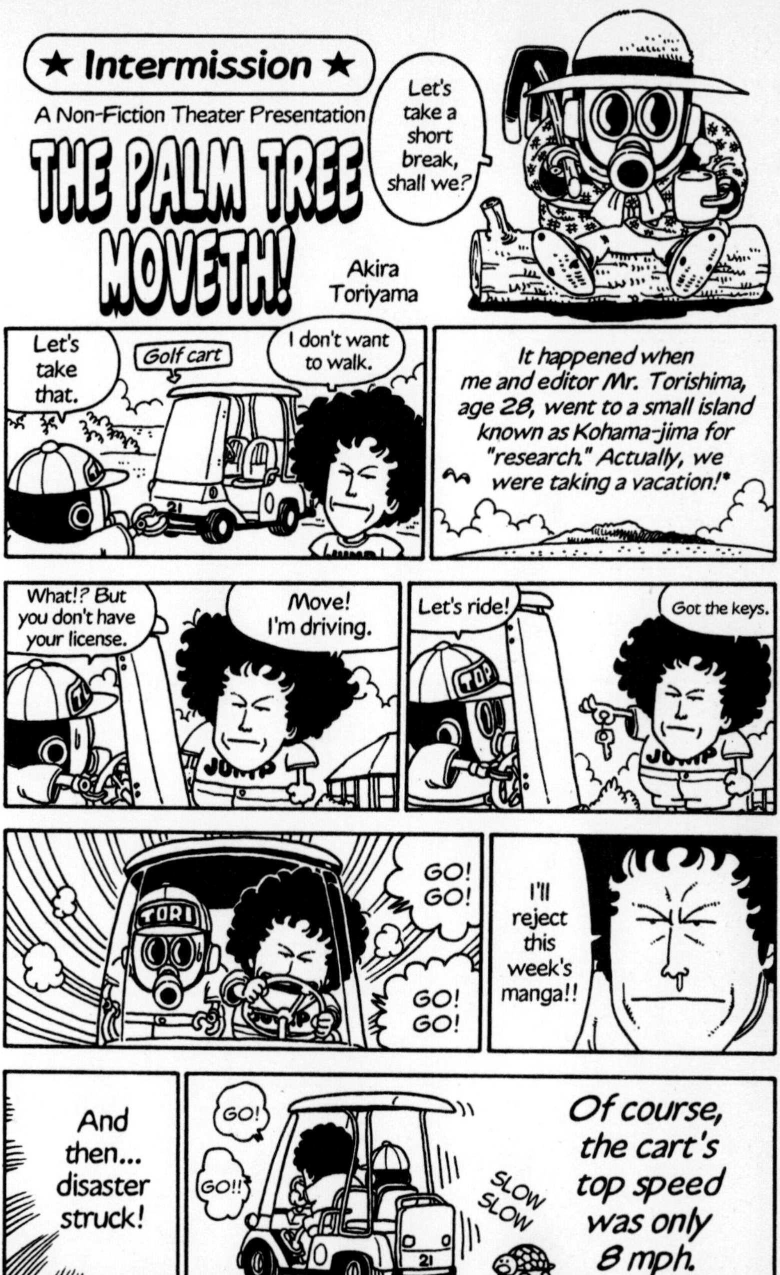
Let's take a short break, shall we?
★ Intermission ★
A Non-Fiction Theater Presentation
THE PALM TREE MOVETH!
Akira Toriyama
It happened when me and editor Mr. Torishima, age 28, went to a small island known as Kohama-jima for "research." Actually, we were taking a vacation!*
I don't want to walk.
Golf cart
Let's take that.
Got the keys.
Let's ride!
Move! I'm driving.
What!? But you don't have your license.
I'll reject this week's manga!!
GO! GO!
GO! GO!
Of course, the cart's top speed was only 8 mph.
SLOW SLOW
GO!
GO!!
And then... disaster struck!

*THE EDITOR WOULD LIKE TO APOLOGIZE FOR ANY MISUNDERSTANDINGS RESULTING FROM THIS AUTHOR'S UTTER LACK OF VISION. THE RESULTS OF THIS VERY SERIOUS BUSINESS TRIP WILL BE REVEALED, IN THEIR FULL GLORY, IN VOLUME 9. THANKS. --EDITOR TORISHIMA

READ THIS WAY

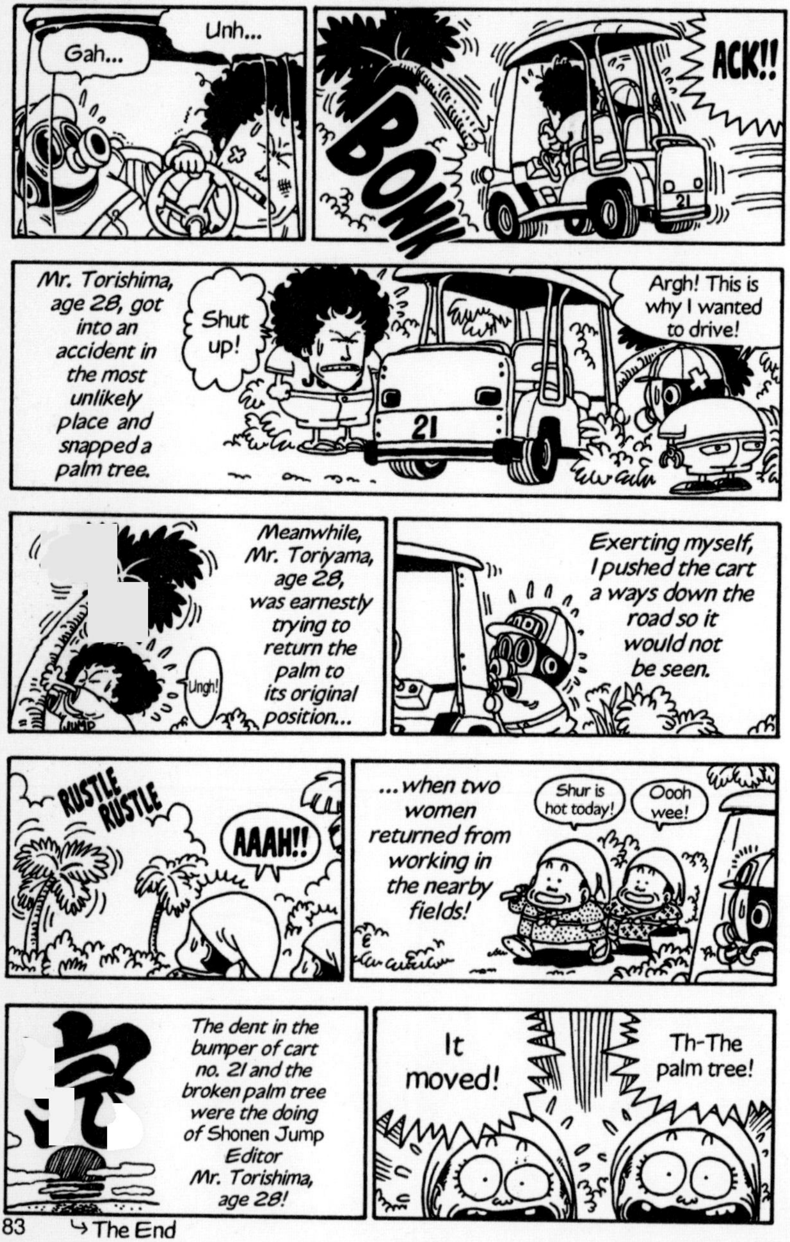

ACK!!
BONK
Unh...
Gah...
Argh! This is why I wanted to drive!
Shut up!
Mr. Torishima, age 28, got into an accident in the most unlikely place and snapped a palm tree.
Exerting myself, I pushed the cart a ways down the road so it would not be seen.
Meanwhile, Mr. Toriyama, age 28, was earnestly trying to return the palm to its original position...
Ungh!
Oooh wee!
Shur is hot today!
...when two women returned from working in the nearby fields!
AAAH!!
RUSTLE RUSTLE
Th-The palm tree!
It moved!
The dent in the bumper of cart no. 21 and the broken palm tree were the doing of Shonen Jump Editor Mr. Torishima, age 28!

↳The End

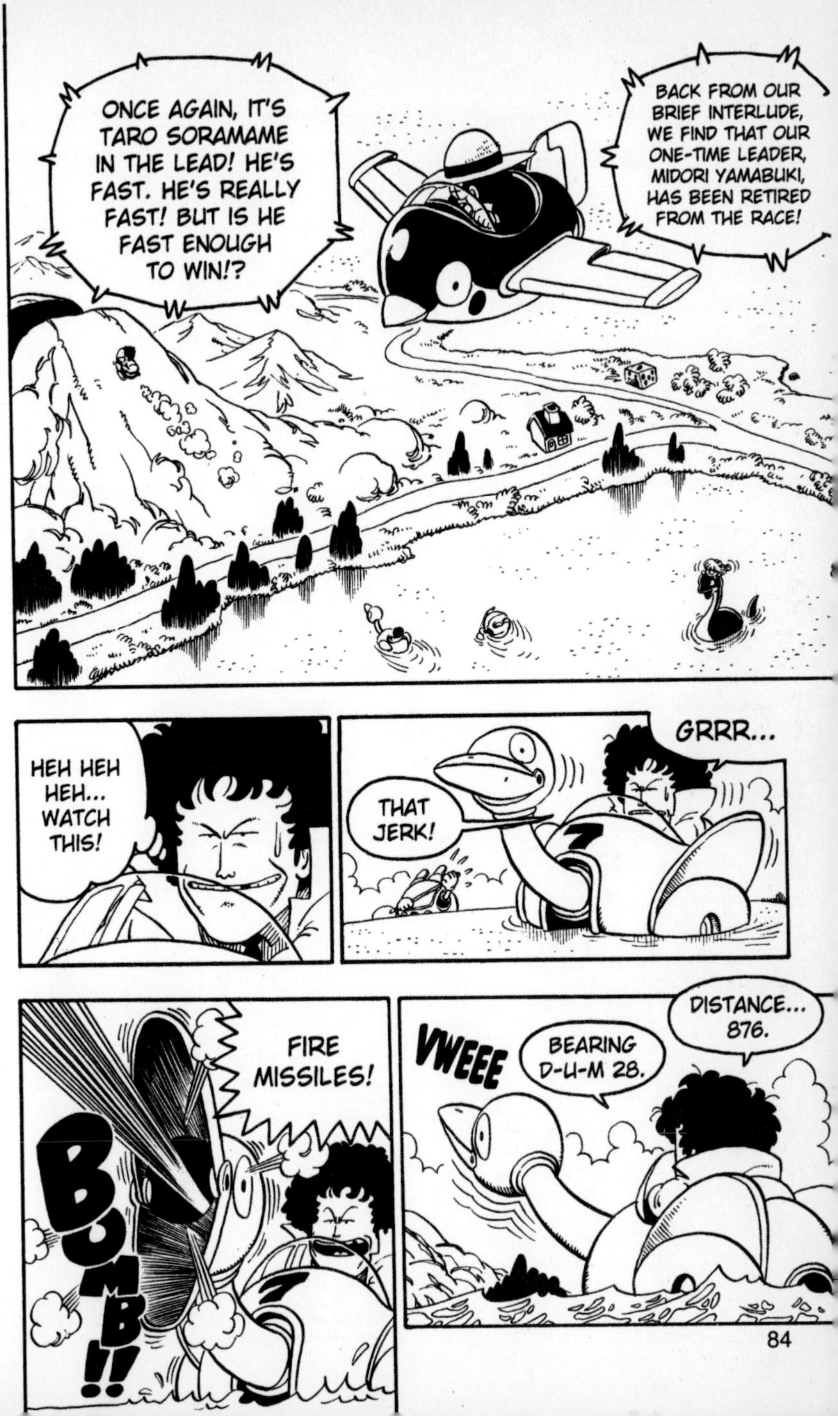
BACK FROM OUR BRIEF INTERLUDE, WE FIND THAT OUR ONE-TIME LEADER, MIDORI YAMABUKI, HAS BEEN RETIRED FROM THE RACE!
ONCE AGAIN, IT'S TARO SORAMAME IN THE LEAD! HE'S FAST. HE'S REALLY FAST! BUT IS HE FAST ENOUGH TO WIN!?
GRRR...
THAT JERK!
HEH HEH HEH... WATCH THIS!
DISTANCE... 876.
BEARING D-U-M 28.
VWEEE
FIRE MISSILES!
BOMB!!

READ THIS WAY

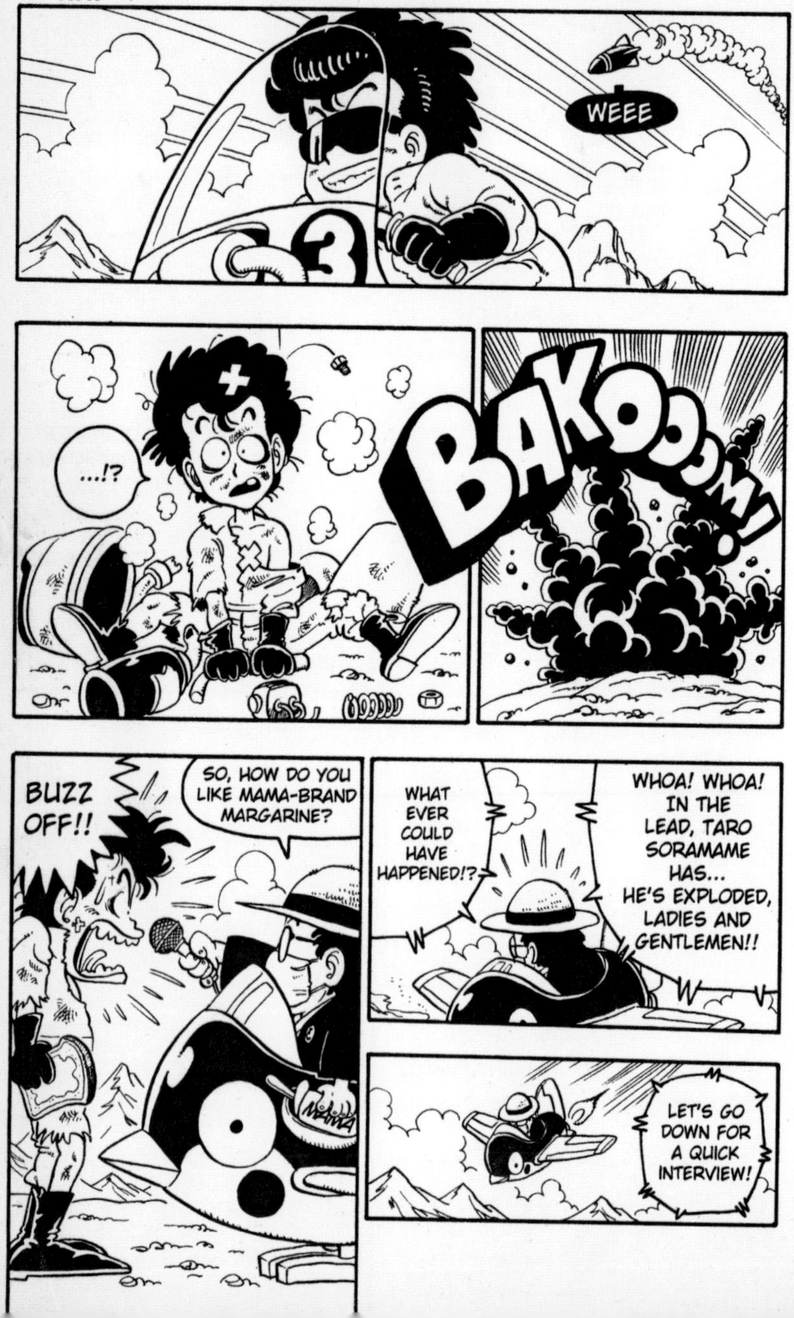
WEEE
BAKOOOM!
...!?
WHOA! WHOA! IN THE LEAD, TARO SORAMAME HAS... HE'S EXPLODED, LADIES AND GENTLEMEN!!
WHAT EVER COULD HAVE HAPPENED!?
LET'S GO DOWN FOR A QUICK INTERVIEW!
SO, HOW DO YOU LIKE MAMA-BRAND MARGARINE?
BUZZ OFF!!
MAMA

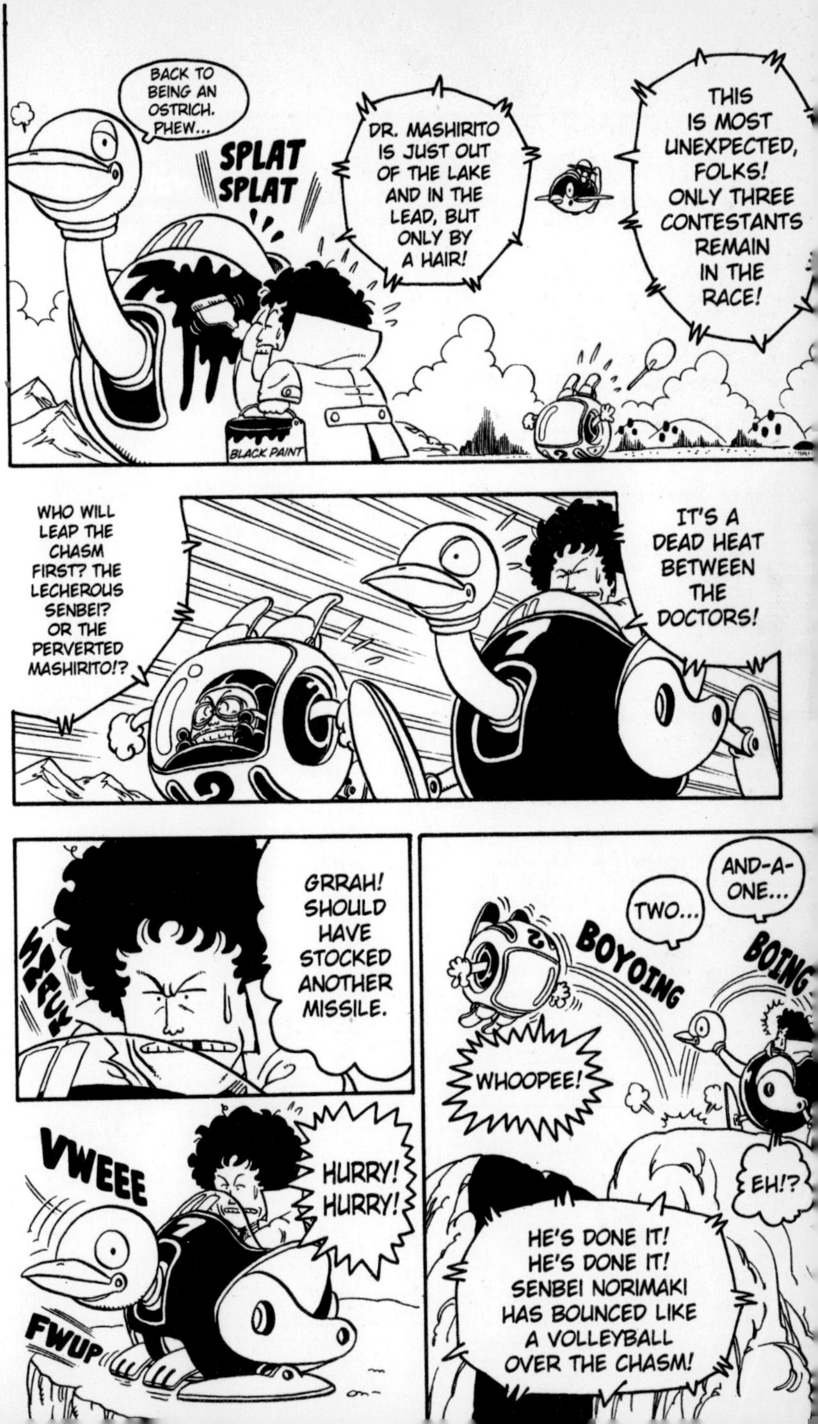
THIS IS MOST UNEXPECTED, FOLKS! ONLY THREE CONTESTANTS REMAIN IN THE RACE!
DR. MASHIRITO IS JUST OUT OF THE LAKE AND IN THE LEAD, BUT ONLY BY A HAIR!
SPLAT SPLAT
BACK TO BEING AN OSTRICH. PHEW...
BLACK PAINT
IT'S A DEAD HEAT BETWEEN THE DOCTORS!
WHO WILL LEAP THE CHASM FIRST? THE LECHEROUS SENBEI? OR THE PERVERTED MASHIRITO!?
AND-A-ONE...
TWO...
BOING
BOYOING
WHOOPEE!
EH!?
HE'S DONE IT! HE'S DONE IT! SENBEI NORIMAKI HAS BOUNCED LIKE A VOLLEYBALL OVER THE CHASM!
GRRAH! SHOULD HAVE STOCKED ANOTHER MISSILE.
HURRY! HURRY!
VWEEE
FWUP

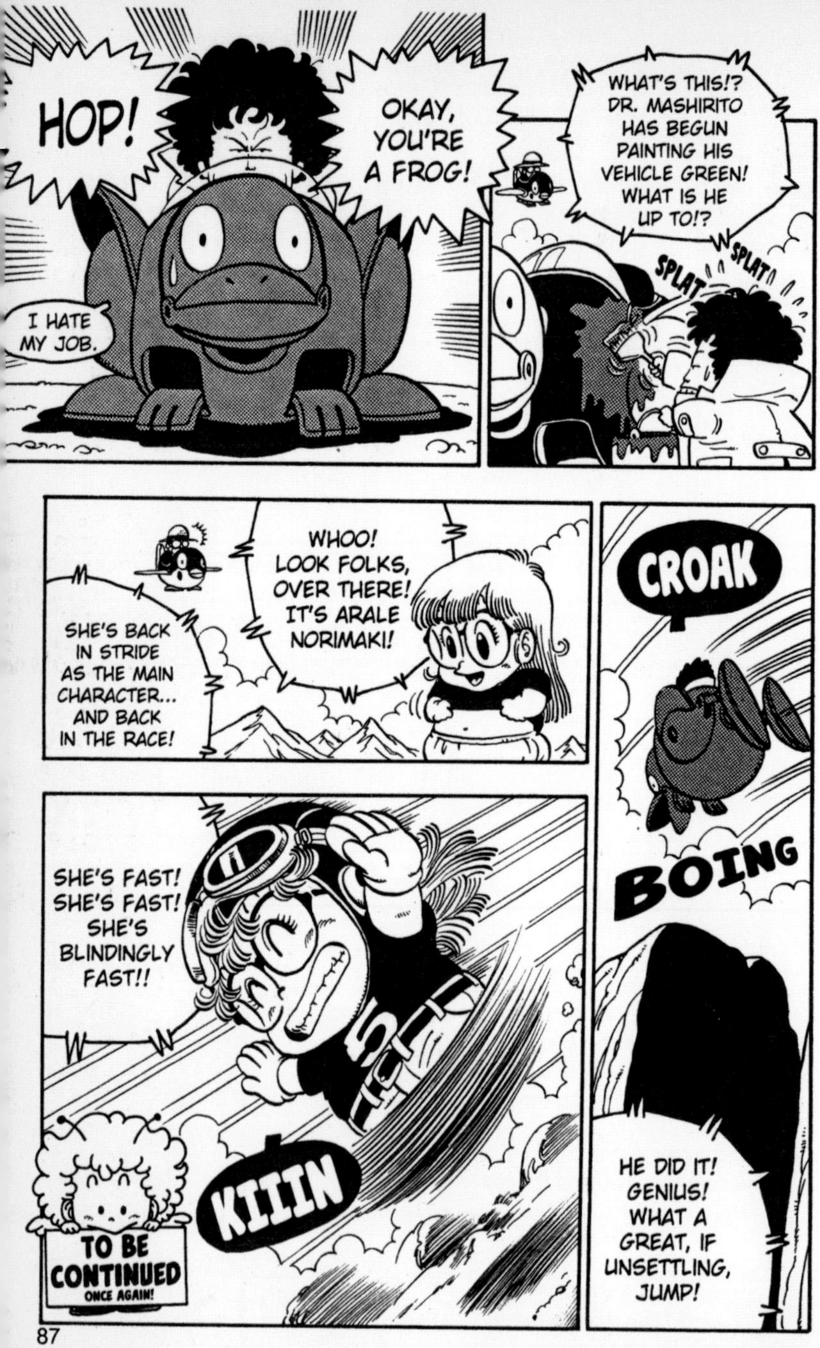
WHAT'S THIS!? DR. MASHIRITO HAS BEGUN PAINTING HIS VEHICLE GREEN! WHAT IS HE UP TO!?
SPLAT
SPLAT
OKAY, YOU'RE A FROG!
HOP!
I HATE MY JOB.
CROAK
BOING
HE DID IT! GENIUS! WHAT A GREAT, IF UNSETTLING, JUMP!
WHOO! LOOK FOLKS, OVER THERE! IT'S ARALE NORIMAKI!
SHE'S BACK IN STRIDE AS THE MAIN CHARACTER... AND BACK IN THE RACE!
SHE'S FAST! SHE'S FAST! SHE'S BLINDINGLY FAST!!
KIIIN
TO BE CONTINUED
ONCE AGAIN!

Penguin Village "I'M NUMBER ONE!" CONTEST

Category: My Genius Frightens Me!

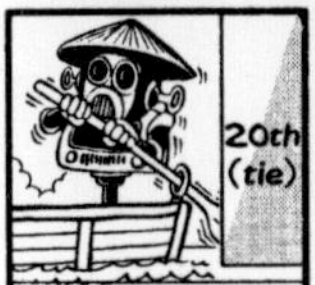

20th (tie)

Roboboat
46 votes

★The mechanical boatman is great!

★He's so slow even I wouldn't get seasick.

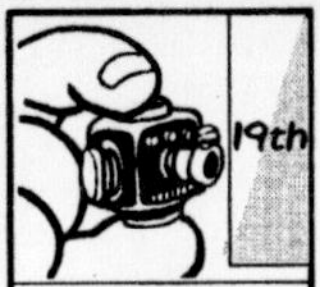

19th

Arale-Eye Television
54 votes

★It's so kinky!

★Who would want this? All you'd get to see is poop all the time!

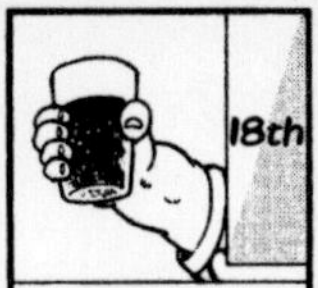

18th

Fall-Down-Go-Boom Love Potion
56 votes

★It was good seeing Senbei work for a change.

★I want this guy in my class to drink it.

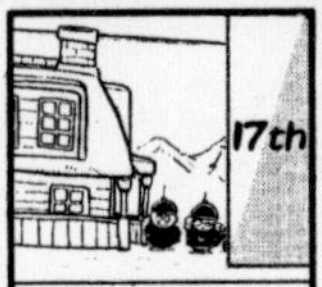

17th

Miniature House
80 votes

★I like that you can do whatever you want with it.

★I would bring over that girl I've always had a crush on.

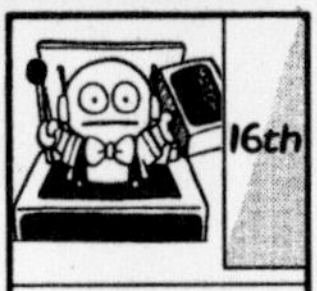

16th

$1 Lighter
84 votes

★I like that you have to put money in to get a light.

★I like that he's polite.

30th	29th	28th	27th	26th	24th (tie)	24th (tie)	23rd	22nd	20th (tie)
The Great Strawberry Panties Caper **6 votes** ★Ridiculously complex	**Walking Jets** **12 votes** ★What do these have to do with walking!?	**K-9 Robot** **16 votes** ★A hip way to shirk his duty!	**Nikochan's Car** **18 votes** ★Only a king would mistake this for a spaceship.	**Youth Serum** **26 votes** ★I'd give this to my dad.	**Boxing Game** **30 votes** ★The gong-bashing referee's the best.	**Robotoriyama** **30 votes** ★That's me, you dummies! Me!	**Cola Fizzjet** **34 votes** ★Nice and simple	**Robbot** **40 votes** ★He's got the look of a scoundrel!	**Invisibility Potion** **46 votes** ★I'd go to the public baths, of course.

I ask for things the Doctor has invented and just look at the junk people send me!

Letsgomobile	268 votes
Senbei Norimaki	160 votes
Gatchan	30 votes

Various other dumb responses:

- Arale's belly-button button
- Arale's finger-spring
- Arale's spare head
- Everything
- Special instant ramen
- The machine that hatched Gatchan
- Arale's power supply, Robovita A
- Ho-yo-yo Bomber

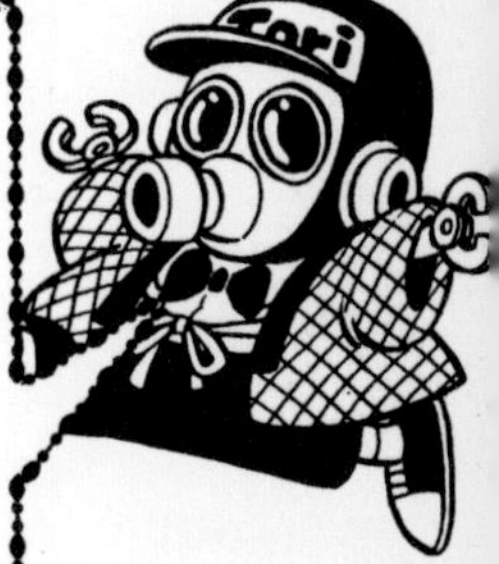
Tori

Penguin Grand Prix
Part 4

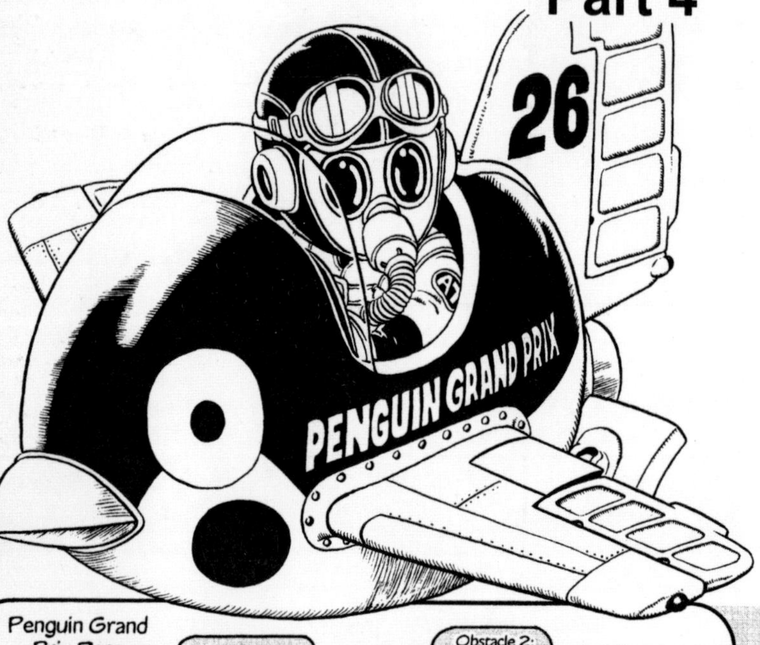
26
PENGUIN GRAND PRIX

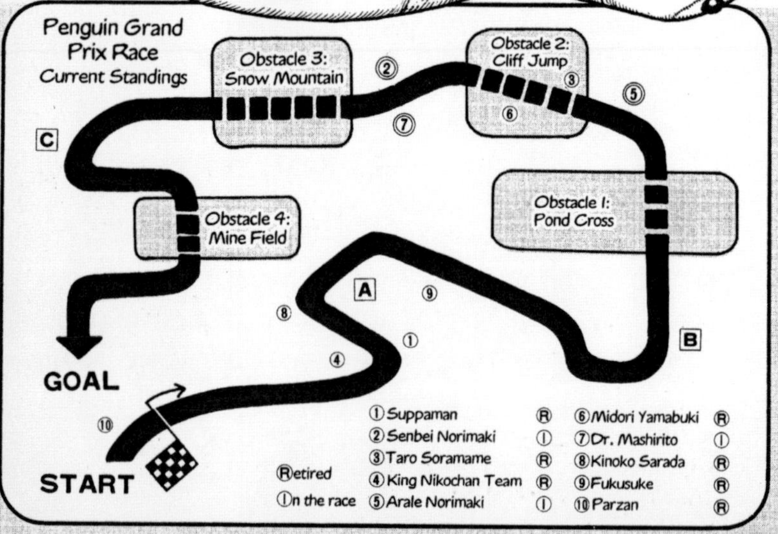
Penguin Grand Prix Race
Current Standings
Obstacle 3: Snow Mountain
Obstacle 2: Cliff Jump
Obstacle 1: Pond Cross
Obstacle 4: Mine Field
A
B
C
GOAL
START
①
②
③
④
⑤
⑥
⑦
⑧
⑨
⑩
Ⓡetired
Ⓘn the race
① Suppaman Ⓡ
② Senbei Norimaki Ⓘ
③ Taro Soramame Ⓡ
④ King Nikochan Team Ⓡ
⑤ Arale Norimaki Ⓘ
⑥ Midori Yamabuki Ⓡ
⑦ Dr. Mashirito Ⓘ
⑧ Kinoko Sarada Ⓡ
⑨ Fukusuke Ⓡ
⑩ Parzan Ⓡ

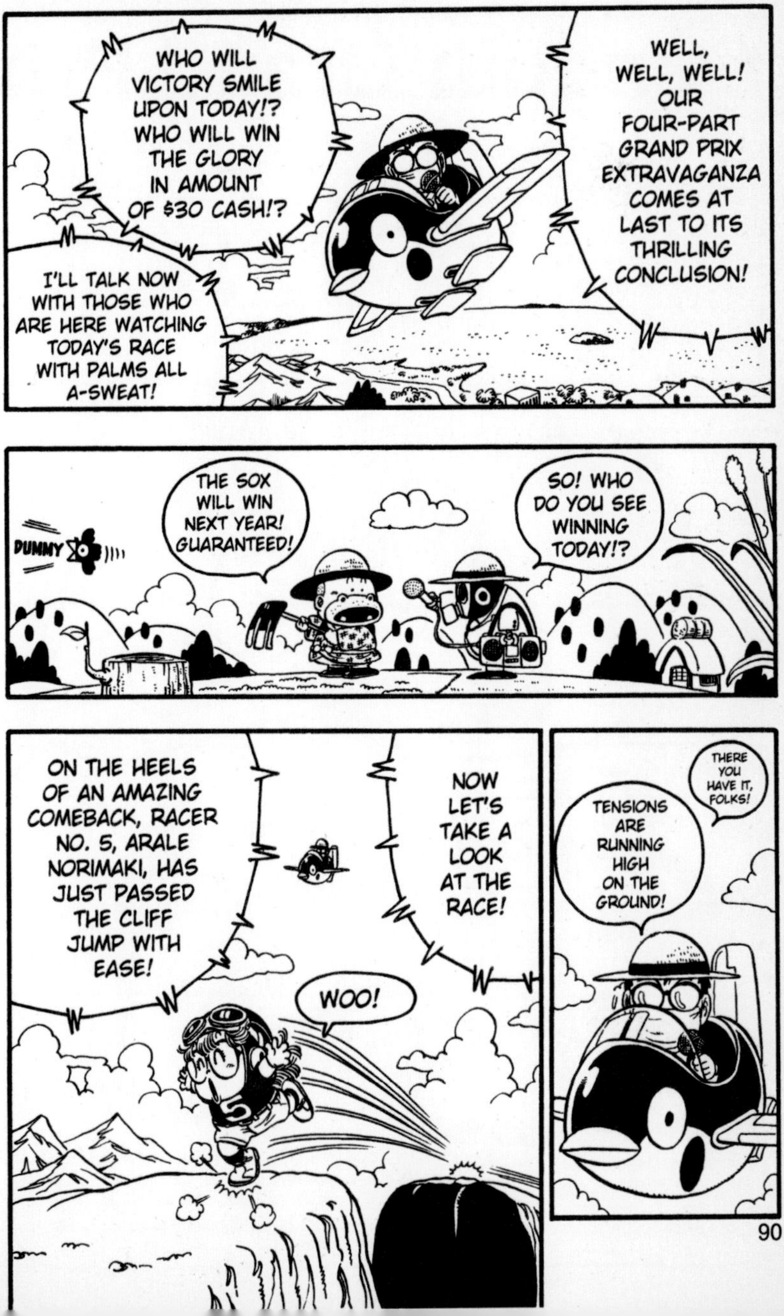
WELL, WELL, WELL! OUR FOUR-PART GRAND PRIX EXTRAVAGANZA COMES AT LAST TO ITS THRILLING CONCLUSION!
WHO WILL VICTORY SMILE UPON TODAY!? WHO WILL WIN THE GLORY IN AMOUNT OF $30 CASH!?
I'LL TALK NOW WITH THOSE WHO ARE HERE WATCHING TODAY'S RACE WITH PALMS ALL A-SWEAT!
SO! WHO DO YOU SEE WINNING TODAY!?
THE SOX WILL WIN NEXT YEAR! GUARANTEED!
DUMMY
THERE YOU HAVE IT, FOLKS!
TENSIONS ARE RUNNING HIGH ON THE GROUND!
NOW LET'S TAKE A LOOK AT THE RACE!
ON THE HEELS OF AN AMAZING COMEBACK, RACER NO. 5, ARALE NORIMAKI, HAS JUST PASSED THE CLIFF JUMP WITH EASE!
WOO!

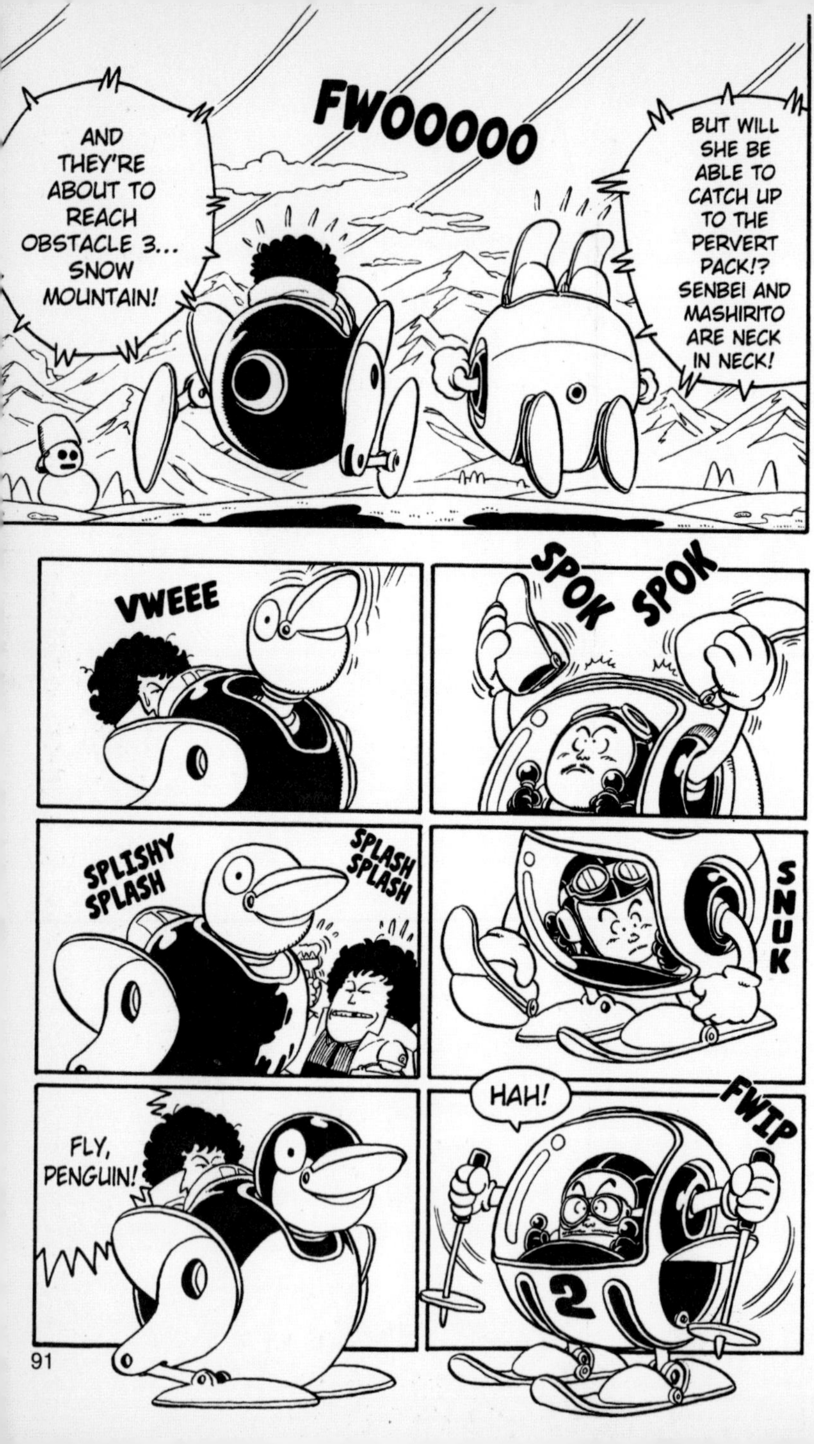
FWOOOOO
BUT WILL SHE BE ABLE TO CATCH UP TO THE PERVERT PACK!? SENBEI AND MASHIRITO ARE NECK IN NECK!
AND THEY'RE ABOUT TO REACH OBSTACLE 3... SNOW MOUNTAIN!
SPOK SPOK
VWEEE
SNUK
SPLASH SPLASH
SPLISHY SPLASH
FWIP
HAH!
FLY, PENGUIN!

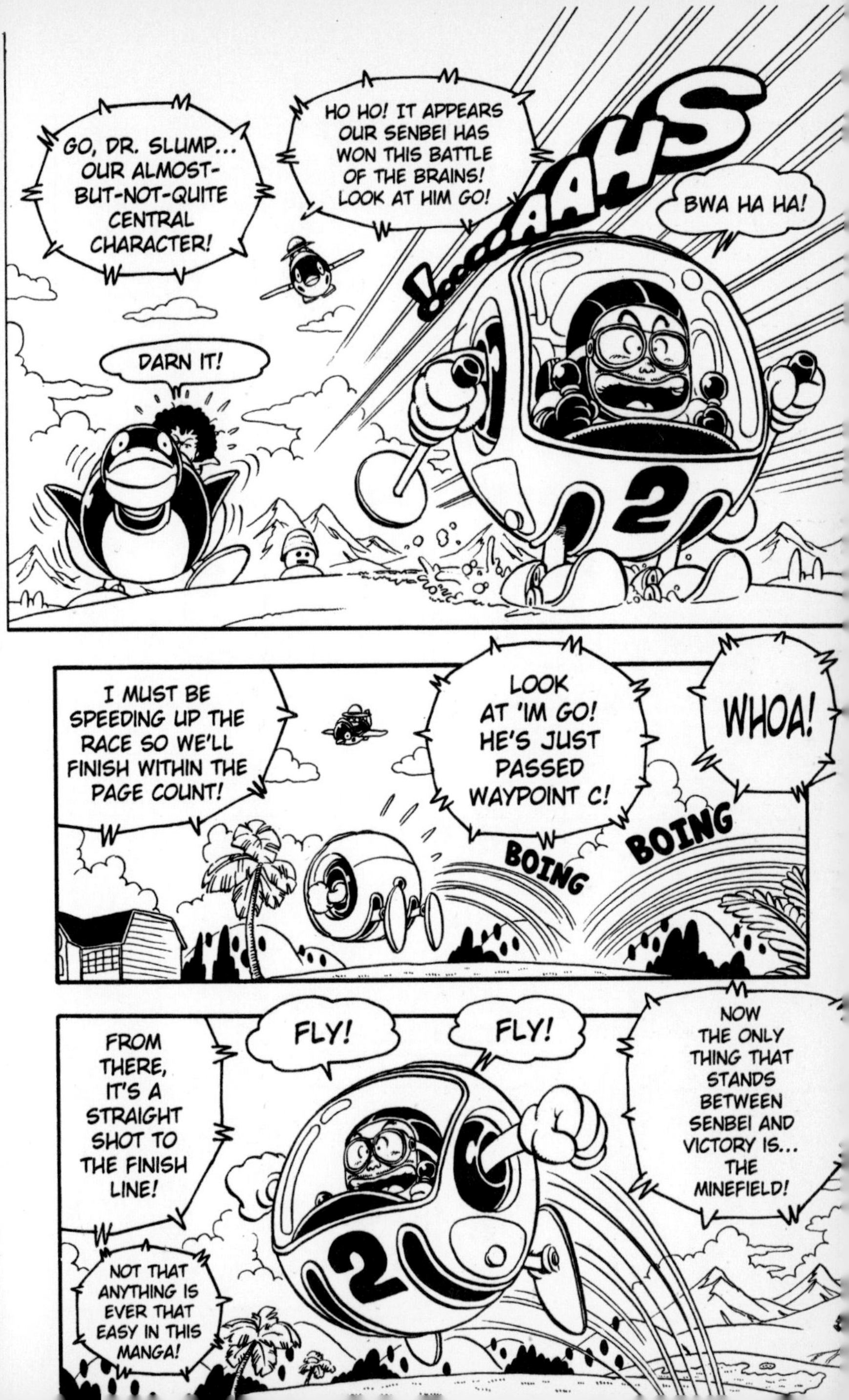
BWA HA HA!
SHAAOOOOO!
HO HO! IT APPEARS OUR SENBEI HAS WON THIS BATTLE OF THE BRAINS! LOOK AT HIM GO!
GO, DR. SLUMP... OUR ALMOST-BUT-NOT-QUITE CENTRAL CHARACTER!
DARN IT!
WHOA!
LOOK AT 'IM GO! HE'S JUST PASSED WAYPOINT C!
BOING
BOING
I MUST BE SPEEDING UP THE RACE SO WE'LL FINISH WITHIN THE PAGE COUNT!
NOW THE ONLY THING THAT STANDS BETWEEN SENBEI AND VICTORY IS... THE MINEFIELD!
FLY!
FLY!
FROM THERE, IT'S A STRAIGHT SHOT TO THE FINISH LINE!
NOT THAT ANYTHING IS EVER THAT EASY IN THIS MANGA!

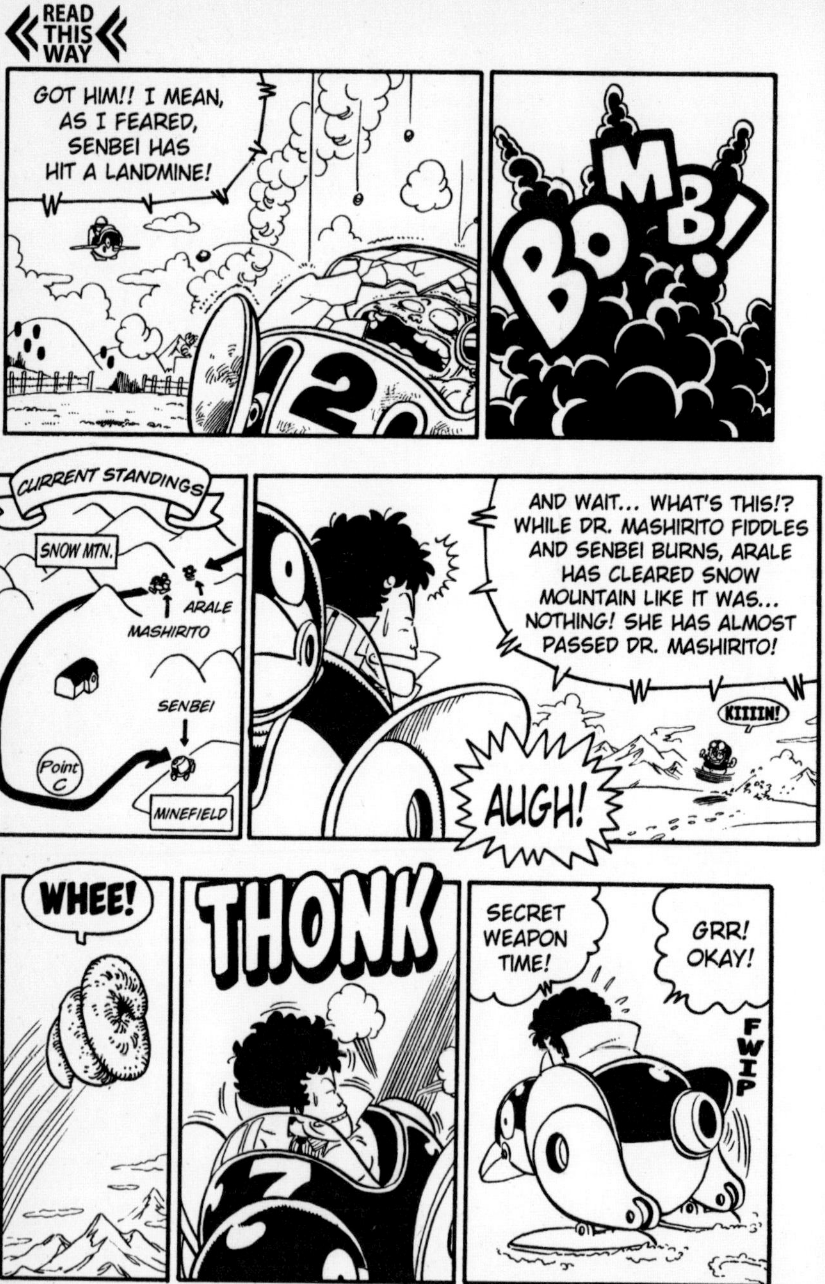
READ THIS WAY
BOMB!
GOT HIM!! I MEAN, AS I FEARED, SENBEI HAS HIT A LANDMINE!
AND WAIT... WHAT'S THIS!? WHILE DR. MASHIRITO FIDDLES AND SENBEI BURNS, ARALE HAS CLEARED SNOW MOUNTAIN LIKE IT WAS... NOTHING! SHE HAS ALMOST PASSED DR. MASHIRITO!
KIIIIN!
AUGH!
CURRENT STANDINGS
SNOW MTN.
ARALE
MASHIRITO
SENBEI
Point C
MINEFIELD
GRR! OKAY!
SECRET WEAPON TIME!
FWIP
THONK
WHEE!

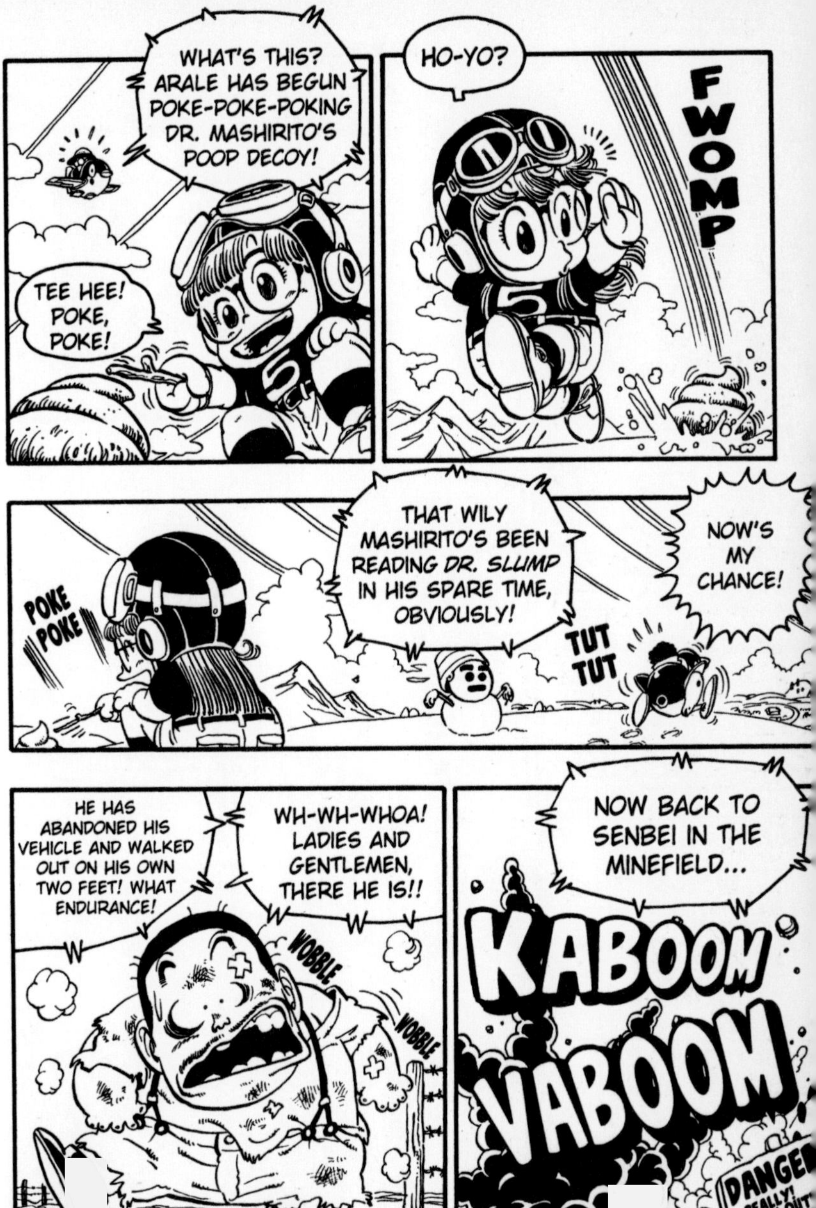
HO-YO?
FWOMP
WHAT'S THIS? ARALE HAS BEGUN POKE-POKE-POKING DR. MASHIRITO'S POOP DECOY!
TEE HEE! POKE, POKE!
NOW'S MY CHANCE!
THAT WILY MASHIRITO'S BEEN READING *DR. SLUMP* IN HIS SPARE TIME, OBVIOUSLY!
TUT TUT
POKE POKE
NOW BACK TO SENBEI IN THE MINEFIELD...
KABOOM
VABOOM
DANGE
REALLY! WATCH OUT
WH-WH-WHOA! LADIES AND GENTLEMEN, THERE HE IS!!
HE HAS ABANDONED HIS VEHICLE AND WALKED OUT ON HIS OWN TWO FEET! WHAT ENDURANCE!
WOBBLE
WOBBLE

READ THIS WAY

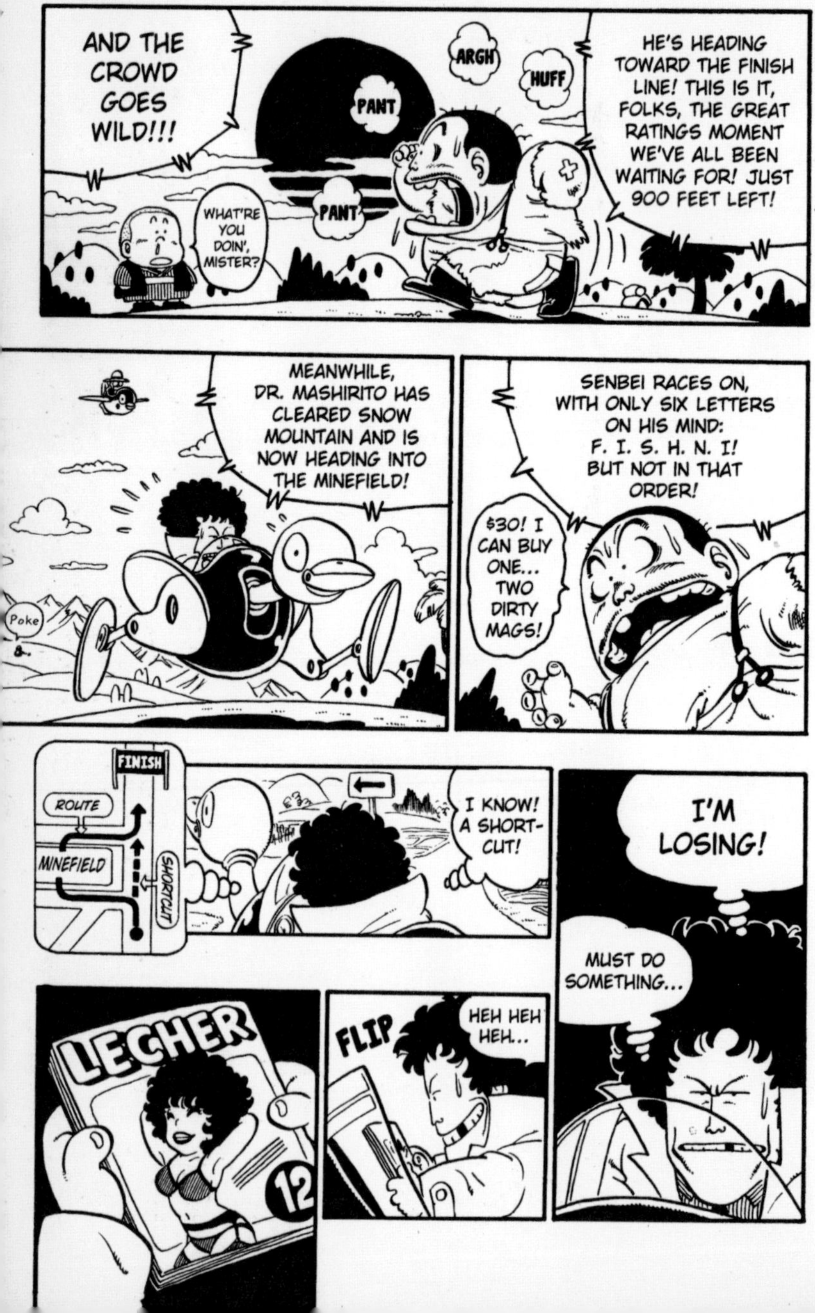
HE'S HEADING TOWARD THE FINISH LINE! THIS IS IT, FOLKS, THE GREAT RATINGS MOMENT WE'VE ALL BEEN WAITING FOR! JUST 900 FEET LEFT!
HUFF
ARGH
PANT
AND THE CROWD GOES WILD!!!
PANT
WHAT'RE YOU DOIN', MISTER?
SENBEI RACES ON, WITH ONLY SIX LETTERS ON HIS MIND: F. I. S. H. N. I! BUT NOT IN THAT ORDER!
$30! I CAN BUY ONE... TWO DIRTY MAGS!
MEANWHILE, DR. MASHIRITO HAS CLEARED SNOW MOUNTAIN AND IS NOW HEADING INTO THE MINEFIELD!
Poke
I'M LOSING!
MUST DO SOMETHING...
I KNOW! A SHORT-CUT!
FINISH
ROUTE
MINEFIELD
SHORTCUT
HEH HEH HEH...
FLIP
LECHER
12

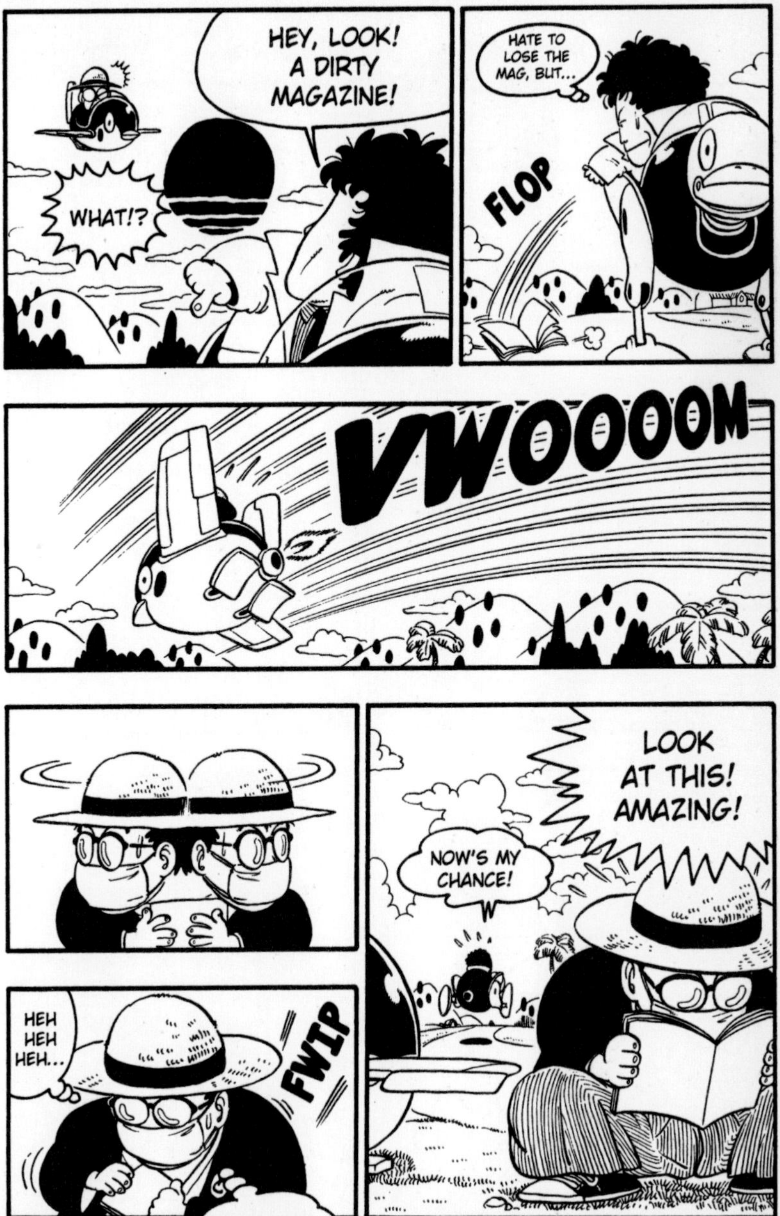
HATE TO LOSE THE MAG, BUT...
FLOP
HEY, LOOK! A DIRTY MAGAZINE!
WHAT!?
VWOOOOM
LOOK AT THIS! AMAZING!
NOW'S MY CHANCE!
FWIP
HEH HEH HEH...
SCORE!

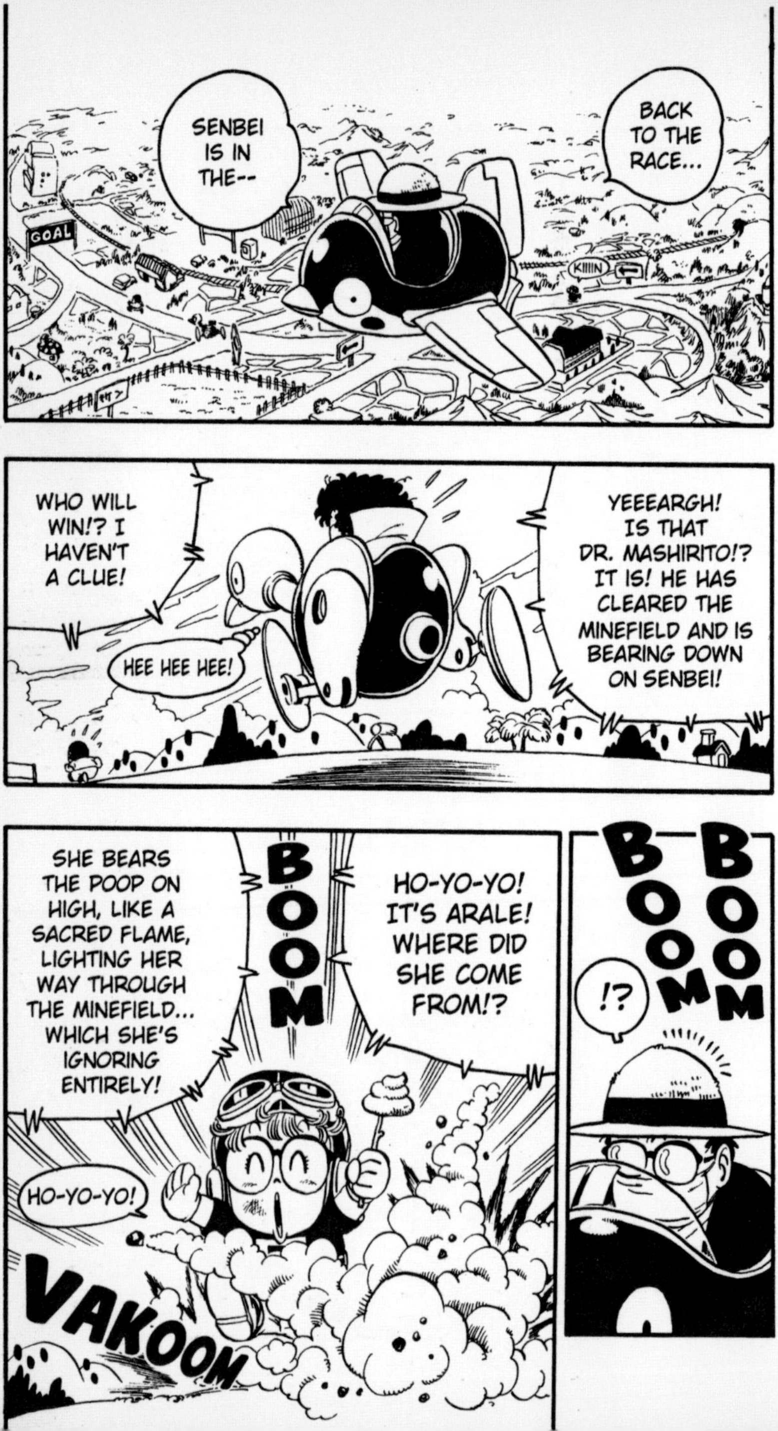
BACK TO THE RACE...
SENBEI IS IN THE--
KIIIN
GOAL
YEEEARGH! IS THAT DR. MASHIRITO!? IT IS! HE HAS CLEARED THE MINEFIELD AND IS BEARING DOWN ON SENBEI!
WHO WILL WIN!? I HAVEN'T A CLUE!
HEE HEE HEE!
BOOM
BOOM
!?
HO-YO-YO! IT'S ARALE! WHERE DID SHE COME FROM!?
BOOM
SHE BEARS THE POOP ON HIGH, LIKE A SACRED FLAME, LIGHTING HER WAY THROUGH THE MINEFIELD... WHICH SHE'S IGNORING ENTIRELY!
HO-YO-YO!
VAKOOM

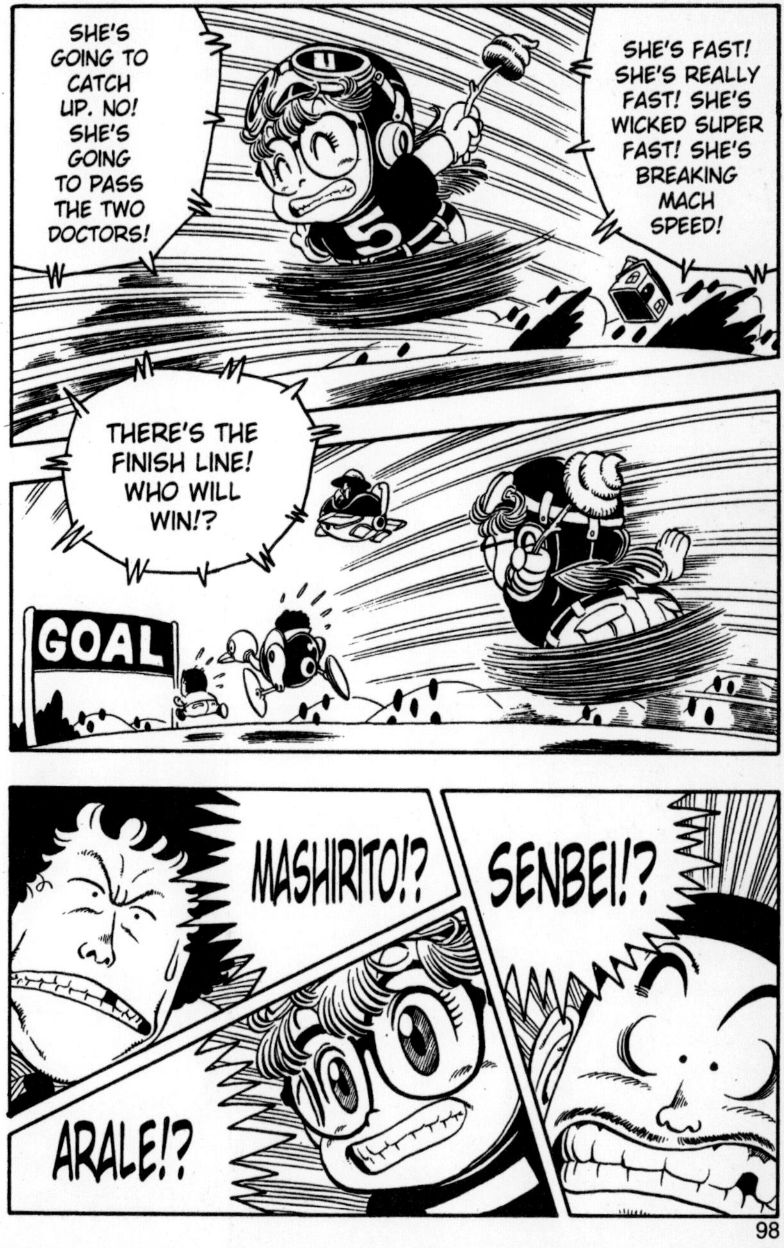
SHE'S FAST! SHE'S REALLY FAST! SHE'S WICKED SUPER FAST! SHE'S BREAKING MACH SPEED!
SHE'S GOING TO CATCH UP. NO! SHE'S GOING TO PASS THE TWO DOCTORS!
THERE'S THE FINISH LINE! WHO WILL WIN!?
GOAL
SENBEI!?
MASHIRITO!?
ARALE!?

READ THIS WAY

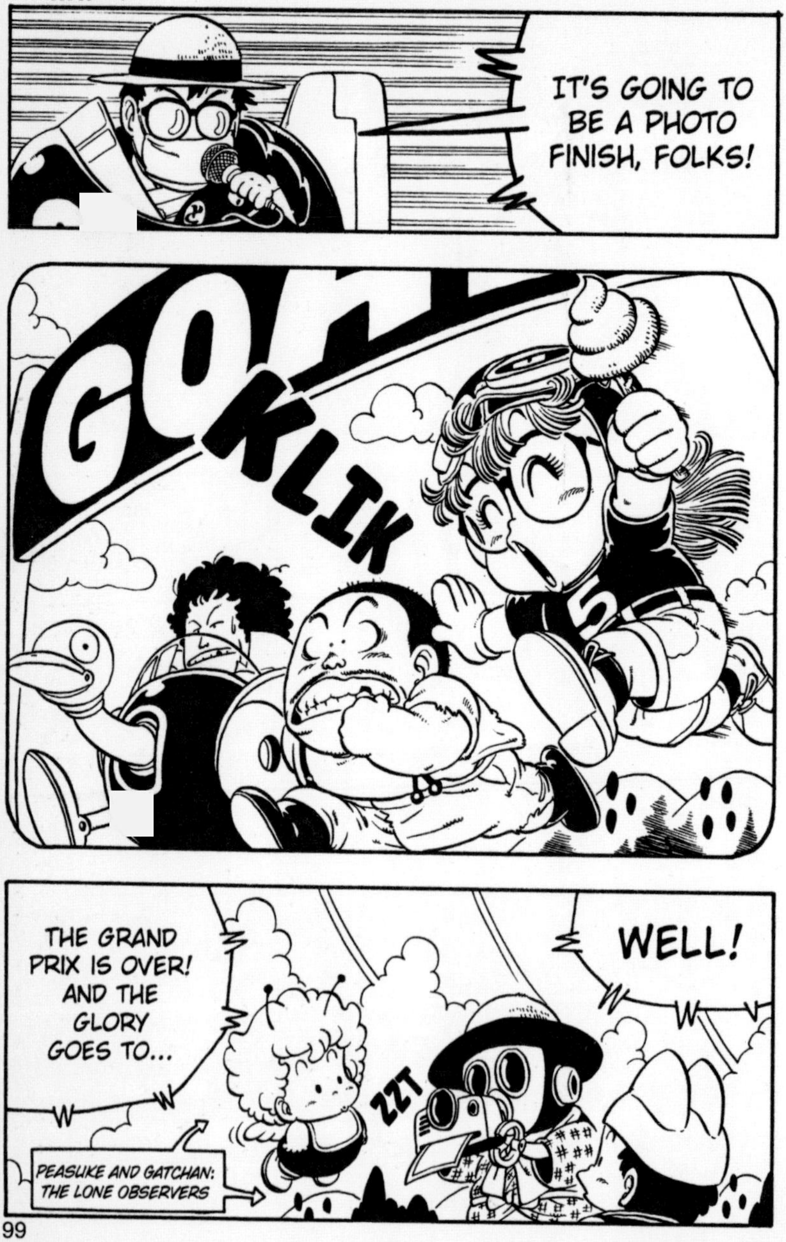
IT'S GOING TO BE A PHOTO FINISH, FOLKS!
KLIK
WELL!
THE GRAND PRIX IS OVER! AND THE GLORY GOES TO...
ZZT
PEASUKE AND GATCHAN: THE LONE OBSERVERS

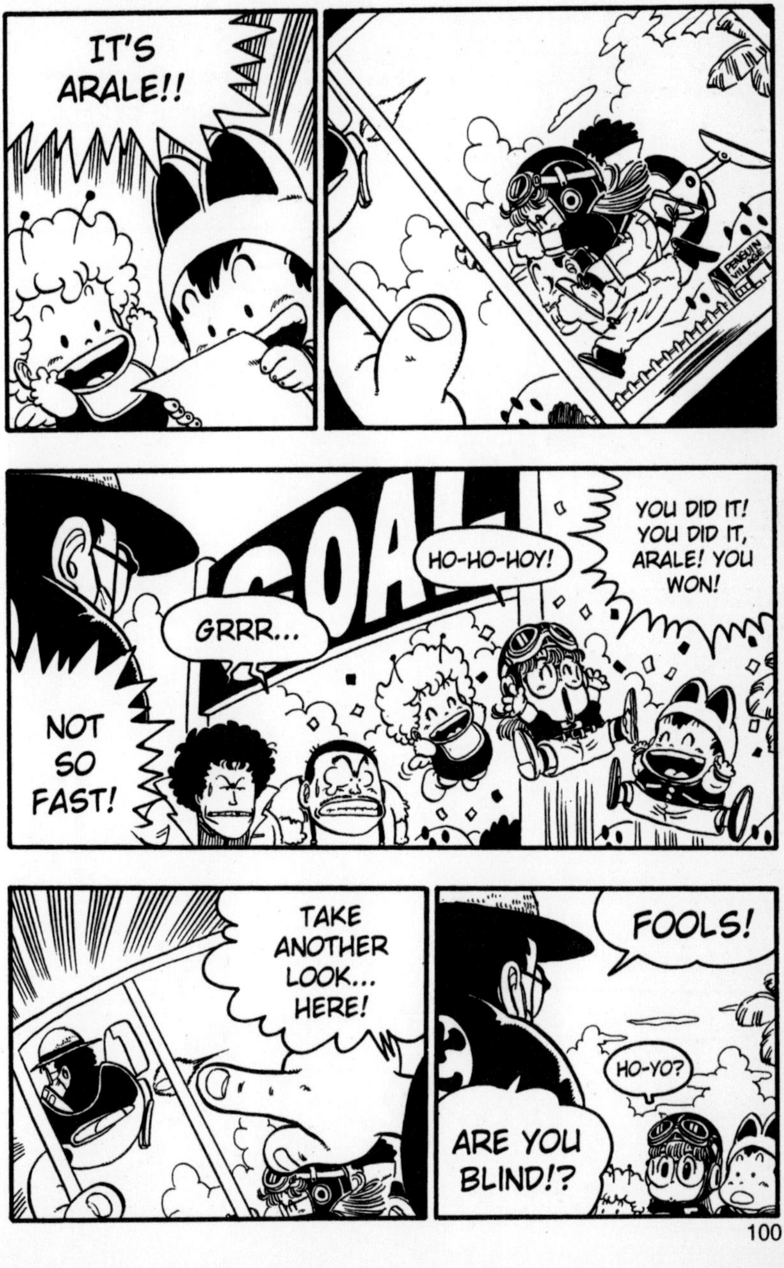
PENGUIN VILLAGE
IT'S ARALE!!
YOU DID IT! YOU DID IT, ARALE! YOU WON!
HO-HO-HOY!
GRRR...
NOT SO FAST!
FOOLS!
HO-YO?
ARE YOU BLIND!?
TAKE ANOTHER LOOK... HERE!

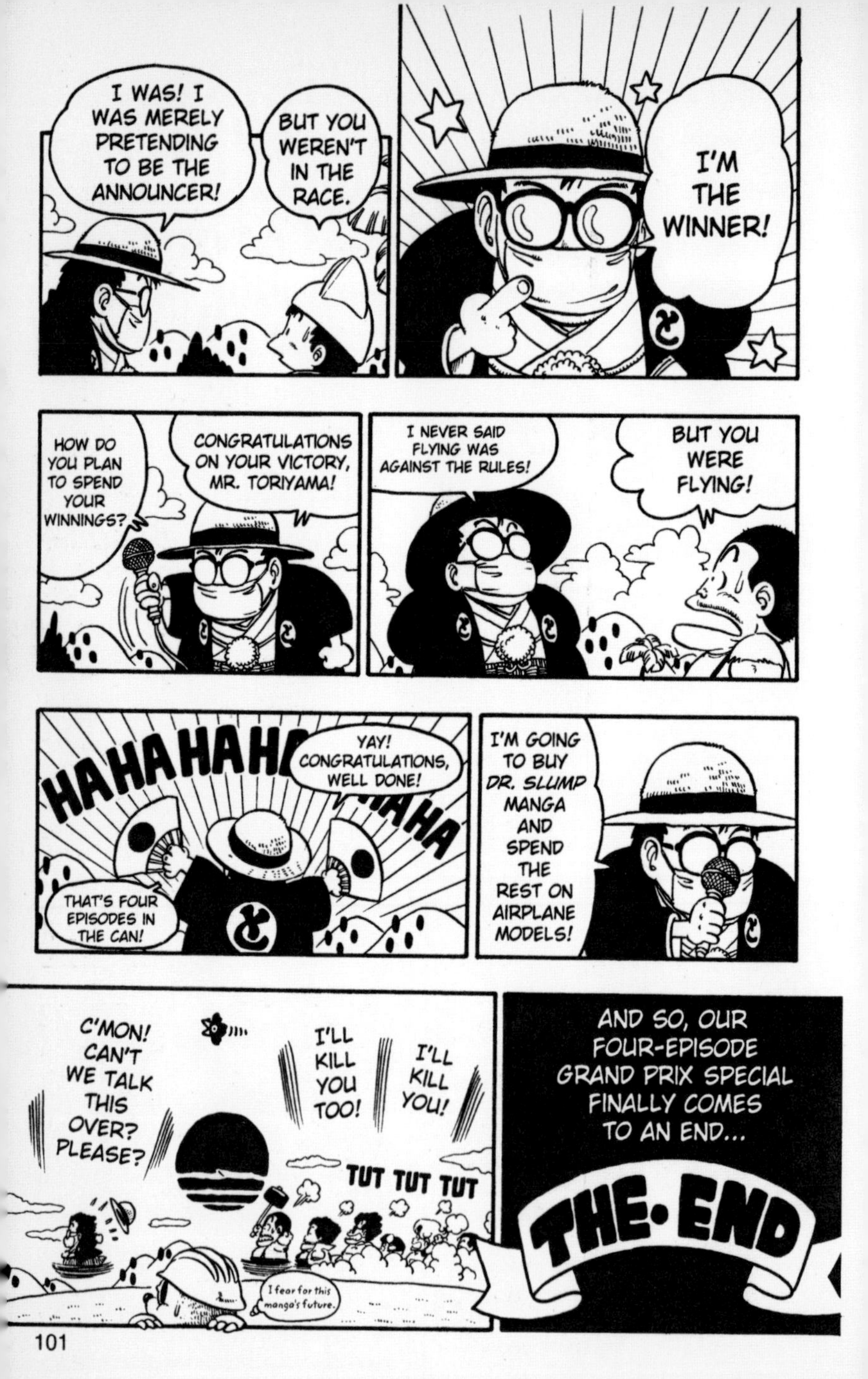
I'M THE WINNER!
BUT YOU WEREN'T IN THE RACE.
I WAS! I WAS MERELY PRETENDING TO BE THE ANNOUNCER!
BUT YOU WERE FLYING!
I NEVER SAID FLYING WAS AGAINST THE RULES!
CONGRATULATIONS ON YOUR VICTORY, MR. TORIYAMA!
HOW DO YOU PLAN TO SPEND YOUR WINNINGS?
I'M GOING TO BUY *DR. SLUMP* MANGA AND SPEND THE REST ON AIRPLANE MODELS!
YAY! CONGRATULATIONS, WELL DONE!
HAHAHAHAHAHAHAHA
THAT'S FOUR EPISODES IN THE CAN!
AND SO, OUR FOUR-EPISODE GRAND PRIX SPECIAL FINALLY COMES TO AN END...
THE END
I'LL KILL YOU!
I'LL KILL YOU TOO!
C'MON! CAN'T WE TALK THIS OVER? PLEASE?
TUT TUT TUT
I fear for this manga's future.

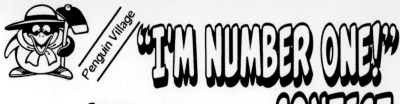

Penguin Village

"I'M NUMBER ONE!" CONTEST

Category:

DUMBEST

Suppaman wins! No contest!

1st
Suppaman
4,700 votes

★His stupidity knows no bounds. ★He makes me ill. Please get rid of him. ★Suppaman is a synonym for "dumb."
★His overconfidence ★His shamelessness
★The only one who doesn't immediately associate the word "dumb" with "Suppaman" is Suppaman himself.
★Why does he have a school bag on his back?
★He's so stoopid. ★Stupid beyond reason.

2nd
King
Nikochan
1,092 votes

★Mistook a toilet for a space rocket. ★Slouchy face
★Build your own dumb spaceship!
★Butt on head = dumb
★How does he know all that slang if he's an alien?
★Always takes the dumbest jobs.
★Hey, space king! You can't do multiplication! Neener, neener!

3rd
Senbei
Norimaki
886 votes

★Has stumpy legs and a scary face, and yet he still chases Ms. Yamabuki.
★Hah! The manga's named after you, and you're not even the main character!
★Has never sold a single invention.
★His name should be Pervcakes Norimaki.
★Always wears the same underpants.

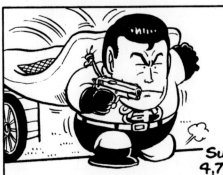

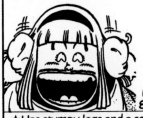

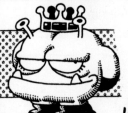

Discover the Countryside

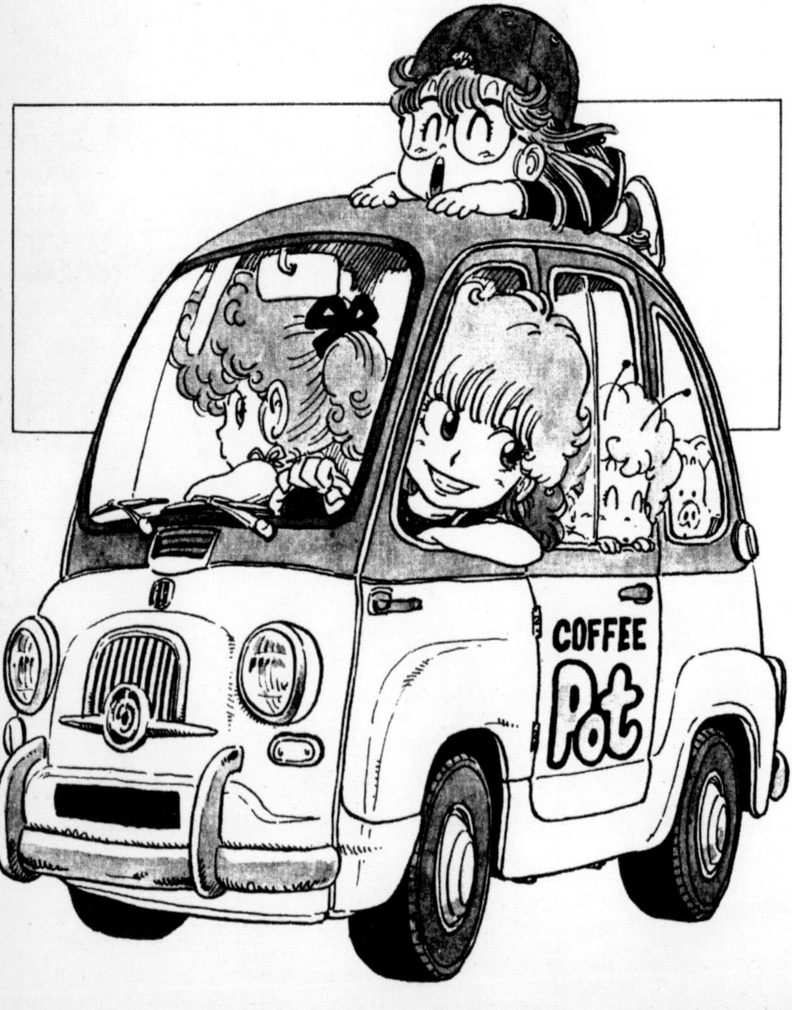
COFFEE
Pot

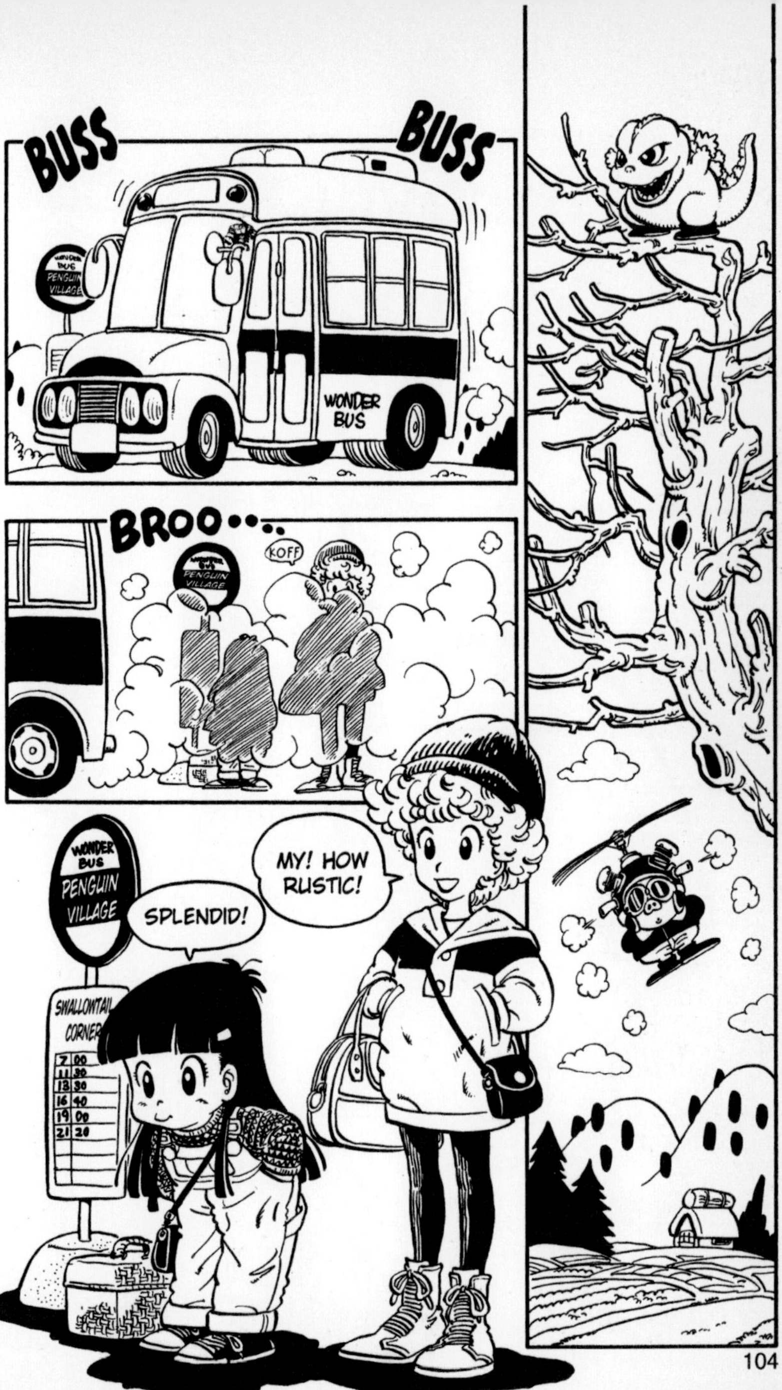
BUSS
BUSS
WONDER BUS
PENGUIN VILLAGE
WONDER BUS
BROO...
KOFF
WONDER BUS
PENGUIN VILLAGE
MY! HOW RUSTIC!
SPLENDID!
SWALLOWTAIL CORNER
7 00
11 30
13 30
16 40
19 00
21 20

READ THIS WAY

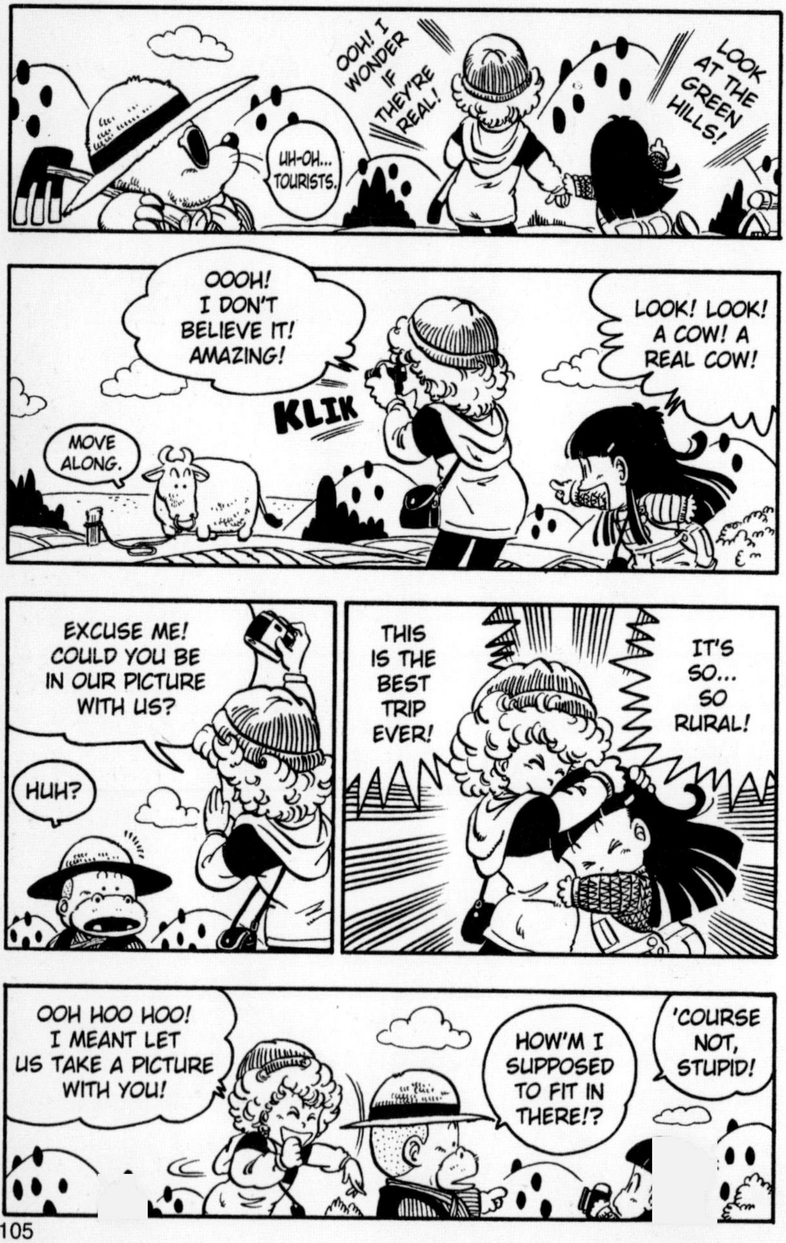
LOOK AT THE GREEN HILLS!
OOH! I WONDER IF THEY'RE REAL!
UH-OH... TOURISTS.
LOOK! LOOK! A COW! A REAL COW!
OOOH! I DON'T BELIEVE IT! AMAZING!
KLIK
MOVE ALONG.
IT'S SO... SO RURAL!
THIS IS THE BEST TRIP EVER!
EXCUSE ME! COULD YOU BE IN OUR PICTURE WITH US?
HUH?
'COURSE NOT, STUPID!
HOW'M I SUPPOSED TO FIT IN THERE!?
OOH HOO HOO! I MEANT LET US TAKE A PICTURE WITH YOU!

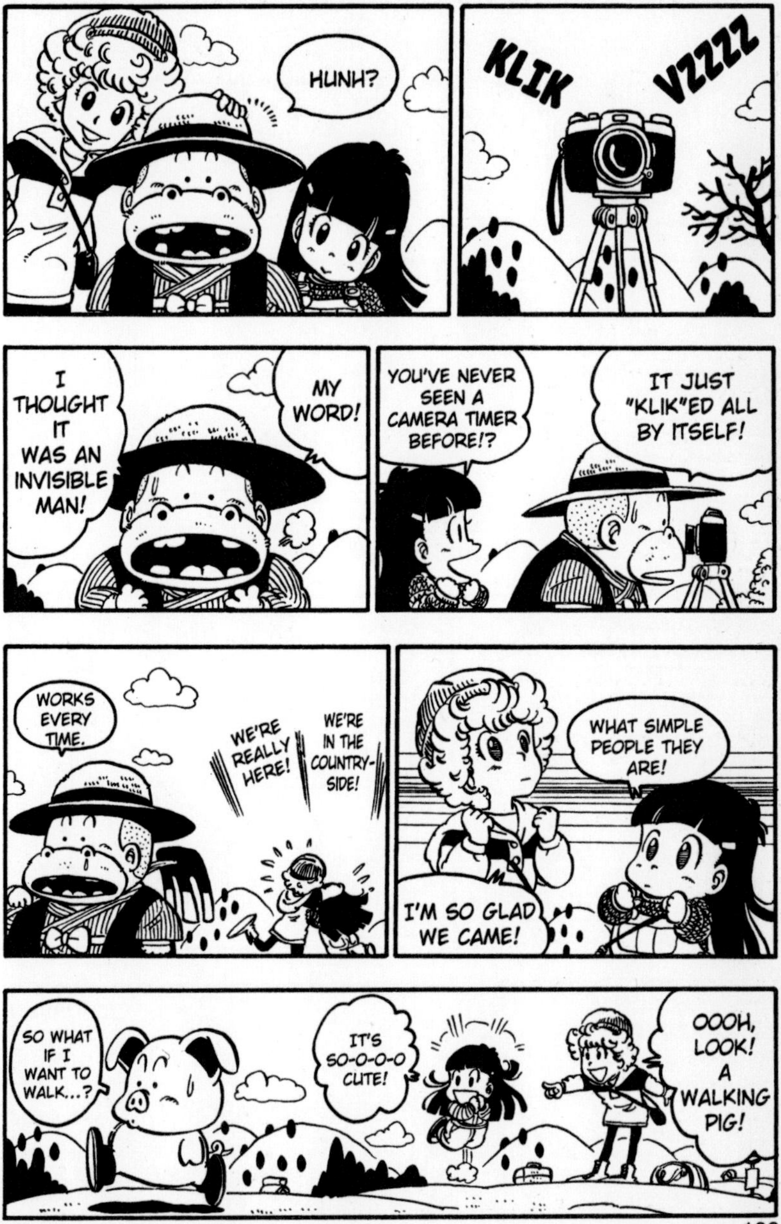
KLIK
VZZZZ
HUNH?
IT JUST "KLIK"ED ALL BY ITSELF!
YOU'VE NEVER SEEN A CAMERA TIMER BEFORE!?
MY WORD!
I THOUGHT IT WAS AN INVISIBLE MAN!
WHAT SIMPLE PEOPLE THEY ARE!
I'M SO GLAD WE CAME!
WE'RE IN THE COUNTRYSIDE!
WE'RE REALLY HERE!
WORKS EVERY TIME.
OOOH, LOOK! A WALKING PIG!
IT'S SO-O-O-O CUTE!
SO WHAT IF I WANT TO WALK...?

READ THIS WAY

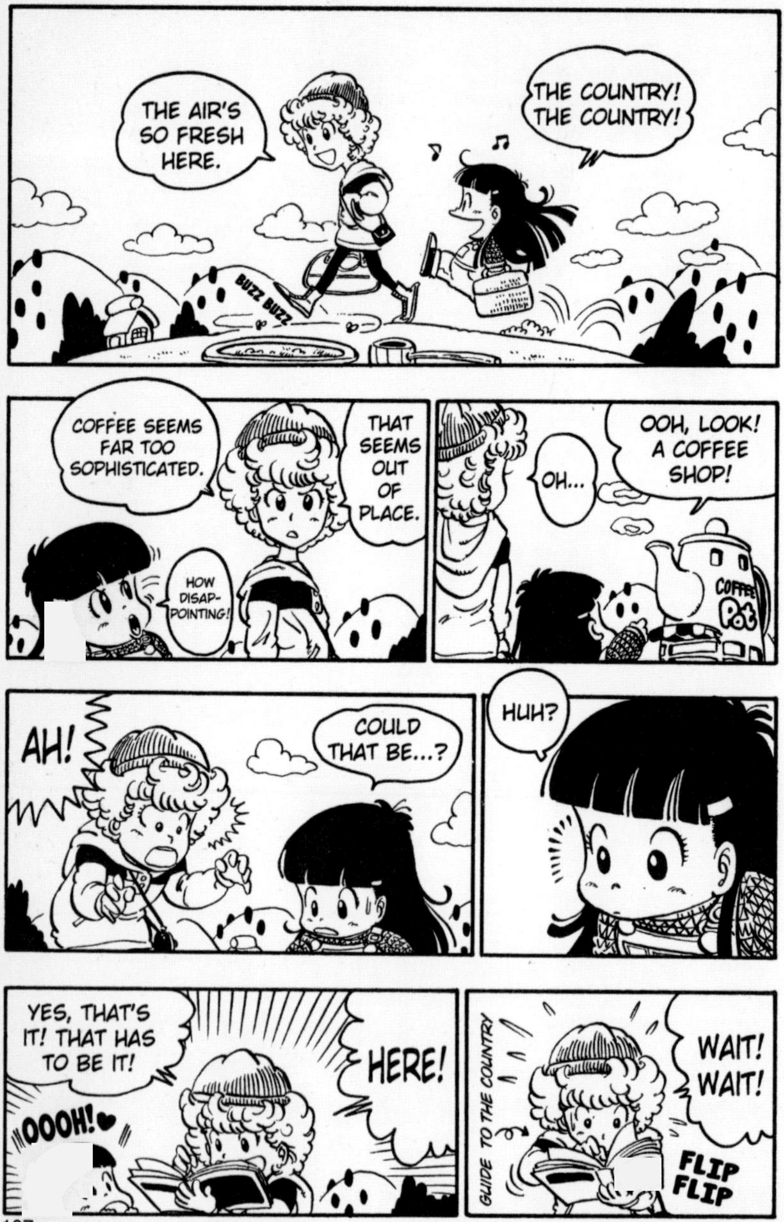
THE COUNTRY! THE COUNTRY!
THE AIR'S SO FRESH HERE.
BUZZ BUZZ
OOH, LOOK! A COFFEE SHOP!
OH...
COFFEE Pot
THAT SEEMS OUT OF PLACE.
COFFEE SEEMS FAR TOO SOPHISTICATED.
HOW DISAP-POINTING!
HUH?
COULD THAT BE...?
AH!
WAIT! WAIT!
GUIDE TO THE COUNTRY
FLIP FLIP
HERE!
YES, THAT'S IT! THAT HAS TO BE IT!
OOOH!♥

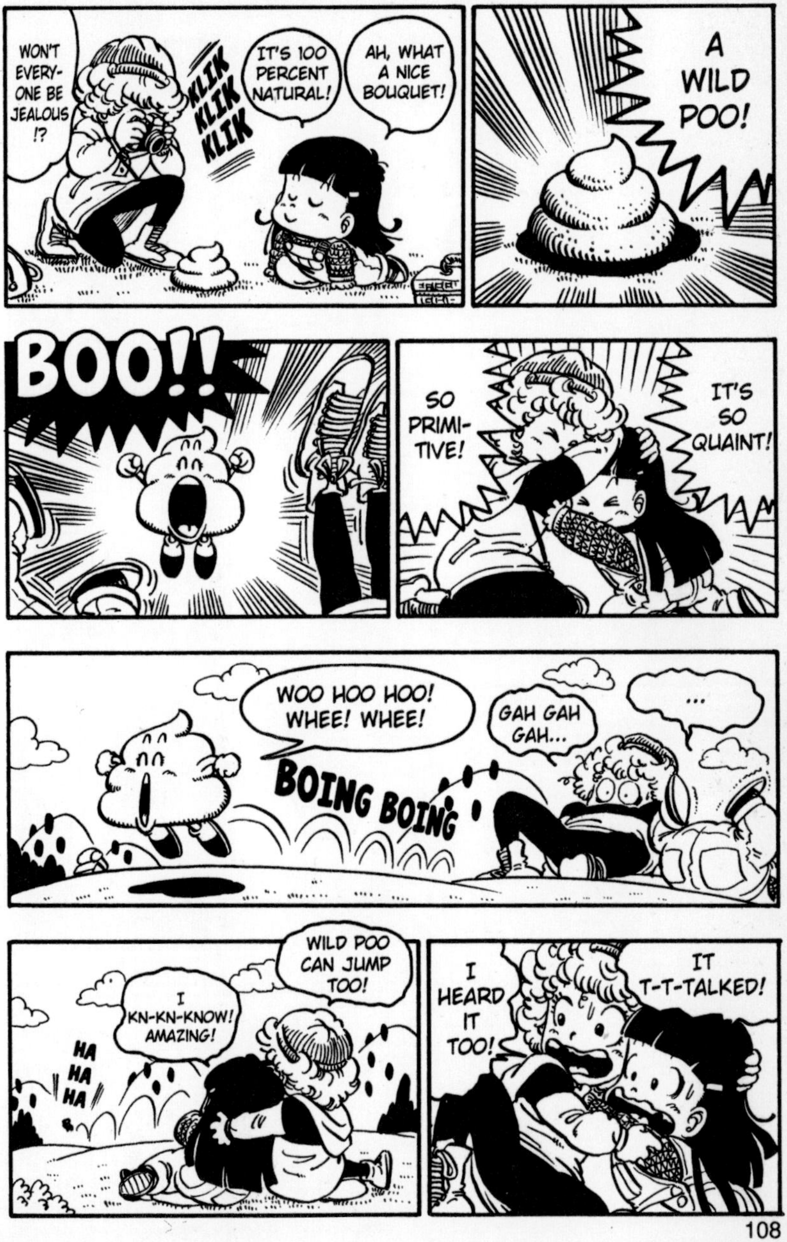
A WILD POO!
AH, WHAT A NICE BOUQUET!
IT'S 100 PERCENT NATURAL!
KLIK KLIK KLIK
WON'T EVERY-ONE BE JEALOUS!?
IT'S SO QUAINT!
SO PRIMI-TIVE!
BOO!!
...
GAH GAH GAH...
WOO HOO HOO! WHEE! WHEE!
BOING BOING
IT T-T-TALKED!
I HEARD IT TOO!
WILD POO CAN JUMP TOO!
I KN-KN-KNOW! AMAZING!
HA HA HA

READ THIS WAY

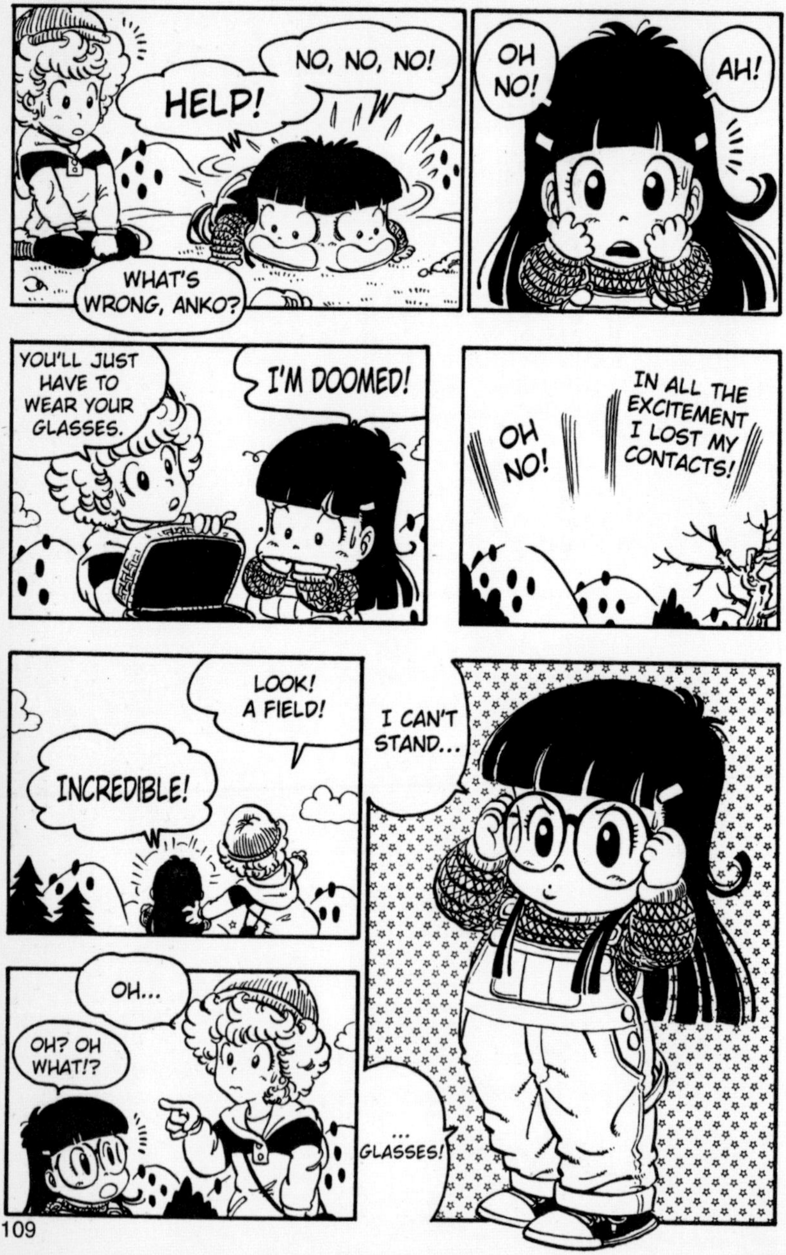
AH!
OH NO!
NO, NO, NO!
HELP!
WHAT'S WRONG, ANKO?
IN ALL THE EXCITEMENT I LOST MY CONTACTS!
OH NO!
I'M DOOMED!
YOU'LL JUST HAVE TO WEAR YOUR GLASSES.
I CAN'T STAND...
...GLASSES!
LOOK! A FIELD!
INCREDIBLE!
OH...
OH? OH WHAT!?

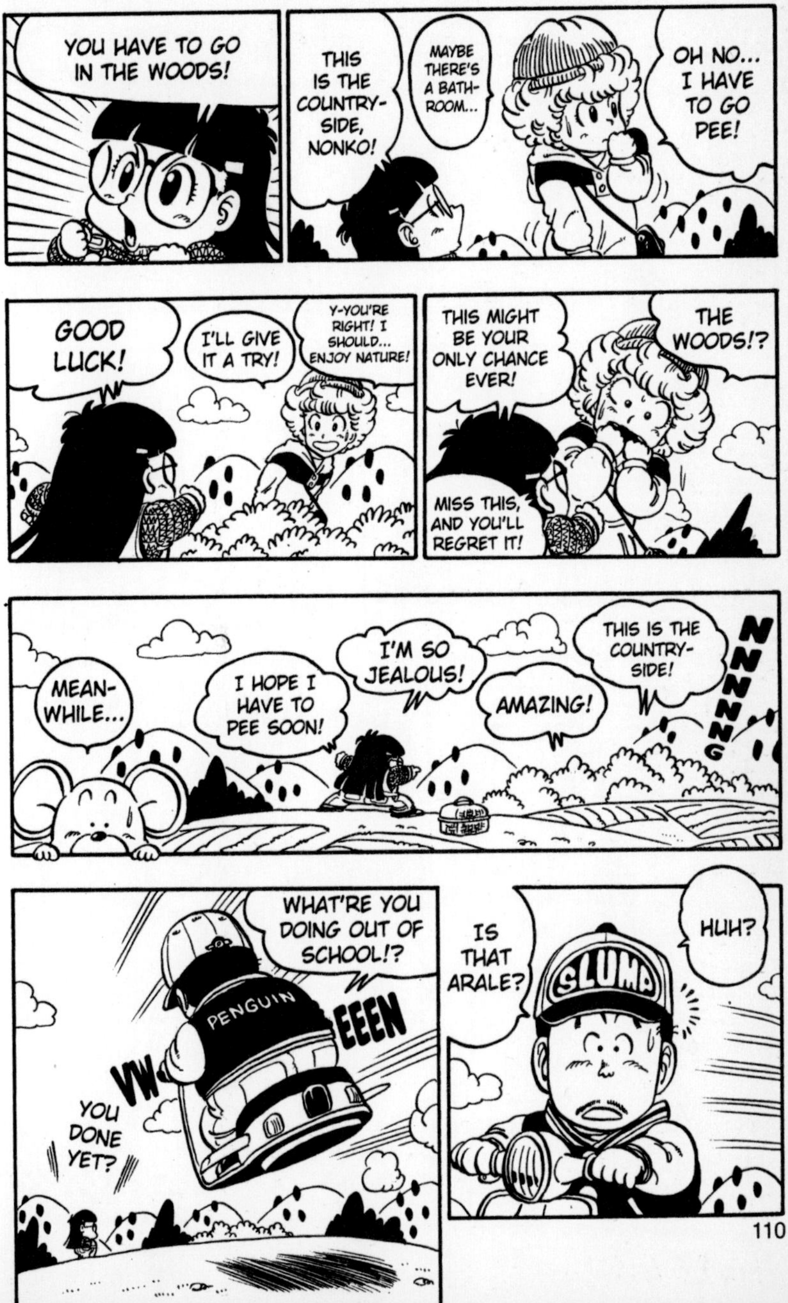
OH NO... I HAVE TO GO PEE!
MAYBE THERE'S A BATHROOM...
THIS IS THE COUNTRYSIDE, NONKO!
YOU HAVE TO GO IN THE WOODS!
THE WOODS!?
THIS MIGHT BE YOUR ONLY CHANCE EVER!
MISS THIS, AND YOU'LL REGRET IT!
Y-YOU'RE RIGHT! I SHOULD... ENJOY NATURE!
I'LL GIVE IT A TRY!
GOOD LUCK!
NNNNNNG
THIS IS THE COUNTRYSIDE!
AMAZING!
I'M SO JEALOUS!
I HOPE I HAVE TO PEE SOON!
MEANWHILE...
HUH?
SLUMP
IS THAT ARALE?
WHAT'RE YOU DOING OUT OF SCHOOL!?
PENGUIN
EEEN
VW
YOU DONE YET?

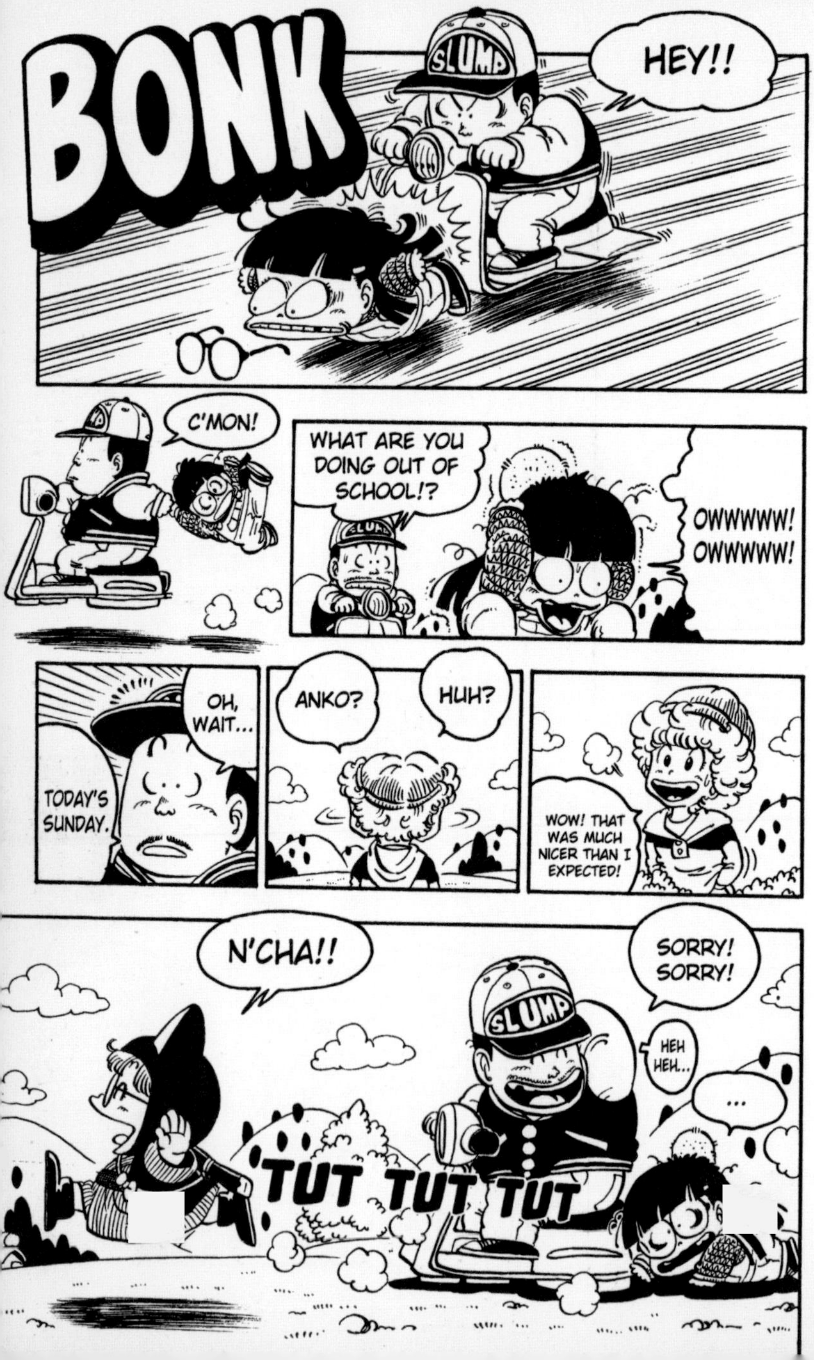
HEY!!
BONK
OWWWWW!
OWWWWW!
WHAT ARE YOU DOING OUT OF SCHOOL!?
C'MON!
WOW! THAT WAS MUCH NICER THAN I EXPECTED!
HUH?
ANKO?
OH, WAIT...
TODAY'S SUNDAY.
SORRY! SORRY!
HEH HEH...
...
N'CHA!!
TUT TUT TUT

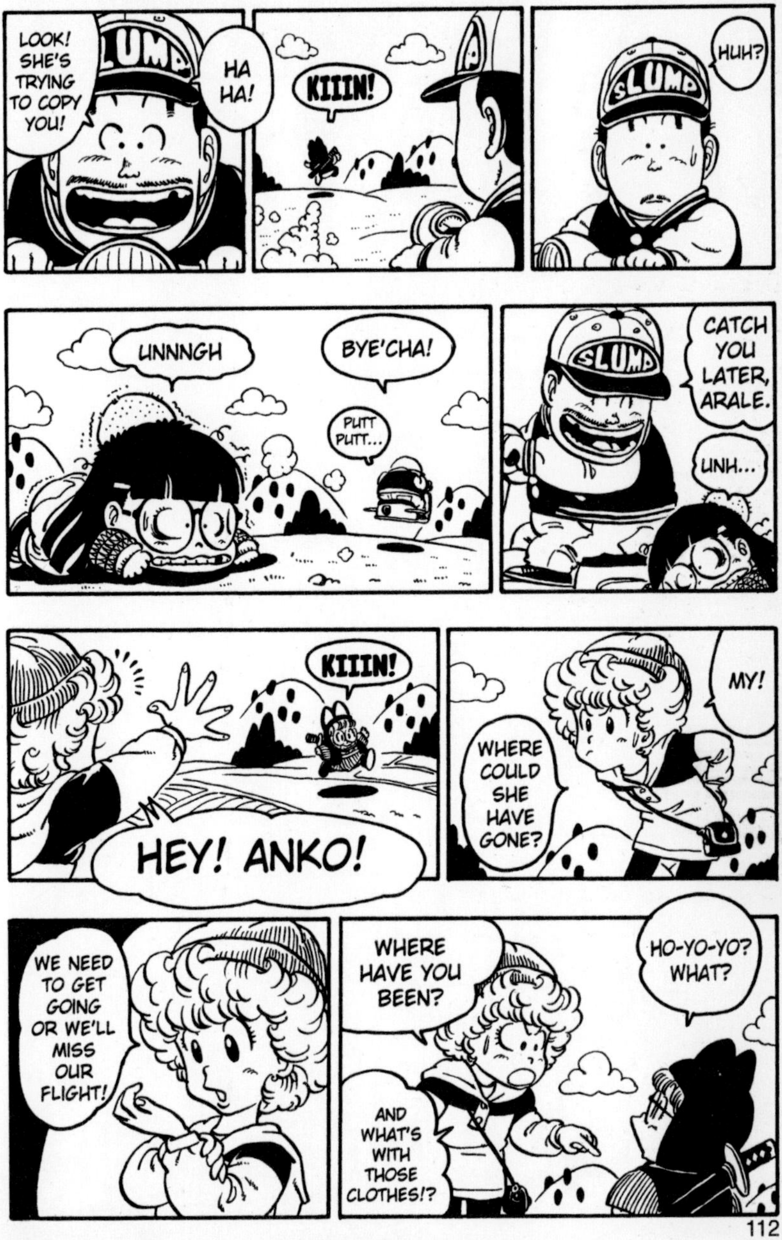
HUH?
KIIIN!
HA HA!
LOOK! SHE'S TRYING TO COPY YOU!
CATCH YOU LATER, ARALE.
UNH...
BYE'CHA!
PUTT PUTT...
UNNNGH
MY!
WHERE COULD SHE HAVE GONE?
KIIIN!
HEY! ANKO!
HO-YO-YO? WHAT?
WHERE HAVE YOU BEEN?
AND WHAT'S WITH THOSE CLOTHES!?
WE NEED TO GET GOING OR WE'LL MISS OUR FLIGHT!

READ THIS WAY

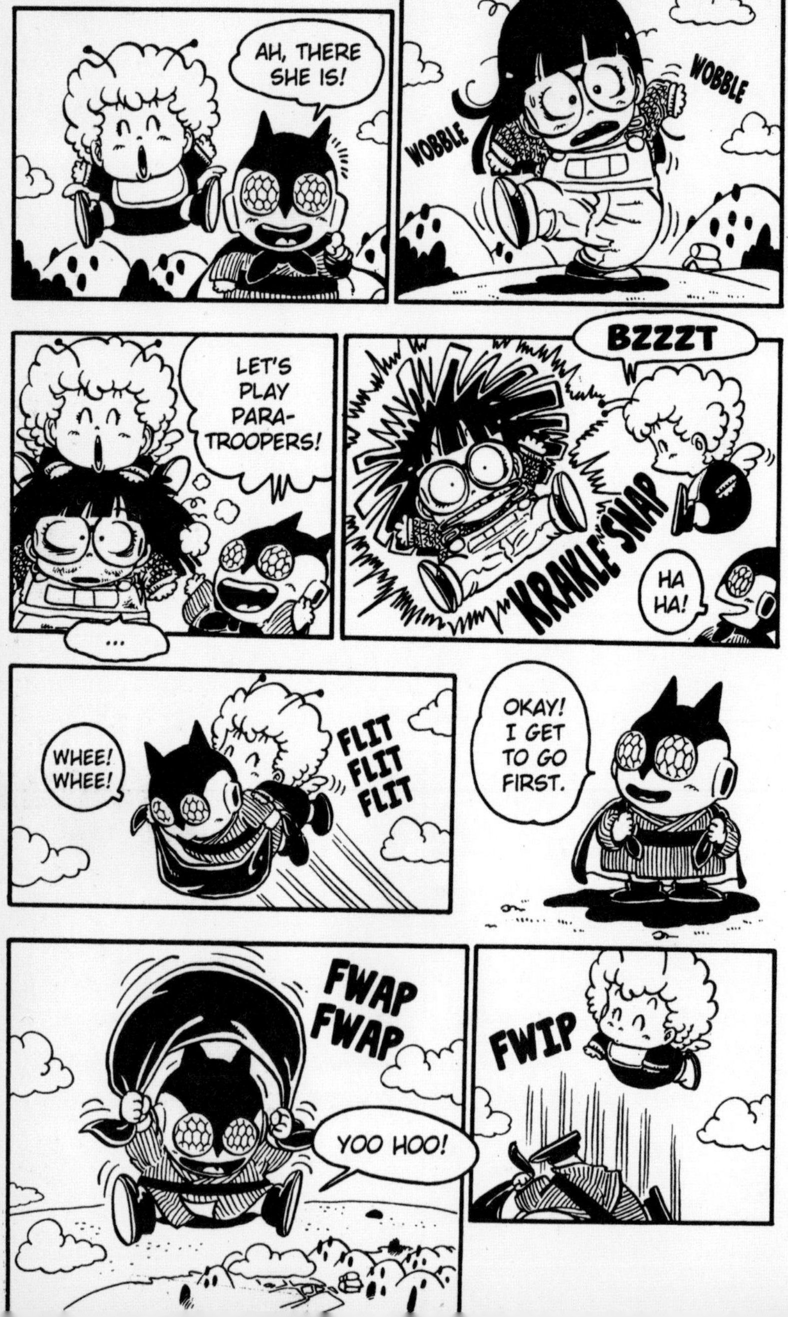
WOBBLE
WOBBLE
AH, THERE SHE IS!
BZZZT
KRAKLE SNAP
HA HA!
LET'S PLAY PARA-TROOPERS!
...
OKAY! I GET TO GO FIRST.
WHEE! WHEE!
FLIT FLIT FLIT
FWIP
FWAP FWAP
YOO HOO!

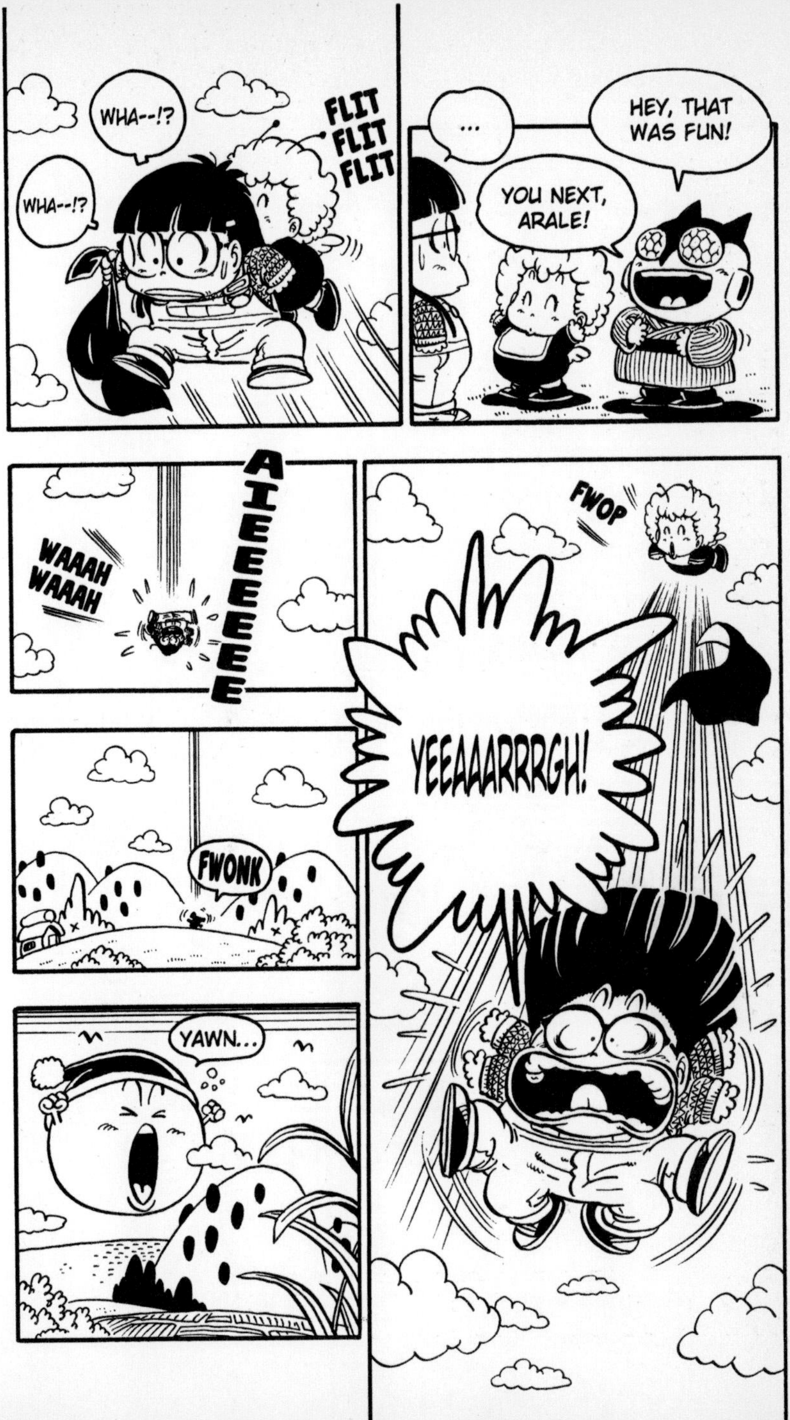
HEY, THAT WAS FUN!
...
YOU NEXT, ARALE!
FLIT FLIT FLIT
WHA--!?
WHA--!?
FWOP
YEEAAARRRGH!
AIEEEEEEE
WAAAH WAAAH
FWONK
YAWN...

READ THIS WAY

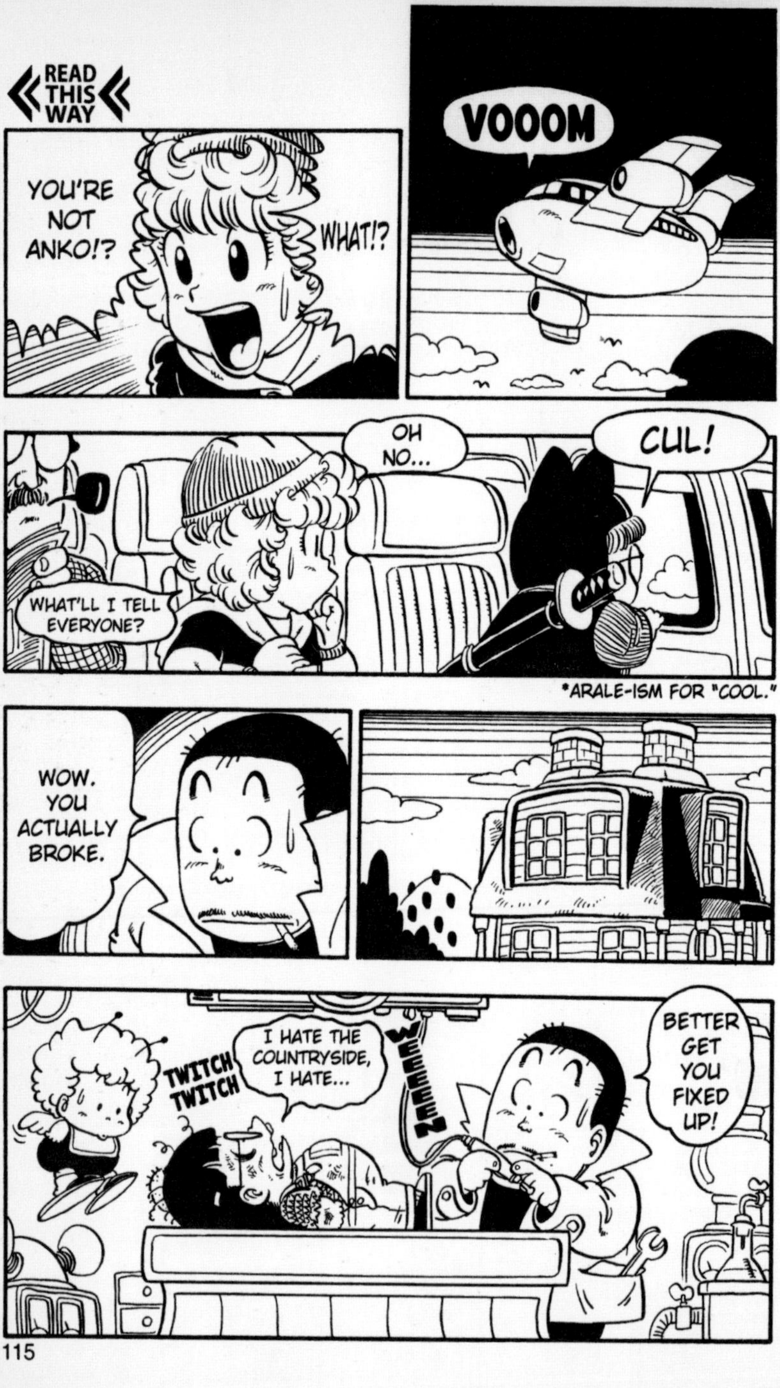

VOOOM
WHAT!?
YOU'RE NOT ANKO!?
CUL!
OH NO...
WHAT'LL I TELL EVERYONE?
WOW. YOU ACTUALLY BROKE.
BETTER GET YOU FIXED UP!
WEEEEEN
I HATE THE COUNTRYSIDE, I HATE...
TWITCH TWITCH

*ARALE-ISM FOR "COOL."

Penguin Village "I'M NUMBER ONE!" CONTEST

Category: DUMBEST

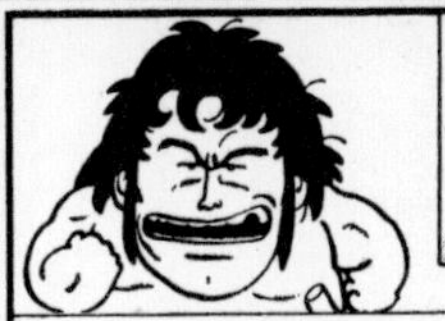

4th

Parzan
774 votes

★Blow your nose once in a while!
★Perv! Gorilla-face! Neener!
★Hardly ever appears in the manga.
★More like "Har!-zan"
★Has a small dingy!

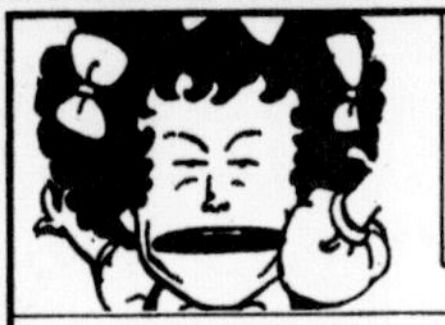

5th

Dr. Mashirito
528 votes

★Thin, lewd-looking eyebrows
★Lame face
★Dummy!
★I sense Toriyama's personal grudge against him.
★He got his hair permed!

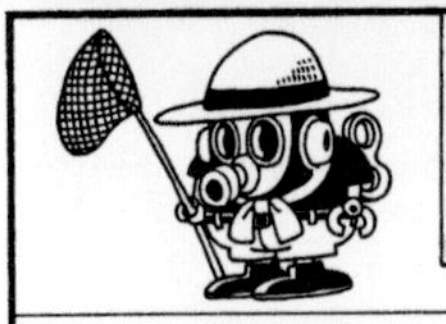

6th

Akira Toriyama
432 votes

★Puts himself in his own manga.
★Creator of all that is dumb
★Laughing stock of the universe
★Total rube!
★Married!? How cheeky!

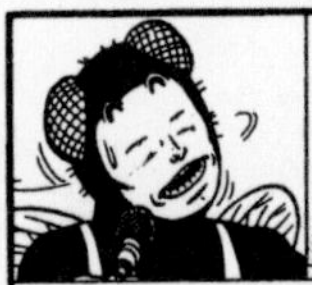

7th

Bubibinman
180 votes

★What's so yummy about poop, you dummy!?
★Hardly showed up after his big debut.
★Utter moron

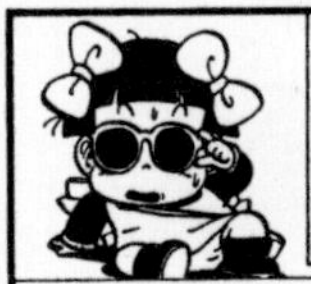

8th

Kinoko Sarada
146 votes

★Is "hip" the only word in your vocabulary!?
★Thinks $4.70 is enough to live on for a whole year.
★That "perm-perm-permanent" song is just dumb.

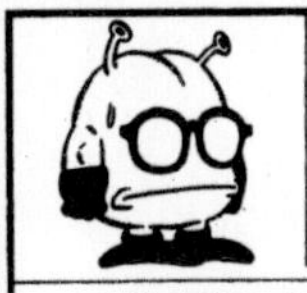

9th

Nikochan's Henchman
140 votes

★Hey! You! Dummy! You don't even have a name!
★Like master, like servant.
★If you're going to disagree, mean it!

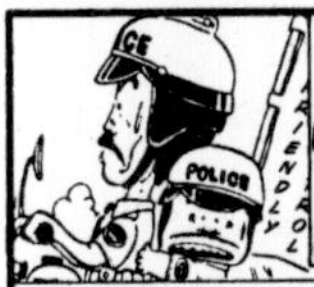
POLICE

10th

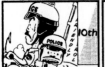

Gala and Pagos
134 votes

★If they didn't freak out every time they saw Arale, they wouldn't get in so many accidents.
★They'll never catch Arale!

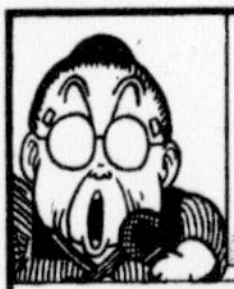

11th

Old Woman Spring
130 votes

★She's always eating those crackers.
★No way can she see anything with those glasses on.

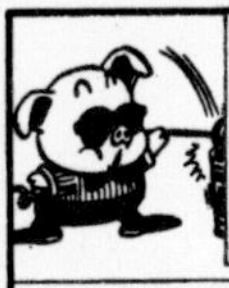

12th

Oinkety Oink
92 votes

★A pig who's a referee!? C'mon!
★Just happens to be around all the time for no good reason.
★A pig who sleeps in a bed!?

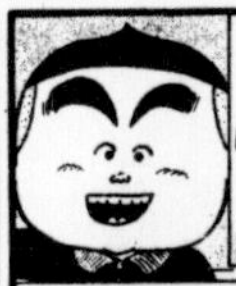

13th

Mr. Daigoro Kurigashira
91 votes

★I pity someone with a head like that.
★He can't touch the top of his own head!
★His head is a chestnut.

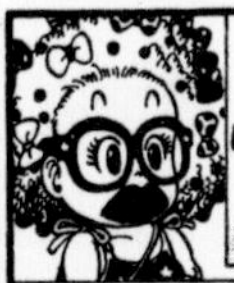

14th

Arale Norimaki
58 votes

★Only an idiot would act like she does.
★Stop poking poop! You're in high school!

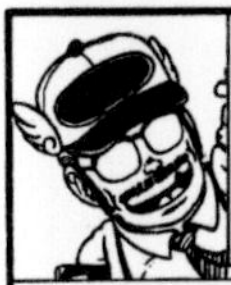

15th

Principal, Penguin Village Junior High
56 votes

★If that's all it takes, even I could be principal!
★Act your age!

Super Driver

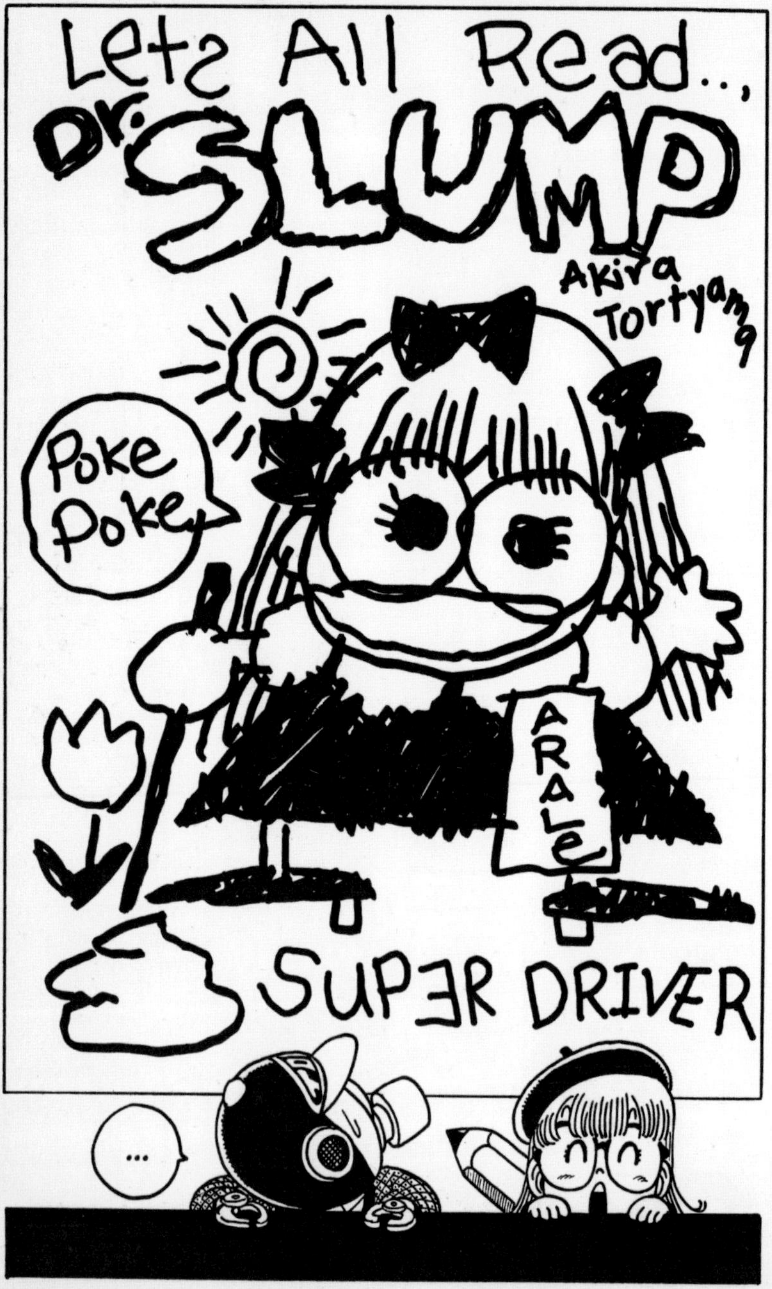
Lets All Read...,
Dr. SLUMP
Akira Toriyama
Poke Poke
ARALe
SUPER DRIVER
...

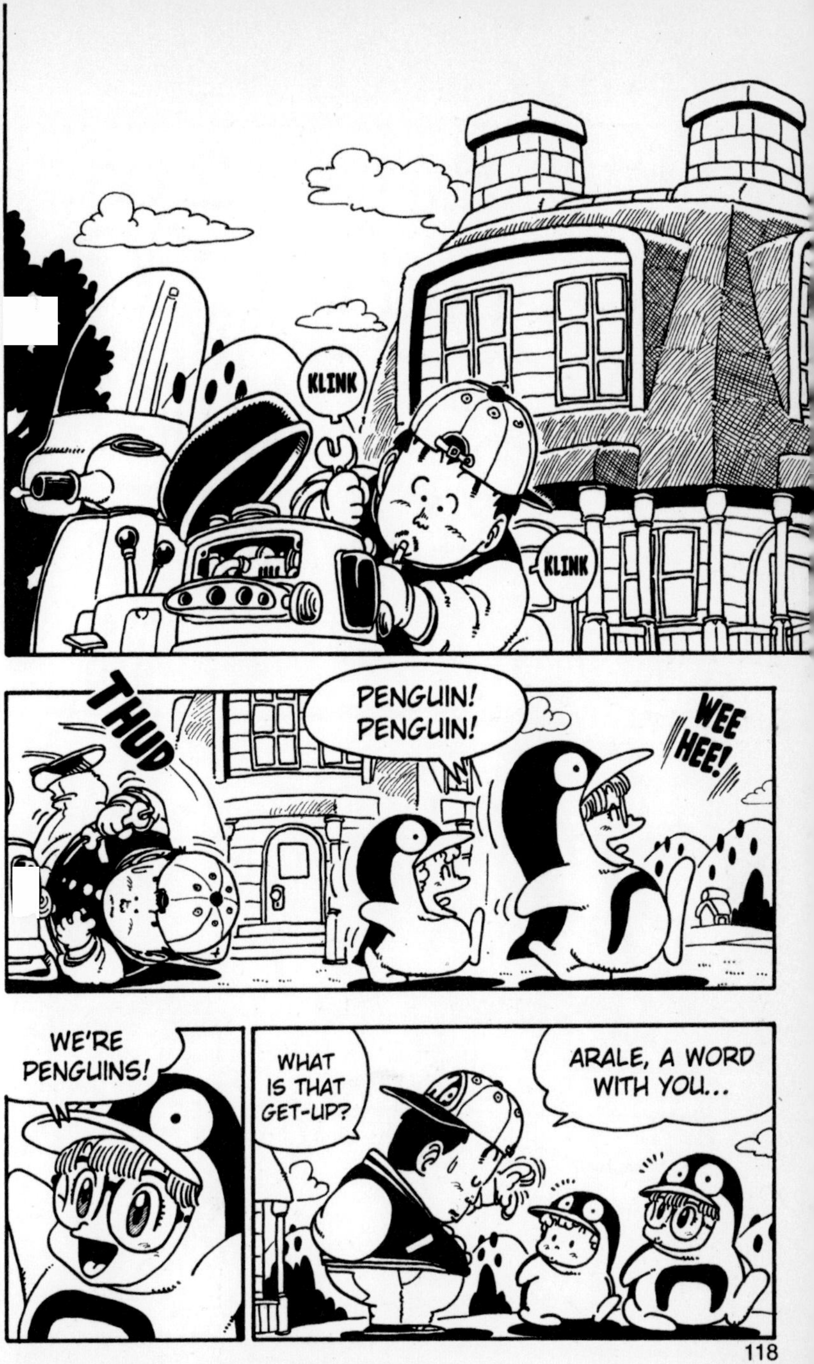
KLINK
KLINK
WEE HEE!
PENGUIN! PENGUIN!
THUD
ARALE, A WORD WITH YOU...
WHAT IS THAT GET-UP?
WE'RE PENGUINS!

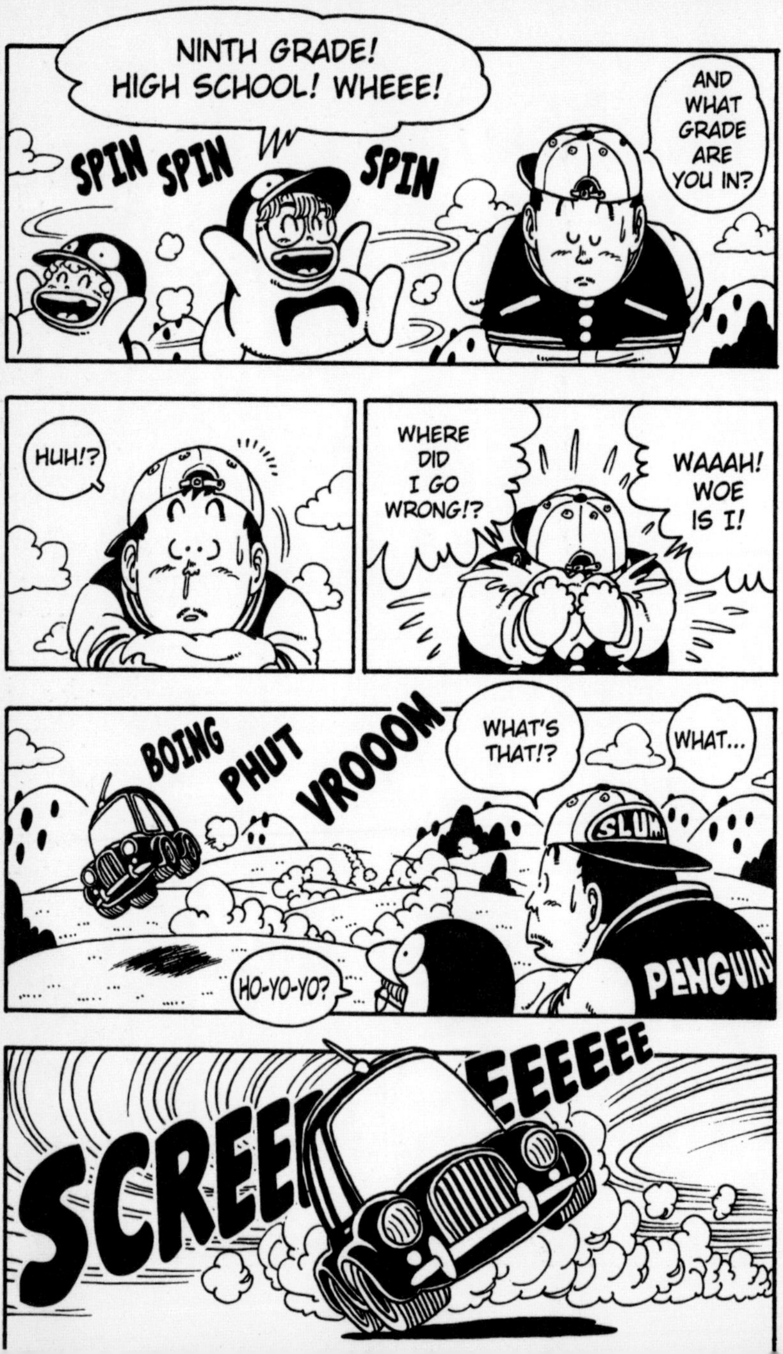
AND WHAT GRADE ARE YOU IN?
NINTH GRADE! HIGH SCHOOL! WHEEE!
SPIN
SPIN
SPIN
WAAAH! WOE IS I!
WHERE DID I GO WRONG!?
HUH!?
WHAT...
WHAT'S THAT!?
SLUM
VROOOM
PHUT
BOING
PENGUIN
HO-YO-YO?
SCREE
EEEEEE

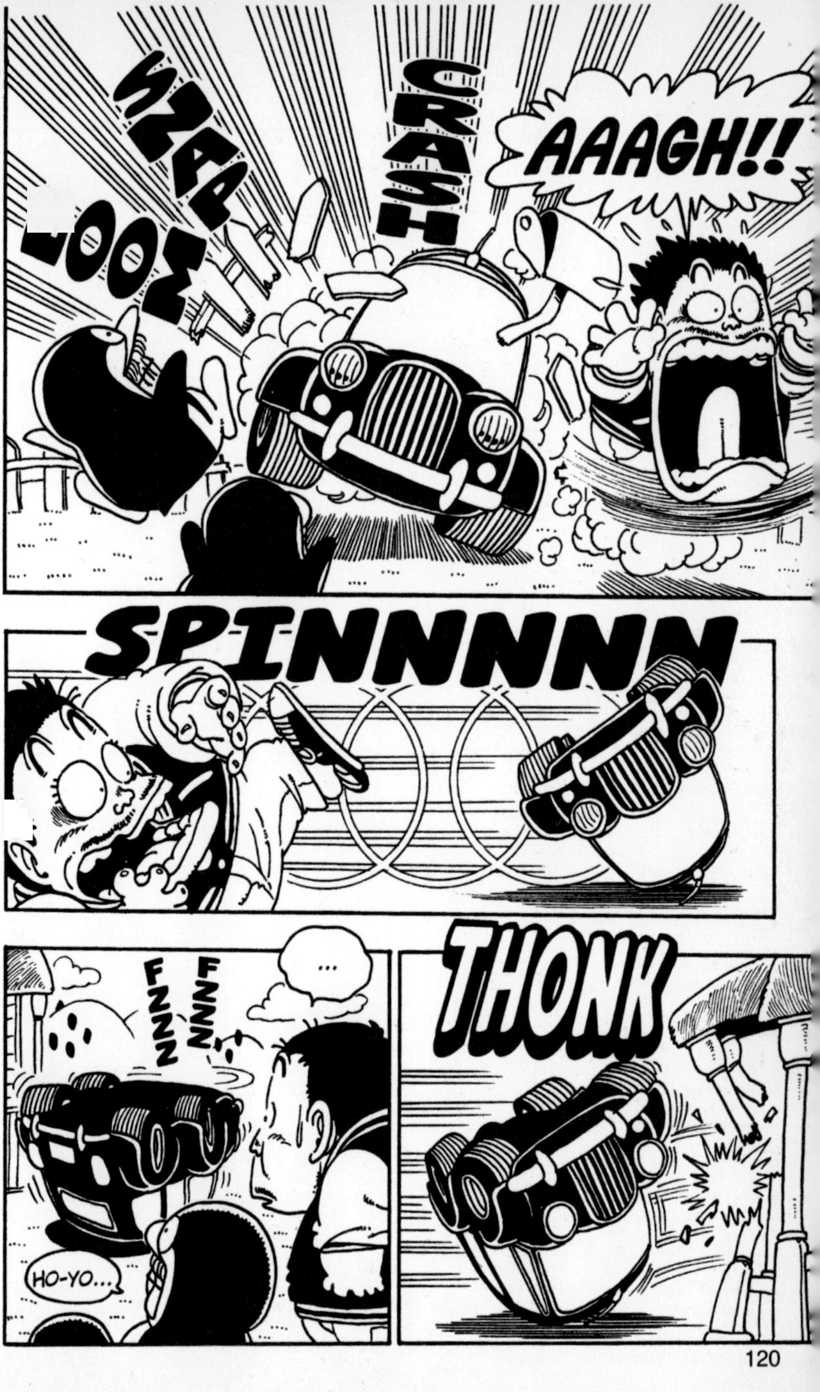
AAAGH!!
CRASH
SNAP
SPINNNNN
THONK
...
FZZZZ
FZZZZ
HO-YO...

READ THIS WAY

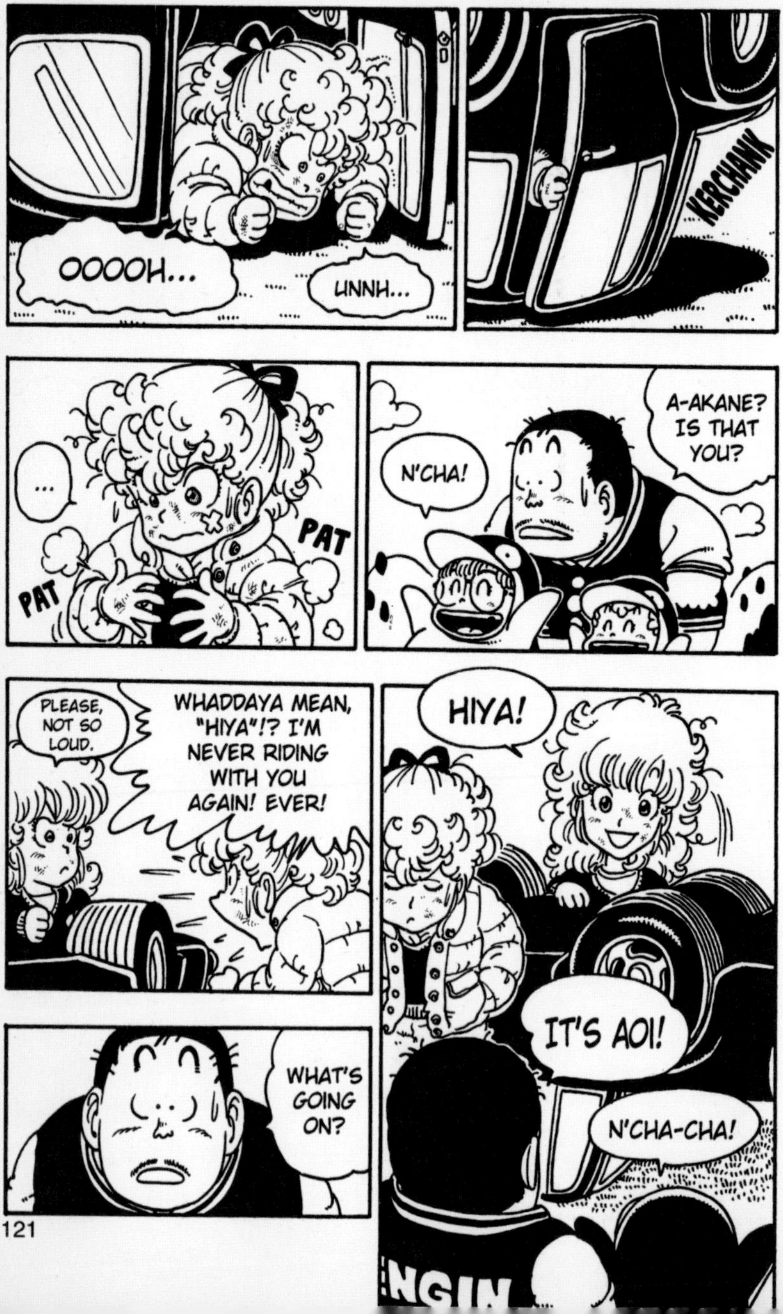
KERCHANK
UNNH...
OOOOH...
A-AKANE? IS THAT YOU?
N'CHA!
...
PAT
PAT
HIYA!
IT'S AOI!
N'CHA-CHA!
WHADDAYA MEAN, "HIYA"!? I'M NEVER RIDING WITH YOU AGAIN! EVER!
PLEASE, NOT SO LOUD.
WHAT'S GOING ON?

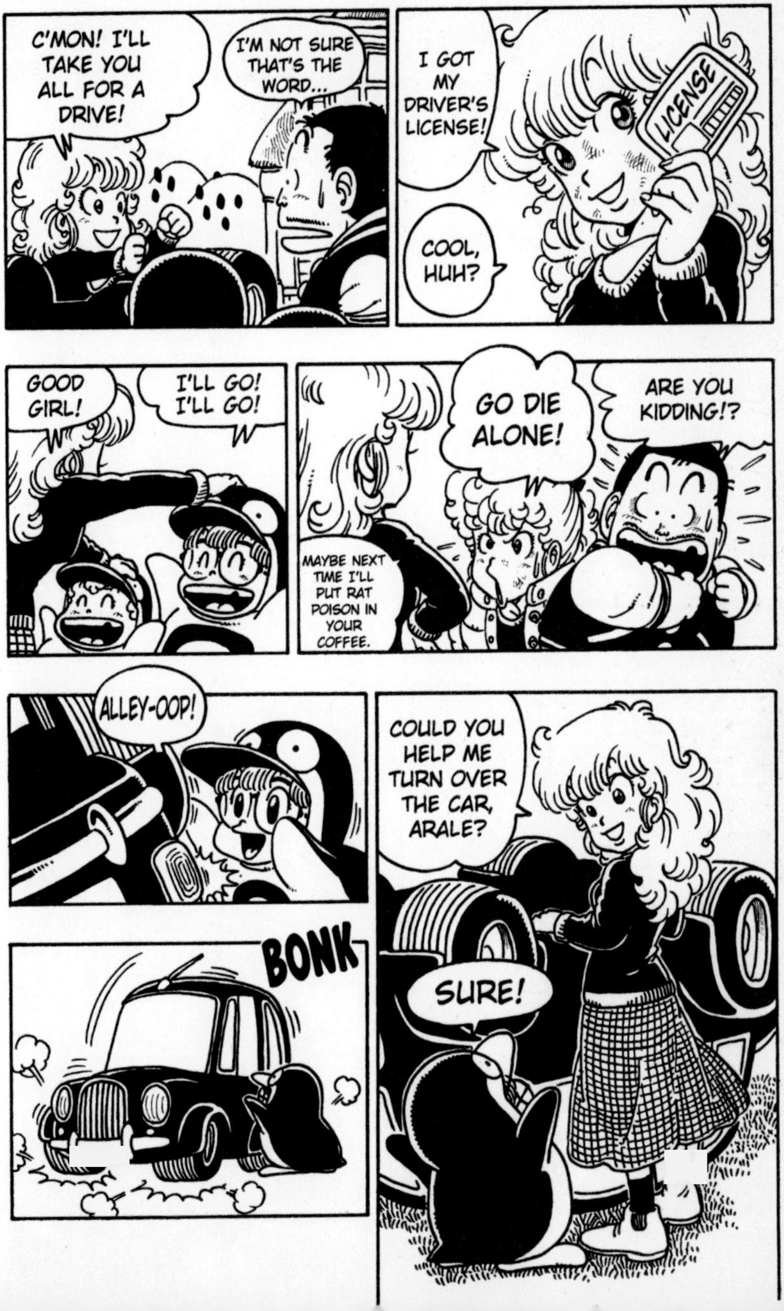
I GOT MY DRIVER'S LICENSE!
LICENSE
COOL, HUH?
C'MON! I'LL TAKE YOU ALL FOR A DRIVE!
I'M NOT SURE THAT'S THE WORD...
ARE YOU KIDDING!?
GO DIE ALONE!
MAYBE NEXT TIME I'LL PUT RAT POISON IN YOUR COFFEE.
I'LL GO! I'LL GO!
GOOD GIRL!
COULD YOU HELP ME TURN OVER THE CAR, ARALE?
SURE!
ALLEY-OOP!
BONK

READ THIS WAY

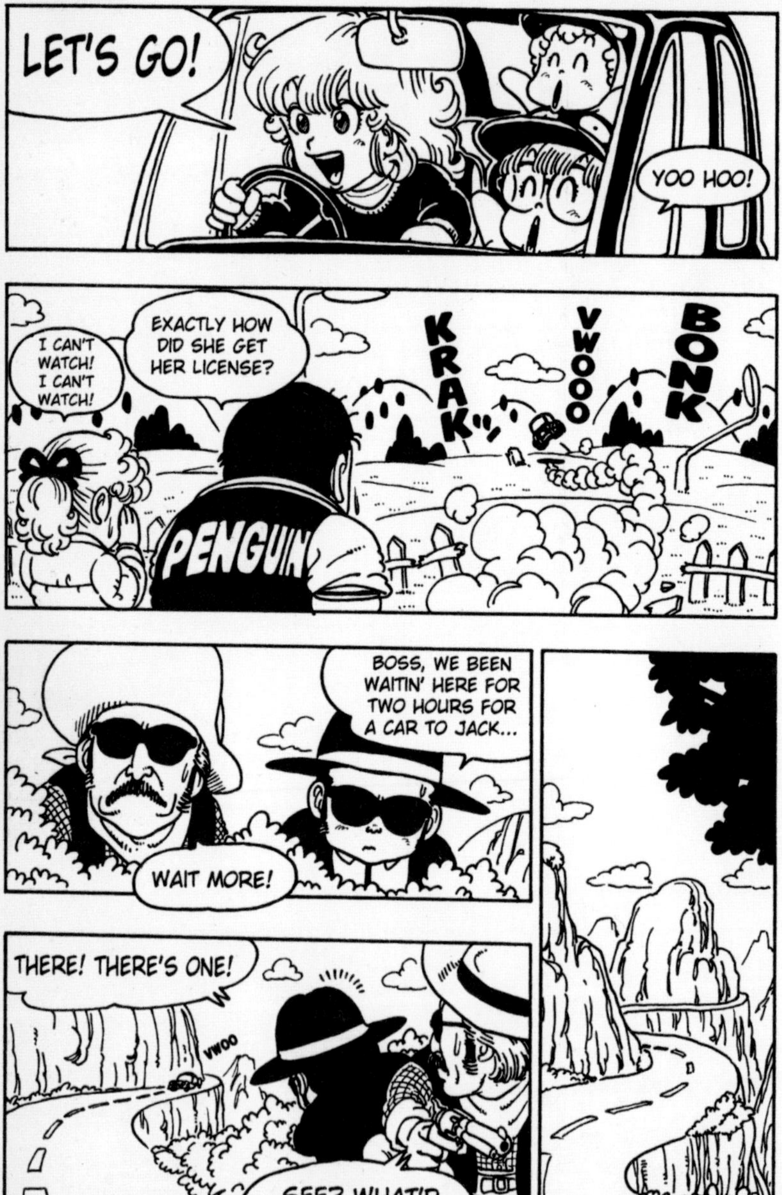
LET'S GO!
YOO HOO!
BONK
VWOOO
KRAK
EXACTLY HOW DID SHE GET HER LICENSE?
I CAN'T WATCH! I CAN'T WATCH!
BOSS, WE BEEN WAITIN' HERE FOR TWO HOURS FOR A CAR TO JACK...
WAIT MORE!
THERE! THERE'S ONE!
VWOO
SEE? WHAT'D I TELL YA?

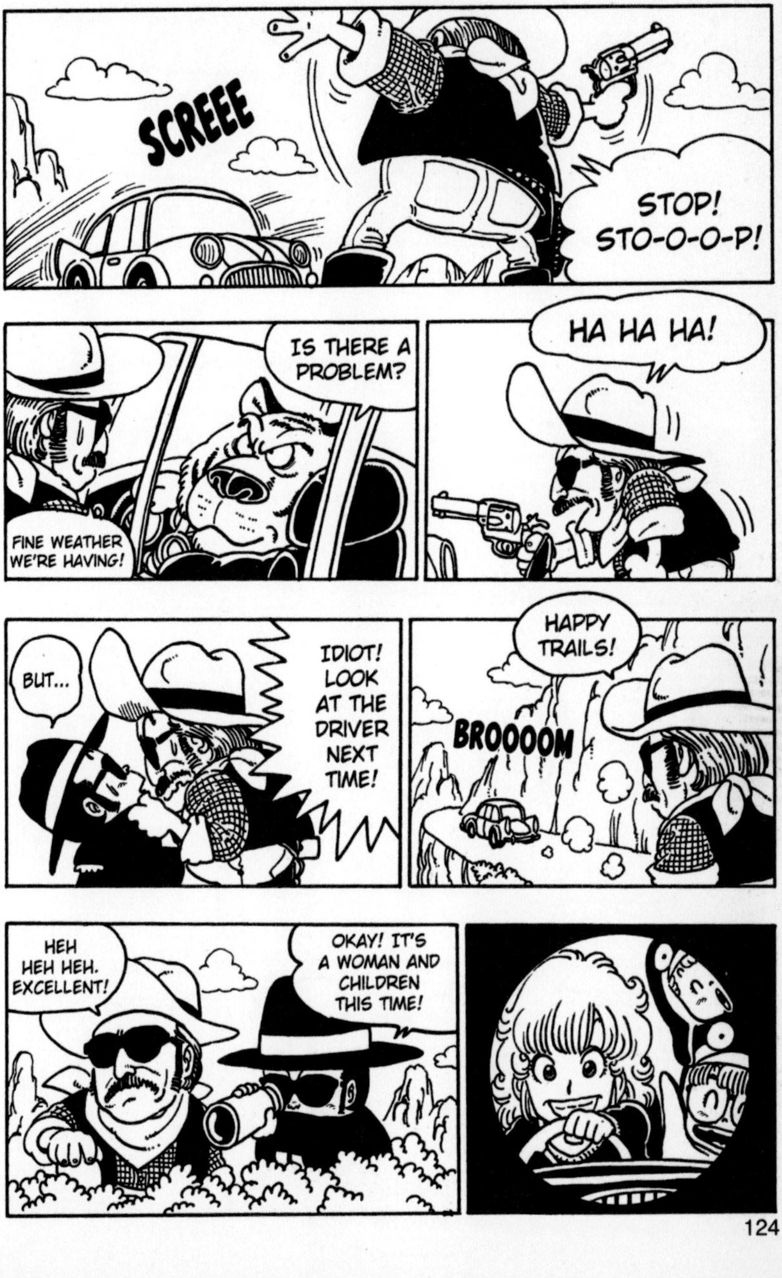
SCREEE
STOP! STO-O-O-P!
HA HA HA!
IS THERE A PROBLEM?
FINE WEATHER WE'RE HAVING!
HAPPY TRAILS!
BROOOOM
IDIOT! LOOK AT THE DRIVER NEXT TIME!
BUT...
OKAY! IT'S A WOMAN AND CHILDREN THIS TIME!
HEH HEH HEH. EXCELLENT!

READ THIS WAY

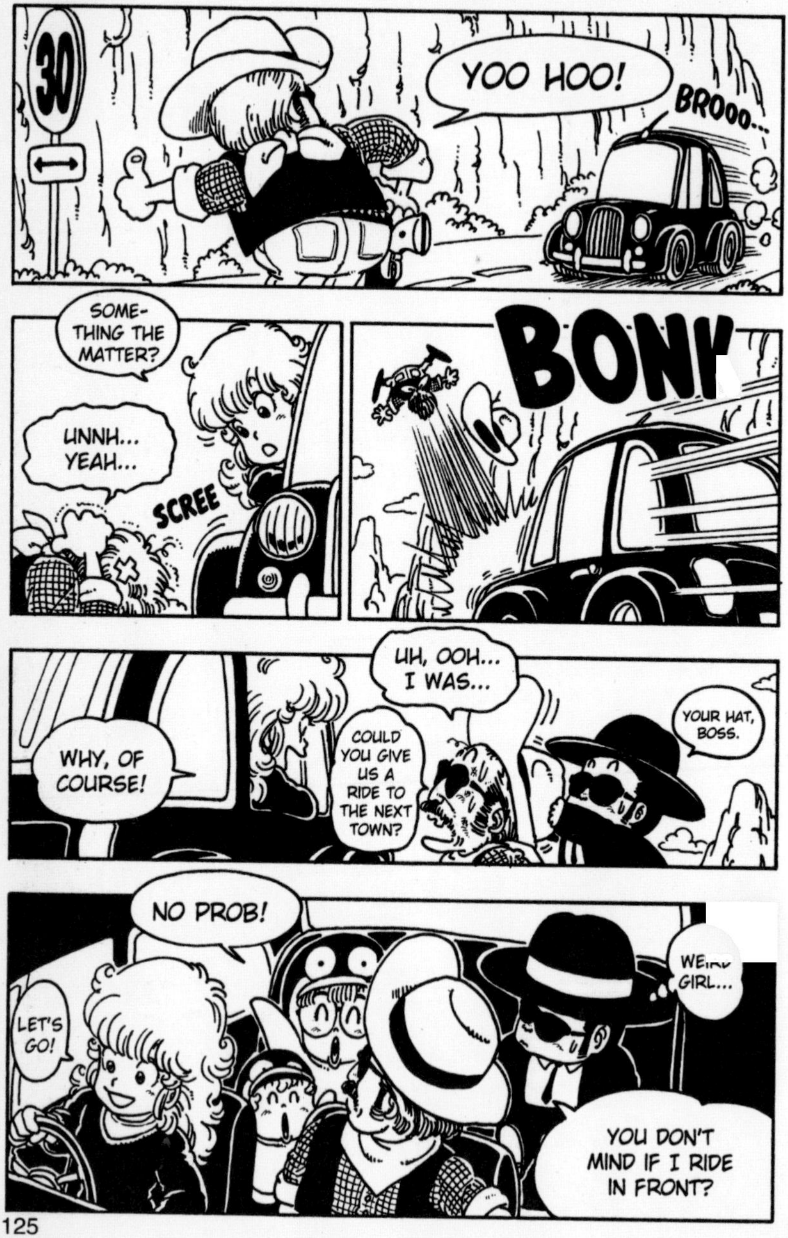

YOO HOO!
BROOO...
BONK
SOME-THING THE MATTER?
UNNH... YEAH...
SCREE
YOUR HAT, BOSS.
UH, OOH... I WAS...
COULD YOU GIVE US A RIDE TO THE NEXT TOWN?
WHY, OF COURSE!
WE GIRL...
NO PROB!
YOU DON'T MIND IF I RIDE IN FRONT?
LET'S GO!

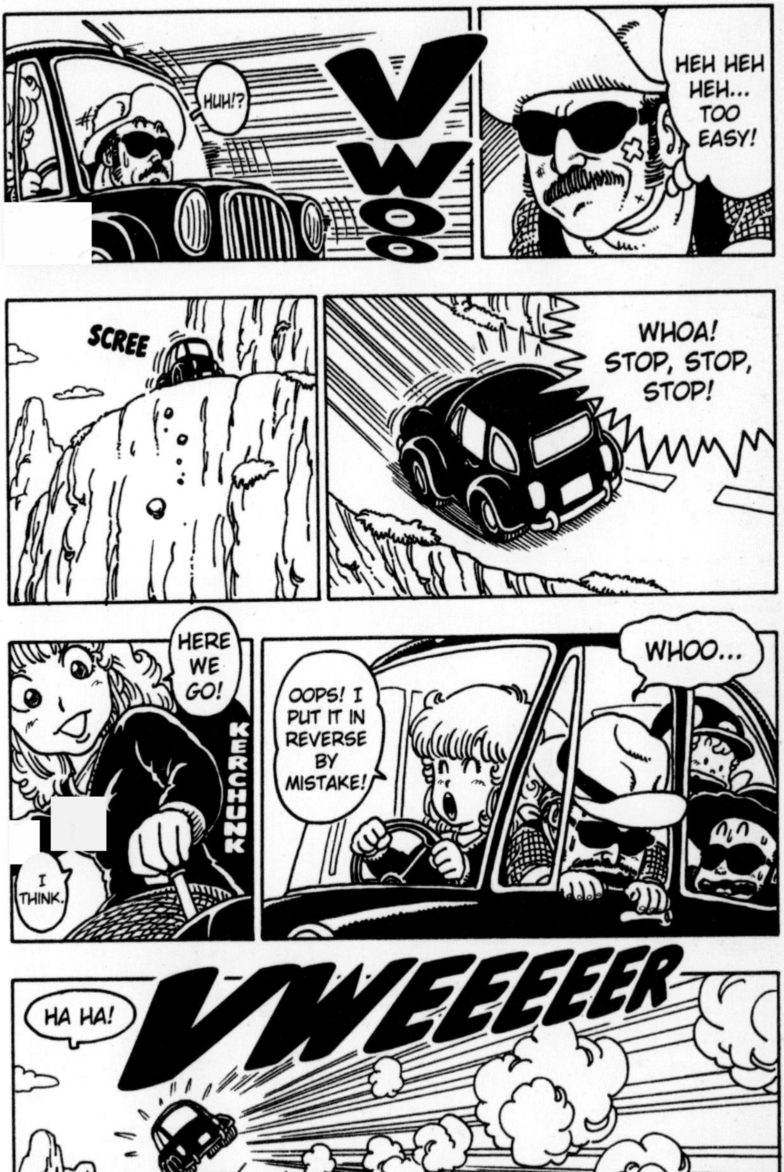
HEH HEH HEH... TOO EASY!
VWOO
HUH!?
WHOA! STOP, STOP, STOP!
SCREE
WHOO...
OOPS! I PUT IT IN REVERSE BY MISTAKE!
HERE WE GO!
KERCHUNK
I THINK.
VWEEEEEER
HA HA!

READ THIS WAY

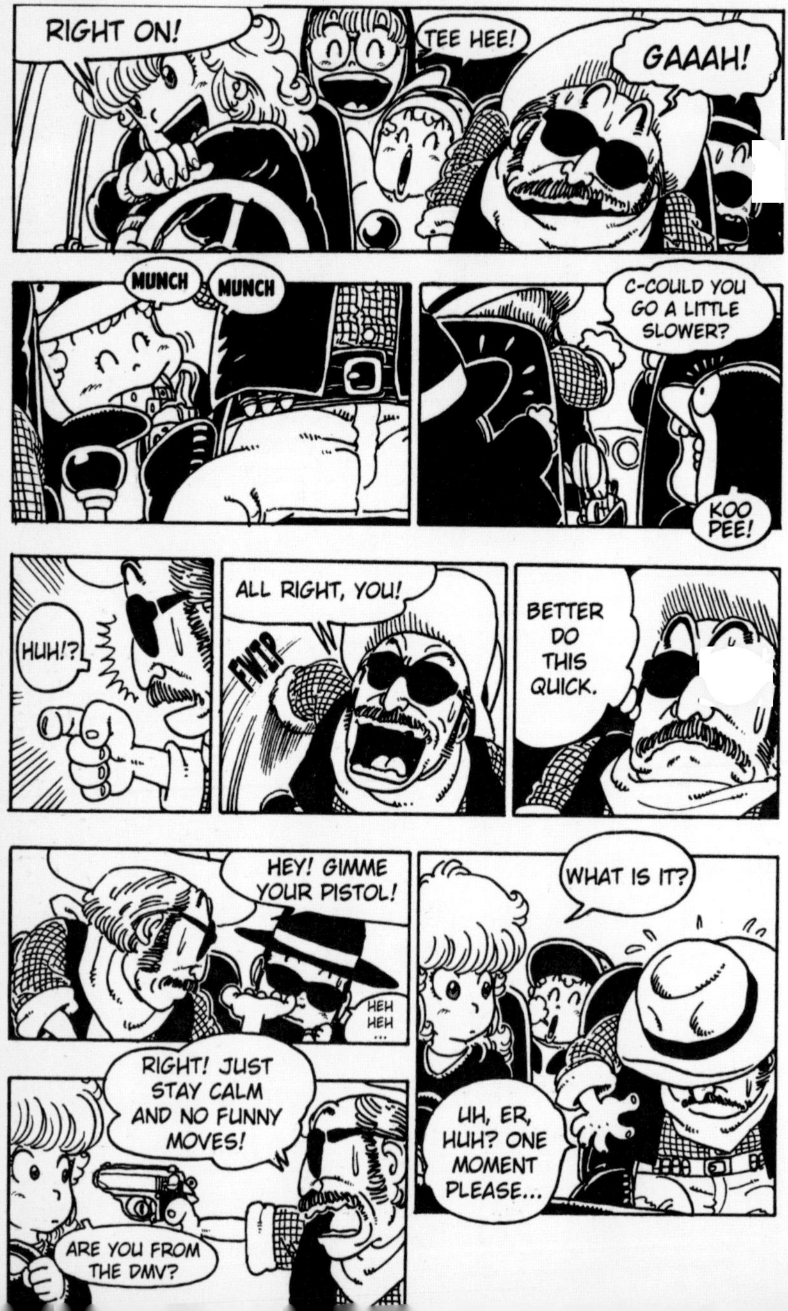
GAAAH!
TEE HEE!
RIGHT ON!
C-COULD YOU GO A LITTLE SLOWER?
KOO PEE!
MUNCH
MUNCH
BETTER DO THIS QUICK.
ALL RIGHT, YOU!
FWIP
HUH!?
WHAT IS IT?
UH, ER, HUH? ONE MOMENT PLEASE...
HEY! GIMME YOUR PISTOL!
HEH HEH ...
RIGHT! JUST STAY CALM AND NO FUNNY MOVES!
ARE YOU FROM THE DMV?

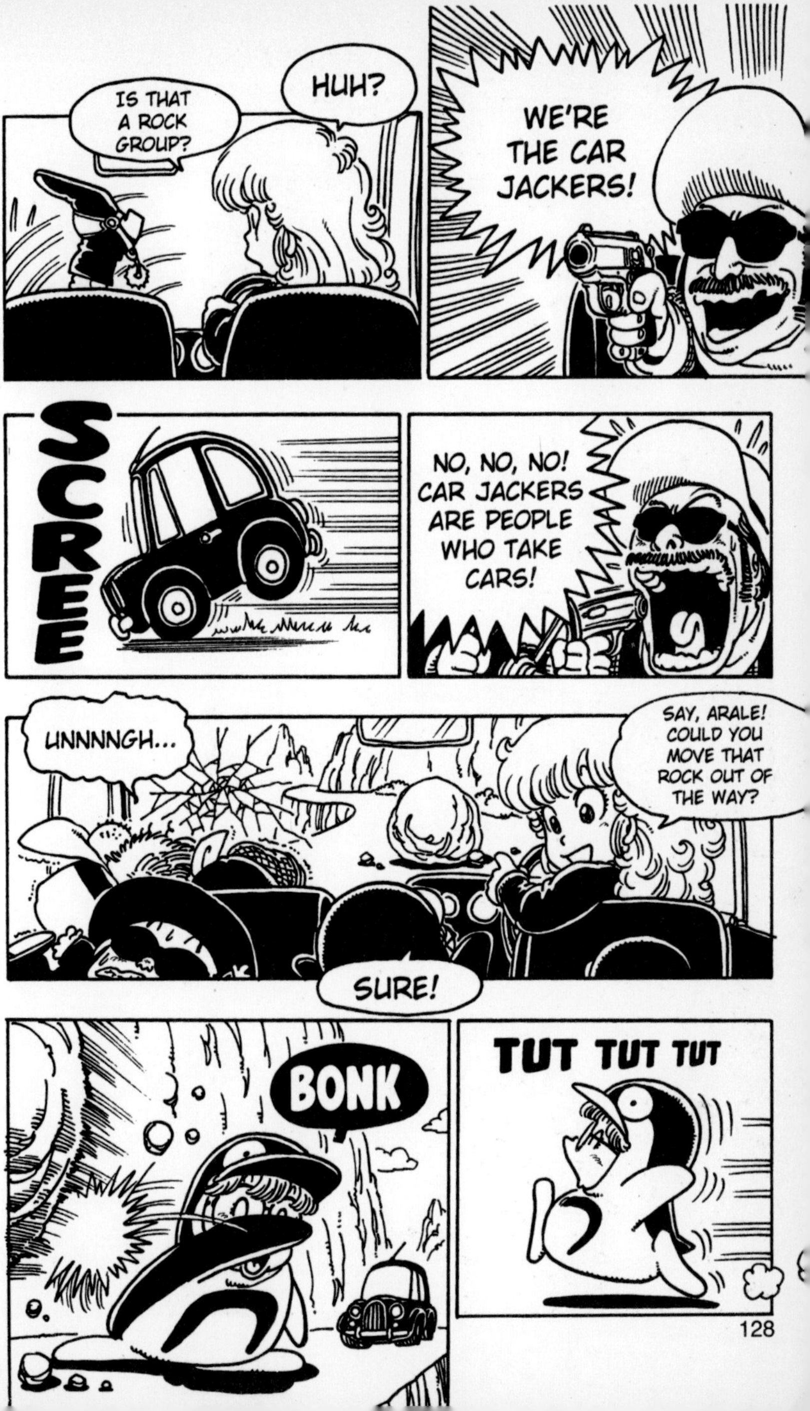

WE'RE THE CAR JACKERS!
HUH?
IS THAT A ROCK GROUP?
NO, NO, NO! CAR JACKERS ARE PEOPLE WHO TAKE CARS!
SCREE
SAY, ARALE! COULD YOU MOVE THAT ROCK OUT OF THE WAY?
UNNNNGH...
SURE!
TUT TUT TUT
BONK

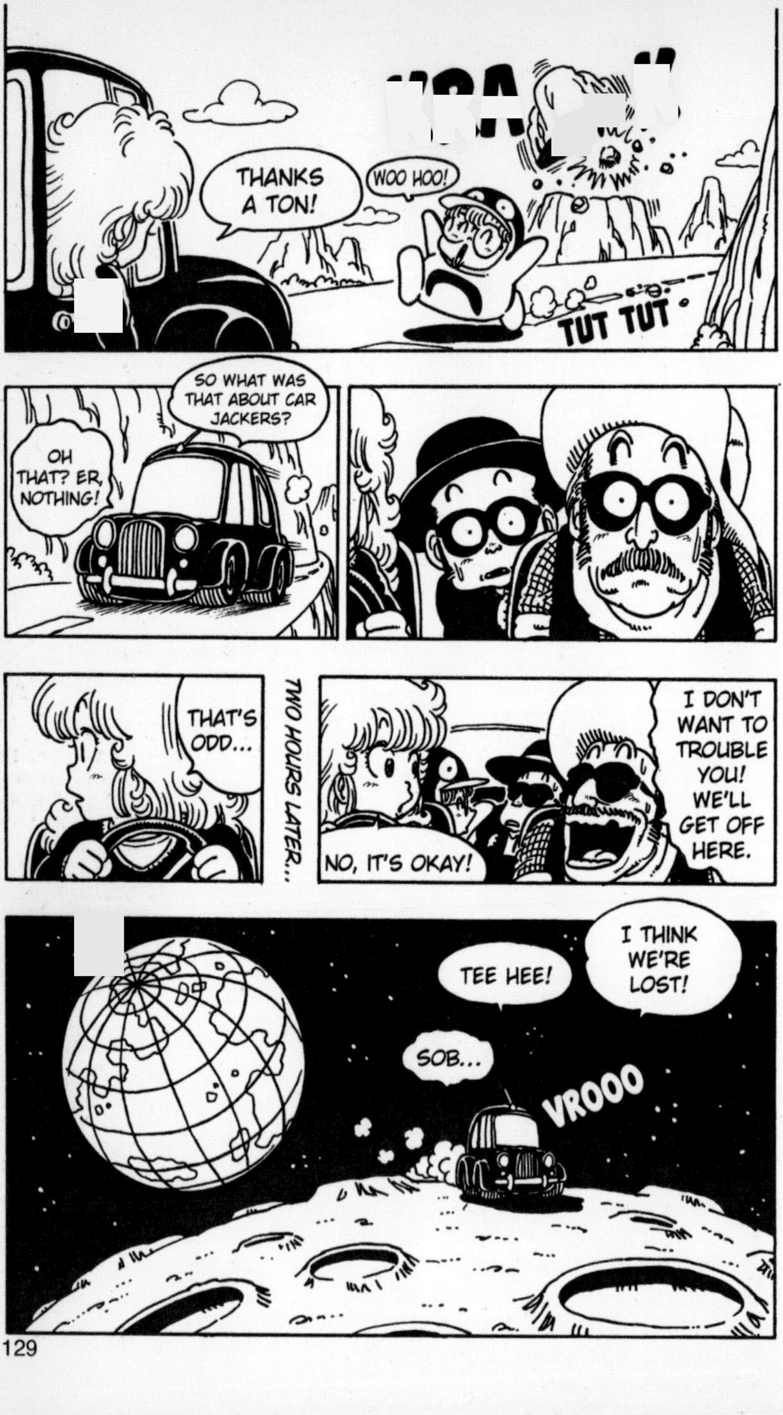
WOO HOO!
THANKS A TON!
TUT TUT
SO WHAT WAS THAT ABOUT CAR JACKERS?
OH THAT? ER, NOTHING!
I DON'T WANT TO TROUBLE YOU! WE'LL GET OFF HERE.
NO, IT'S OKAY!
TWO HOURS LATER...
THAT'S ODD...
I THINK WE'RE LOST!
TEE HEE!
SOB...
VROOO

Penguin Village **"I'M NUMBER ONE!" CONTEST** Category: Dumbest

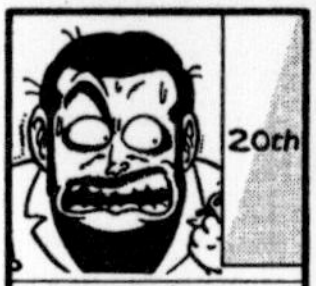 20th	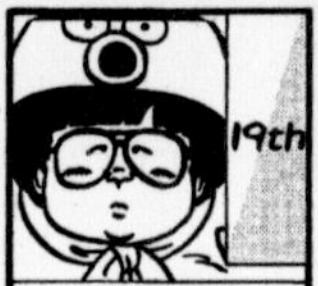 19th	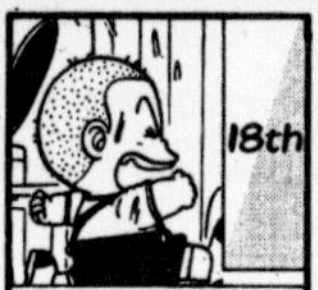 18th	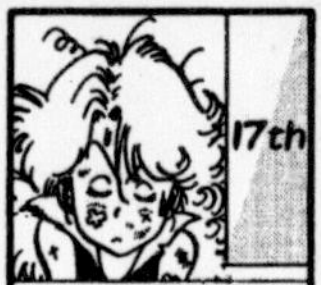 17th	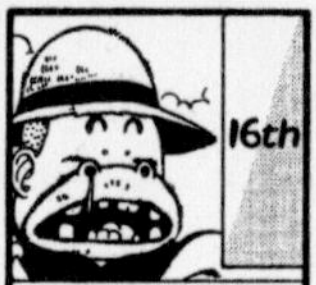 16th
The Shiverman 35 votes ★Sucking a fly in through your nose and spitting it out is the epitome of dumb. ★This guy's a killer? He should be fired.	**Octo-Ball Makusa 36 votes** ★His bumpkin face! ★His dopey look makes me weep. ★Whoever he's based on must be dumb.	**Peasuke Soramame 38 votes** ★High school students shouldn't wear kindergarten backpacks. ★What a crybaby!	**Midori Norimaki (neé Yamabuki) 40 votes** ★Only an idiot would marry that idiot Senbei! ★She seems dumber of late.	**Farmer guy 50 votes** ★That dumb hippo face of his wins hands down. ★Clearly not all there.

29th (tie)	29th (tie)	26th (tie)	26th (tie)	26th (tie)	24th (tie)	24th (tie)	22nd (tie)	22nd (tie)	21st
Mr. Skop 20 votes ★Penguin Village rubbed off on him.	**Kintaman (Koita Ojo) 20 votes** ★Transforms for no good reason.	**The Entire Penguin Village Police Force 22 votes** ★Completely useless	**Miyamoto Musashi* 22 votes** ★Musashi in junior high!? *A famous Japanese swordsman	**Penguin Village Police Dept. 22 votes** ★Utterly useless	**Bank Robber 24 votes** ★He's dumb to go up against Arale.	**Tsun Tsuku-Tsun 40 votes** ★Doesn't think Penguin Village is strange at all.	**Gatchan 26 votes** ★You'd have to be dumb to live at the Norimakis'.	**Poop 26 votes** ★Poop shouldn't be able to talk.	**Taro Soramame 34 votes** ★Always in Akane's shadow.

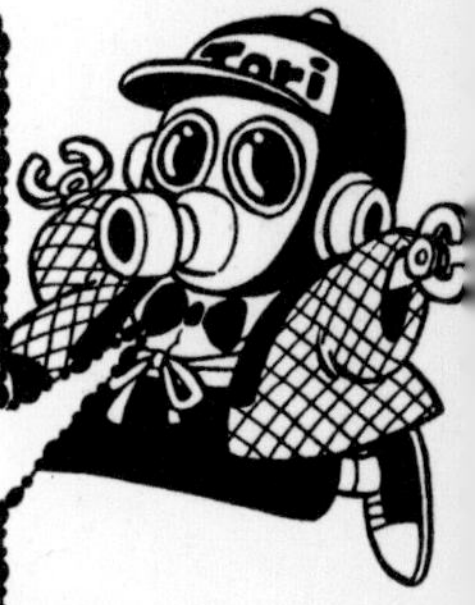

Tori

Whaaaaaooh! The few, the dumb, the rest of the responses! Check them out!

- Anyone passing through Penguin Village
- Torishima
- The lovely trio
- Good Mornooning!
- The women's clothing salesclerk in Volume 1
- The fly killed by Dr. Mashirito's bug spray
- King Nikochan's tall boots
- The stars over Penguin Village
- The 8th Grade athletic team
- Kinoko's radio-cassette player
- Senbei's old man

Our Little House

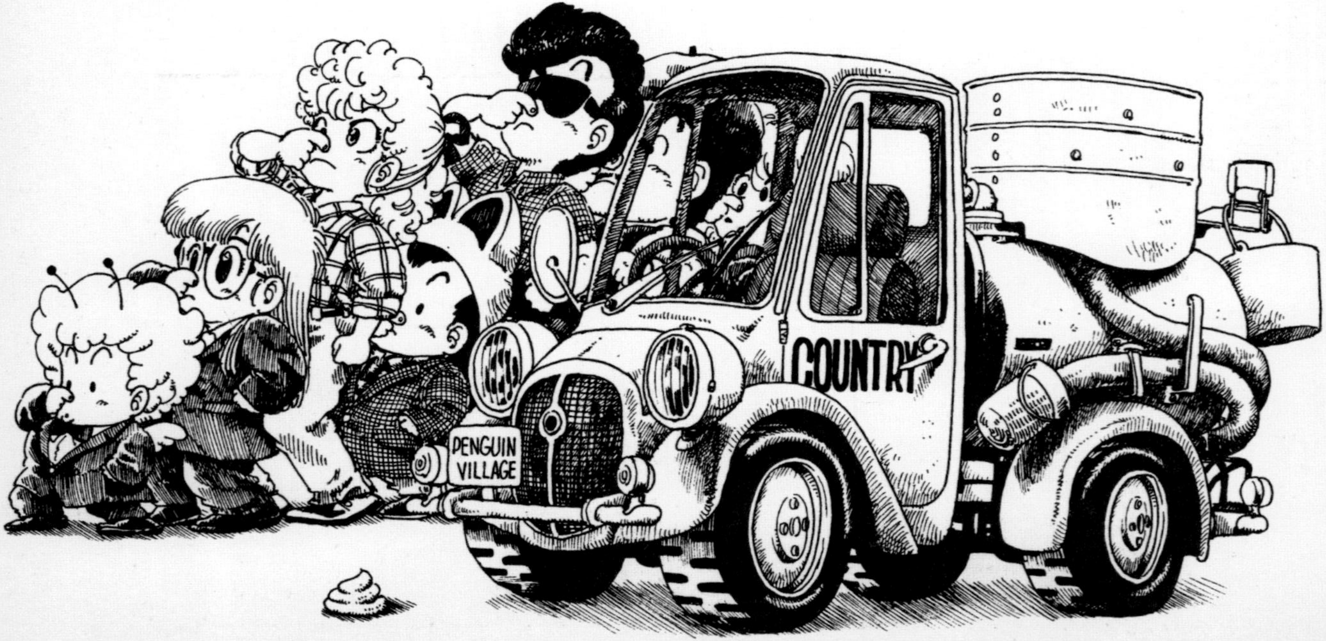
PENGUIN VILLAGE
COUNTRY

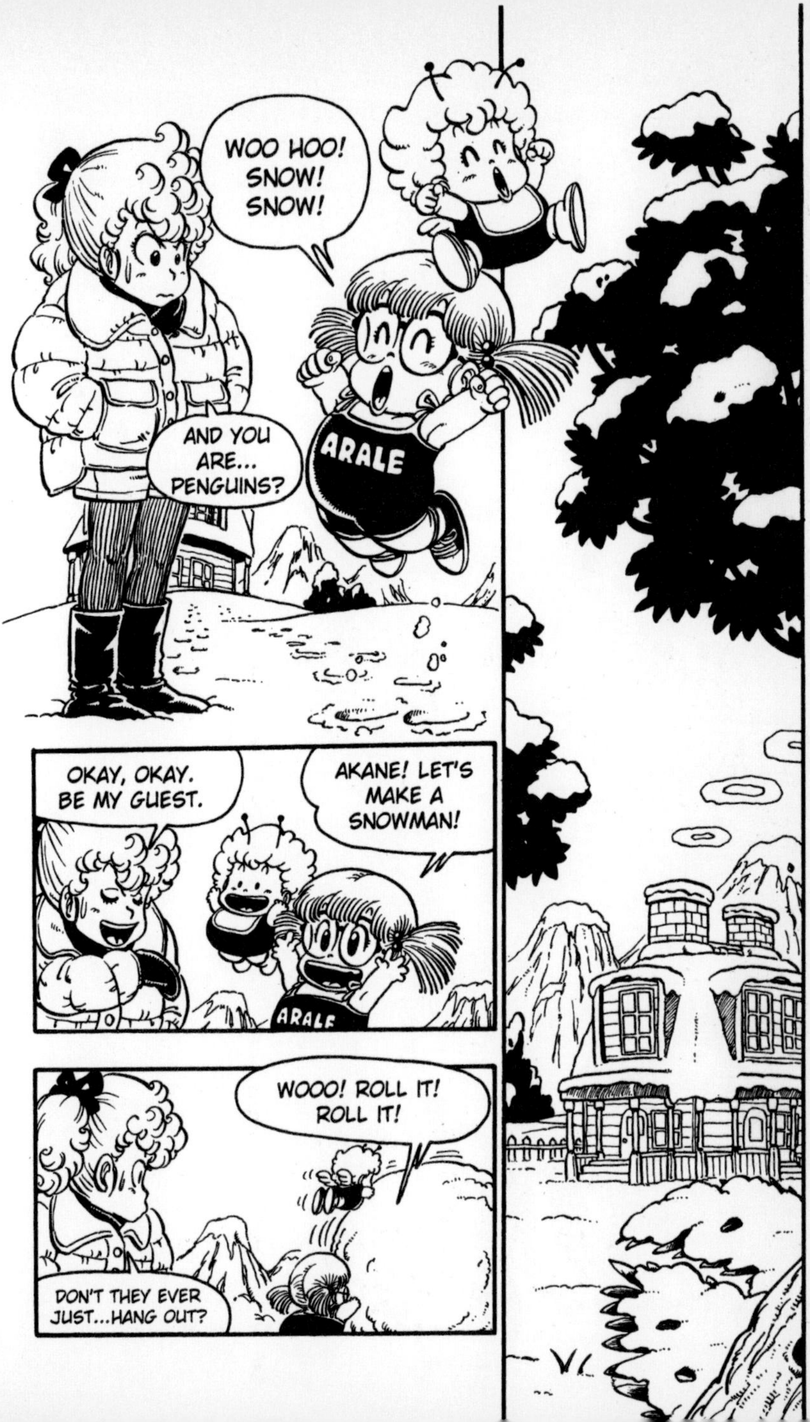
WOO HOO! SNOW! SNOW!
AND YOU ARE... PENGUINS?
ARALE
AKANE! LET'S MAKE A SNOWMAN!
OKAY, OKAY. BE MY GUEST.
ARALE
WOOO! ROLL IT! ROLL IT!
DON'T THEY EVER JUST...HANG OUT?

READ THIS WAY

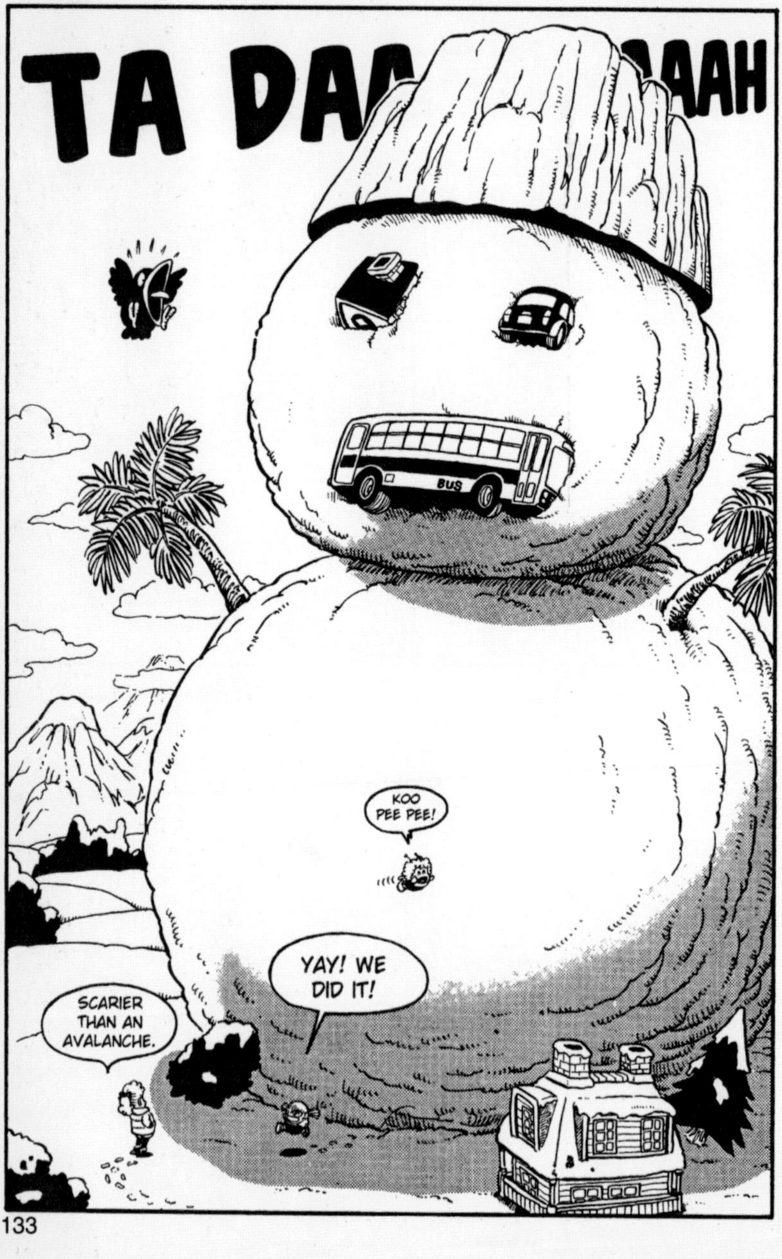
TA DAA AAAH
BUS
KOO PEE PEE!
YAY! WE DID IT!
SCARIER THAN AN AVALANCHE.

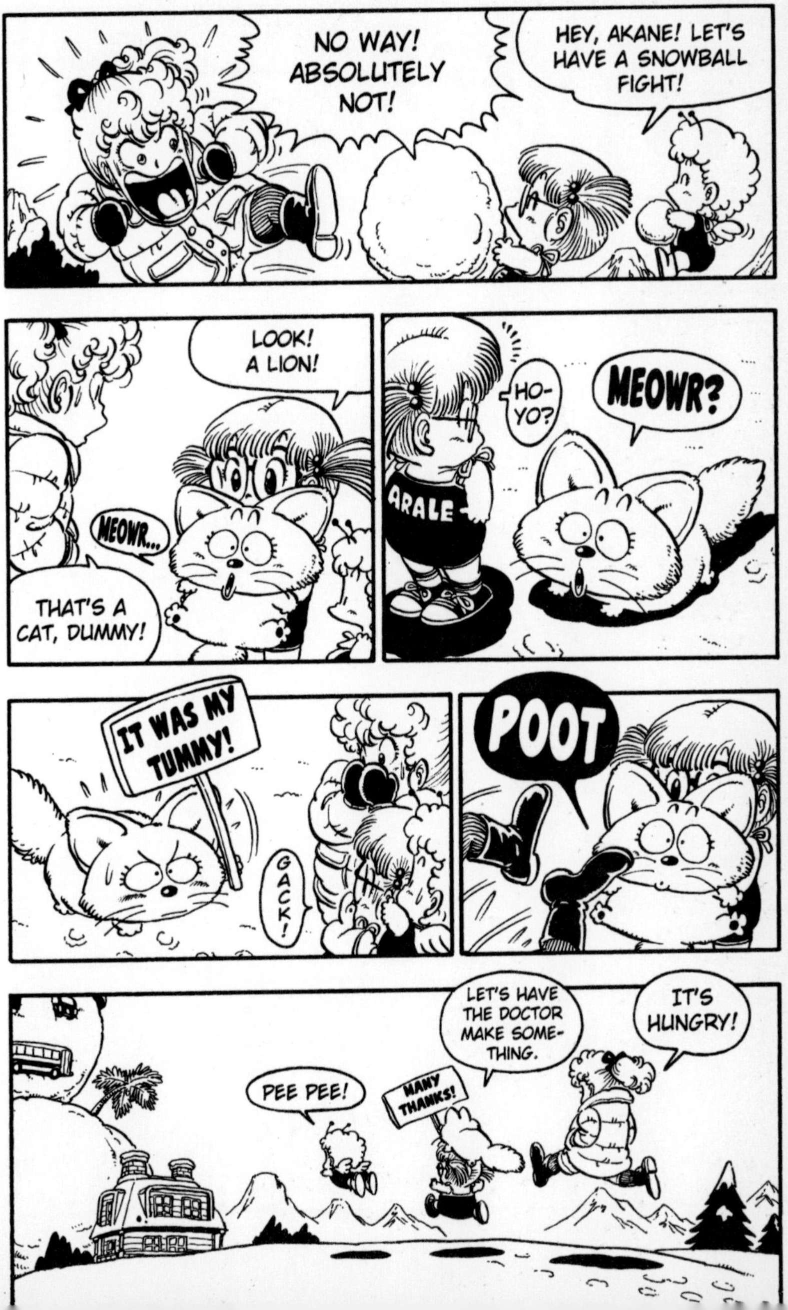
HEY, AKANE! LET'S HAVE A SNOWBALL FIGHT!
NO WAY! ABSOLUTELY NOT!
MEOWR?
HO-YO?
LOOK! A LION!
MEOWR...
THAT'S A CAT, DUMMY!
POOT
IT WAS MY TUMMY!
GACK!
IT'S HUNGRY!
LET'S HAVE THE DOCTOR MAKE SOMETHING.
MANY THANKS!
PEE PEE!

READ THIS WAY

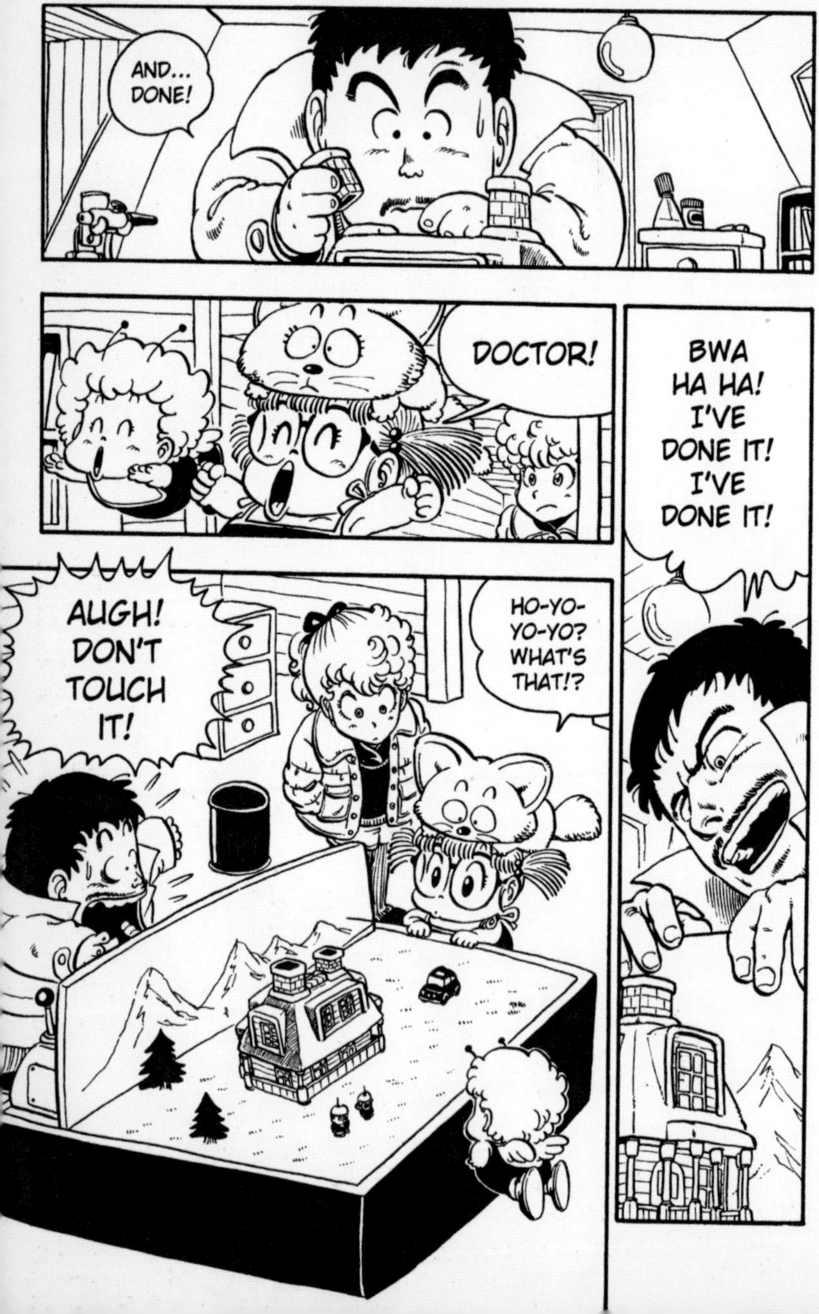
AND... DONE!
BWA HA HA! I'VE DONE IT! I'VE DONE IT!
DOCTOR!
HO-YO-YO-YO? WHAT'S THAT!?
AUGH! DON'T TOUCH IT!

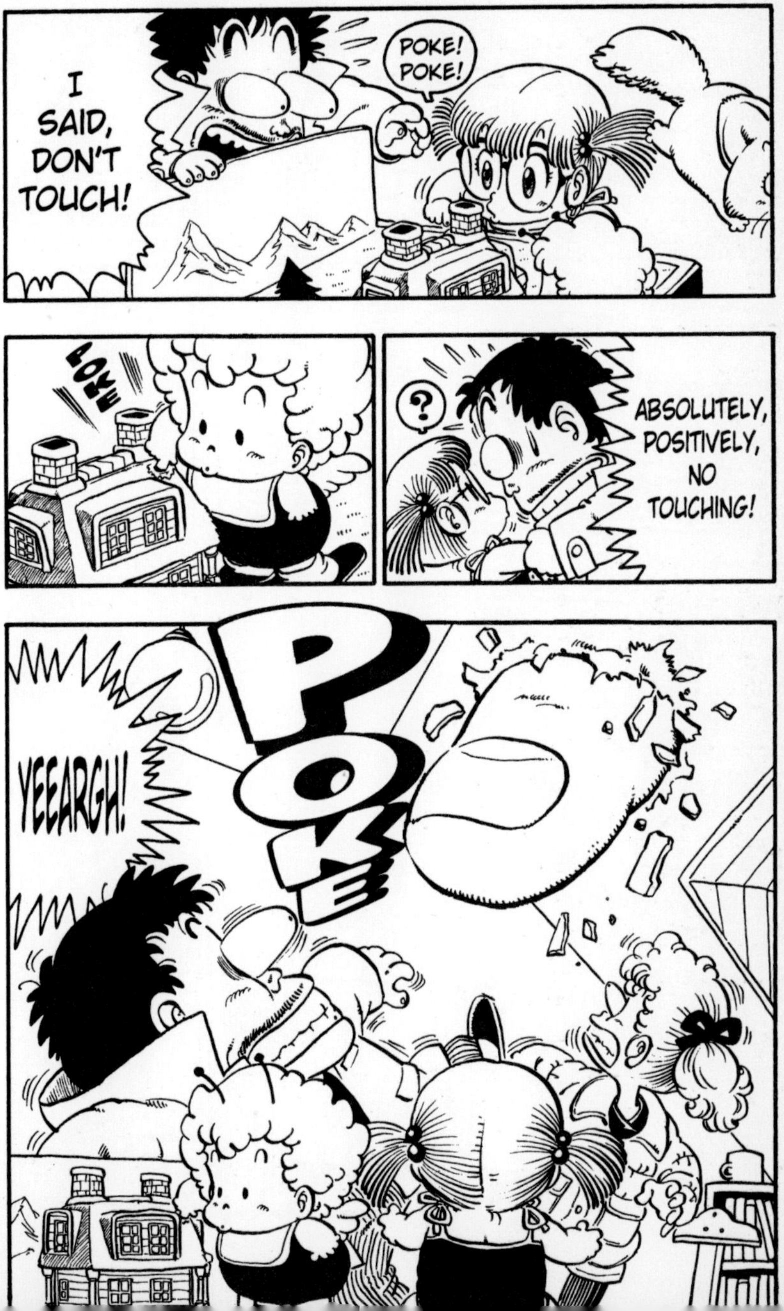
POKE! POKE!
I SAID, DON'T TOUCH!
?
ABSOLUTELY, POSITIVELY, NO TOUCHING!
POKE
POKE
YEEARGH!

READ THIS WAY

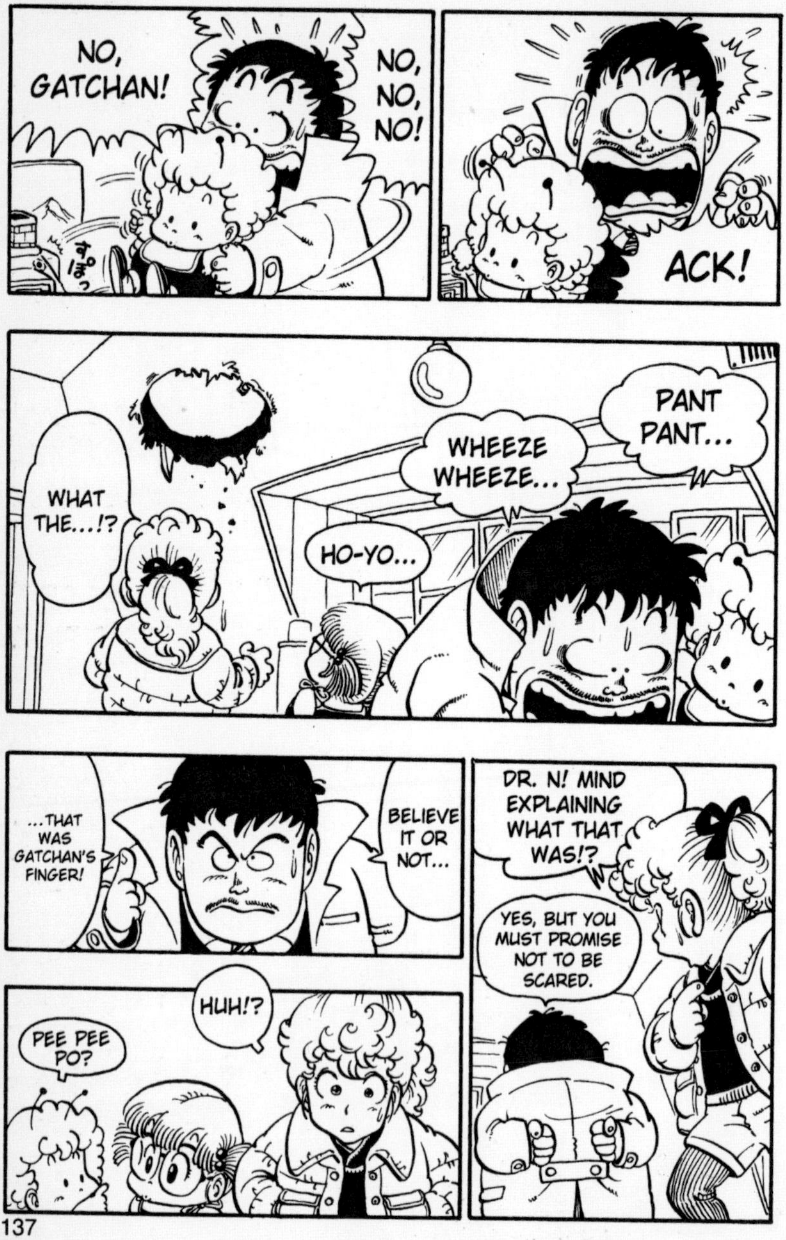
ACK!
NO, NO, NO!
NO, GATCHAN!
すぽっ
PANT PANT...
WHEEZE WHEEZE...
HO-YO...
WHAT THE...!?
DR. N! MIND EXPLAINING WHAT THAT WAS!?
YES, BUT YOU MUST PROMISE NOT TO BE SCARED.
BELIEVE IT OR NOT...
...THAT WAS GATCHAN'S FINGER!
HUH!?
PEE PEE PO?

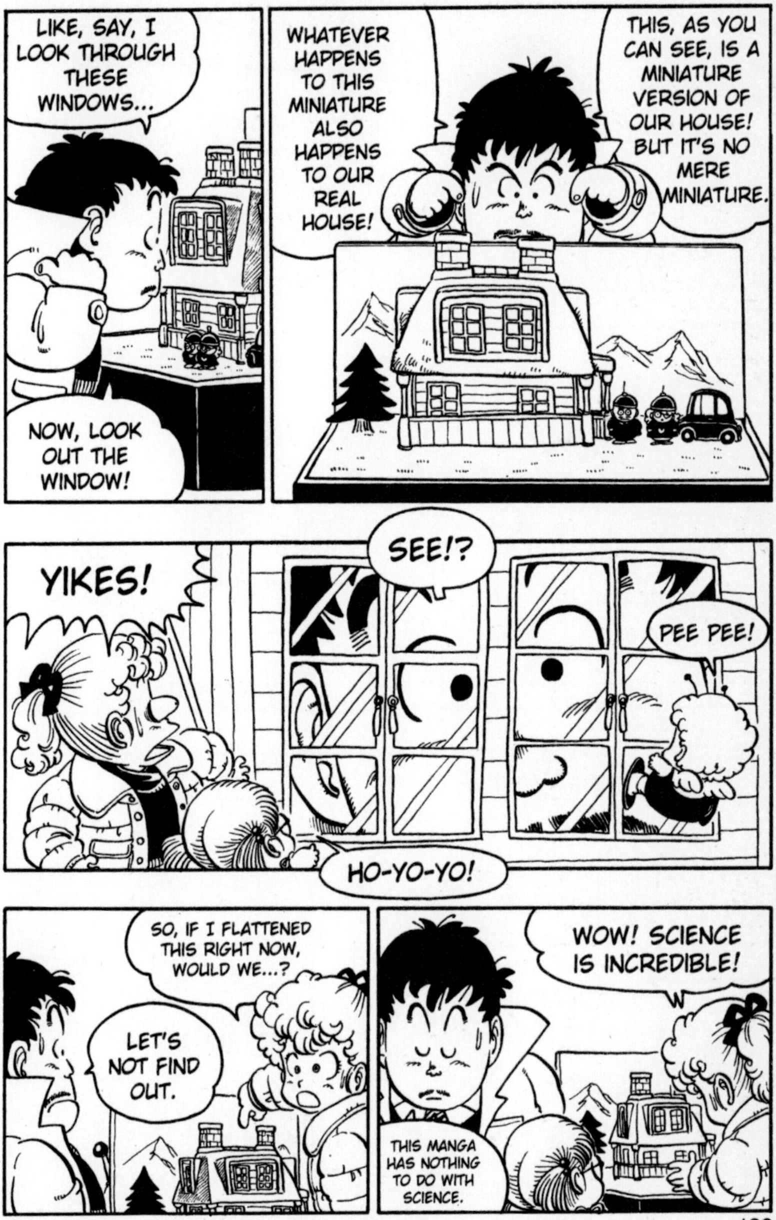
THIS, AS YOU CAN SEE, IS A MINIATURE VERSION OF OUR HOUSE! BUT IT'S NO MERE MINIATURE.
WHATEVER HAPPENS TO THIS MINIATURE ALSO HAPPENS TO OUR REAL HOUSE!
LIKE, SAY, I LOOK THROUGH THESE WINDOWS...
NOW, LOOK OUT THE WINDOW!
SEE!?
PEE PEE!
YIKES!
HO-YO-YO!
WOW! SCIENCE IS INCREDIBLE!
THIS MANGA HAS NOTHING TO DO WITH SCIENCE.
SO, IF I FLATTENED THIS RIGHT NOW, WOULD WE...?
LET'S NOT FIND OUT.

READ THIS WAY

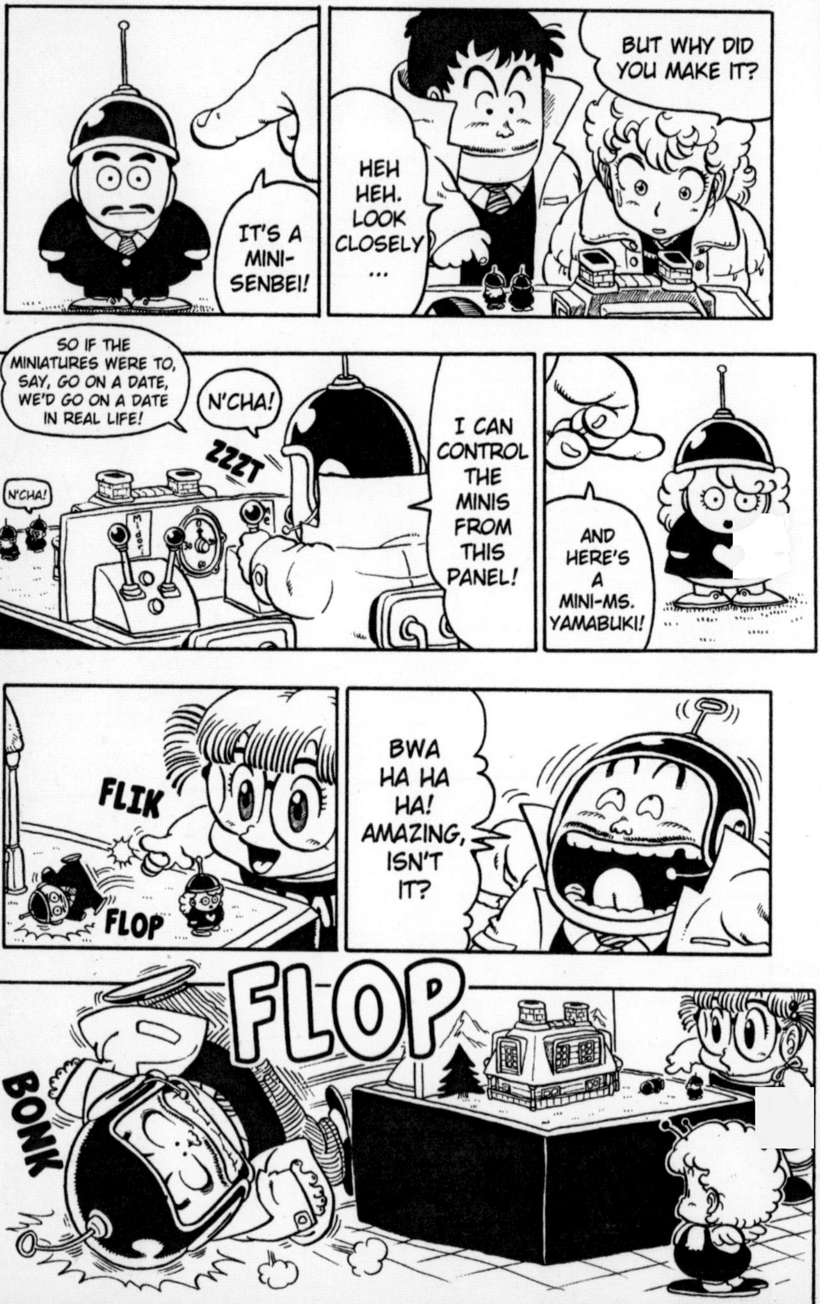
BUT WHY DID YOU MAKE IT?
HEH HEH. LOOK CLOSELY ...
IT'S A MINI-SENBEI!
AND HERE'S A MINI-MS. YAMABUKI!
I CAN CONTROL THE MINIS FROM THIS PANEL!
N'CHA!
SO IF THE MINIATURES WERE TO, SAY, GO ON A DATE, WE'D GO ON A DATE IN REAL LIFE!
ZZZT
N'CHA!
BWA HA HA HA! AMAZING, ISN'T IT?
FLIK
FLOP
FLOP
BONK

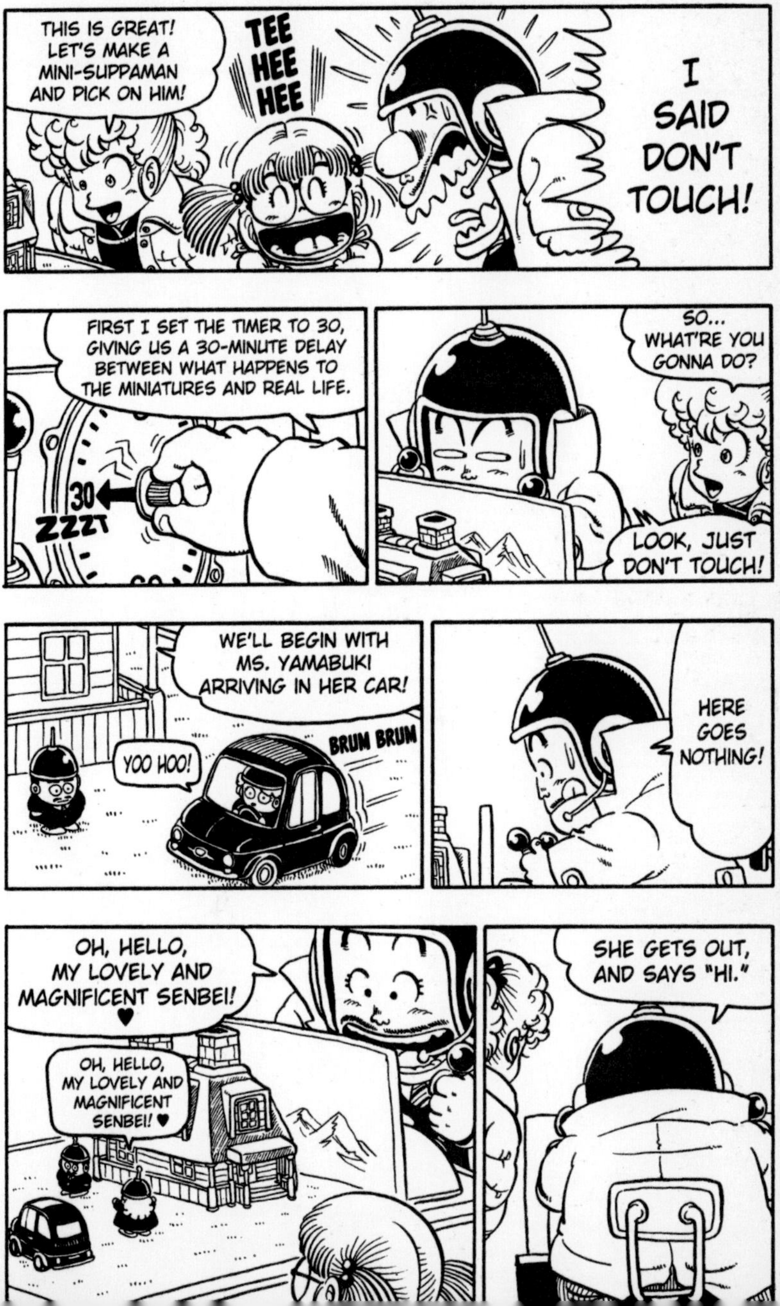
I SAID DON'T TOUCH!
TEE HEE HEE
THIS IS GREAT! LET'S MAKE A MINI-SUPPAMAN AND PICK ON HIM!
SO... WHAT'RE YOU GONNA DO?
LOOK, JUST DON'T TOUCH!
FIRST I SET THE TIMER TO 30, GIVING US A 30-MINUTE DELAY BETWEEN WHAT HAPPENS TO THE MINIATURES AND REAL LIFE.
30
ZZZT
HERE GOES NOTHING!
WE'LL BEGIN WITH MS. YAMABUKI ARRIVING IN HER CAR!
BRUM BRUM
YOO HOO!
SHE GETS OUT, AND SAYS "HI."
OH, HELLO, MY LOVELY AND MAGNIFICENT SENBEI! ♥
OH, HELLO, MY LOVELY AND MAGNIFICENT SENBEI! ♥

READ THIS WAY

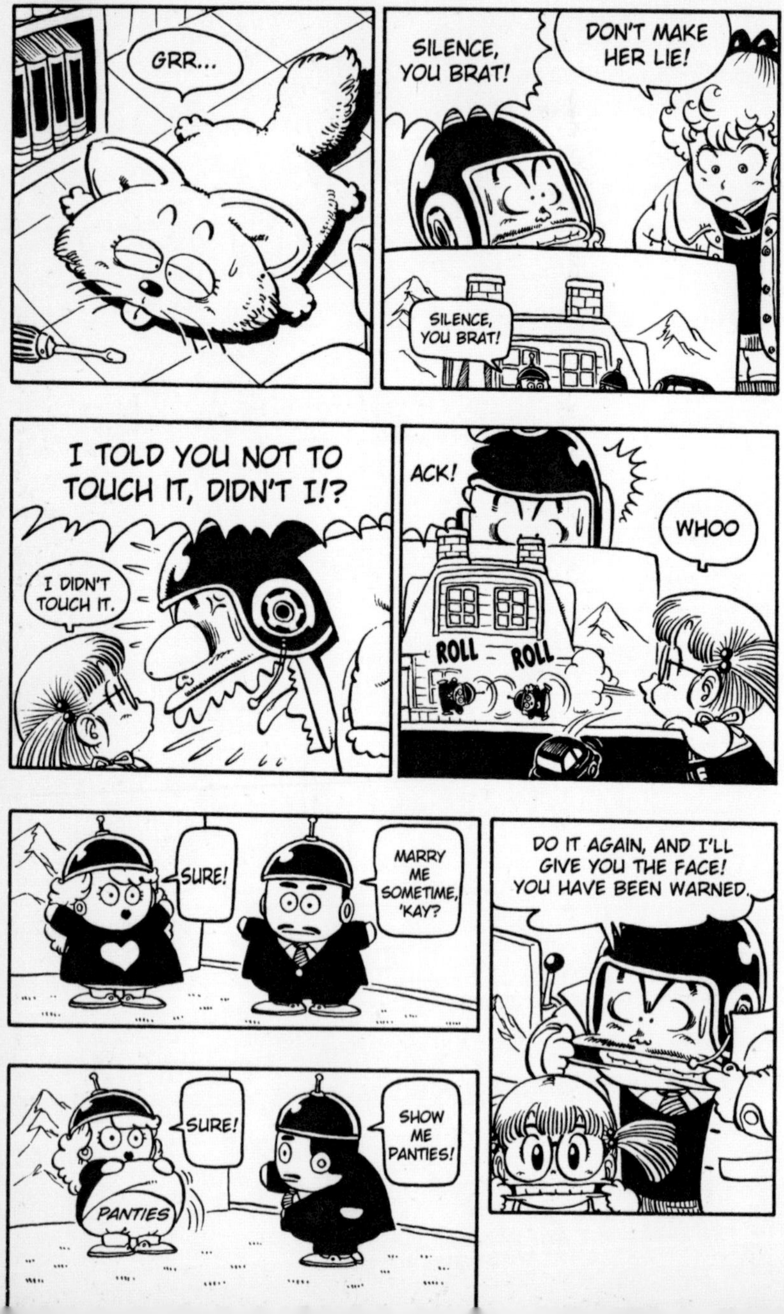
DON'T MAKE HER LIE!
SILENCE, YOU BRAT!
SILENCE, YOU BRAT!
GRR...
WHOO
ACK!
ROLL ROLL
I TOLD YOU NOT TO TOUCH IT, DIDN'T I!?
I DIDN'T TOUCH IT.
DO IT AGAIN, AND I'LL GIVE YOU THE FACE! YOU HAVE BEEN WARNED.
MARRY ME SOMETIME, 'KAY?
SURE!
SHOW ME PANTIES!
SURE!
PANTIES

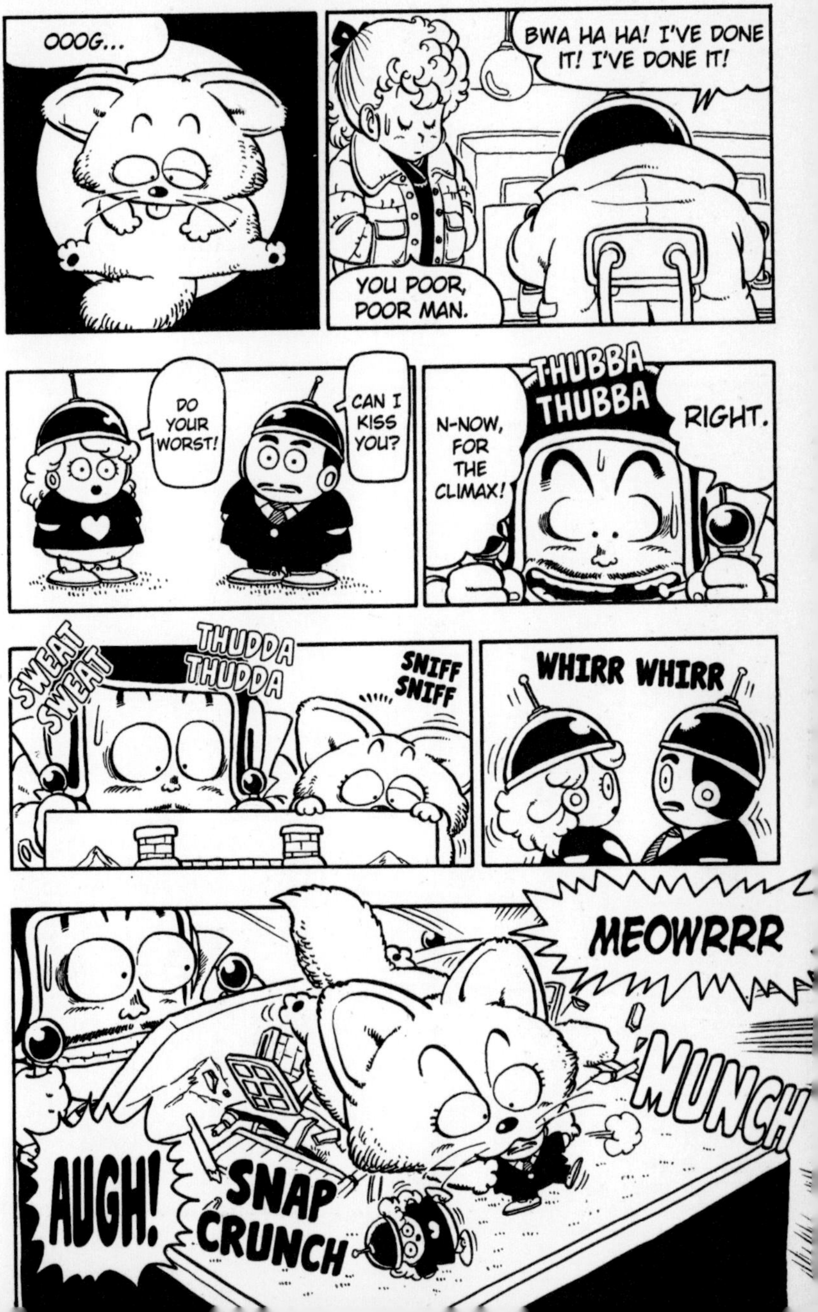
BWA HA HA! I'VE DONE IT! I'VE DONE IT!
YOU POOR, POOR MAN.
OOOG...
THUBBA THUBBA
RIGHT.
N-NOW, FOR THE CLIMAX!
CAN I KISS YOU?
DO YOUR WORST!
WHIRR WHIRR
SNIFF SNIFF
THUDDA THUDDA
SWEAT SWEAT
MEOWRRR
MUNCH
SNAP CRUNCH
AUGH!

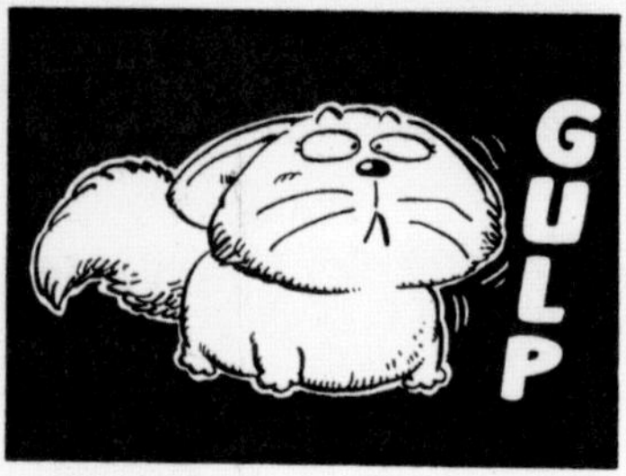
GULP

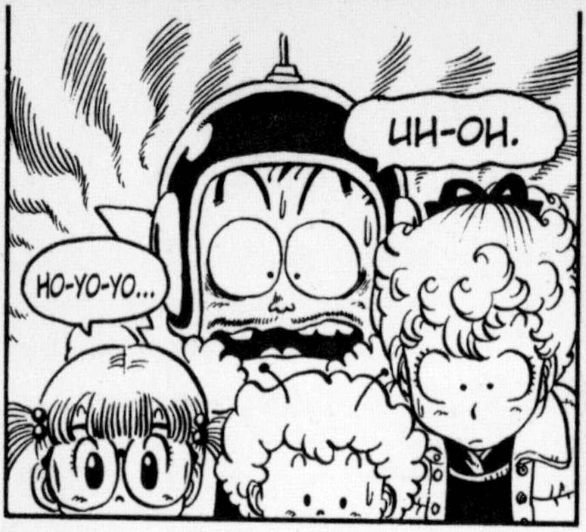
UH-OH.
HO-YO-YO...

THIRTY MINUTES LATER...

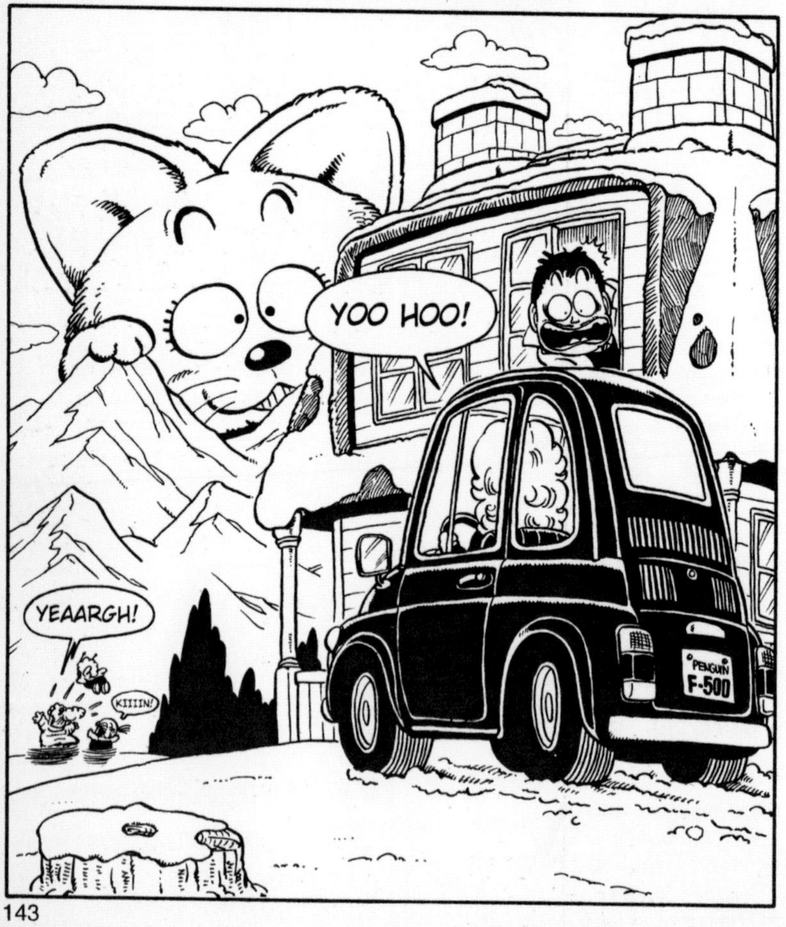
YOO HOO!
PENGUIN
F-500
YEAARGH!
KIIIIN!

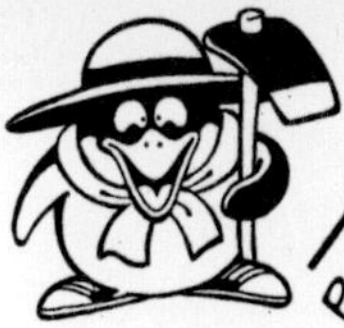

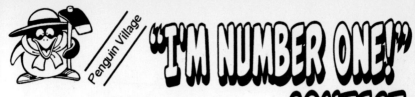

Penguin Village

"I'M NUMBER ONE!" CONTEST

Category:

RIDICULOUS

Poop and the Sun are neck and neck!

1st

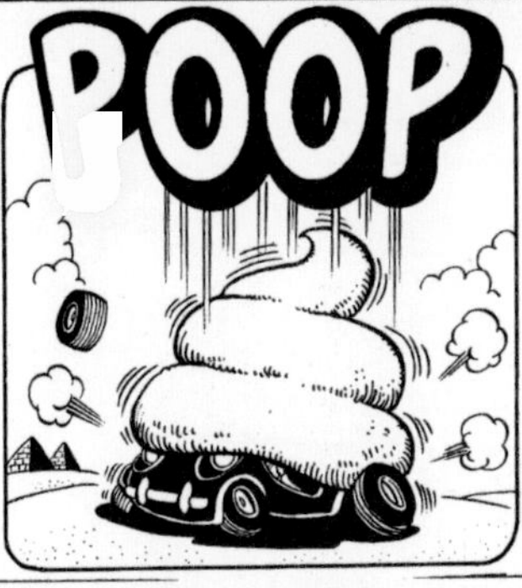
POOP

Poop
1,524 votes

- ★No one knows who pooped, but it's always there! Ridiculous!
- ★Always perfectly formed.
- ★I've never seen poop that big!
- ★Who would have thought I'd fall in love with poop!

2nd

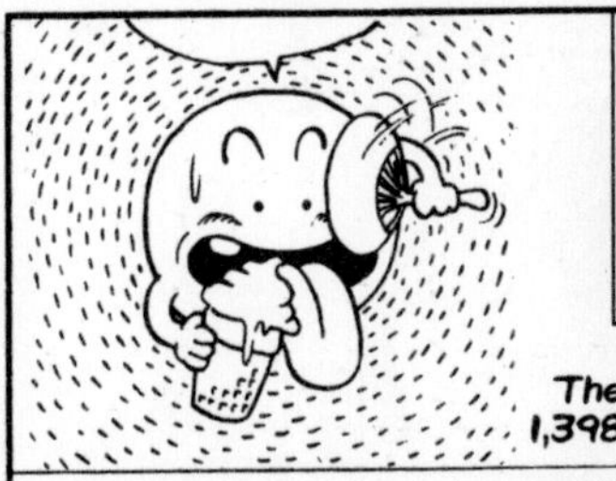

The Sun
1,398 votes

- ★The most obviously ridiculous.
- ★Always says the same thing! Ridiculous!
- ★That dumb look when he brushes his teeth.
- ★Don't oversleep! You're the Sun, for crying out loud!
- ★A Sun that eats ice cream...
- ★I wish **we** had a Sun like that.

3rd

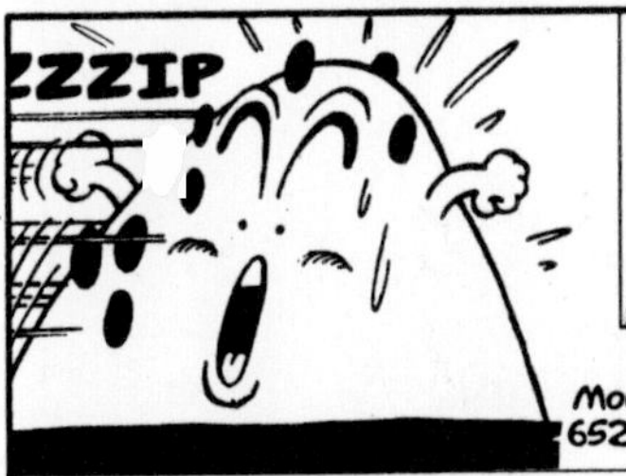
ZZZIP

Mountain
652 votes

- ★A mountain that sweats. Ridiculous!
- ★The blotches on it that are supposed to be trees.
- ★Why a mountain? Why?
- ★You only draw that mountain 'cause it's easy.
- ★The curve of its slope is exquisite.

Penguin Village Wars: Part 1

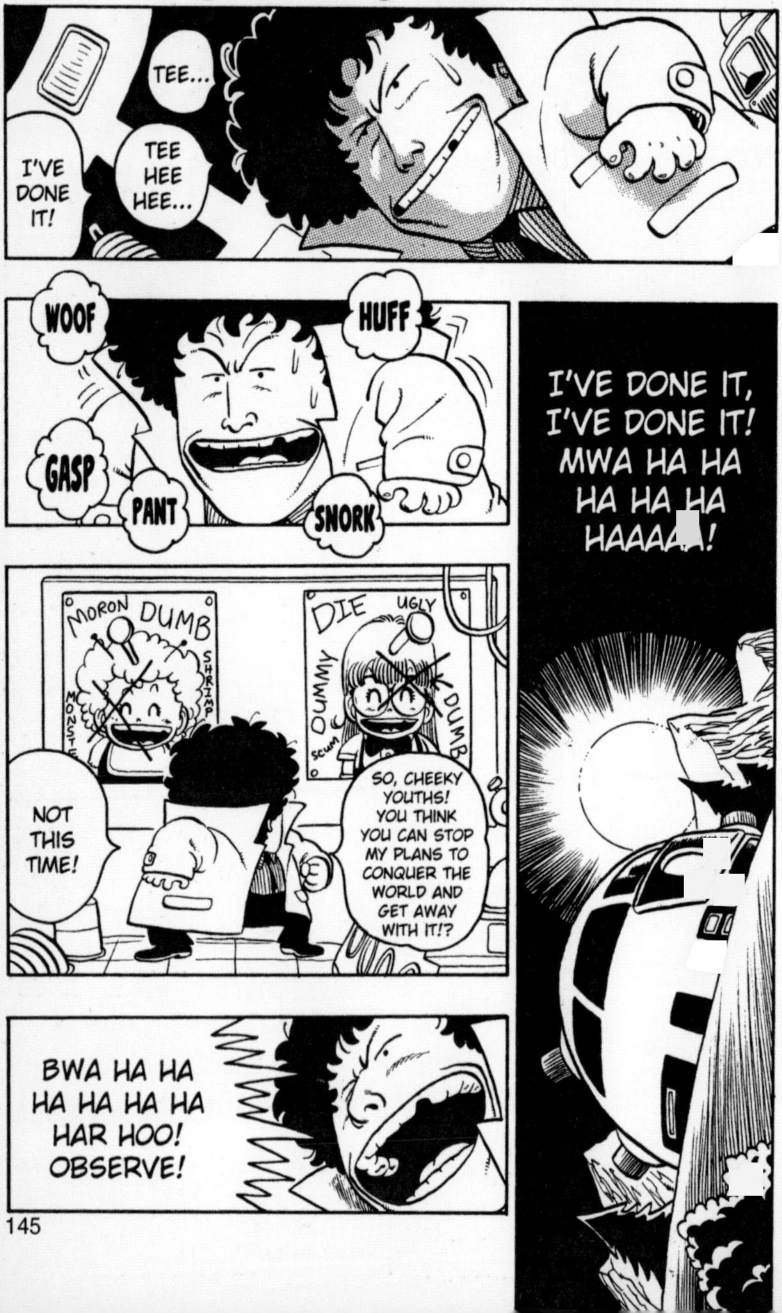

TEE...
TEE HEE HEE...
I'VE DONE IT!
I'VE DONE IT, I'VE DONE IT! MWA HA HA HA HA HA HAAAAA!
HUFF
WOOF
SNORK
PANT
GASP
DIE
UGLY
DUMMY
DUMB
scum
MORON
DUMB
SHRIMP
MONSTE
SO, CHEEKY YOUTHS! YOU THINK YOU CAN STOP MY PLANS TO CONQUER THE WORLD AND GET AWAY WITH IT!?
NOT THIS TIME!
BWA HA HA HA HA HA HA HAR HOO! OBSERVE!

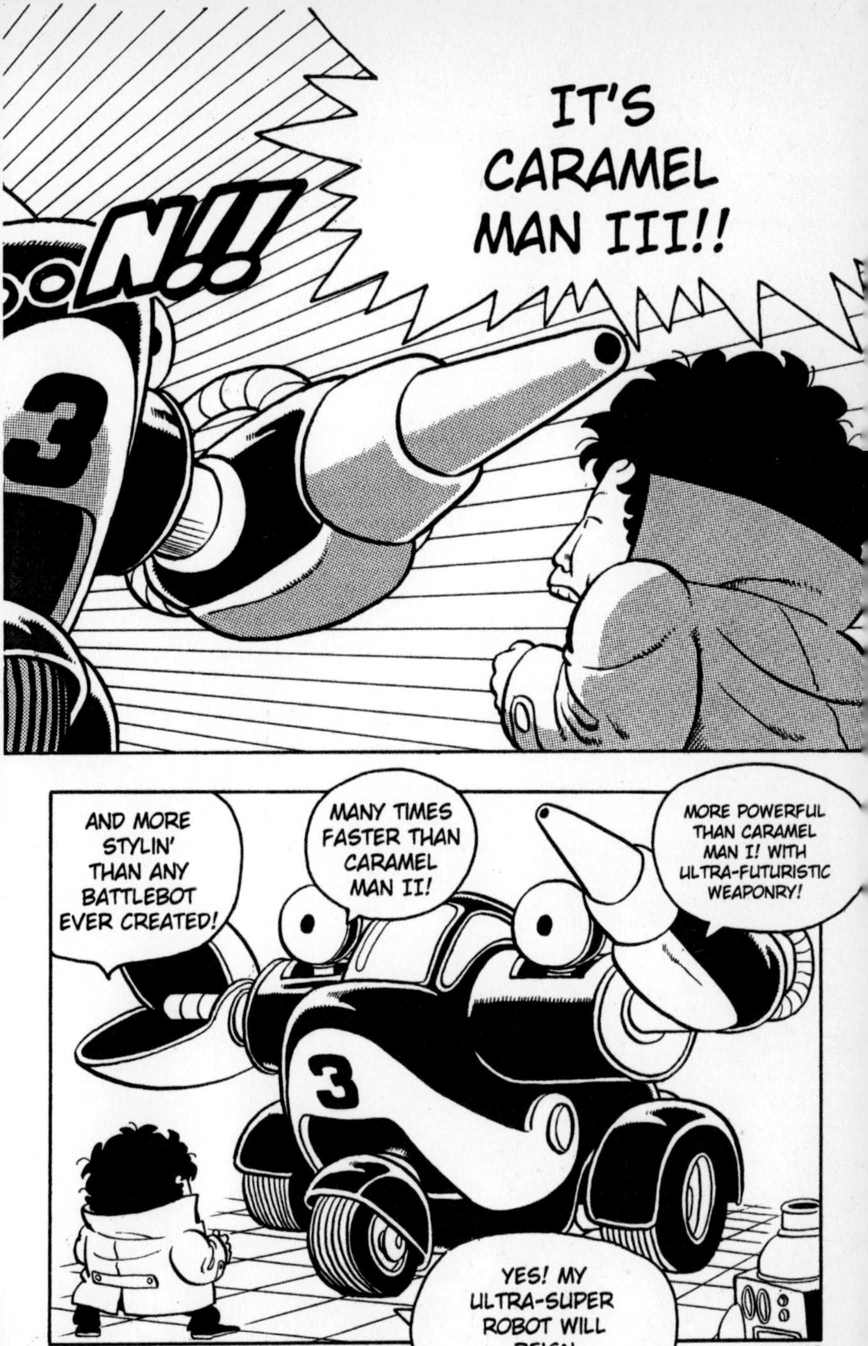

OON!!
IT'S CARAMEL MAN III!!
MORE POWERFUL THAN CARAMEL MAN I! WITH ULTRA-FUTURISTIC WEAPONRY!
MANY TIMES FASTER THAN CARAMEL MAN II!
AND MORE STYLIN' THAN ANY BATTLEBOT EVER CREATED!
YES! MY ULTRA-SUPER ROBOT WILL REIGN SUPREME!

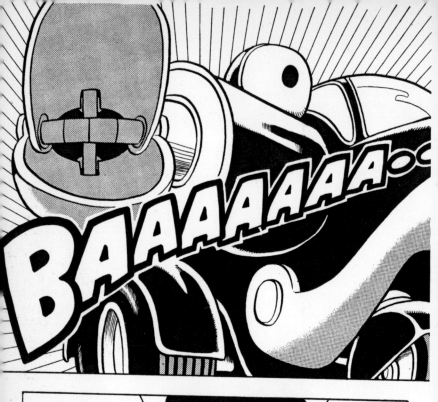

BAAAAAAA ∞∞

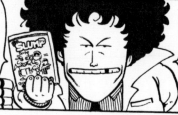

GENIUS THAT I AM, I READ VOLUMES 1 TO 3 OF *DR. SLUMP* AND CONCOCTED A PLAN!

BUT FIRST, I MUST DEAL WITH THOSE FIENDISH KIDS!

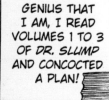

FIRST, FOR THAT WINGED RUNT THAT EATS EVERYTHING...

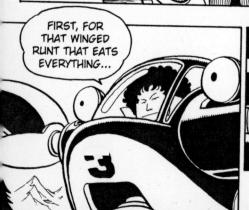

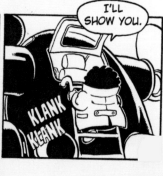

I'LL SHOW YOU.

KLANK KLANK

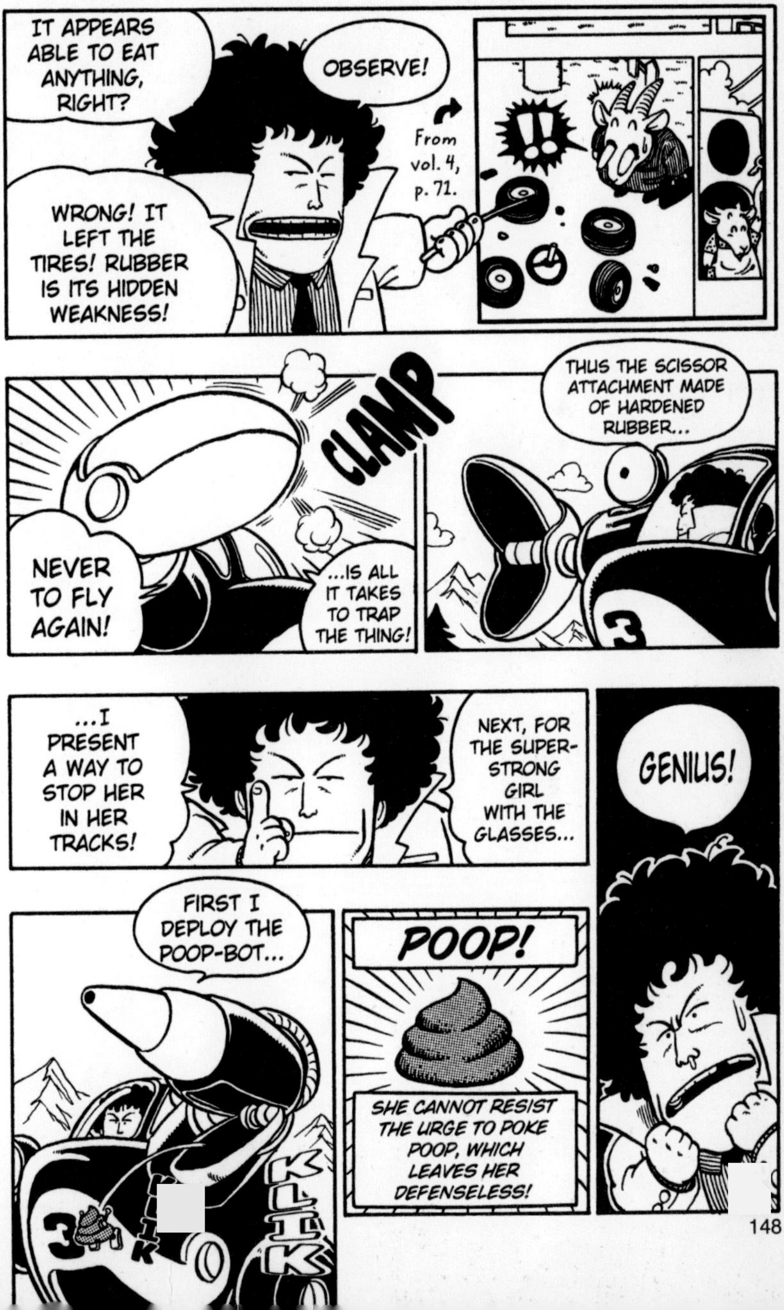
!!
From vol. 4, p. 71.
OBSERVE!
IT APPEARS ABLE TO EAT ANYTHING, RIGHT?
WRONG! IT LEFT THE TIRES! RUBBER IS ITS HIDDEN WEAKNESS!
THUS THE SCISSOR ATTACHMENT MADE OF HARDENED RUBBER...
CLAMP
...IS ALL IT TAKES TO TRAP THE THING!
NEVER TO FLY AGAIN!
GENIUS!
NEXT, FOR THE SUPER-STRONG GIRL WITH THE GLASSES...
...I PRESENT A WAY TO STOP HER IN HER TRACKS!
POOP!
SHE CANNOT RESIST THE URGE TO POKE POOP, WHICH LEAVES HER DEFENSELESS!
FIRST I DEPLOY THE POOP-BOT...
KLIK
KLIK

READ THIS WAY

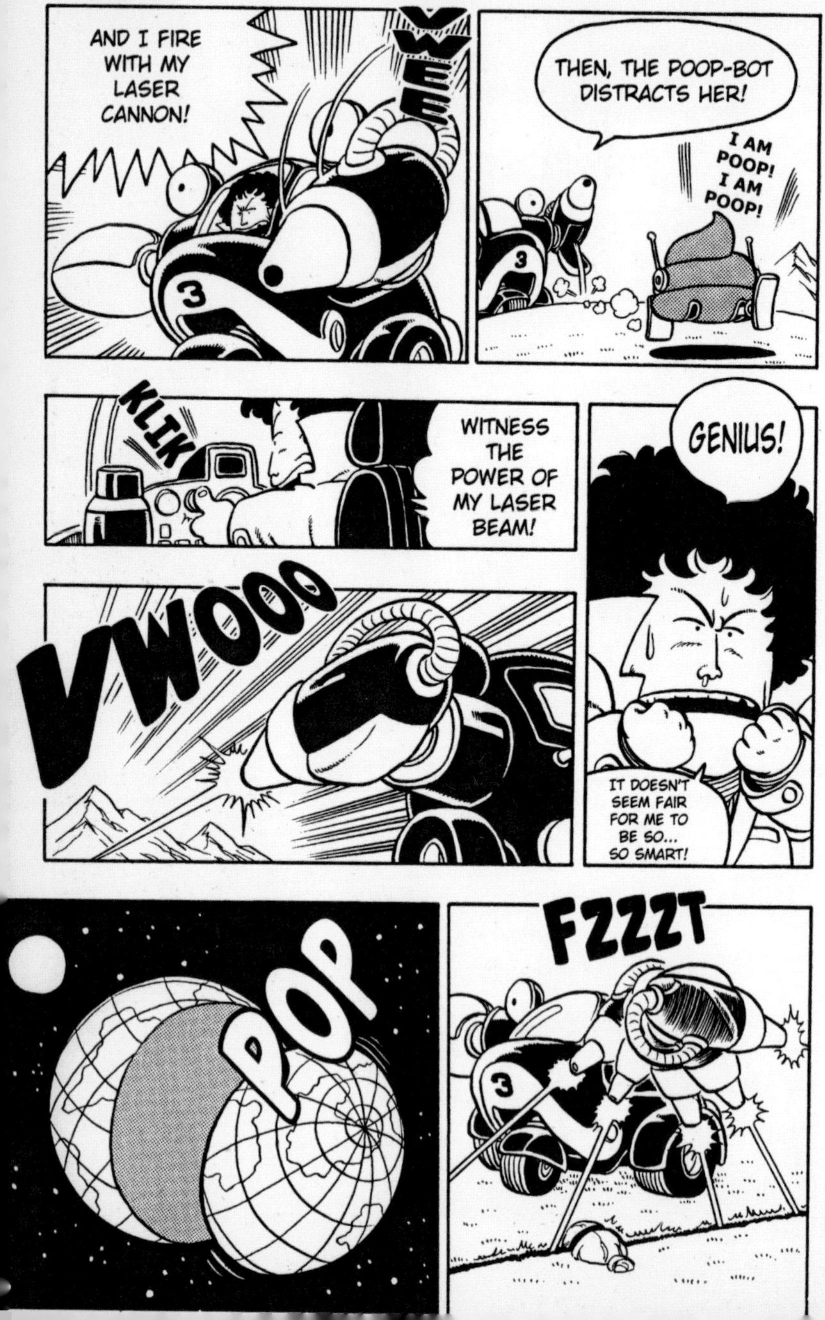
THEN, THE POOP-BOT DISTRACTS HER!
I AM POOP! I AM POOP!
AND I FIRE WITH MY LASER CANNON!
WEE
GENIUS!
IT DOESN'T SEEM FAIR FOR ME TO BE SO... SO SMART!
KLIK
WITNESS THE POWER OF MY LASER BEAM!
VWOOO
FZZZT
POP

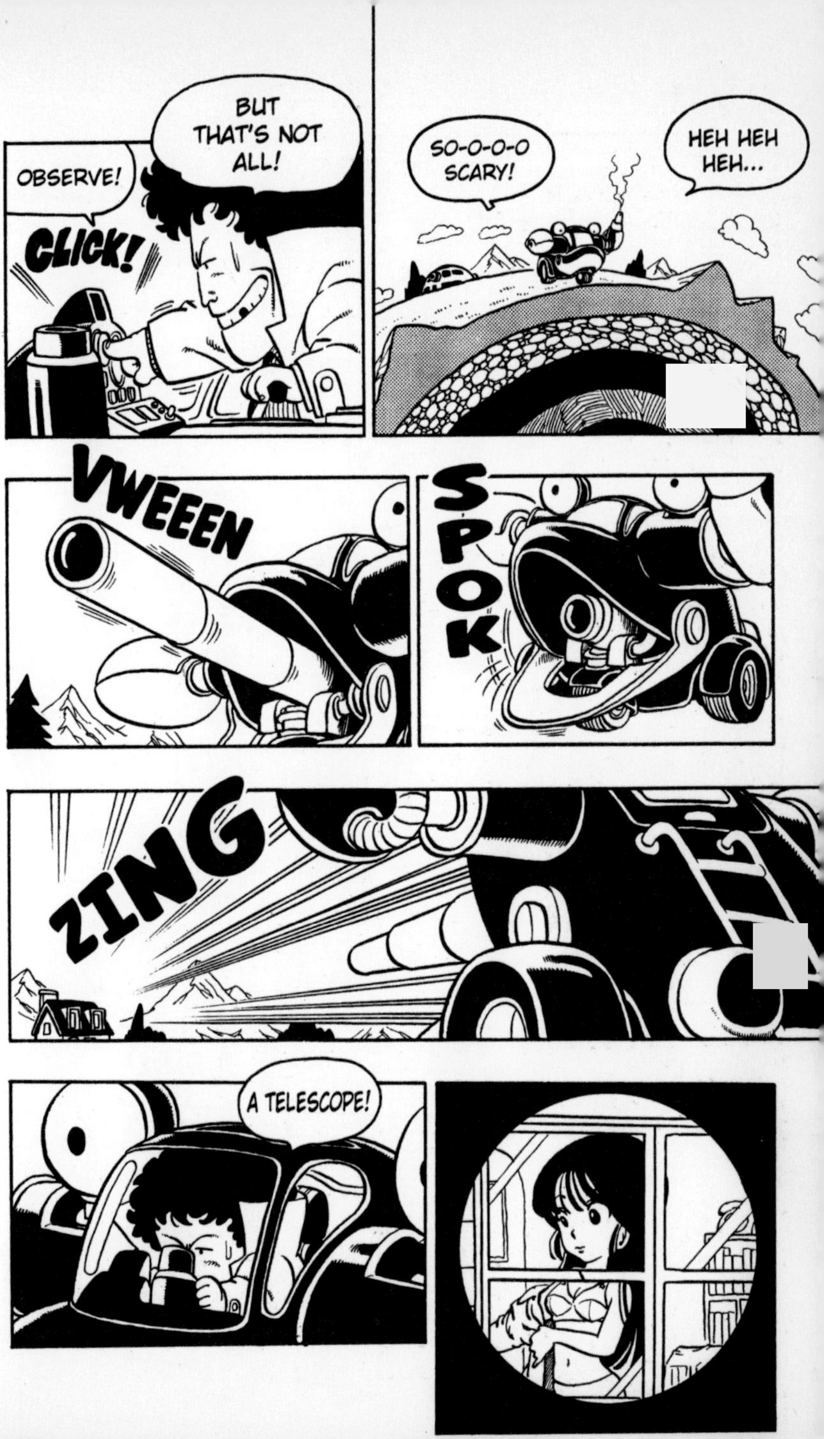
HEH HEH HEH...
SO-O-O-O SCARY!
BUT THAT'S NOT ALL!
OBSERVE!
CLICK!
SPOK
VWEEEN
ZING
A TELESCOPE!

READ THIS WAY

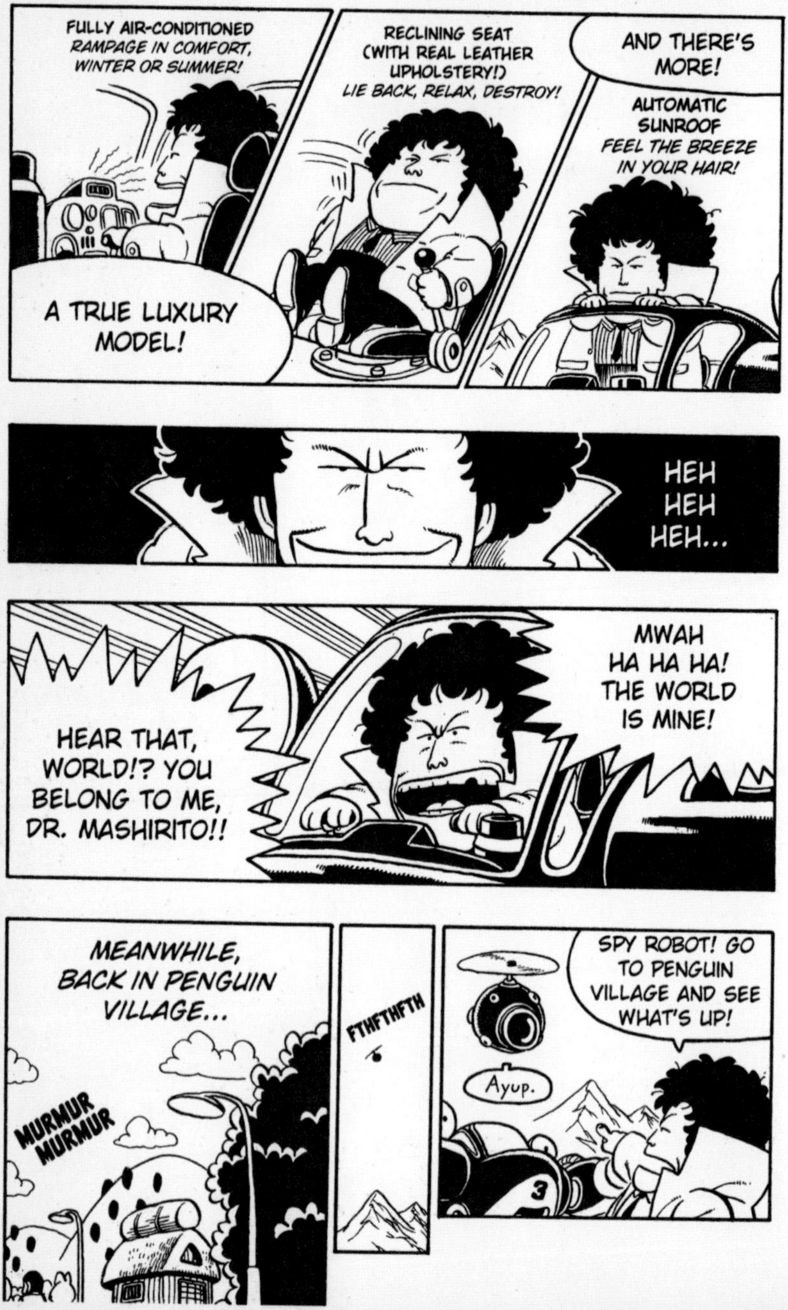
AND THERE'S MORE!
AUTOMATIC SUNROOF FEEL THE BREEZE IN YOUR HAIR!
RECLINING SEAT (WITH REAL LEATHER UPHOLSTERY!) LIE BACK, RELAX, DESTROY!
FULLY AIR-CONDITIONED RAMPAGE IN COMFORT, WINTER OR SUMMER!
A TRUE LUXURY MODEL!
HEH HEH HEH...
MWAH HA HA HA! THE WORLD IS MINE!
HEAR THAT, WORLD!? YOU BELONG TO ME, DR. MASHIRITO!!
SPY ROBOT! GO TO PENGUIN VILLAGE AND SEE WHAT'S UP!
Ayup.
FTHFTHFTH
MEANWHILE, BACK IN PENGUIN VILLAGE...
MURMUR MURMUR

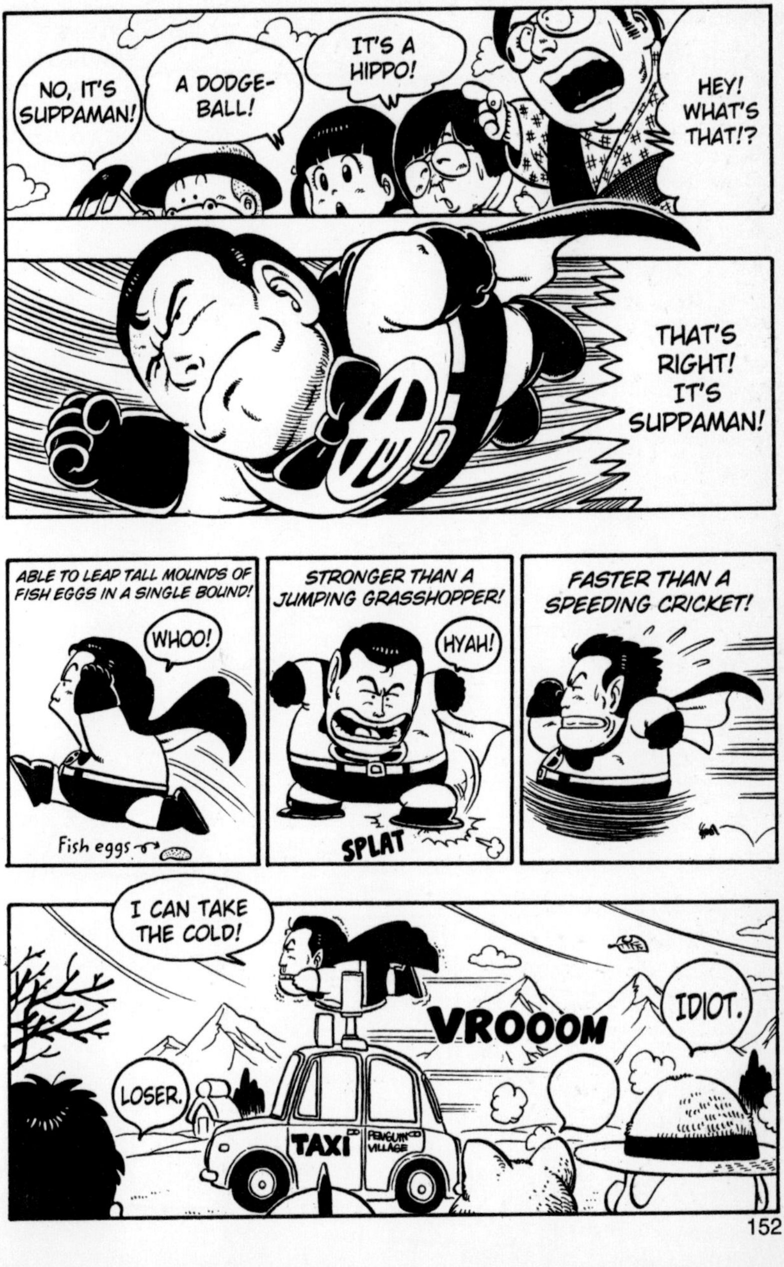
HEY! WHAT'S THAT!?
IT'S A HIPPO!
A DODGE-BALL!
NO, IT'S SUPPAMAN!
THAT'S RIGHT! IT'S SUPPAMAN!
FASTER THAN A SPEEDING CRICKET!
STRONGER THAN A JUMPING GRASSHOPPER!
HYAH!
SPLAT
ABLE TO LEAP TALL MOUNDS OF FISH EGGS IN A SINGLE BOUND!
WHOO!
Fish eggs
IDIOT.
I CAN TAKE THE COLD!
VROOOM
TAXI
PENGUIN VILLAGE
LOSER.

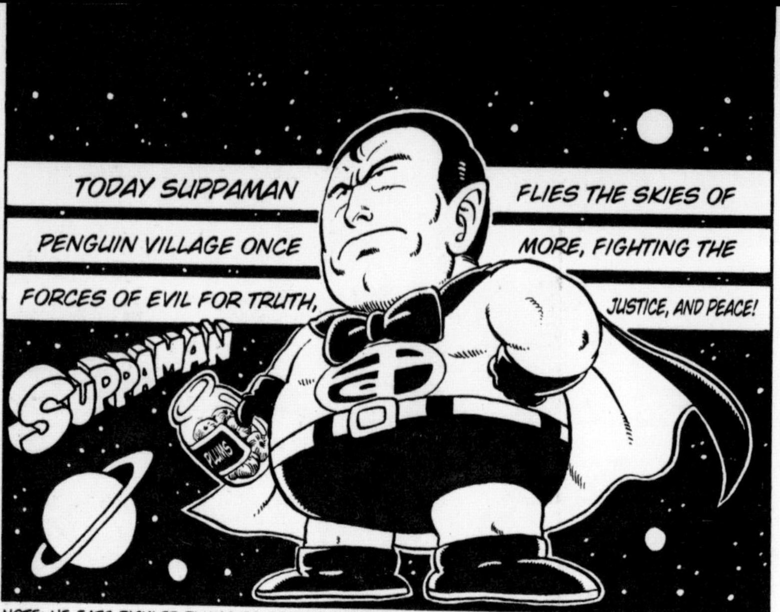
TODAY SUPPAMAN FLIES THE SKIES OF PENGUIN VILLAGE ONCE MORE, FIGHTING THE FORCES OF EVIL FOR TRUTH, JUSTICE, AND PEACE!
SUPPAMAN
PLUMS

NOTE: HE EATS PICKLED PLUMS TO BECOME SUPPAMAN (*SUPPA* MEANS "SOUR" IN JAPANESE).

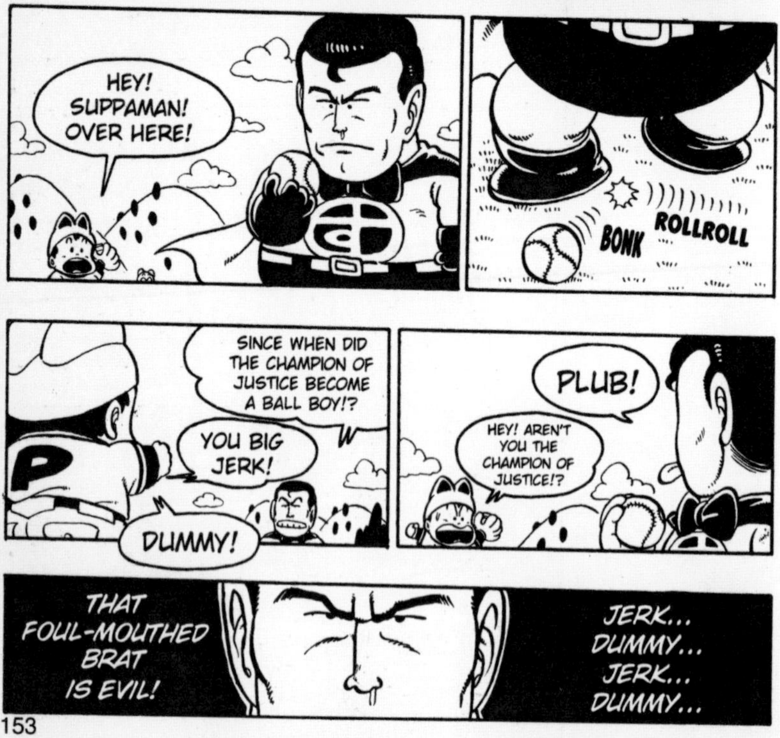
BONK
ROLLROLL
HEY! SUPPAMAN! OVER HERE!
PLUB!
HEY! AREN'T YOU THE CHAMPION OF JUSTICE!?
SINCE WHEN DID THE CHAMPION OF JUSTICE BECOME A BALL BOY!?
YOU BIG JERK!
DUMMY!
JERK... DUMMY... JERK... DUMMY...
THAT FOUL-MOUTHED BRAT IS EVIL!

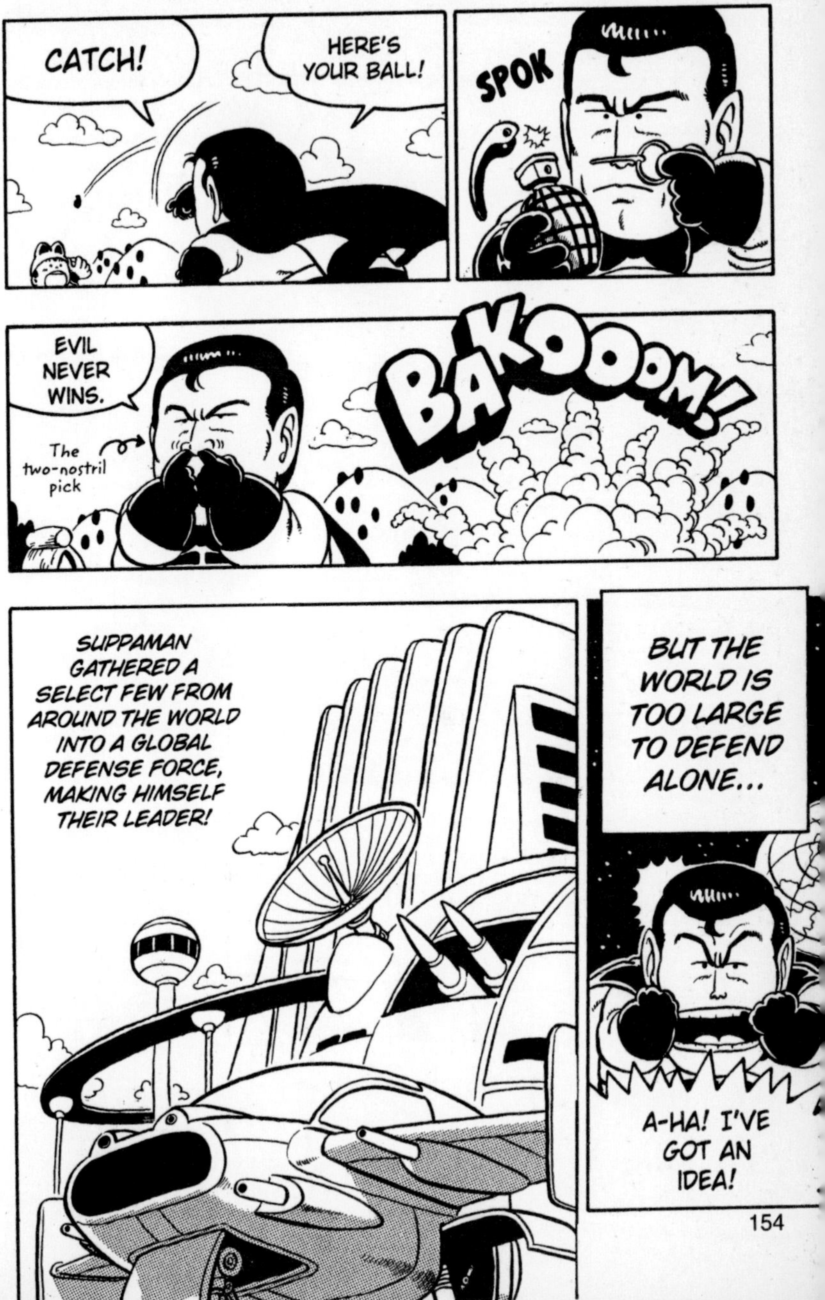
SPOK
HERE'S YOUR BALL!
CATCH!
BAKOOOM!
EVIL NEVER WINS.
The two-nostril pick
BUT THE WORLD IS TOO LARGE TO DEFEND ALONE...
A-HA! I'VE GOT AN IDEA!
SUPPAMAN GATHERED A SELECT FEW FROM AROUND THE WORLD INTO A GLOBAL DEFENSE FORCE, MAKING HIMSELF THEIR LEADER!

READ THIS WAY

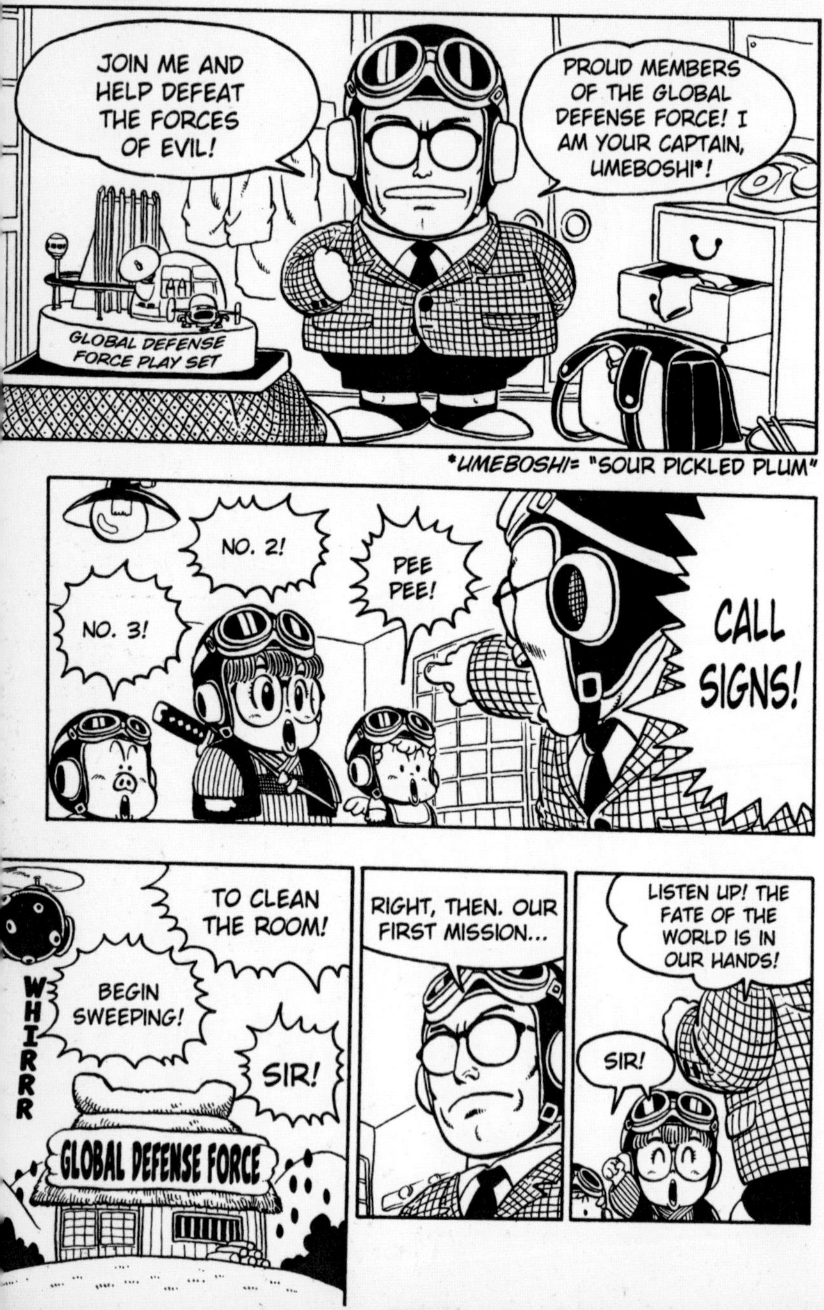
PROUD MEMBERS OF THE GLOBAL DEFENSE FORCE! I AM YOUR CAPTAIN, UMEBOSHI*!
JOIN ME AND HELP DEFEAT THE FORCES OF EVIL!
GLOBAL DEFENSE FORCE PLAY SET
*UMEBOSHI= "SOUR PICKLED PLUM"
CALL SIGNS!
PEE PEE!
NO. 2!
NO. 3!
LISTEN UP! THE FATE OF THE WORLD IS IN OUR HANDS!
SIR!
RIGHT, THEN. OUR FIRST MISSION...
TO CLEAN THE ROOM!
BEGIN SWEEPING!
SIR!
WHIRRR
GLOBAL DEFENSE FORCE

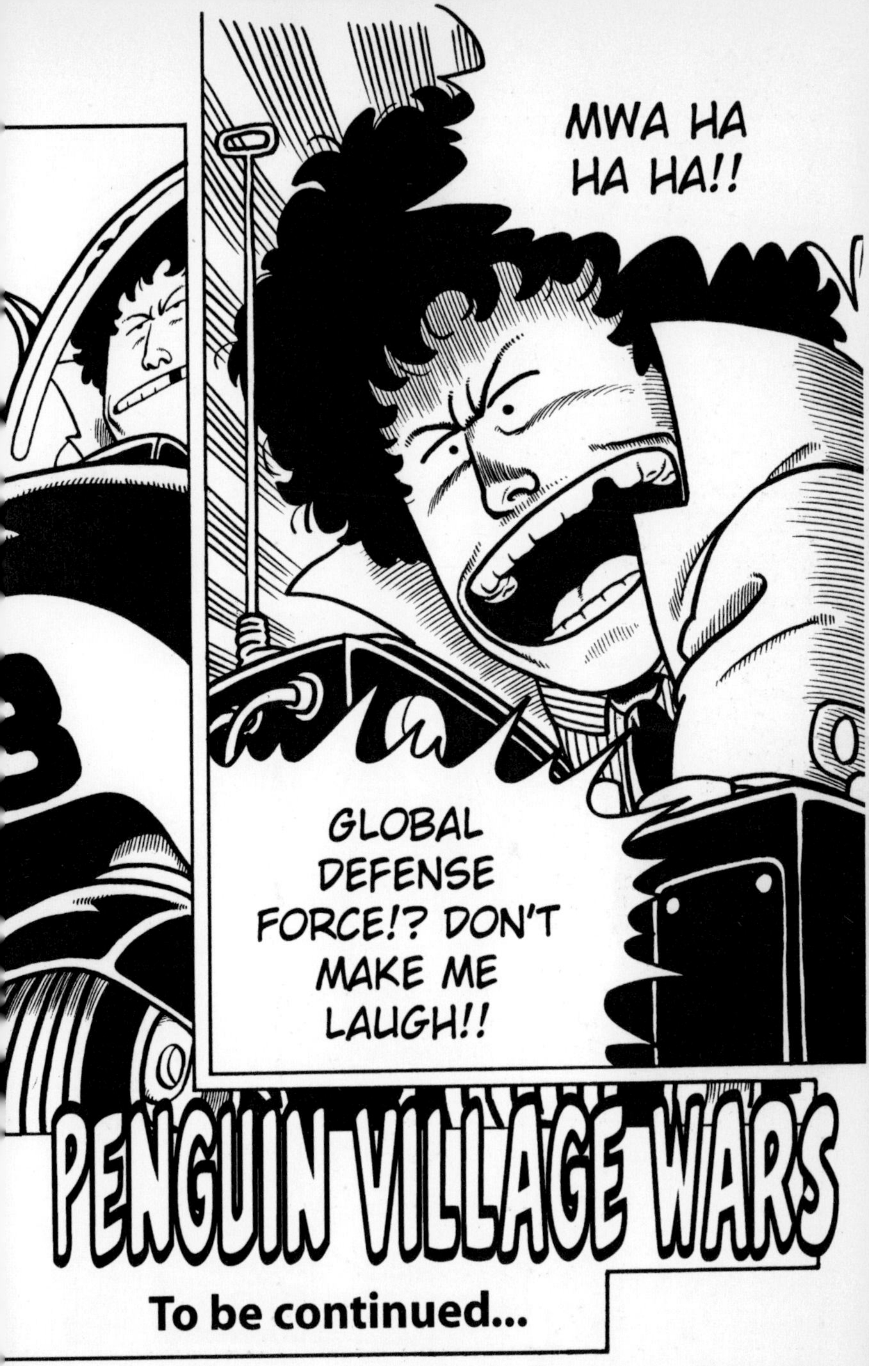
MWA HA HA HA!!
GLOBAL DEFENSE FORCE!? DON'T MAKE ME LAUGH!!
PENGUIN VILLAGE WARS
To be continued...

READ THIS WAY

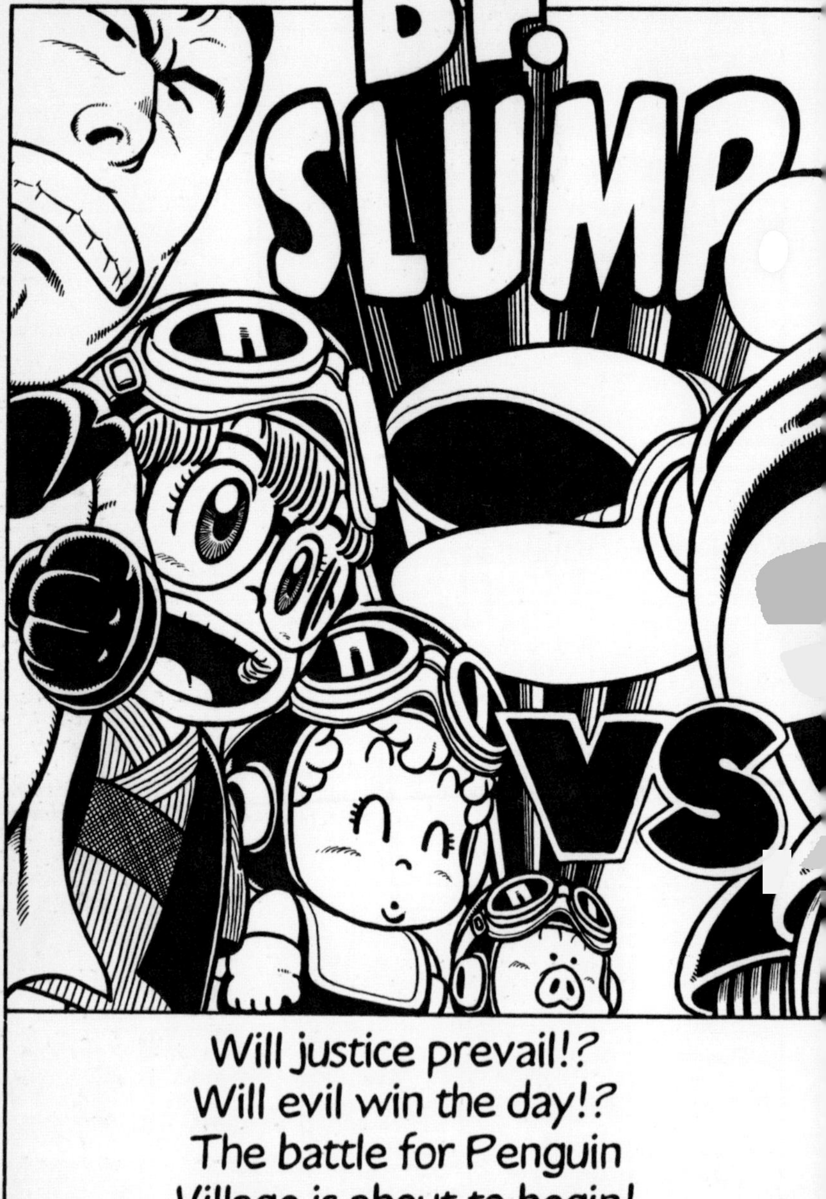
Dr. SLUMP
VS
Will justice prevail!?
Will evil win the day!?
The battle for Penguin
Village is about to begin!

Penguin Village "I'M NUMBER ONE!" CONTEST Category: Ridiculous

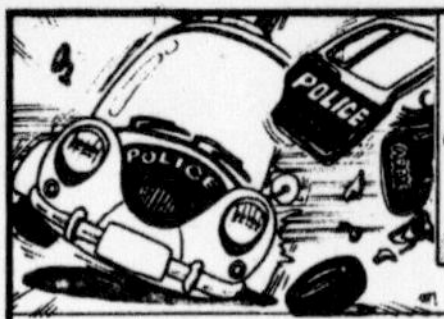
POLICE
POLICE

4th

Police Cruiser
300 votes

★Poor car, always getting destroyed by Arale.
★No matter how many times she destroys it, it always comes back. Incredible!

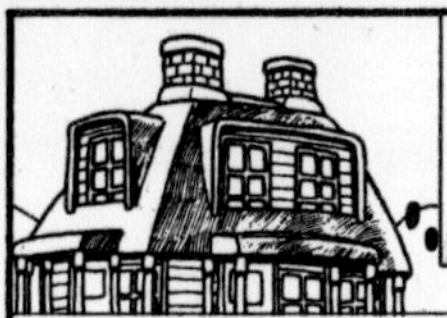

5th

The Norimaki Residence
294 votes

★Ridiculous on account of its occupants.
★Destroyed time and time again, yet it's always back to normal in the next chapter. Ridiculous construction.
★Such a happy household, it must be dumb.

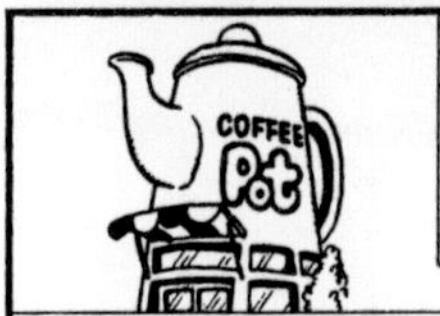
COFFEE
Pot

6th

The Coffee Pot
286 votes

★I like the cute puffs of steam.
★I would go there every day.
★I would like to drink Aoi's coffee some day.

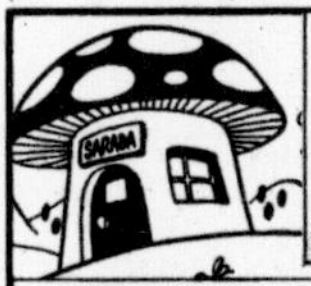
SARADA

7th

Kinoko Sarada's House
232 votes

★It changed shape between its first and second appearances.
★It looks like a mushroom. How dumb!

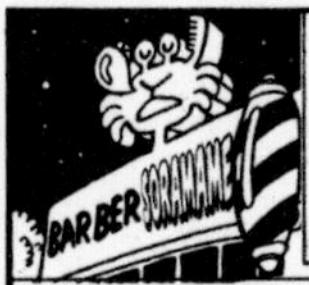
BARBER SORAMAME

8th

Barbershop Soramame
228 votes

★I like the crab logo, and the fact that there are never any customers.
★It's Taro's house; it has to be cool!

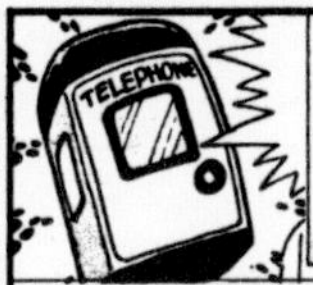
TELEPHONE

9th

The Phone Booth
222 votes

★No one uses it, except for Suppaman.
★Where are the telephone poles, huh?

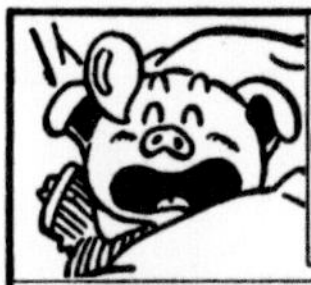

10th

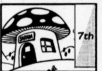

Oinkity Oink
218 votes

★Always a completely different character each time. Ridiculous!
★When he admits he loves Betty in the next town over.

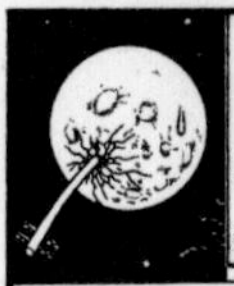

11th (tie)

The Moon
210 votes

★Destroyed by Arale on each of its rare appearances.
★Completely overshadowed by the Sun's popularity.

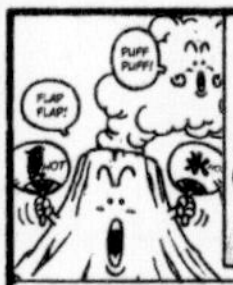
PUFF PUFF!
FLAP FLAP!

11th (tie)

Mt. Flapflap
210 votes

★That dumb face, and those dumb fans.
★Wherever Chivil and Witchey live has to be ridiculous.

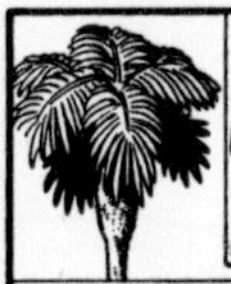

13th

The Palm Tree
152 votes

★It's amazing to find a tropical tree in Penguin Village, where it snows!

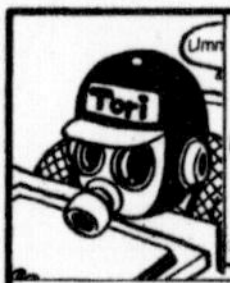
Umm
Tori

14th

Akira Toriyama
148 votes

★Always writes that dumb manga.
★Ignoramus
★Fool
★Snotty-nosed reject
★Eat poop, freak.

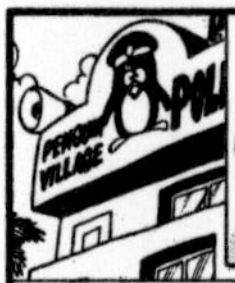
PENGUIN VILLAGE
POL

15th

Penguin Village Police Dept.
120 votes

★Completely useless and therefore, ridiculous.
★Needless

Penguin Village Wars: Part 2

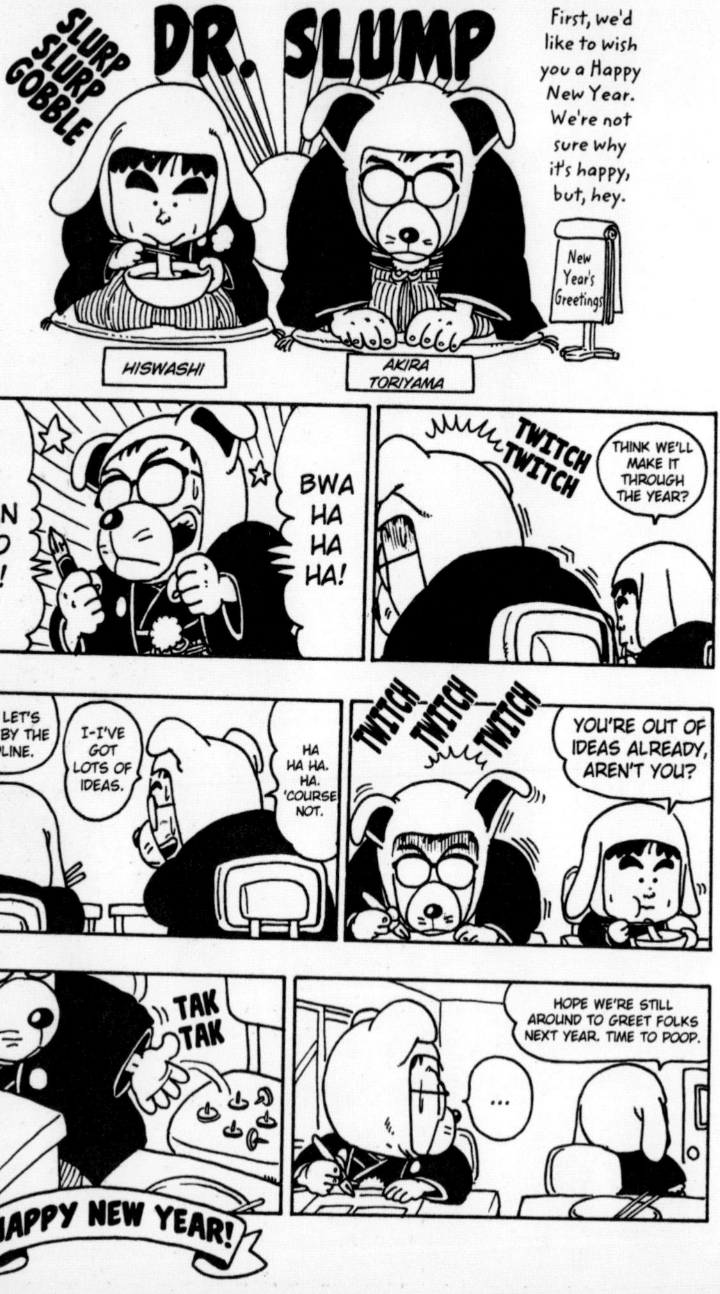
First, we'd like to wish you a Happy New Year. We're not sure why it's happy, but, hey.
DR. SLUMP
SLURP SLURP GOBBLE
New Year's Greetings
AKIRA TORIYAMA
HISWASHI
TWITCH TWITCH
THINK WE'LL MAKE IT THROUGH THE YEAR?
BWA HA HA HA!
I CAN DO IT!
TWITCH TWITCH TWITCH
YOU'RE OUT OF IDEAS ALREADY, AREN'T YOU?
HA HA HA. HA. 'COURSE NOT.
I-I'VE GOT LOTS OF IDEAS.
THEN LET'S FINISH BY THE DEADLINE.
HOPE WE'RE STILL AROUND TO GREET FOLKS NEXT YEAR. TIME TO POOP.
...
TAK TAK
TACKS
HAPPY NEW YEAR!

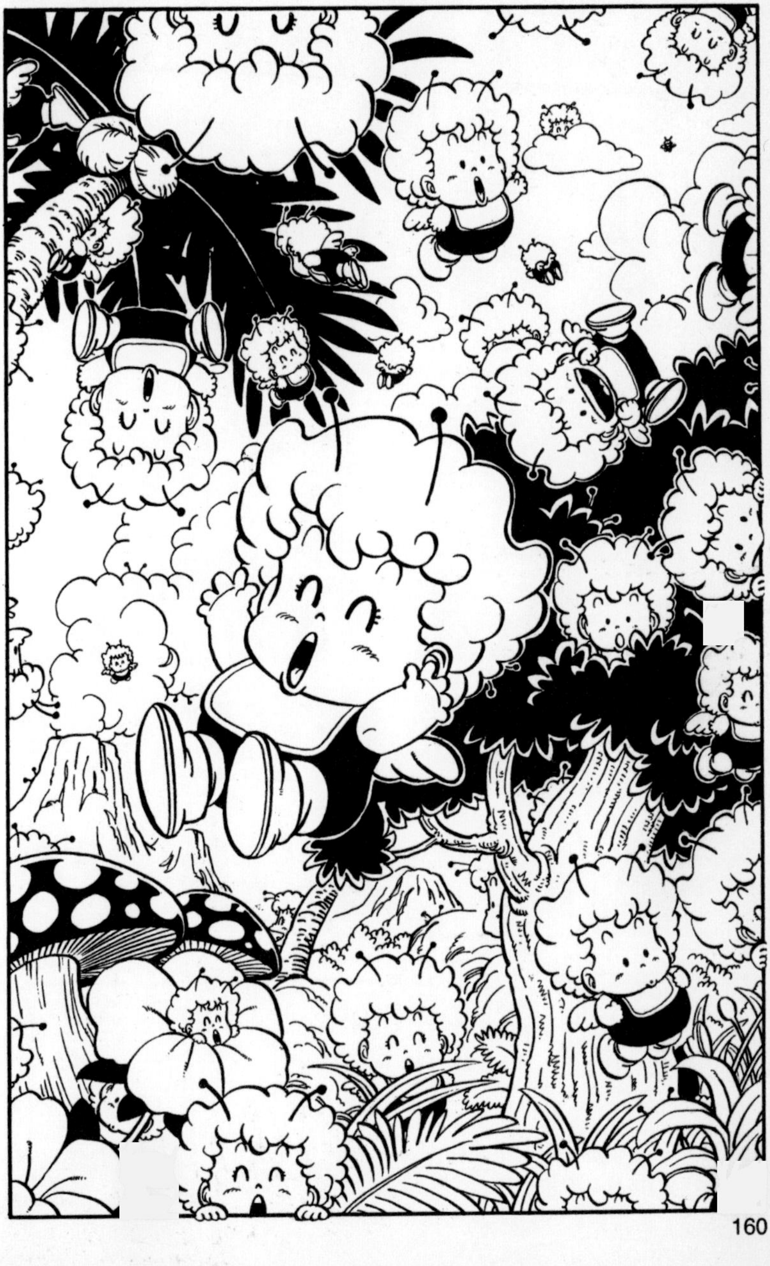

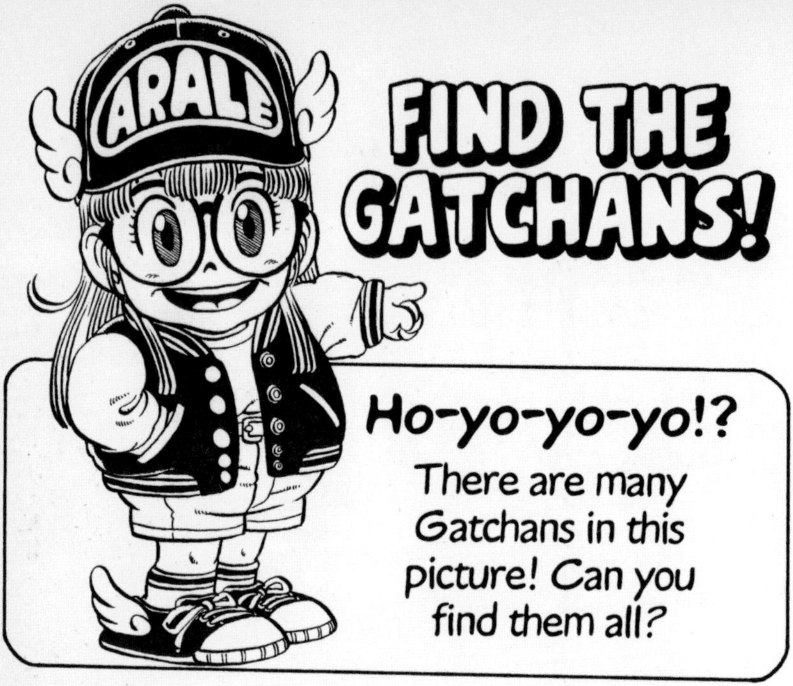
FIND THE GATCHANS!
Ho-yo-yo-yo!?
There are many Gatchans in this picture! Can you find them all?

Penguin Village Wars
Part 2

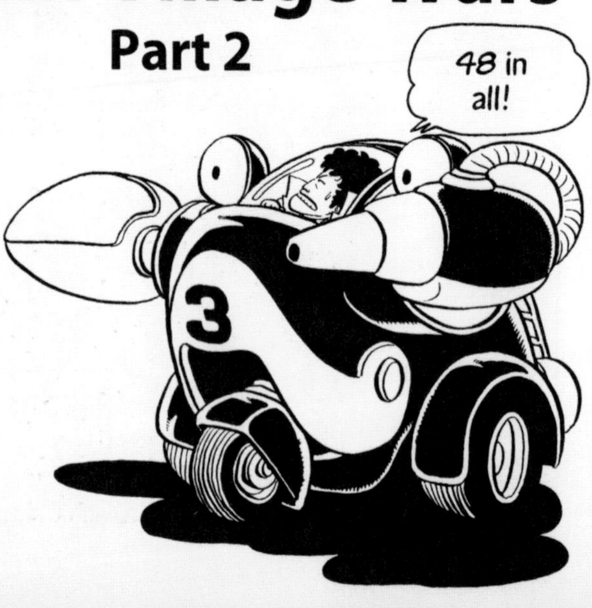
48 in all!

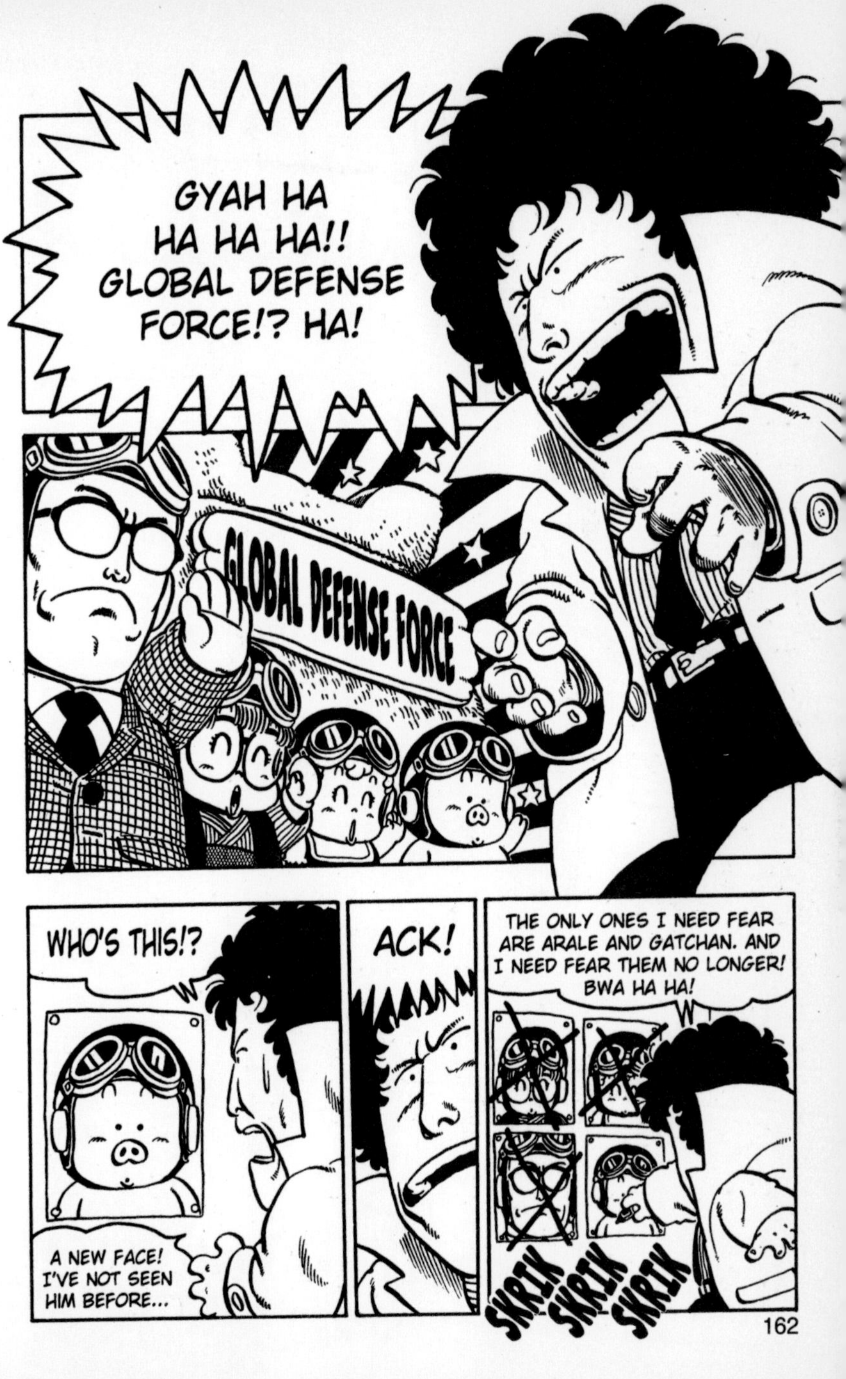
GYAH HA HA HA HA!! GLOBAL DEFENSE FORCE!? HA!
GLOBAL DEFENSE FORCE
THE ONLY ONES I NEED FEAR ARE ARALE AND GATCHAN. AND I NEED FEAR THEM NO LONGER! BWA HA HA!
SKRIK SKRIK SKRIK
ACK!
WHO'S THIS!?
A NEW FACE! I'VE NOT SEEN HIM BEFORE...

READ THIS WAY

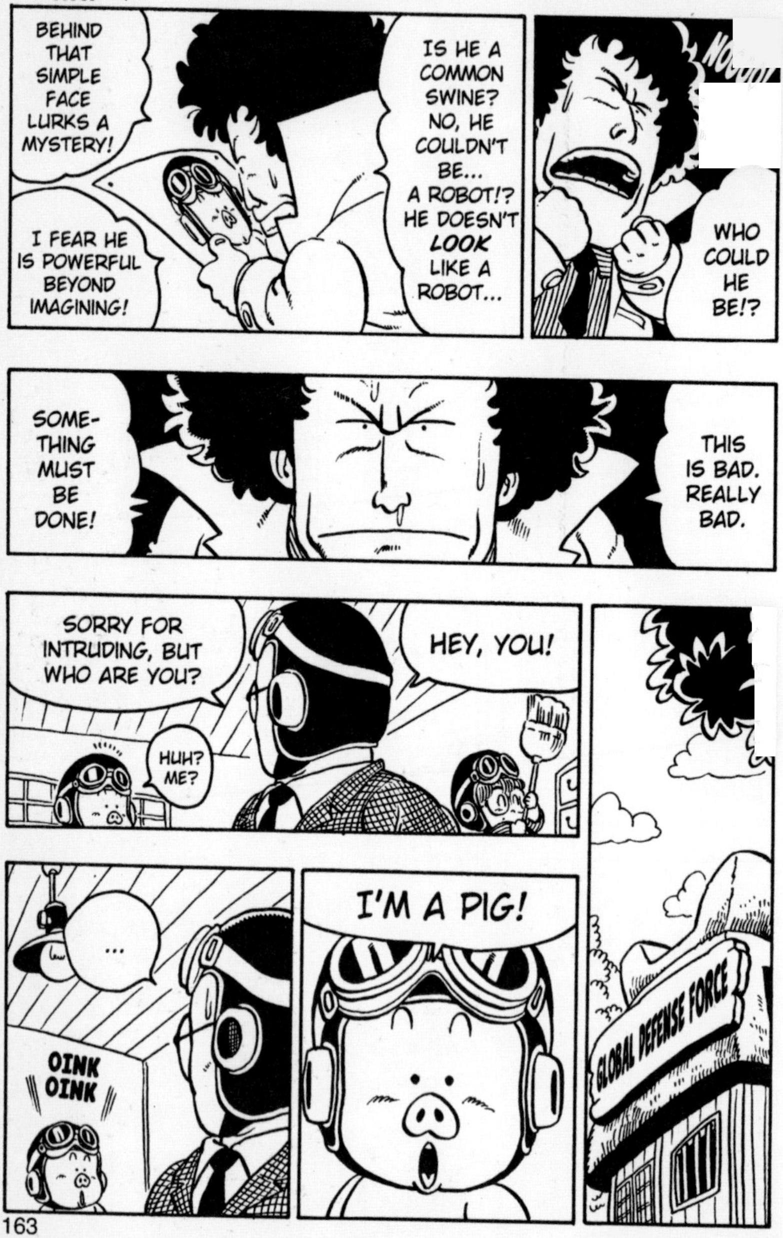
WHO COULD HE BE!?
IS HE A COMMON SWINE? NO, HE COULDN'T BE... A ROBOT!? HE DOESN'T LOOK LIKE A ROBOT...
BEHIND THAT SIMPLE FACE LURKS A MYSTERY!
I FEAR HE IS POWERFUL BEYOND IMAGINING!
THIS IS BAD. REALLY BAD.
SOME-THING MUST BE DONE!
GLOBAL DEFENSE FORCE
HEY, YOU!
SORRY FOR INTRUDING, BUT WHO ARE YOU?
HUH? ME?
I'M A PIG!
...
OINK OINK

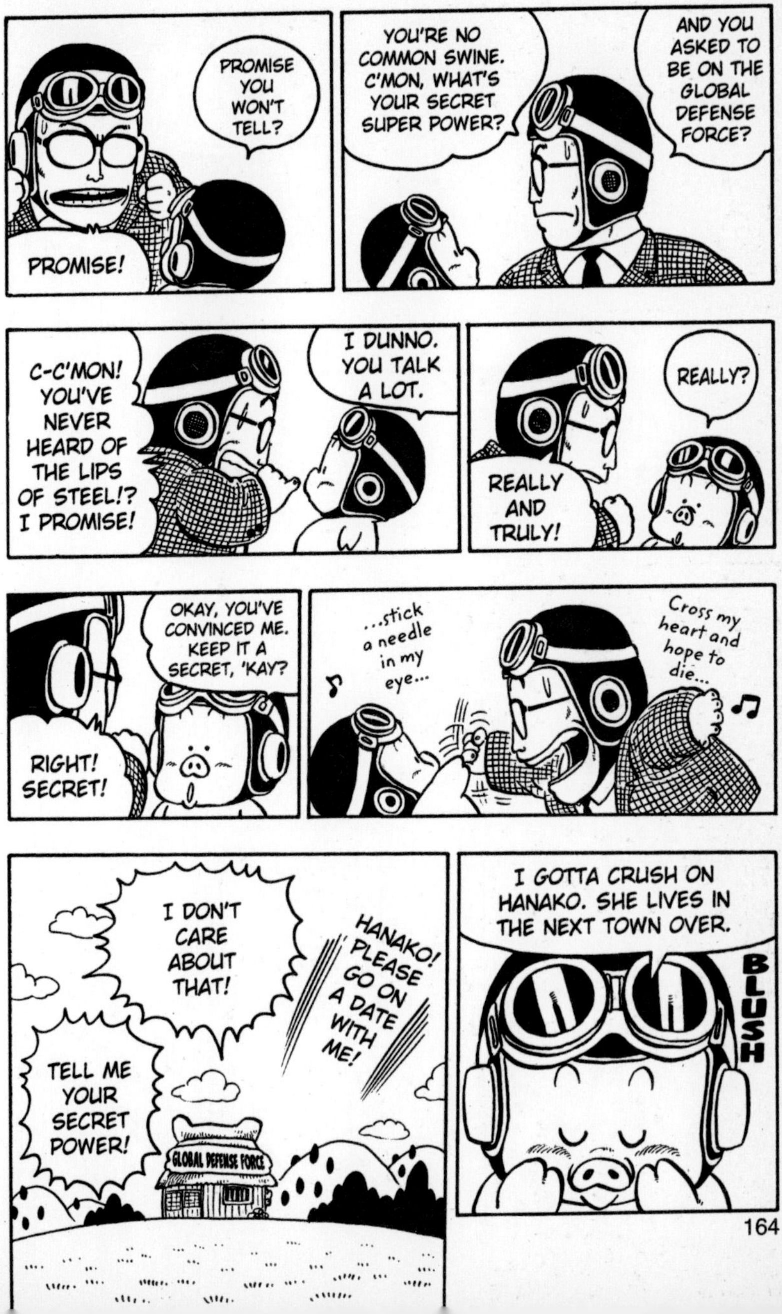
AND YOU ASKED TO BE ON THE GLOBAL DEFENSE FORCE?
YOU'RE NO COMMON SWINE. C'MON, WHAT'S YOUR SECRET SUPER POWER?
PROMISE YOU WON'T TELL?
PROMISE!
REALLY?
REALLY AND TRULY!
I DUNNO. YOU TALK A LOT.
C-C'MON! YOU'VE NEVER HEARD OF THE LIPS OF STEEL!? I PROMISE!
Cross my heart and hope to die...
...stick a needle in my eye...
OKAY, YOU'VE CONVINCED ME. KEEP IT A SECRET, 'KAY?
RIGHT! SECRET!
I GOTTA CRUSH ON HANAKO. SHE LIVES IN THE NEXT TOWN OVER.
BLUSH
HANAKO! PLEASE GO ON A DATE WITH ME!
I DON'T CARE ABOUT THAT!
TELL ME YOUR SECRET POWER!
GLOBAL DEFENSE FORCE

READ THIS WAY

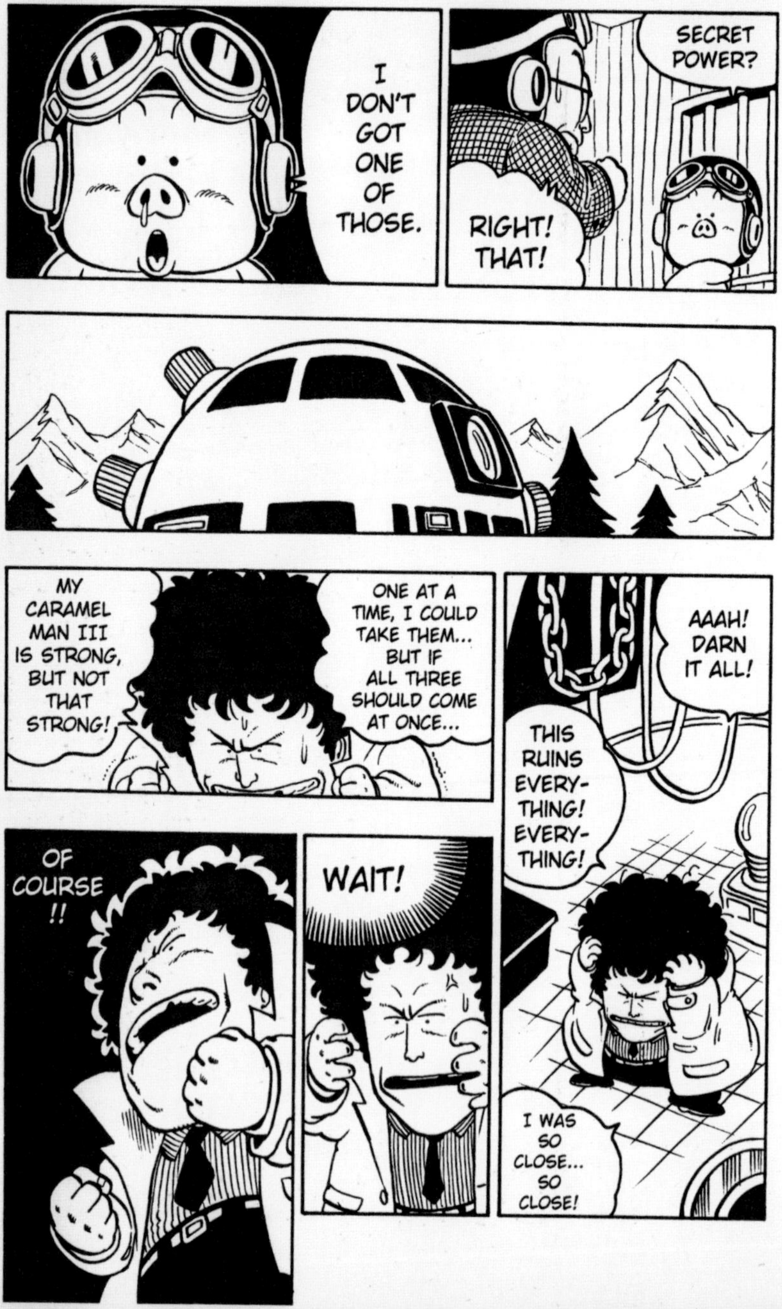
SECRET POWER?
RIGHT! THAT!
I DON'T GOT ONE OF THOSE.
AAAH! DARN IT ALL!
THIS RUINS EVERY-THING! EVERY-THING!
I WAS SO CLOSE... SO CLOSE!
ONE AT A TIME, I COULD TAKE THEM... BUT IF ALL THREE SHOULD COME AT ONCE...
MY CARAMEL MAN III IS STRONG, BUT NOT THAT STRONG!
WAIT!
OF COURSE !!

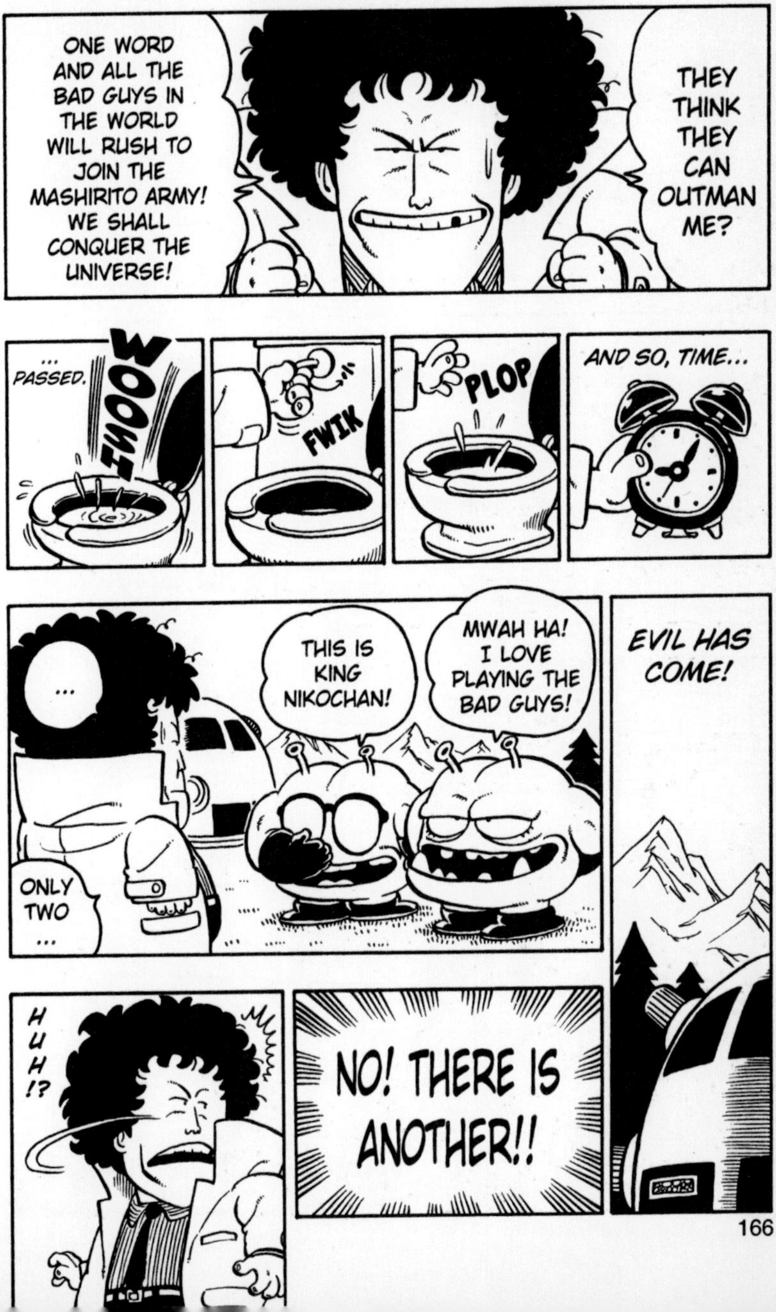
THEY THINK THEY CAN OUTMAN ME?
ONE WORD AND ALL THE BAD GUYS IN THE WORLD WILL RUSH TO JOIN THE MASHIRITO ARMY! WE SHALL CONQUER THE UNIVERSE!
AND SO, TIME...
PLOP
FWIK
WOOOSH
... PASSED.
EVIL HAS COME!
MWAH HA! I LOVE PLAYING THE BAD GUYS!
THIS IS KING NIKOCHAN!
...
ONLY TWO ...
NO! THERE IS ANOTHER!!
HUH!?

READ THIS WAY

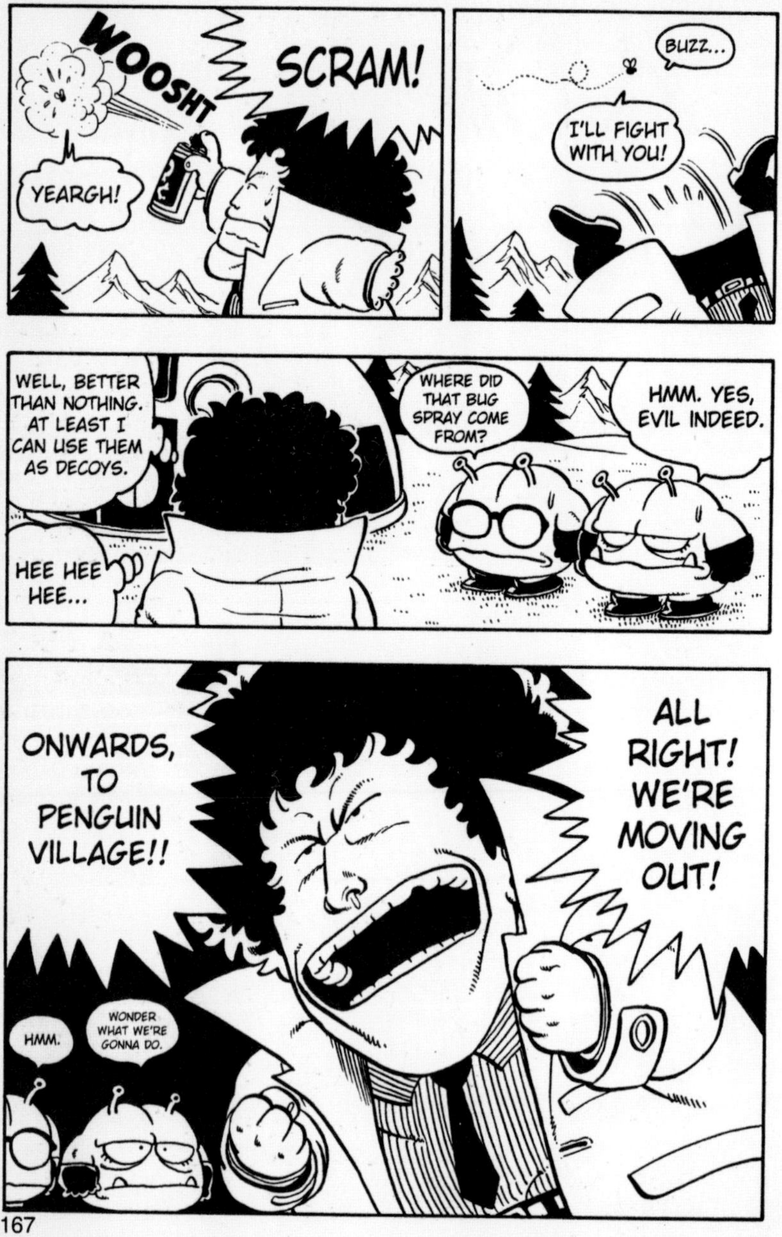
BUZZ...
I'LL FIGHT WITH YOU!
WOOSHT
SCRAM!
YEARGH!
HMM. YES, EVIL INDEED.
WHERE DID THAT BUG SPRAY COME FROM?
WELL, BETTER THAN NOTHING. AT LEAST I CAN USE THEM AS DECOYS.
HEE HEE HEE...
ALL RIGHT! WE'RE MOVING OUT!
ONWARDS, TO PENGUIN VILLAGE!!
WONDER WHAT WE'RE GONNA DO.
HMM.

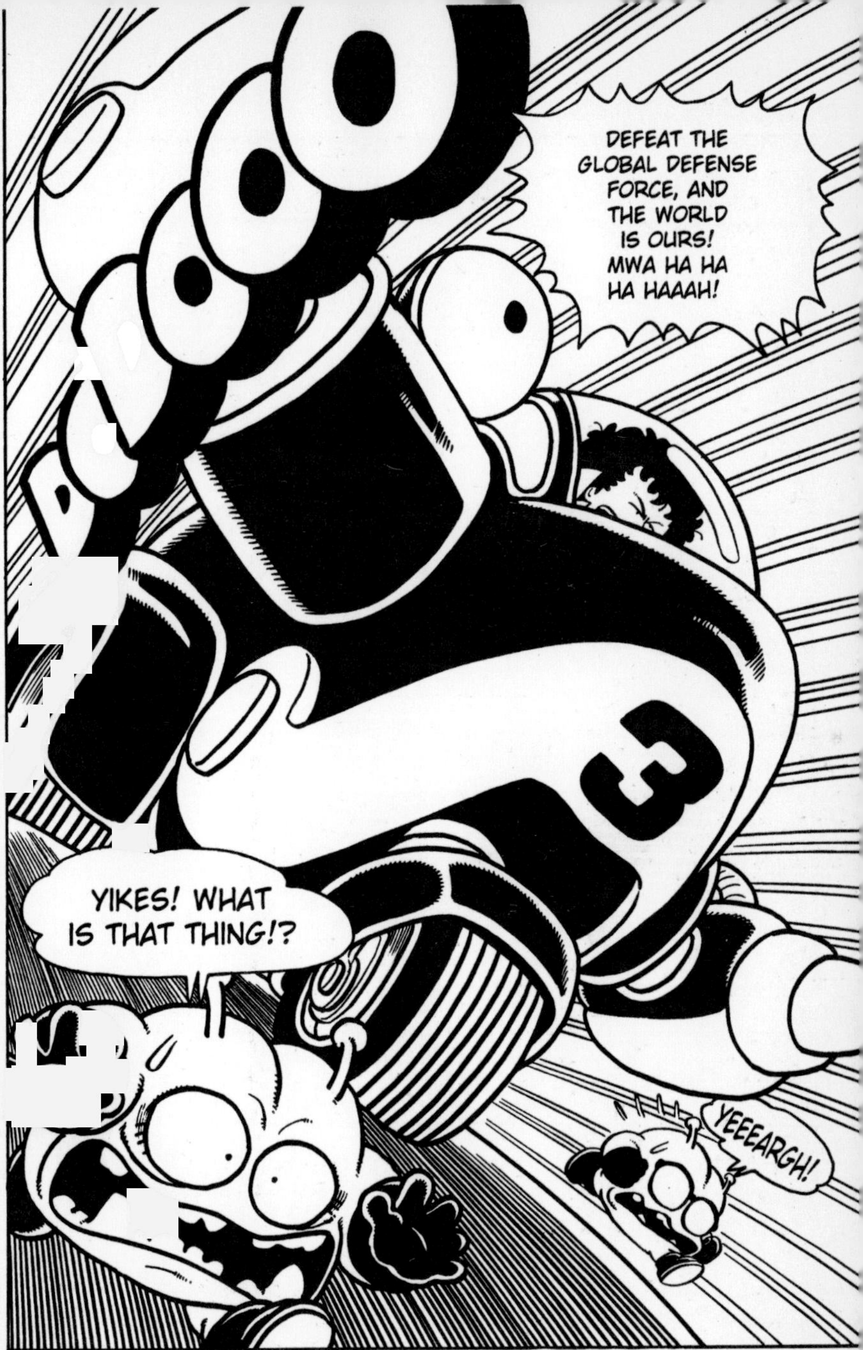
DEFEAT THE GLOBAL DEFENSE FORCE, AND THE WORLD IS OURS! MWA HA HA HA HAAAH!
YEEEARGH!
YIKES! WHAT IS THAT THING!?

READ THIS WAY

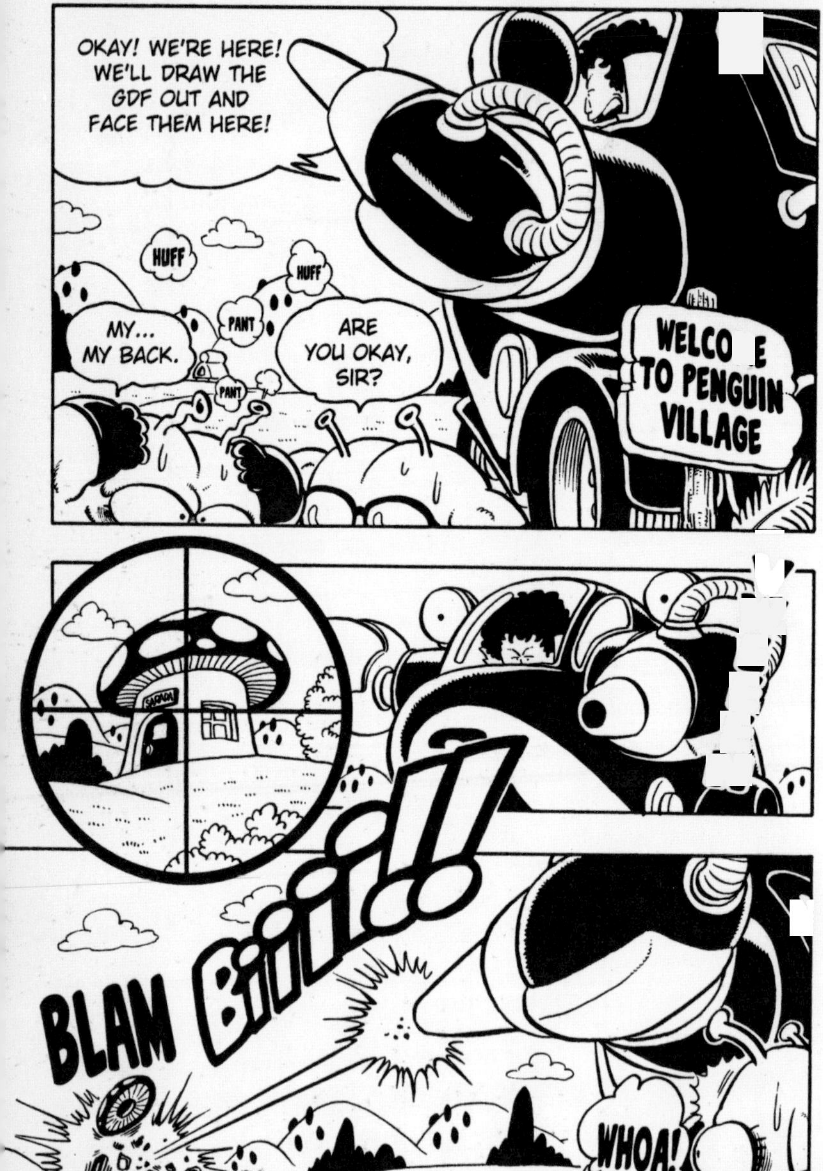
OKAY! WE'RE HERE! WE'LL DRAW THE GDF OUT AND FACE THEM HERE!
WELCO E TO PENGUIN VILLAGE
HUFF
HUFF
ARE YOU OKAY, SIR?
PANT
MY... MY BACK.
PANT
WHOA!
BLAM

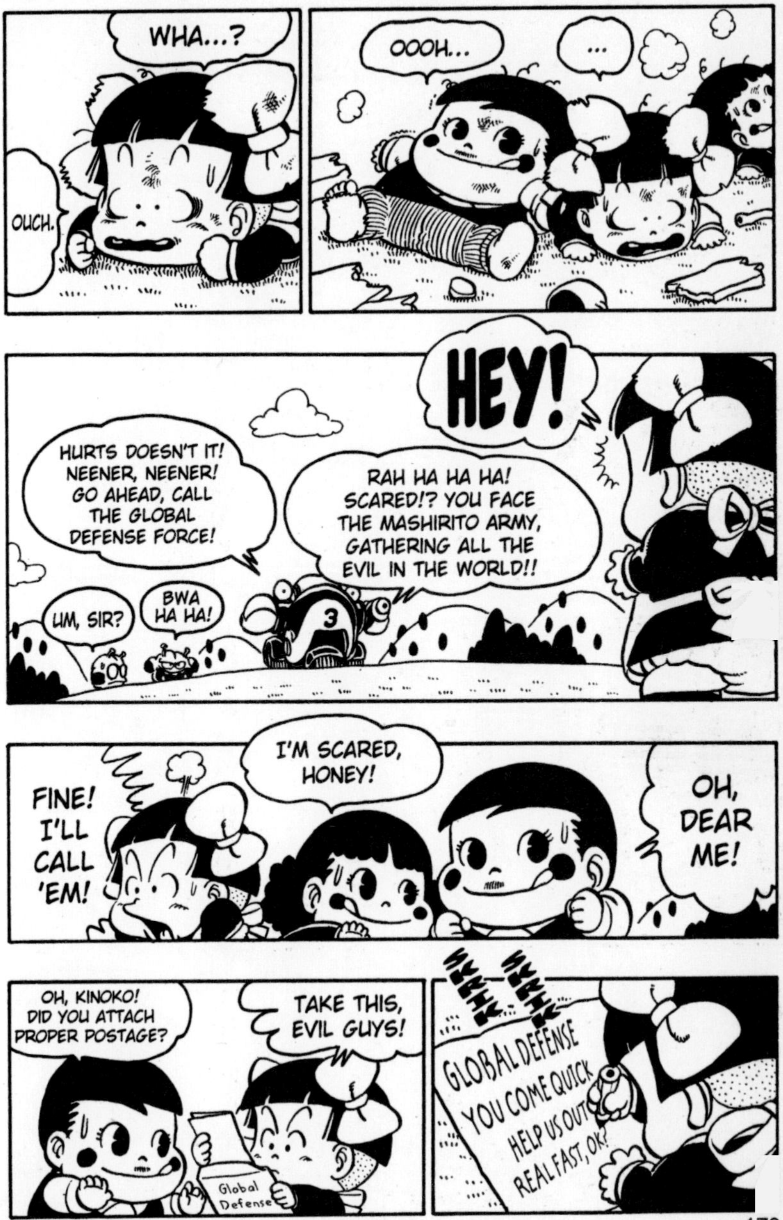
...
OOOH...
WHA...?
OUCH.
HEY!
RAH HA HA HA! SCARED!? YOU FACE THE MASHIRITO ARMY, GATHERING ALL THE EVIL IN THE WORLD!!
HURTS DOESN'T IT! NEENER, NEENER! GO AHEAD, CALL THE GLOBAL DEFENSE FORCE!
BWA HA HA!
UM, SIR?
3
OH, DEAR ME!
I'M SCARED, HONEY!
FINE! I'LL CALL 'EM!
SKRIK SKRIK
GLOBAL DEFENSE
YOU COME QUICK
HELP US OUT
REAL FAST, OK?
TAKE THIS, EVIL GUYS!
OH, KINOKO! DID YOU ATTACH PROPER POSTAGE?
Global Defense

READ THIS WAY

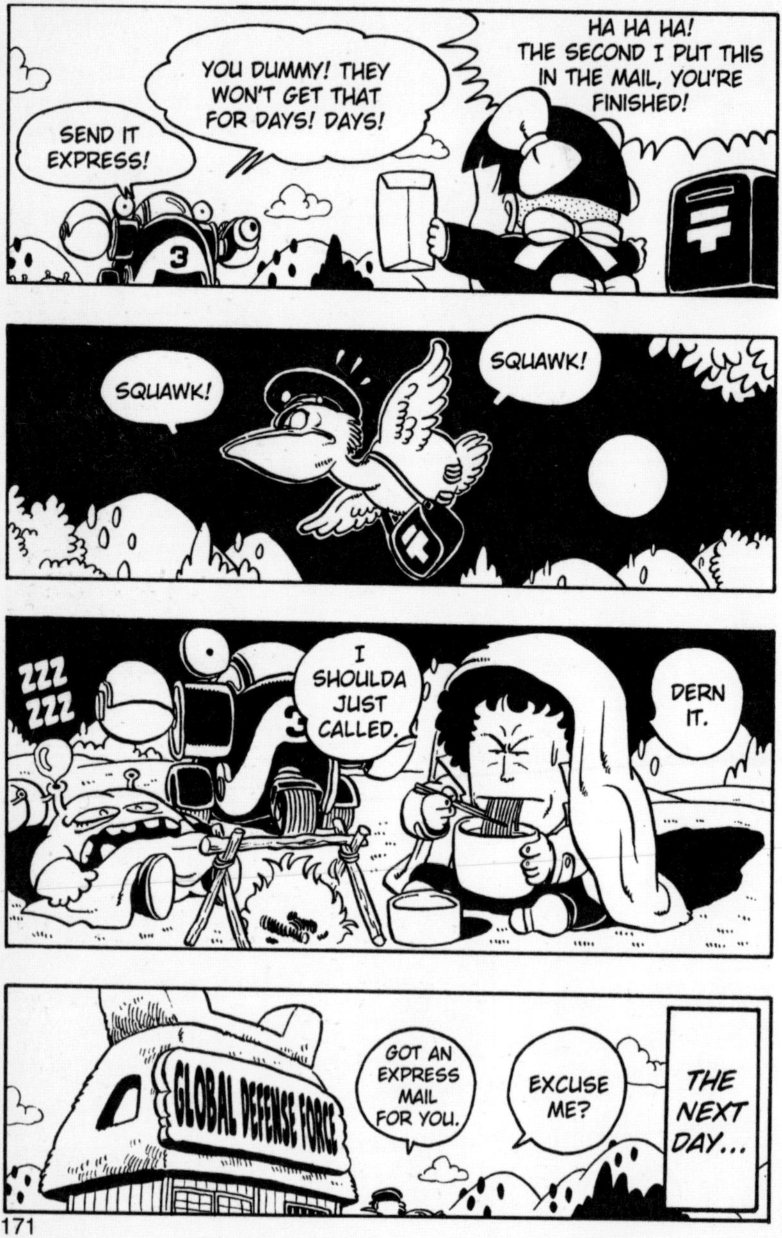
HA HA HA! THE SECOND I PUT THIS IN THE MAIL, YOU'RE FINISHED!
YOU DUMMY! THEY WON'T GET THAT FOR DAYS! DAYS!
SEND IT EXPRESS!
SQUAWK!
SQUAWK!
DERN IT.
I SHOULDA JUST CALLED.
ZZZ ZZZ
THE NEXT DAY...
EXCUSE ME?
GOT AN EXPRESS MAIL FOR YOU.
GLOBAL DEFENSE FORCE

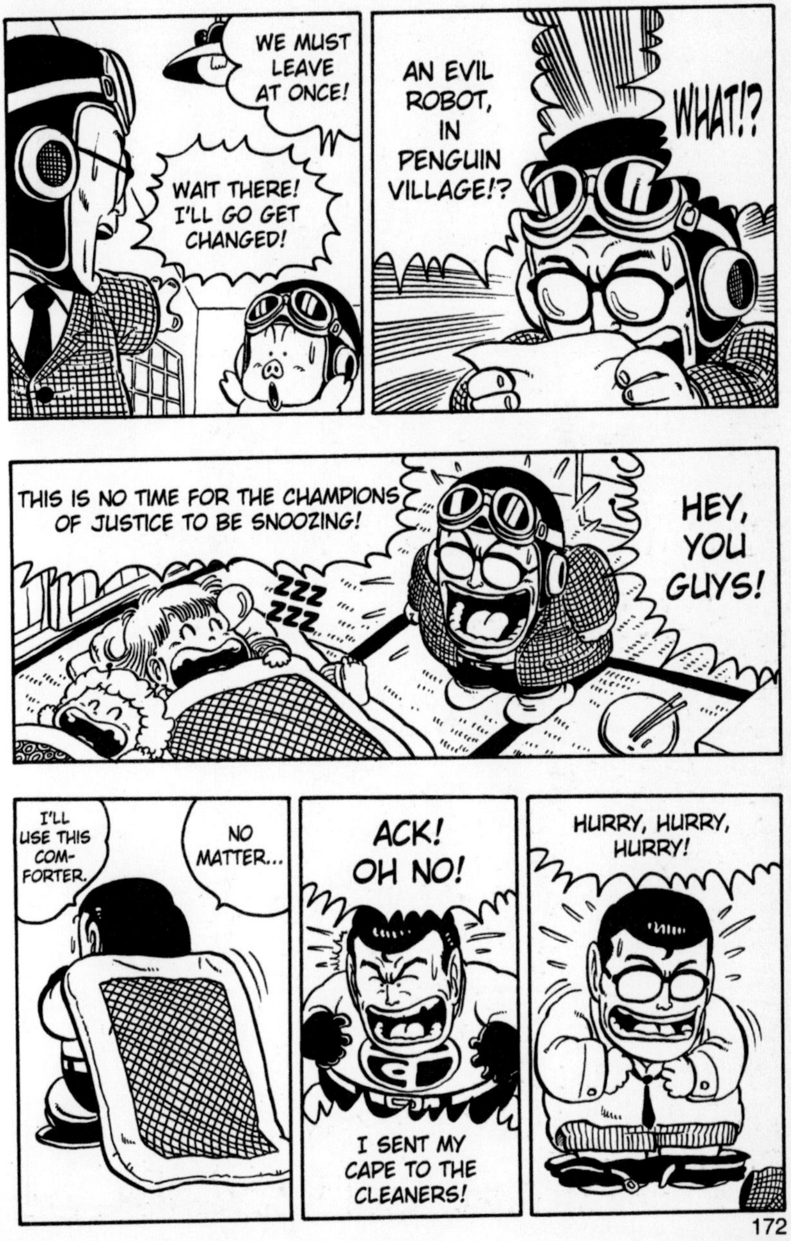
WHAT!?
AN EVIL ROBOT, IN PENGUIN VILLAGE!?
WE MUST LEAVE AT ONCE!
WAIT THERE! I'LL GO GET CHANGED!
HEY, YOU GUYS!
THIS IS NO TIME FOR THE CHAMPIONS OF JUSTICE TO BE SNOOZING!
ZZZ ZZZ
HURRY, HURRY, HURRY!
ACK! OH NO!
I SENT MY CAPE TO THE CLEANERS!
NO MATTER...
I'LL USE THIS COM-FORTER.

READ THIS WAY

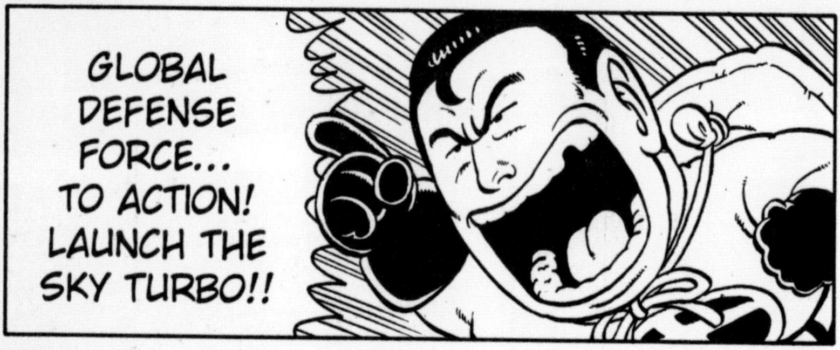
GLOBAL DEFENSE FORCE... TO ACTION! LAUNCH THE SKY TURBO!!

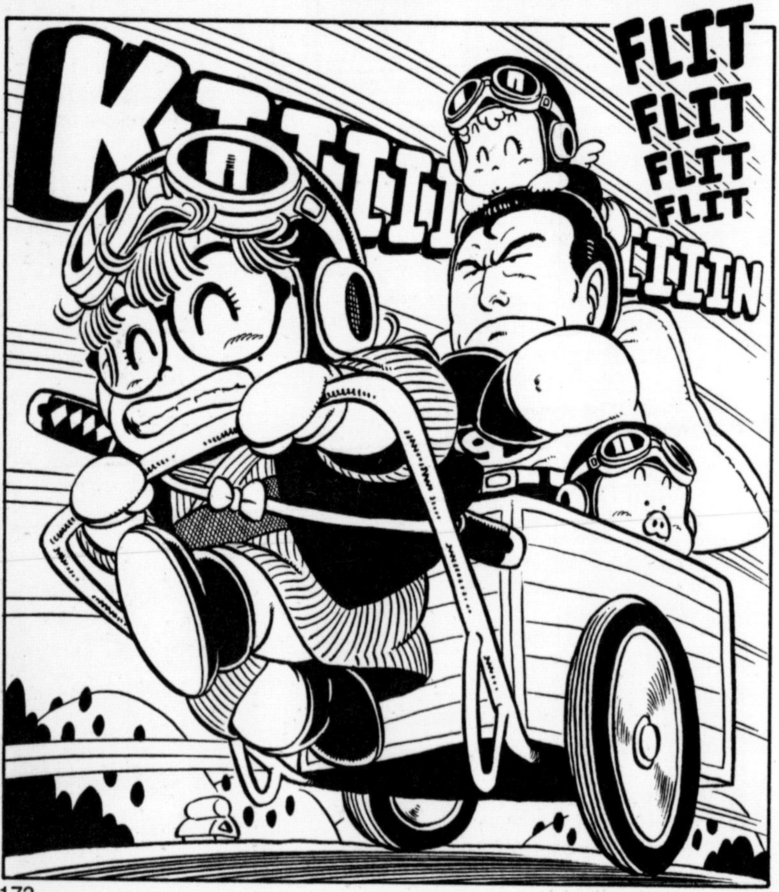
FLIT
FLIT
FLIT
FLIT
KIIIIIIIIIN

Penguin Village "I'M NUMBER ONE!" CONTEST Category: Ridiculous

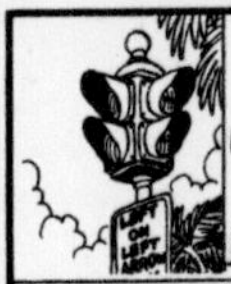
LEFT ON LEFT ARROW

16th

Traffic Light
118 votes
★Impossible to tell between red and green, which is silly, but it looks cute.

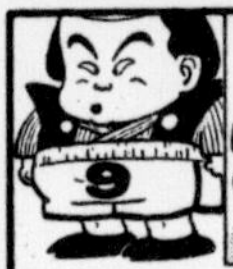
9

17th (tie)

Running Socks
112 votes
★When one falls off you run around in a circle. How dumb!

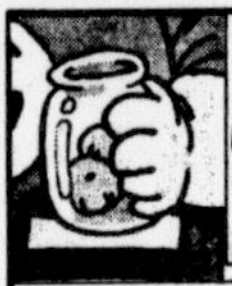

17th (tie)

Suppaman's Pickled Plums
112 votes
★In the anime, there's always the same number of plums in the jar, no matter how many he eats!

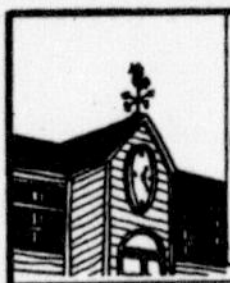

19th

Penguin Village Junior High
96 votes
★A principal on roller skates? Ridiculous!

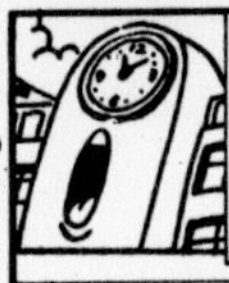

20th

Penguin Village High
84 votes
★The school looks like a face.
★I wish I didn't have to take a test to get into high school.*

21st Anguirus Apartments
22nd Suppaman's backpack
23rd Kinoko's radio-cassette player
24th All of Penguin Village
25th Barbershop Soramame's crab sign/the vending machine
27th Old woman Spring's cigarette shop
28th Kinoko Sarada's tricycle
29th The bank
30th The trees on the mountains
31st Ultraman/Arale Norimaki/Akane Kimidori's hair ribbon
34th The rocks in Penguin Village
35th Arale's glasses/King Nikochan's spaceship
37th The clouds/Arale's pumpkin panties
38th The night

Yeeearrgh! There were over 173 entries in the "ridiculous" category! How'm I supposed to write down all of them!?

- The poop-poking stick
- Suppaman's runny nose
- King Nikochan's wild poo
- The front covers of *Dr. Slump*
- Arale's drawings
- Senbei's perverted side
- The Norimaki toilet and phone
- Dr. Mashirito's laboratory
- The desks at the school
- The plum tree that appeared near the Norimaki house, then just as quickly disappeared.
- Anything anyone says in Penguin Village

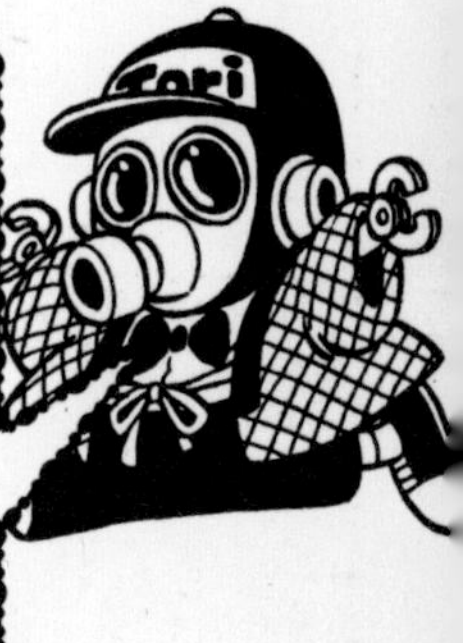
Tori

*In Japan, you have to take a test to get into high school!

Penguin Village Wars: Part 3

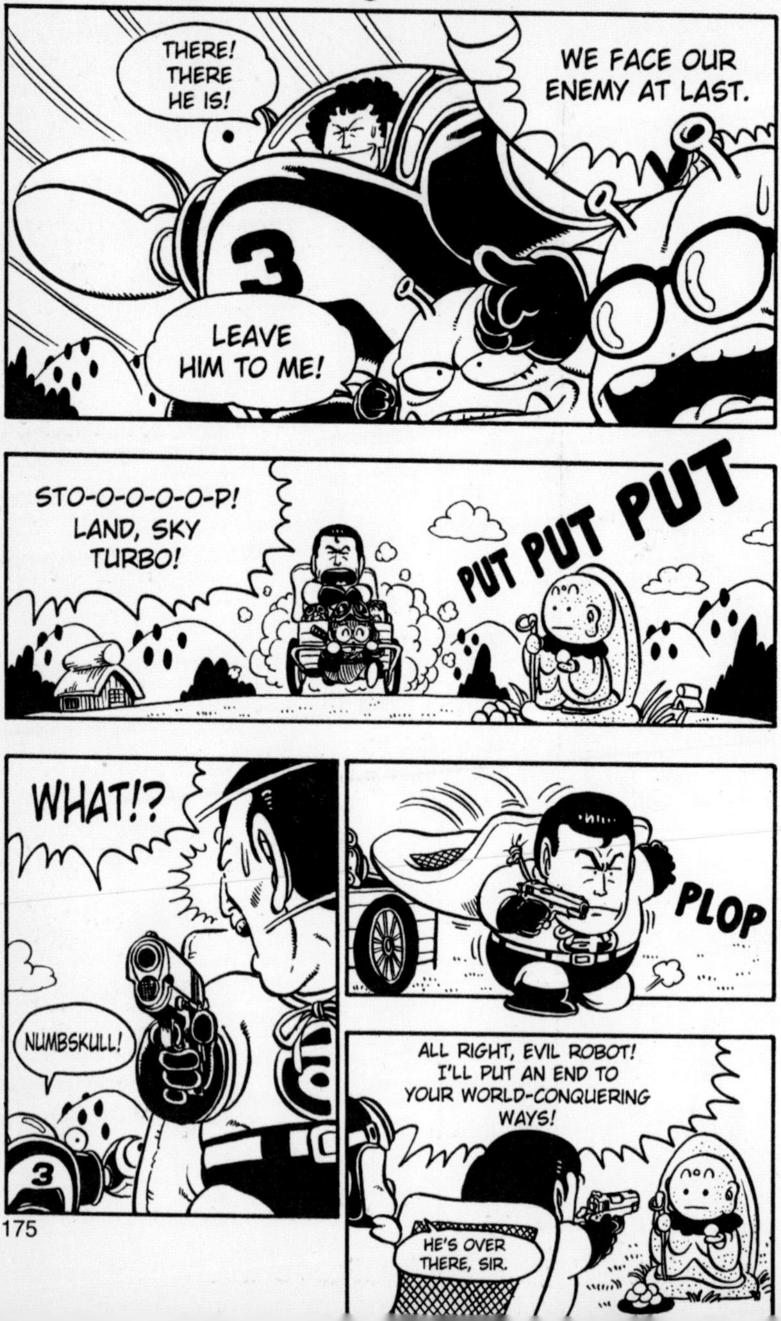
WE FACE OUR ENEMY AT LAST.
THERE! THERE HE IS!
LEAVE HIM TO ME!
PUT PUT PUT
STO-O-O-O-O-P! LAND, SKY TURBO!
PLOP
ALL RIGHT, EVIL ROBOT! I'LL PUT AN END TO YOUR WORLD-CONQUERING WAYS!
HE'S OVER THERE, SIR.
WHAT!?
NUMBSKULL!

THE CHAMPIONS OF JUSTICE

THE FORCES OF EVIL

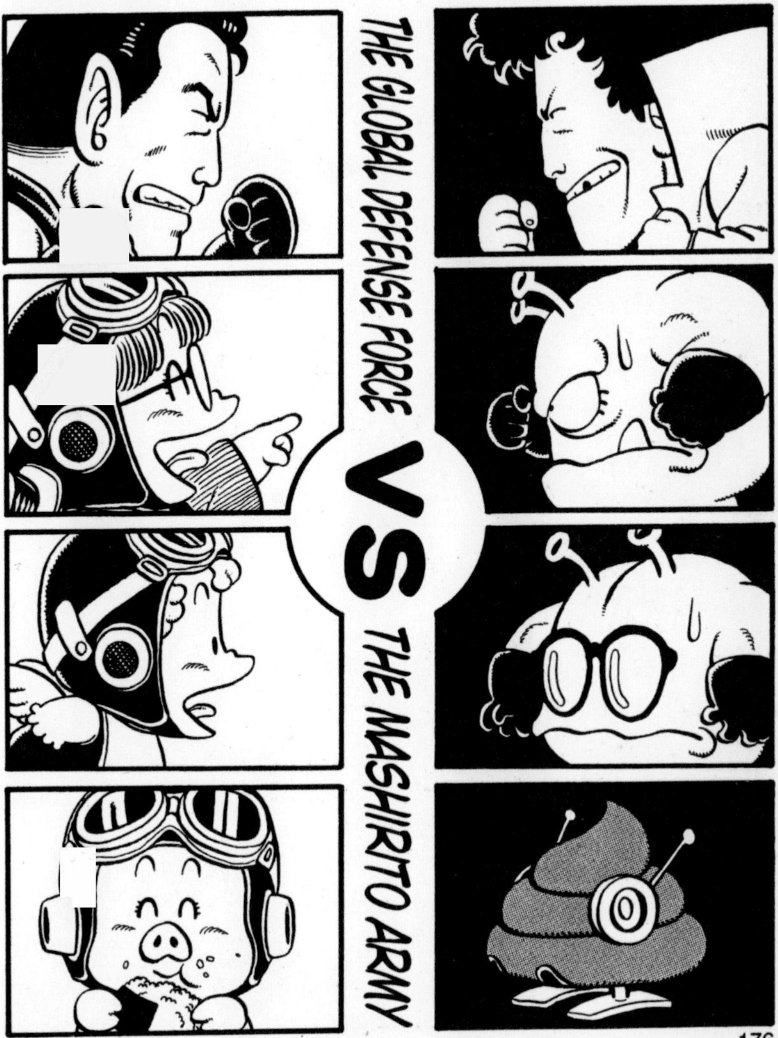
THE GLOBAL DEFENSE FORCE
VS
THE MASHIRITO ARMY

Penguin Village Wars
Part 3

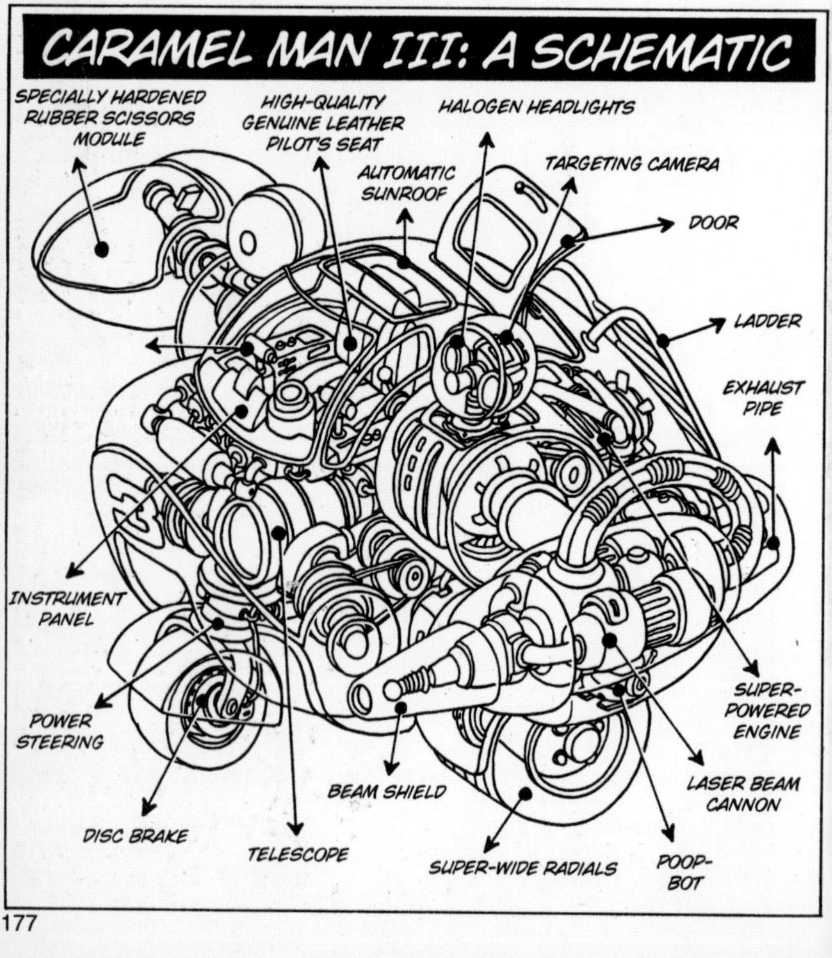
CARAMEL MAN III: A SCHEMATIC
SPECIALLY HARDENED RUBBER SCISSORS MODULE
HIGH-QUALITY GENUINE LEATHER PILOT'S SEAT
HALOGEN HEADLIGHTS
AUTOMATIC SUNROOF
TARGETING CAMERA
DOOR
LADDER
EXHAUST PIPE
INSTRUMENT PANEL
SUPER-POWERED ENGINE
POWER STEERING
LASER BEAM CANNON
BEAM SHIELD
DISC BRAKE
TELESCOPE
SUPER-WIDE RADIALS
POOP-BOT

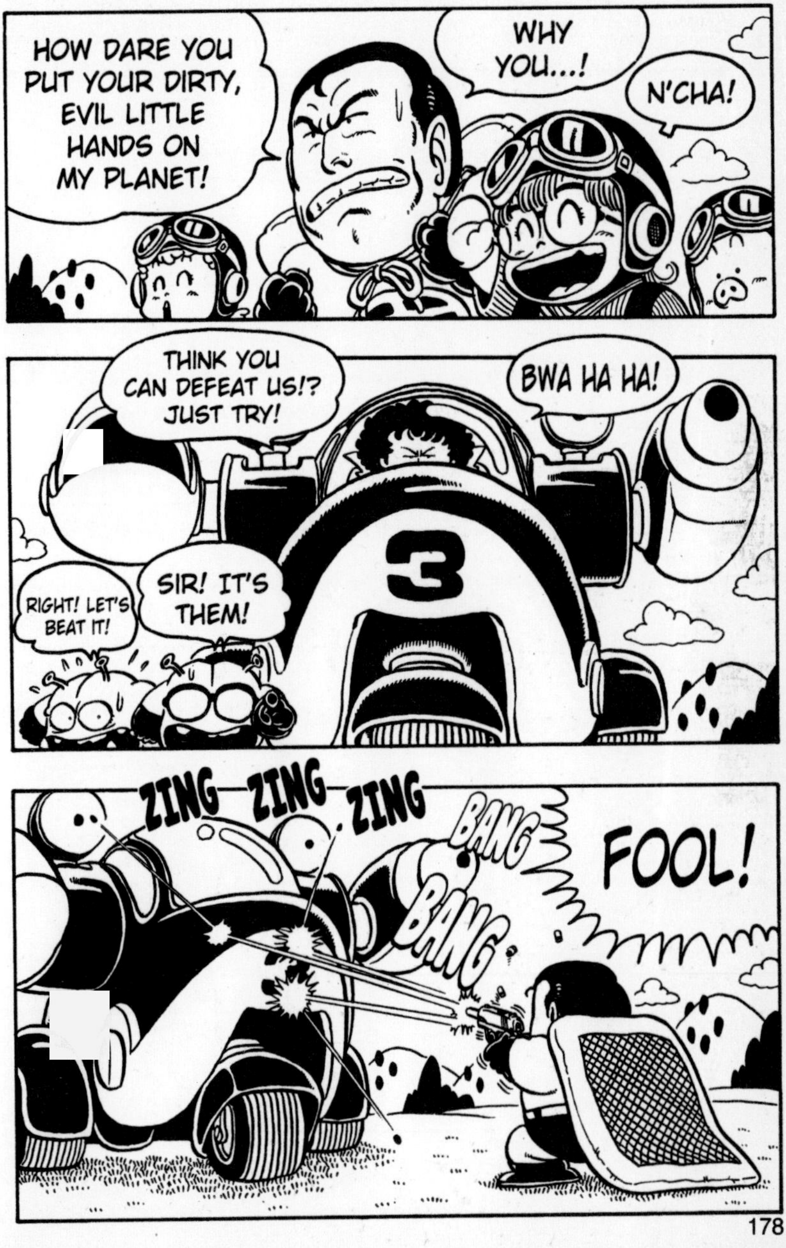

WHY YOU...!
N'CHA!
HOW DARE YOU PUT YOUR DIRTY, EVIL LITTLE HANDS ON MY PLANET!
BWA HA HA!
THINK YOU CAN DEFEAT US!? JUST TRY!
SIR! IT'S THEM!
RIGHT! LET'S BEAT IT!
FOOL!
BANG
BANG
ZING ZING ZING

READ THIS WAY

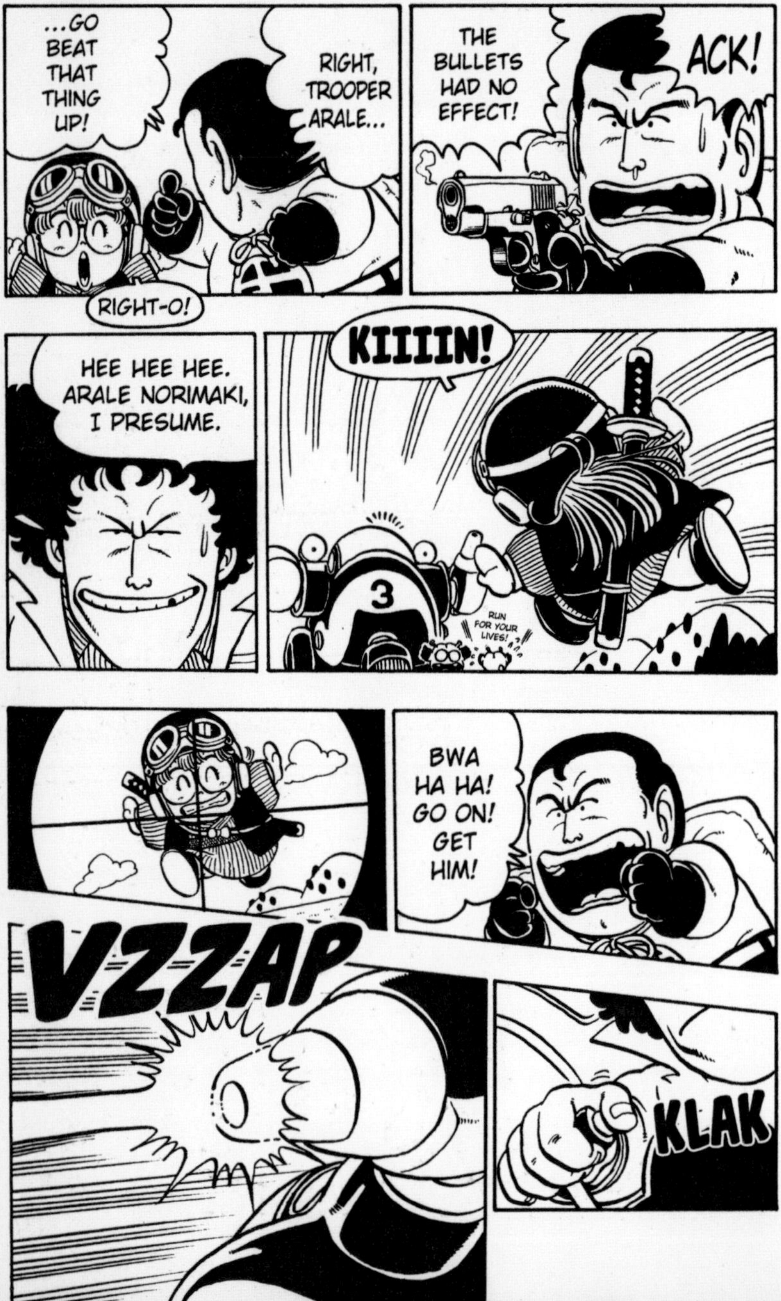
ACK!
THE BULLETS HAD NO EFFECT!
RIGHT, TROOPER ARALE...
...GO BEAT THAT THING UP!
RIGHT-O!
KIIIIN!
RUN FOR YOUR LIVES!
HEE HEE HEE. ARALE NORIMAKI, I PRESUME.
BWA HA HA! GO ON! GET HIM!
KLAK
VZZAP

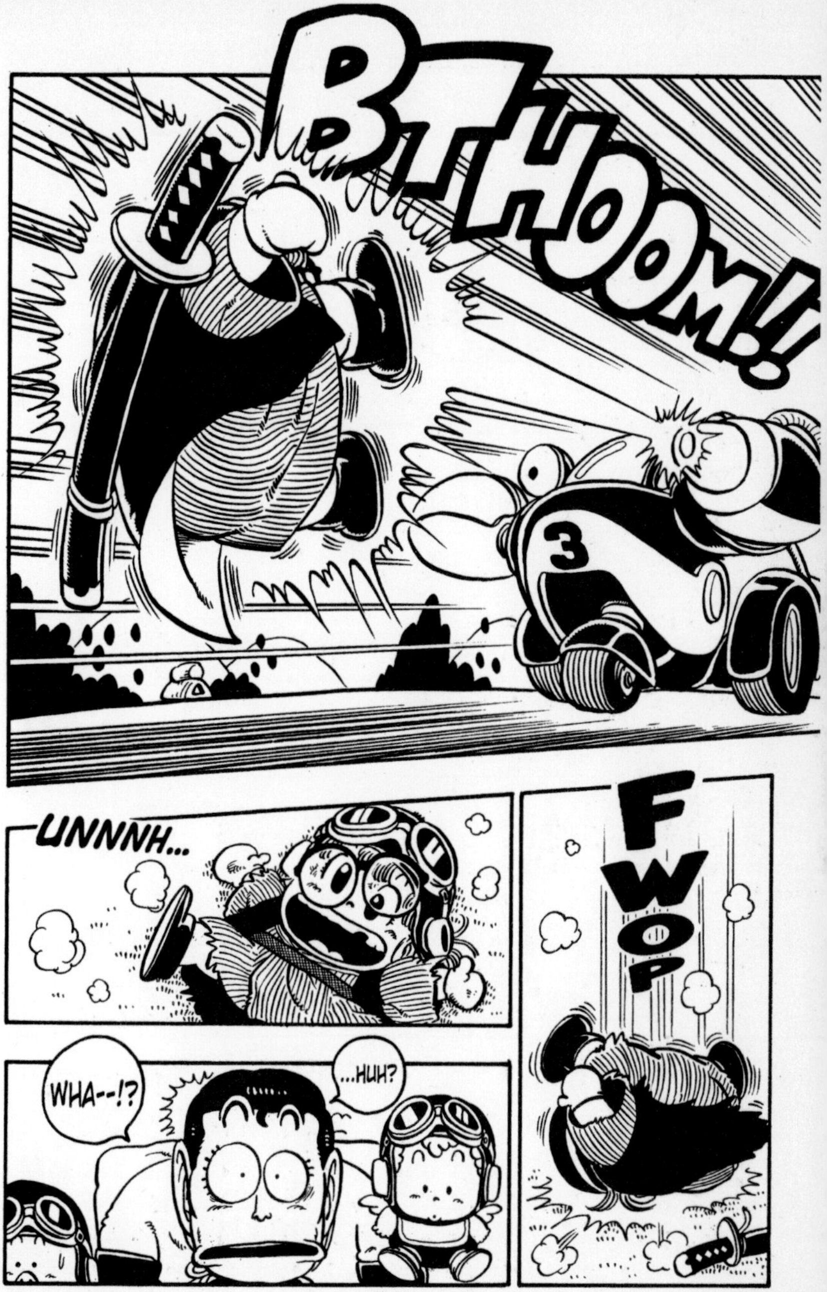
BHOOM!!
FWOP
UNNNH...
...HUH?
WHA--!?

READ THIS WAY

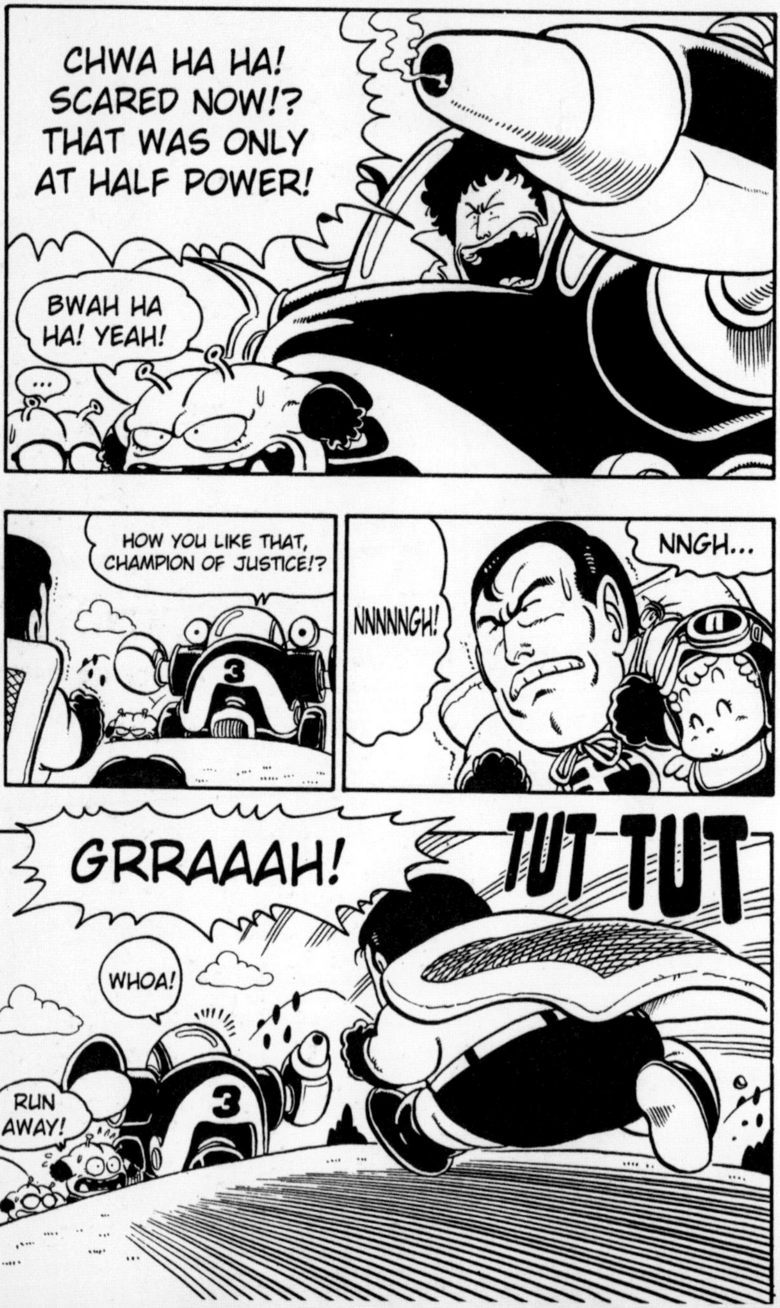

CHWA HA HA! SCARED NOW!? THAT WAS ONLY AT HALF POWER!
BWAH HA HA! YEAH!
...
NNGH...
NNNNNGH!
HOW YOU LIKE THAT, CHAMPION OF JUSTICE!?
TUT TUT
GRRAAAH!
WHOA!
RUN AWAY!

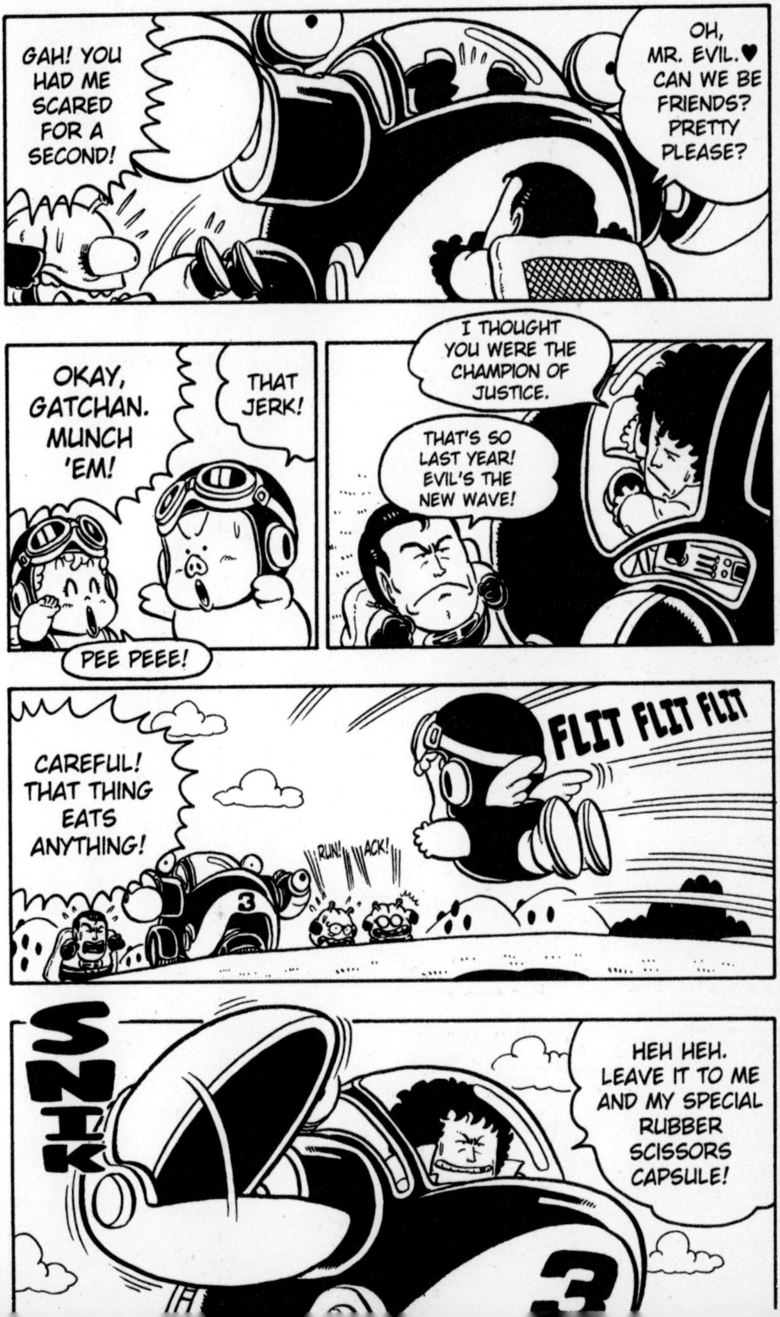
OH, MR. EVIL.♥ CAN WE BE FRIENDS? PRETTY PLEASE?
GAH! YOU HAD ME SCARED FOR A SECOND!
I THOUGHT YOU WERE THE CHAMPION OF JUSTICE.
THAT'S SO LAST YEAR! EVIL'S THE NEW WAVE!
THAT JERK!
OKAY, GATCHAN. MUNCH 'EM!
PEE PEEE!
FLIT FLIT FLIT
ACK!
RUN!
CAREFUL! THAT THING EATS ANYTHING!
HEH HEH. LEAVE IT TO ME AND MY SPECIAL RUBBER SCISSORS CAPSULE!
SNIK

READ THIS WAY

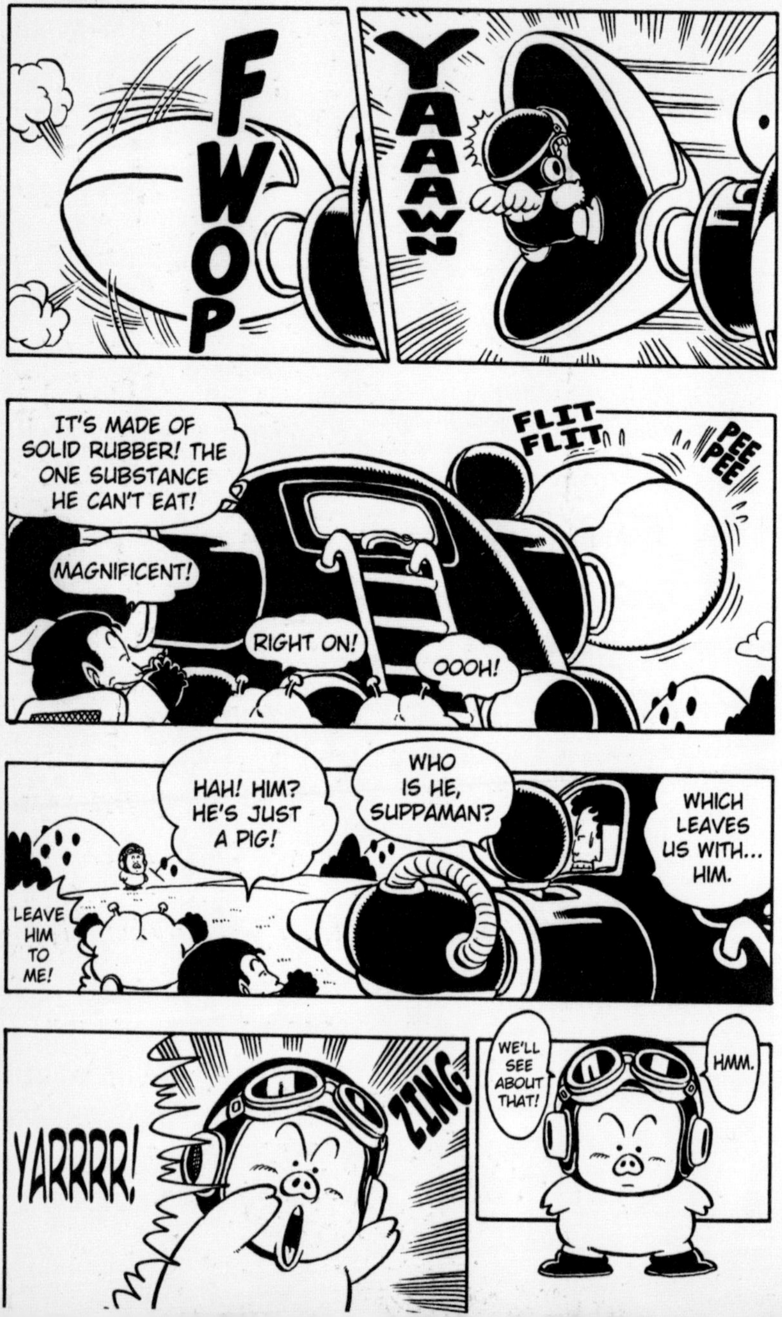
YAAAWN
FWOP
PEE PEE
FLIT FLIT
IT'S MADE OF SOLID RUBBER! THE ONE SUBSTANCE HE CAN'T EAT!
MAGNIFICENT!
OOOH!
RIGHT ON!
WHICH LEAVES US WITH... HIM.
WHO IS HE, SUPPAMAN?
HAH! HIM? HE'S JUST A PIG!
LEAVE HIM TO ME!
HMM.
WE'LL SEE ABOUT THAT!
ZING
YARRRR!

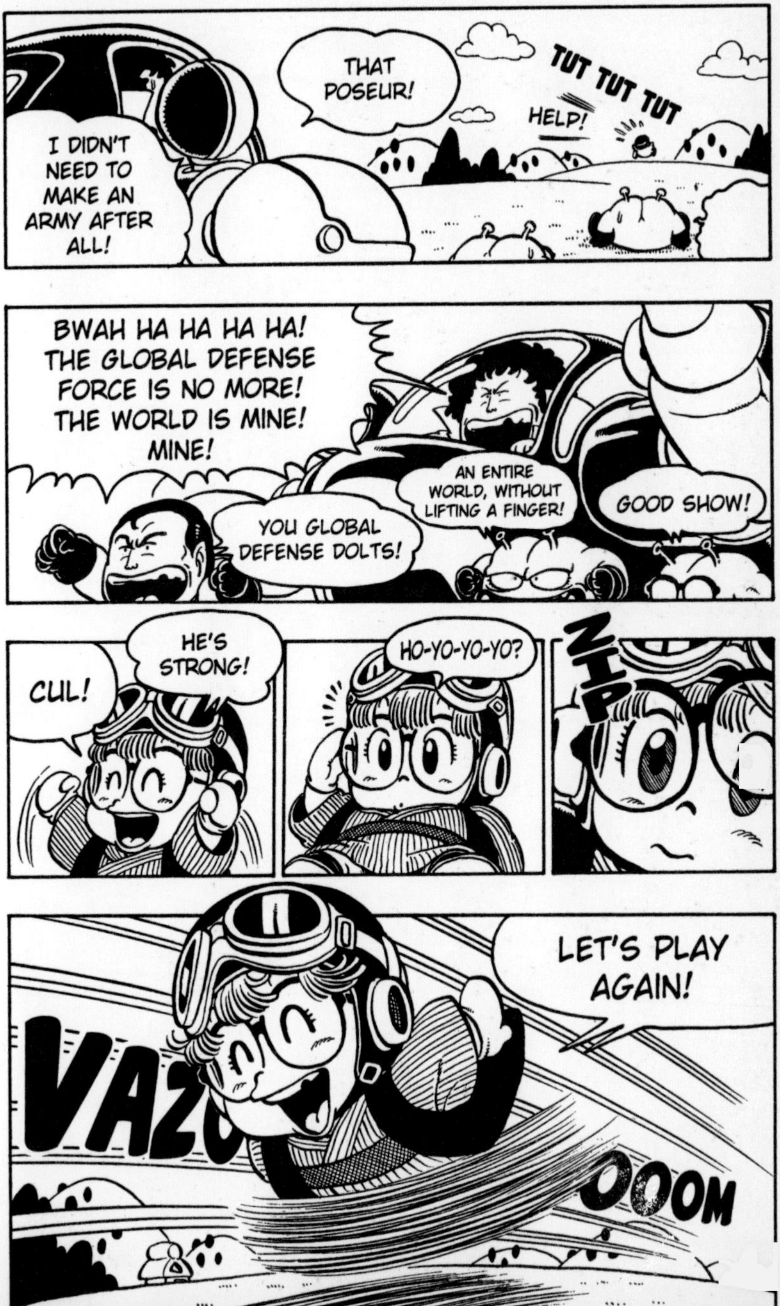
TUT TUT TUT
HELP!
THAT POSEUR!
I DIDN'T NEED TO MAKE AN ARMY AFTER ALL!
BWAH HA HA HA HA! THE GLOBAL DEFENSE FORCE IS NO MORE! THE WORLD IS MINE! MINE!
GOOD SHOW!
AN ENTIRE WORLD, WITHOUT LIFTING A FINGER!
YOU GLOBAL DEFENSE DOLTS!
ZIP
HO-YO-YO-YO?
HE'S STRONG!
CUL!
LET'S PLAY AGAIN!
VAZOOOOM

READ THIS WAY

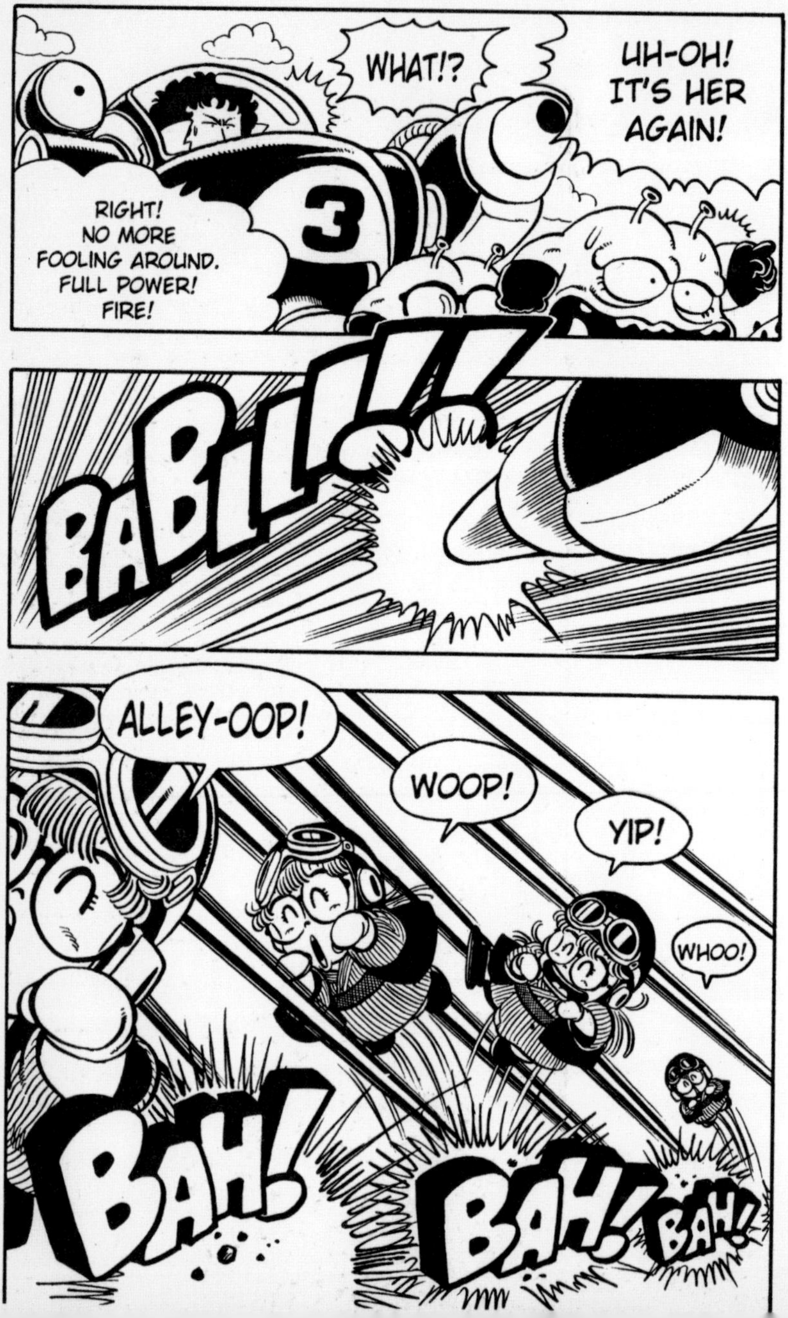
UH-OH! IT'S HER AGAIN!
WHAT!?
RIGHT! NO MORE FOOLING AROUND. FULL POWER! FIRE!
BABII!!
YIP!
WOOP!
ALLEY-OOP!
WHOO!
BAH!
BAH!
BAH!

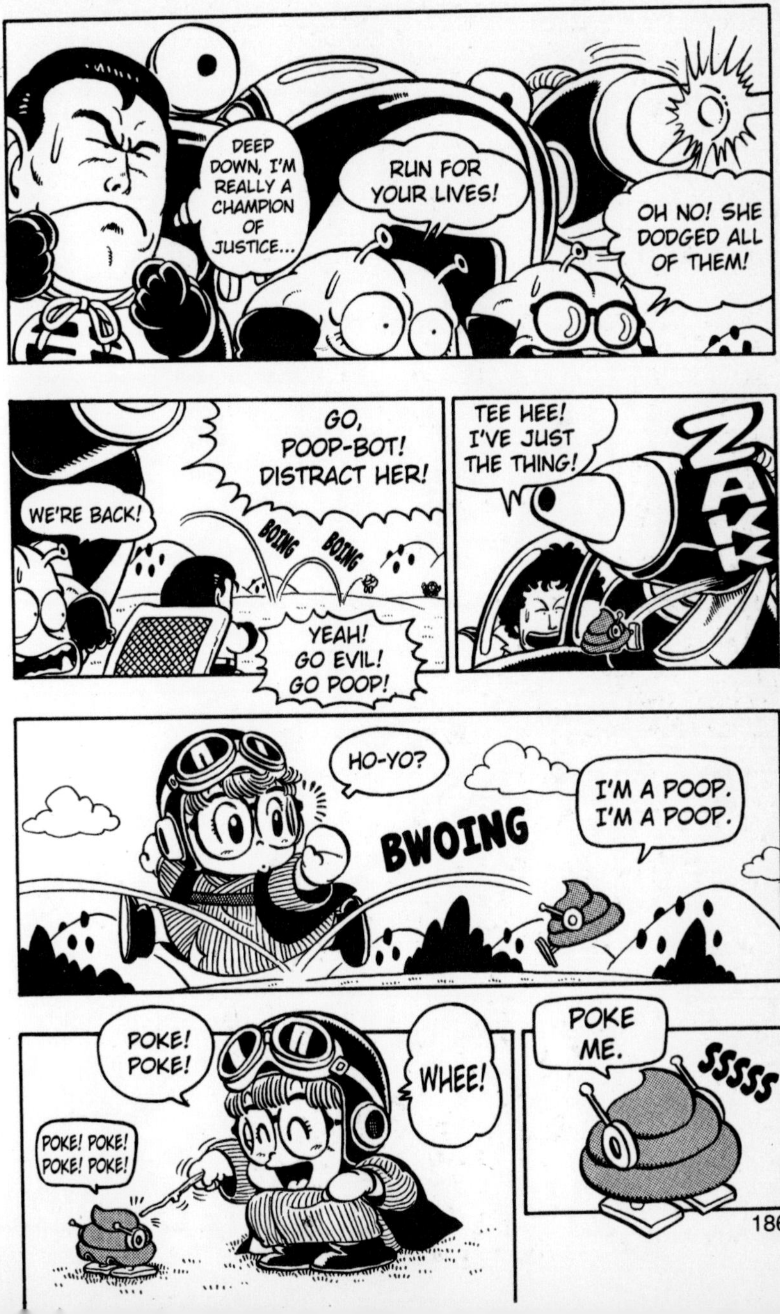
OH NO! SHE DODGED ALL OF THEM!
RUN FOR YOUR LIVES!
DEEP DOWN, I'M REALLY A CHAMPION OF JUSTICE...
ZAKK
TEE HEE! I'VE JUST THE THING!
GO, POOP-BOT! DISTRACT HER!
WE'RE BACK!
BOING
BOING
YEAH! GO EVIL! GO POOP!
I'M A POOP. I'M A POOP.
BWOING
HO-YO?
POKE ME.
SSSSS
WHEE!
POKE! POKE!
POKE! POKE! POKE! POKE!

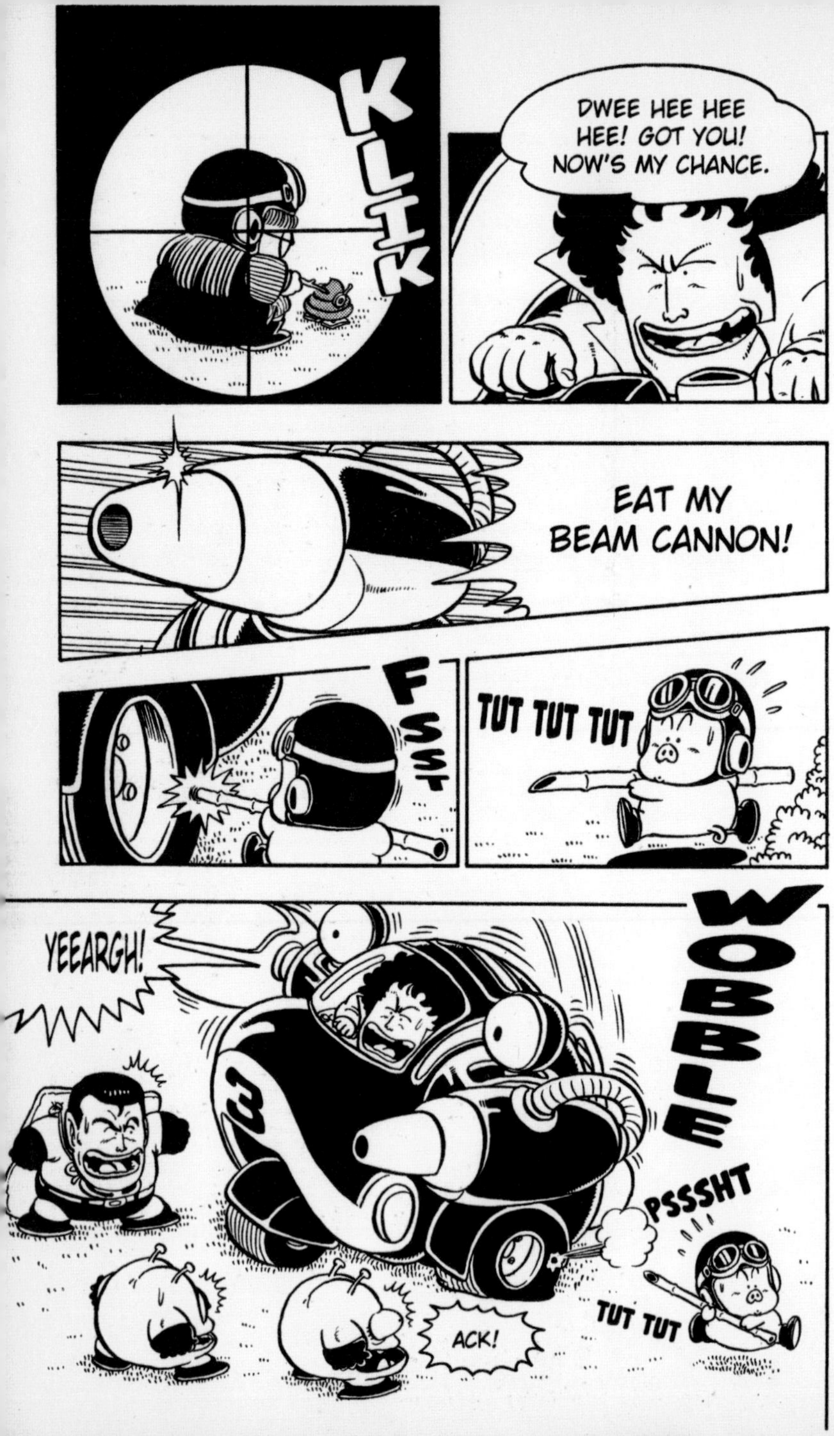
DWEE HEE HEE HEE! GOT YOU! NOW'S MY CHANCE.
KLIK
EAT MY BEAM CANNON!
TUT TUT TUT
FSSST
WOBBLE
YEEARGH!
PSSSHT
TUT TUT
ACK!

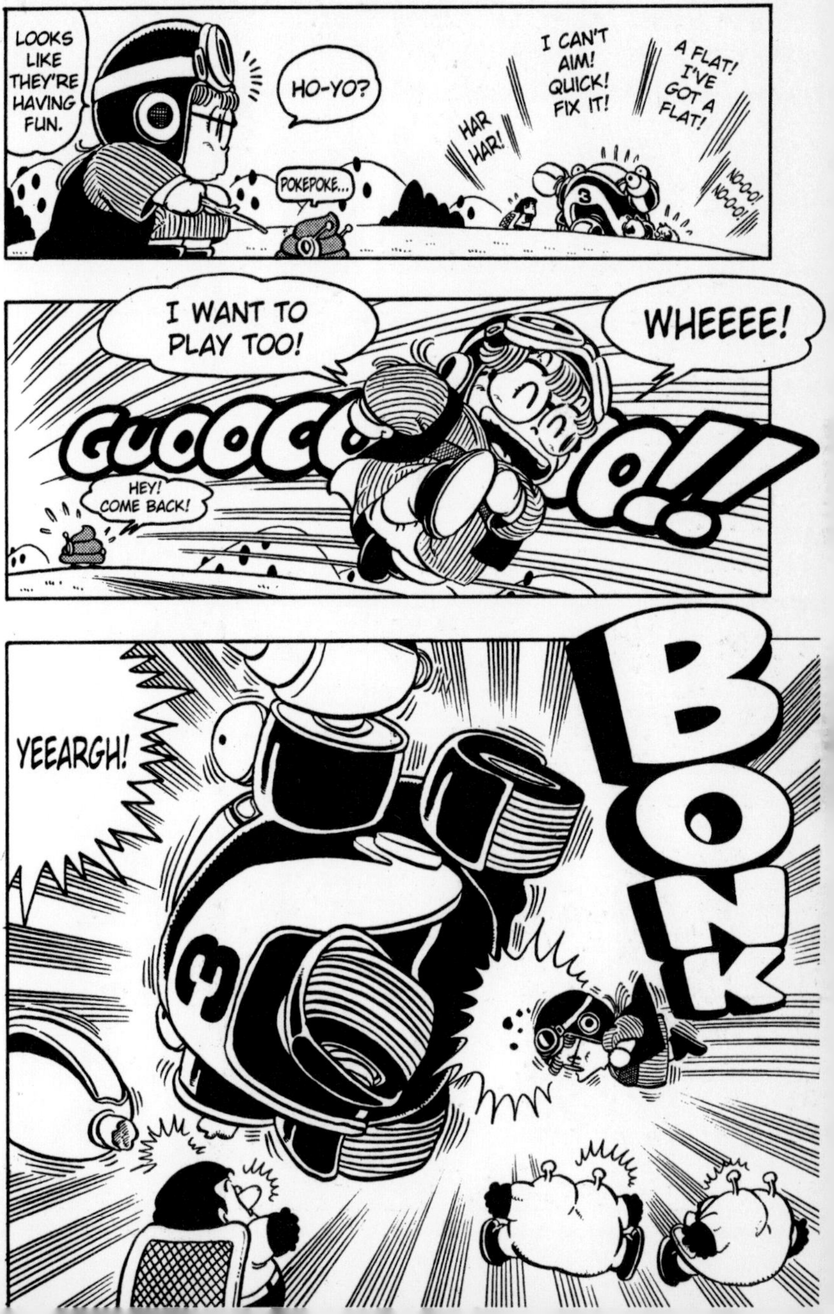
A FLAT! I'VE GOT A FLAT!
NO-O-O! NO-O-O!
I CAN'T AIM! QUICK! FIX IT!
HAR HAR!
HO-YO?
POKEPOKE...
LOOKS LIKE THEY'RE HAVING FUN.
WHEEEE!
I WANT TO PLAY TOO!
HEY! COME BACK!
BONK
YEEARGH!

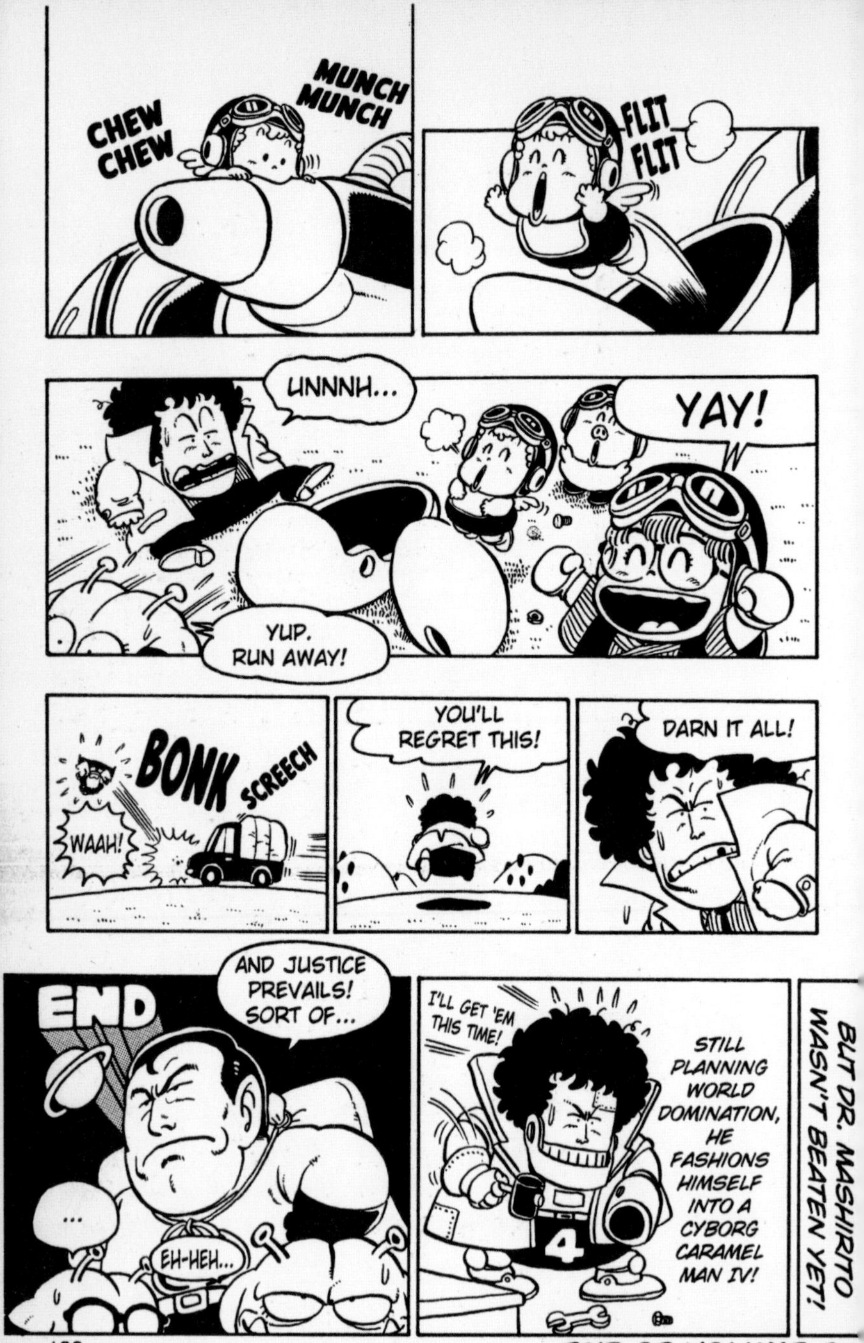
FLIT
FLIT
MUNCH
MUNCH
CHEW
CHEW
YAY!
UNNNH...
YUP.
RUN AWAY!
DARN IT ALL!
YOU'LL
REGRET THIS!
SCREECH
BONK
WAAH!
BUT DR. MASHIRITO
WASN'T BEATEN YET!
STILL
PLANNING
WORLD
DOMINATION,
HE
FASHIONS
HIMSELF
INTO A
CYBORG
CARAMEL
MAN IV!
I'LL GET 'EM
THIS TIME!
4
AND JUSTICE
PREVAILS!
SORT OF...
END
...
EH-HEH...

END OF VOLUME 8

In The Next Volume

Senbei's bachelor days are finally over, but the nightmare has only just begun. Will he and his new bride, Midori, survive the onslaught of flying cats, menacing apes and other creatures of the animal kingdom that now stand in the way of their happiness?

Available in September 2006!

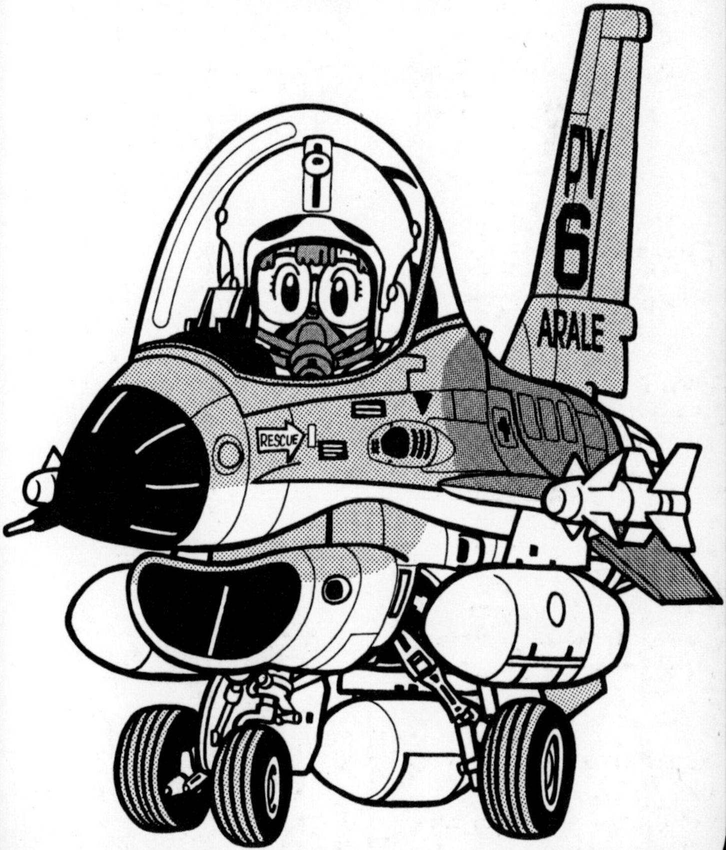
PV
6
ARALE
RESCUE

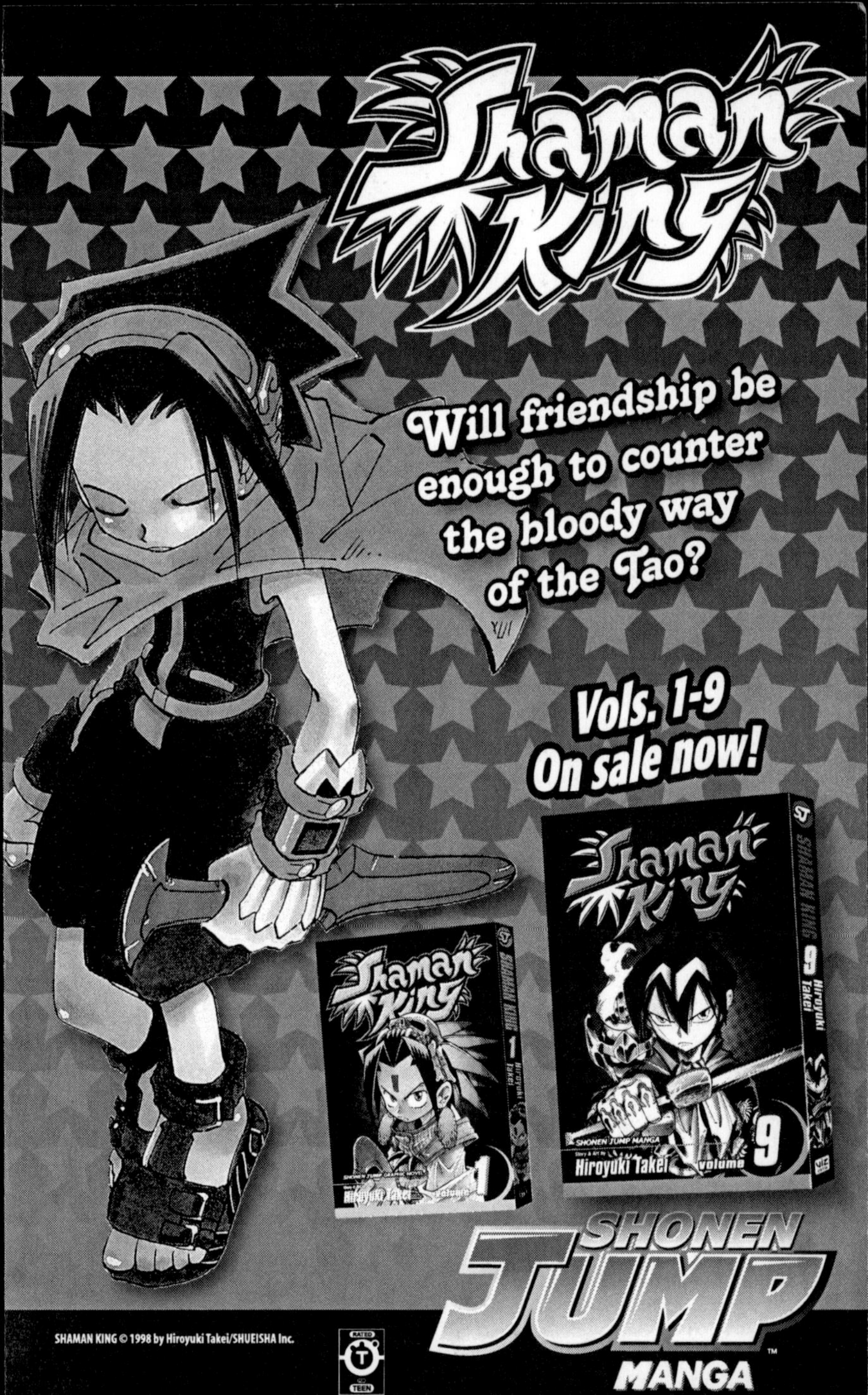

Shaman King
Will friendship be enough to counter the bloody way of the Tao?
Vols. 1-9
On sale now!
SHONEN JUMP MANGA
SHAMAN KING © 1998 by Hiroyuki Takei/SHUEISHA Inc.
RATED T TEEN

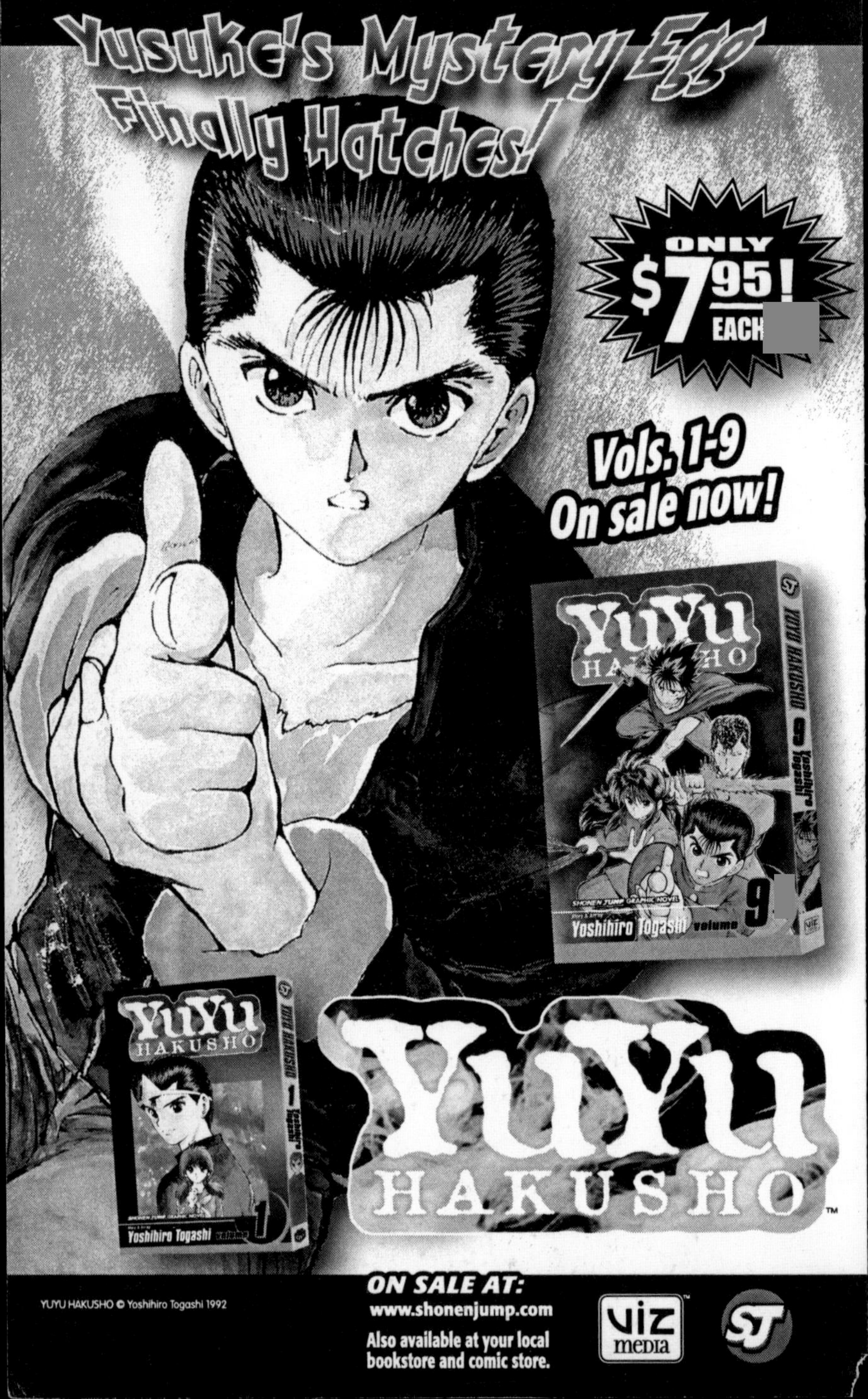
Yusuke's Mystery Egg Finally Hatches!
ONLY $7.95! EACH
Vols. 1-9 On sale now!
YuYu HAKUSHO
Yoshihiro Togashi volume 9
YuYu HAKUSHO
Yoshihiro Togashi volume 1
YuYu HAKUSHO™
ON SALE AT:
www.shonenjump.com
Also available at your local bookstore and comic store.
YUYU HAKUSHO © Yoshihiro Togashi 1992

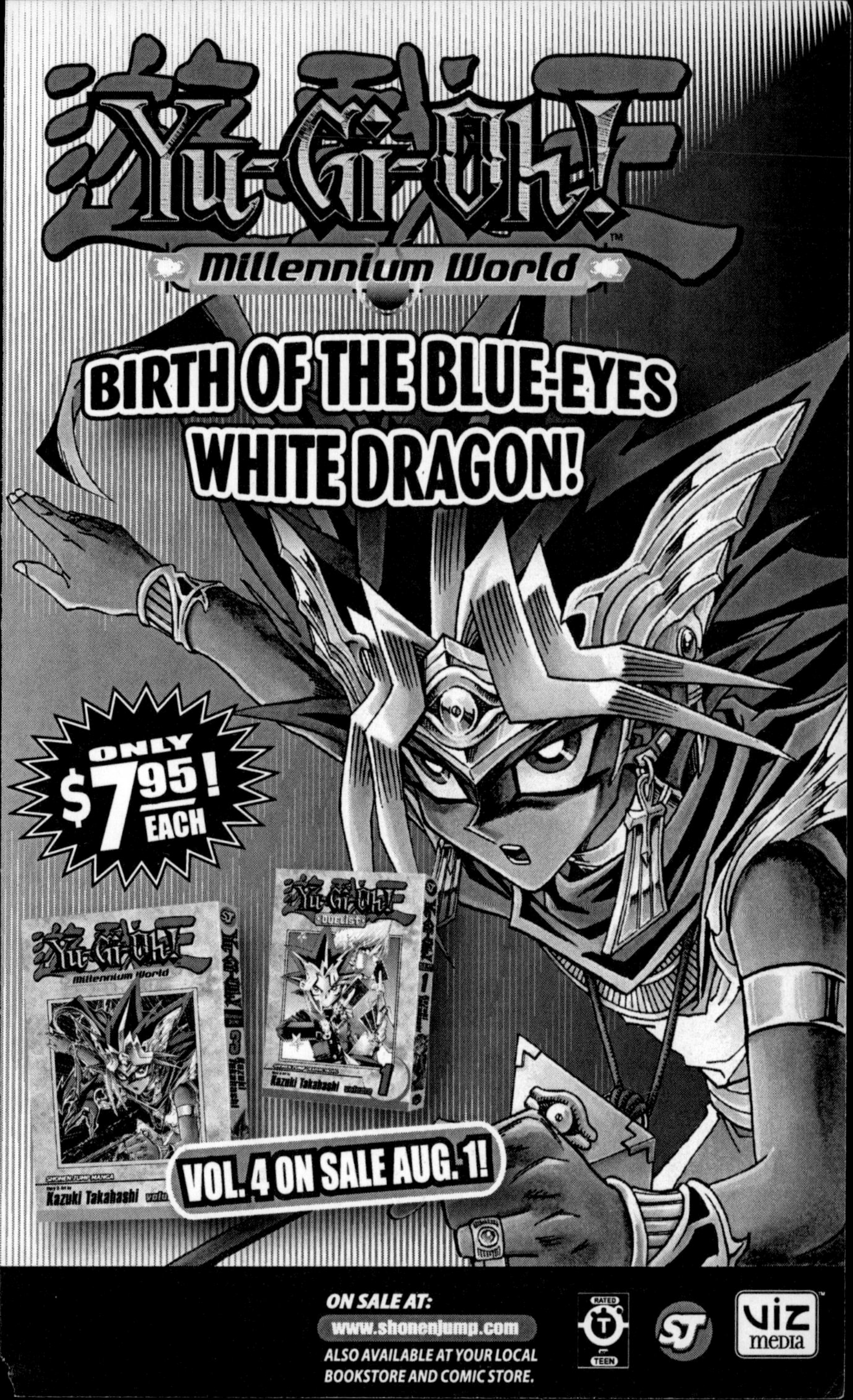
YU-GI-OH!
Millennium World
BIRTH OF THE BLUE-EYES WHITE DRAGON!
ONLY $7.95! EACH
YU-GI-OH! Millennium World
Kazuki Takahashi
YU-GI-OH! DUELIST
Kazuki Takahashi
VOL. 4 ON SALE AUG. 1!
ON SALE AT:
www.shonenjump.com
ALSO AVAILABLE AT YOUR LOCAL BOOKSTORE AND COMIC STORE.
RATED T TEEN
SJ
VIZ media

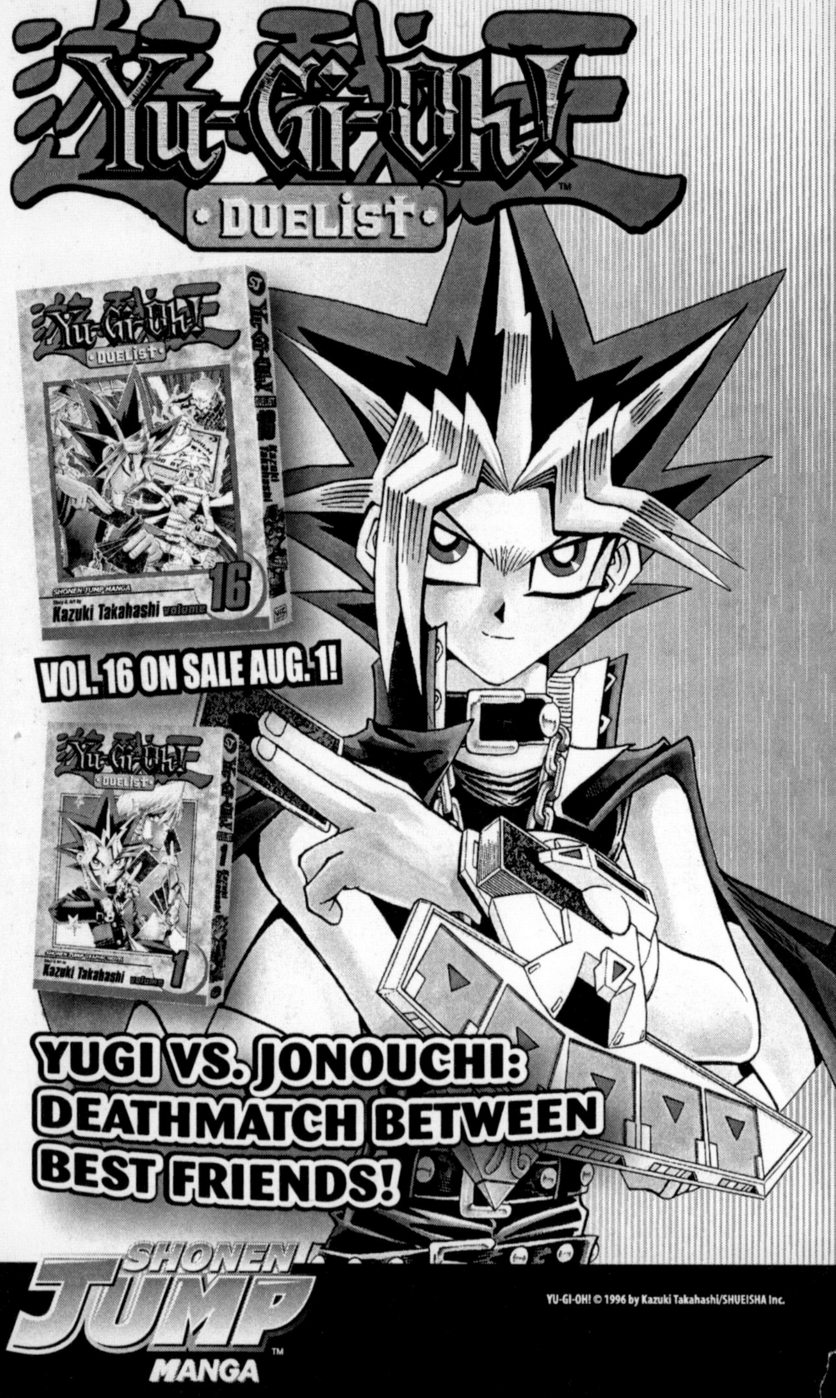
YU-GI-OH!™
DUELIST
Kazuki Takahashi
16
VOL. 16 ON SALE AUG. 1!
Kazuki Takahashi
1
YUGI VS. JONOUCHI: DEATHMATCH BETWEEN BEST FRIENDS!
SHONEN JUMP™ MANGA
YU-GI-OH! © 1996 by Kazuki Takahashi/SHUEISHA Inc.

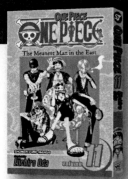
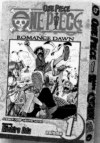

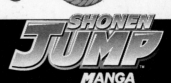

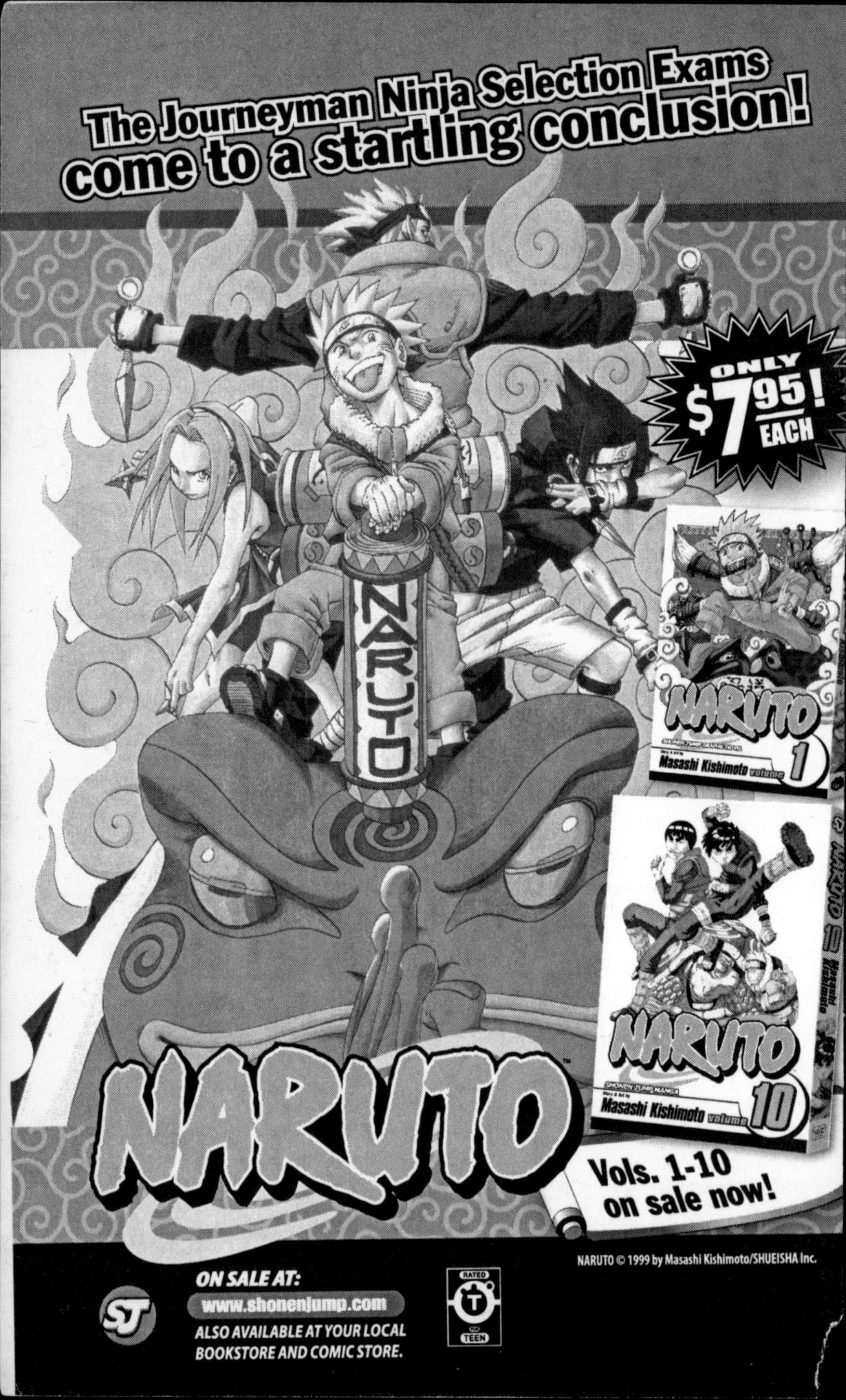
The Journeyman Ninja Selection Exams come to a startling conclusion!
ONLY $7.95! EACH
NARUTO
NARUTO
Masashi Kishimoto volume 1
NARUTO
SHONEN JUMP MANGA
Masashi Kishimoto volume 10
NARUTO
Vols. 1-10 on sale now!
NARUTO © 1999 by Masashi Kishimoto/SHUEISHA Inc.
ON SALE AT:
www.shonenjump.com
ALSO AVAILABLE AT YOUR LOCAL BOOKSTORE AND COMIC STORE.
RATED T TEEN

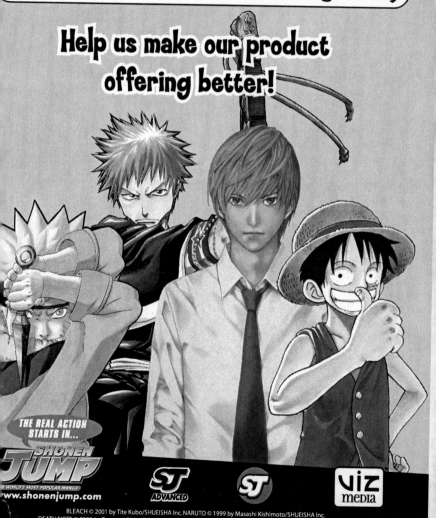

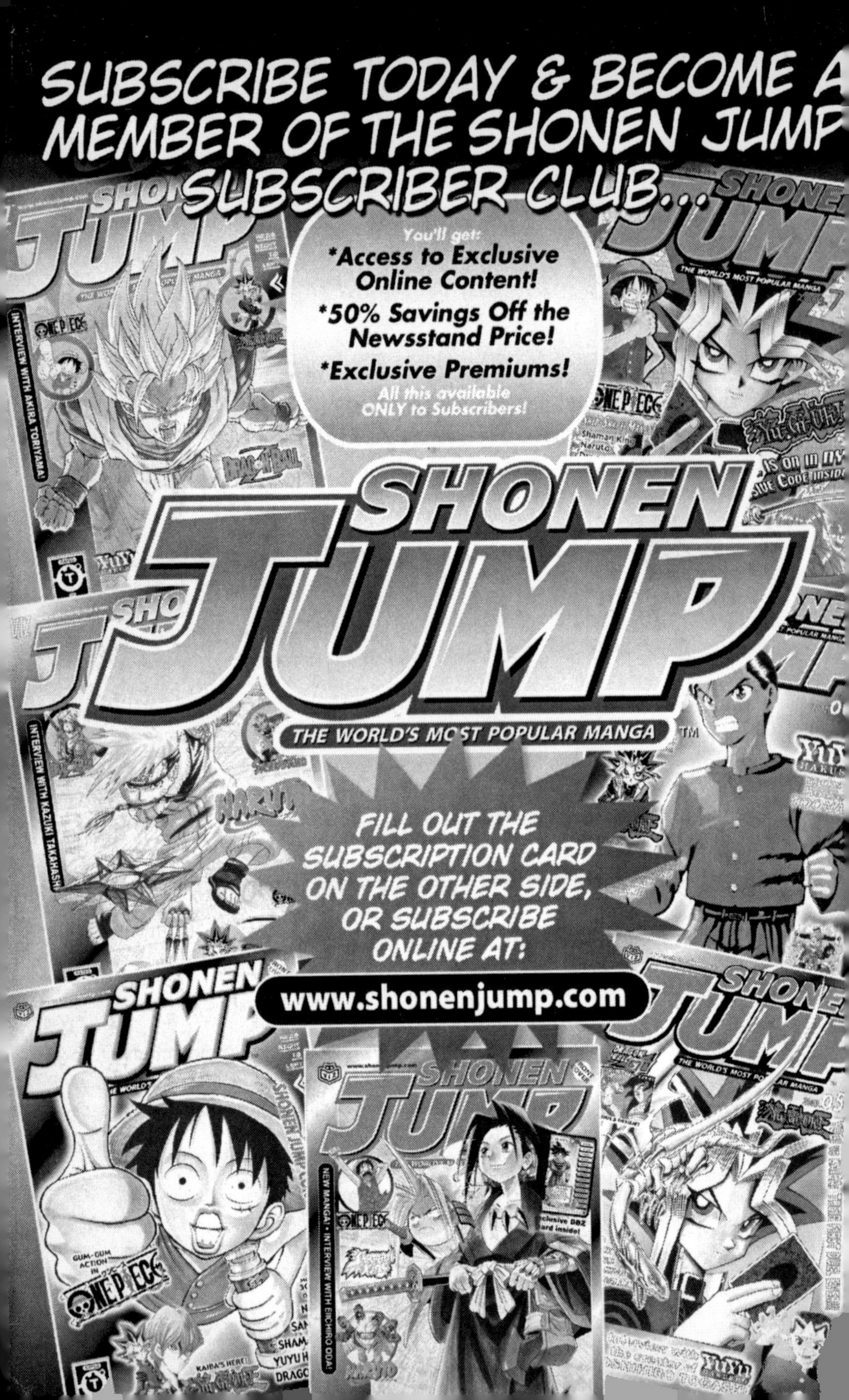

SUBSCRIBE TODAY & BECOME A MEMBER OF THE SHONEN JUMP SUBSCRIBER CLUB...
You'll get:
*Access to Exclusive Online Content!
*50% Savings Off the Newsstand Price!
*Exclusive Premiums!
All this available ONLY to Subscribers!
SHONEN JUMP
THE WORLD'S MOST POPULAR MANGA
TM
FILL OUT THE SUBSCRIPTION CARD ON THE OTHER SIDE, OR SUBSCRIBE ONLINE AT:
www.shonenjump.com